THE BACKGROUND OF ANTI-ENGLISH

FEELING IN GERMANY, 1890-1902

THE BACKGROUND OF ANTI-ENGLISH FEELING IN GERMANY, 1890-1902

BY

PAULINE RELYEA ANDERSON

1969

OCTAGON BOOKS

New York

Reprinted 1969
by special arrangement with Pauline Relyea Anderson

OCTAGON BOOKS
A DIVISION OF FARRAR, STRAUS & GIROUX, INC.
19 Union Square West
New York, N. Y. 10003

AM

LIBRARY OF CONGRESS CATALOG CARD NUMBER: 78-86268

Printed in U.S.A. by
TAYLOR PUBLISHING COMPANY
DALLAS, TEXAS

To the Memory
OF
ECKART KEHR

PREFACE

This study is the result of research begun in Germany in 1931 under a fellowship from Bryn Mawr College, where it was accepted in 1937 as a doctoral thesis. The atmosphere of the Republic was stimulating and helpful to my work and I take this opportunity to thank the German professors, archivists, and citizens who encouraged me, both directly with materials and suggestions and indirectly by conversation. The newspaper and periodical files, chamber of commerce reports, and the handbooks of certain organizations, which form the bulk of the source materials for the study, were found in Germany. Other materials are largely available in this country. No use has been made of unpublished records, with the exception of a few references personally given me and acknowledged in the text. My original intention had been to make a similar study for anti-German opinion in England. It will be evident why I have confined myself to Germany. Moreover, I have wished primarily to try out a method of handling public opinion rather than to exhaust a problem of research.

My special gratitude is due the late Dr. Eckart Kehr, who in Germany and subsequently in this country gave me inestimable help in mapping out my work. I wish likewise to acknowledge with warmth the aid which I have received from the volumes of Dr. Alfred Vagts and from his criticism of the manuscript of my work.

In addition to my gratitude to Bryn Mawr College for its grant, I wish to express my sincere thanks to Professor Howard L. Gray, under whose direction the work was originally begun. He has shown unfailing interest in it and has carefully criticized the form and improved the style. My gratitude is also due to Professor Max Dietz, who has made many valuable corrections and suggestions in regard to translations from the German and style in general. Lastly, I wish to acknowledge the encouragement and criticism given by my husband, Professor Eugene N. Anderson.

PAULINE RELYEA ANDERSON.

Sperryville,
August, 1938.

TABLE OF CONTENTS

INTRODUCTION

The history of the relations between Germany and England during the last part of the preceding and the first years of this century has hitherto been largely written by diplomatic historians. To lay bare the origins and evolution of pre-war alliances, to judge the character of statesmen and diplomats, and to assess responsibility for the catastrophe of 1914 have proved such absorbing problems that historians have neglected investigation of the forces behind diplomacy. Although the documentary collections published by the various post-war governments represent only a selection from the Foreign Archives, historians have ignored the nature and importance of the omitted material. Denied access to the unpublished documents, they have been slow to close the gaps in their knowledge by referring to available material from which the background of the period can be reconstructed.[1] They have used neither histories of parties nor those of large industrial enterprises; they have not examined the reports of the chambers of commerce or the archives of large towns; and they have seldom consulted the writings of the economists, sociologists, and political theorists of the period, who, whenever they held teaching posts, were important members of the state bureaucracy, and whose conclusions in any case grew out of the age in which they lived.[2]

---

[1] Dr. Alfred Vagts in his work, *Deutschland und die Vereinigten Staaten in der Weltpolitik* (London, 1935), represents perhaps best the few who have recently attempted to approach foreign policy through a study of domestic policy and history. In addition Dr. Vagts has had extensive access to unpublished Foreign Office documents. Friedrich Meinecke has given, in accordance with his method of *Ideengeschichte*, much valuable material for understanding the history of Germany in the nineteenth century. Yet in his book, *Die Geschichte des deutsch-englischen Bündnis-Problems, 1890-1901* (Munich and Berlin, 1927), Professor Meinecke has written merely diplomatic history. Only in the last chapter does he indicate problems arising from domestic conditions, which he might have considered throughout.

[2] Here may be mentioned the works of Max Weber, of the contributors to *Schmollers Jahrbuch*, and to the *Schriften des Vereins für Sozialpolitik*, all subsequently referred to more specifically.

Foreign policy is, however, not determined in accordance with diplomatic considerations alone. Both democratic and autocratic states arrive at their foreign policies by conscious and often unconscious regard for the dominant interests within the state. The men who are responsible for foreign policy cannot isolate themselves from the ideologies and material conditions peculiar to the country, the age, the caste or group of which they are a part.[3] The power of the ruling groups, moreover, as was the case in Germany, may be sufficiently great to control the thinking of a bureaucratic official. It may happen that more than one powerful group in a state claims consideration from the Foreign Office. When the interests of two such groups are in sharp conflict, the Foreign Office may for a time during a deadlock secure control and direct affairs through a small clique. But even this small group of officials will not resort to an ideal policy reflecting only the best interests of the whole people; its tradition will be too strong. More often a compromise between or among conflicting groups will be reached. In this case the objectives stand out less clearly than is the case with the objectives of a single group, and again the Foreign Office has more scope. It must, however, in the end satisfy these dominant groups; hence its activity cannot range far from a given line. In general, if a foreign policy suggested by one group, such as close friendship or alliance with England, proves contrary to the interests and hence to the foreign policy of a group stronger in numbers, wealth, and political influence, the government will find it impossible to adopt such a policy without coming to terms with the latter group. If no agreement proves possible, the policy will in all probability be relinquished and yet a third sought. If, on the other hand, the second group agrees in principle to the policy of the first group but at the same time obstructs the execution of the policy by making (in other fields) demands inconsistent with it, the government will be forced into an embarrassing situation. It will have to reopen the issue or become completely opportunist. Such considerations make it desirable to begin the study of foreign policy with an analysis of domestic politics. Otherwise the motivation of the former remains obscure.

[3] Emil Lederer, "Das oekonomische Element und die politischen Ideen im modernen Parteiwesen," *Zeitschrift für Politik,* V (1912), 535 ff.

In a country like pre-war Germany, where vested social and economic interests were very strong, it is particularly important to examine foreign policy in this realistic way. An illustration may be given. Historians have almost unanimously considered the year 1890 a turning point in German foreign policy and have ascribed the tragedy of 1914 in part to the change then made. When, however, the foreign policy of the years 1890 to 1902 is viewed in the light of party interests, commercial tendencies, and other internal problems, the question is reopened. The cutting of the wire to St. Petersburg and the gradual estrangement from England suggest themselves as possible results of changes already under way in the Bismarkian Reich. The forces responsible for imperial policy in 1890 did not differ from those of a decade before. In fact, at the end of the 'seventies the Iron Chancellor turned to protectionism, a movement greatly intensified in the period under survey. In giving up the policy of free-trade he was influenced by the Central Union of German Industrialists and by the Prussian Agrarians. Already at that time the Agrarians, less and less able to export large supplies of grain, were formulating those arguments which they used so effectively in the Bülow era. Even then they revealed antagonisms to other countries; they felt angry at England because of the loss of their market in Great Britain, angry at America for supplanting them in this market, and angry at America and Russia for supplying Germany with cheaper wheat and rye than they could themselves produce. Although Bülow came to be known as the " agricultural Chancellor," Bismarck in 1879 was so convinced of the Agrarians' need that he threatened to deprive industry of protection unless agriculture was protected as well.[4] At the same time the industrialists felt the pressure of English iron competition and forced up tariffs against it. Later when these interests grew stronger politically and demanded further protection, the more outspoken antagonism to England and America developed. In addition to turning to protection Bismarck was induced to inaugurate a colonial policy. Even while he harbored misgivings as to the effect on Anglo-German relations, he took another step toward imperialism by acquiring footholds for Germany abroad. Although

[4] Siegfried von Kardorff, *Wilhelm von Kardorff: Ein nationaler Parlamentarier im Zeitalter Bismarcks und Wilhelms II* (Berlin, 1936), p. 145.

his motives were not anti-English, the results of his policy were bound to affect relations with England, if only because the interests behind German imperialism would chafe at English imperialistic preëminence.

Thus a consideration of internal forces reveals that the change in foreign policy after 1890 was more superficial than real. Caprivi's foreign policy embodied not so much a radical change in direction as a return to earlier Bismarckian principles and a resistance to imperialism. Caprivi reduced friction with England by the Zanzibar-Helgoland Treaty and by giving up colonial expansion. Through commercial treaties with lowered tariff rates, he sought to strengthen good relations with Russia and other countries by means of economic ties. His failure and the subsequent development of foreign policy under Bülow can only be understood by reference to the history of industrial and agricultural interests and to the political, social, and economic problems of the post-Bismarckian Reich.

Historians who treat foreign policy as something apart frequently make the mistake of handling public opinion in the same way. It is necessary to distinguish between the public opinion of different groups, to relate the opinion of a group to its own peculiar interests, and to allow for the extravagance of professional chauvinists, nationalists, and their opponents. Public opinion, moreover, does not always proclaim frankly the interests which it represents, but appeals to the " general welfare " or to " national interests." Thus at times the arguments of ardent nationalists and patriots, however unintentionally, conceal special interests. Large propaganda societies which concern themselves with foreign relations are, therefore, doubly dangerous: they enlist sincere and insincere followers, and it is difficult for the uninitiated to distinguish between the two sorts. This was often the case with those who fostered anti-English opinion in Germany between 1890 and 1902. For example, a part of the support for anti-English propaganda came from men who wished primarily to bring about the passage of the naval laws. For such persons and interests, whether they actually were or were not anti-English, a national enmity furthered naval plans.

It is well known that the world criticized England severely at the time of the Boer War. This criticism sprang from real sympathy with the Boers; but with it were also mixed the fear or jealousy of England, the desire for colonial gain, and a variety of other feelings, about which there has been facile generalization. Though these generalizations may contain much truth, it is far more informing to analyze the details of anti-English reaction in Germany, where it had wide import. The analysis raises among others the question whether Anglophobia in any measure determined the failure of the proposal for an Anglo-German alliance. To answer this question it is necessary to examine Anglophobia intensively, that is, to consider public opinion not so much as it appears on the surface but rather as it appears when each important group is scrutinized. It is necessary to ascertain the interests of various groups, their positions in the social, economic, and political body; for these factors conditioned their attitudes to the questions of the day. Analysis of the forces behind public opinion necessarily widens our understanding of it, disclosing fine shades of difference. Thus one cannot appraise the public opinion of the Agrarian-Conservative group, whether regarding England or America, without acquaintance with the Agrarians themselves.

Some historians have attempted to simplify the Anglo-German problem by taking commercial rivalry as a primary cause of ill-feeling. Antagonism in Germany to England was not confined, however, to industrial and commercial interests; there is in this matter no clear cut example of economic determinism. The antagonism was partly inherent in the nature of the ideologies and institutions of the two countries, in their political and social systems, and in their imperialisms.[5] Nothing disclosed this more, so it seemed to Germans, than the Boer War. Nor did unsatisfactory economic conditions at home drive Germany to new colonial activity; rather this activity coincided with the high point of German prosperity, which seemed to reinforce the eagerness of public opinion and of government for imperialism. One may safely say that considerable Anglophobia sprang from the exuberance of prosperous times. Morally bolstered by Admiral Mahan's writings and impelled by national optimism German thought was centering about

[5] Dr. Vagts has studied German-American relations and has come to the same conclusion regarding them. See Vagts, *op. cit.*, *passim*.

the idea of Power (*Macht*). Max Weber, a famous sociologist of
the period, wrote that the time was approaching " when only Power
can decide the share of each country in the economic control of the
earth and therewith the space in which the population of each,
especially the workers, has to operate." [6] In pre-war Germany the
eagerness for Power was perhaps more potent than commercial
rivalry.

In any study of public opinion the question arises as to the
influence of it on executive officials and through them on foreign
policy. To assert that in pre-war Germany the government controlled, rather than was controlled by, public opinion does not
answer the question. It is still important to ascertain the views of
the higher bureaucrats and of the Emperor and to compare these
views with the fundamental demands of the groups which created
public opinion. Even when the government opposed (or yielded to)
a momentary outburst of feeling in the press, it may have done
so without deviating essentially from the demands of certain dominant groups. Such proves to have been the case in Germany, where
influential interest-groups coöperated in the *Sammlung* (organized
in 1897) for political log-rolling and largely directed policy. The
government could not depart far from the path laid down by these
interests, even when the whole press, including the organs of the
Sammlung, seemed at the moment to demand otherwise. To have
done so would have disturbed the socio-political balance and neces-
sitated a change of officials.

Finally, in order to be able to appraise foreign policy and public
opinion correctly, it is essential to know something of the political
and economic atmosphere of the period. The late eighteen-nineties
all over the world ushered in a period of great imperialistic activity.
It is doubtful whether any great state, in spite of the attendant
disadvantages, could have remained aloof from it. Certainly, an
ambitious nation like Germany with an expanding industry, a
rapidly growing population, and an active Emperor who prided
himself on being a man of his time would not lag behind her friends
and enemies. Yet ventures involving ways of thought so new and a

---

[6] Max Weber, *Gutachten zur Flottenumfrage der Allgemeinen Zeitung,*
1897, cited by Vagts, *op. cit.,* I, xiii, note 1. See also Theodor Heuss,
Friedrich Naumann (Stuttgart and Berlin, 1937), p. 139.

programme so different from past ones was bound to create new and complicated external and internal problems. This correlation between imperialism and internal affairs has become increasingly evident. Recent writers like Alfred Vagts in *Deutschland und die Vereinigten Staaten in der Weltpolitik* and William L. Langer in *The Diplomacy of Imperialism* have placed diplomacy in close conjunction with its background.[7] For a work on Anglophobia in Germany this relation is doubly important, first, because the imperialism of the period gave rise to events which directly aroused anti-English feeling and, secondly, because only the exaggerated nationalism of the imperialists can explain the unusual virulence of that feeling.

The new wave of imperialism coincided with a worldwide upturn in the business cycle.[8] After the long depression of the early nineties renewed industrial and commercial activity produced confidence and enthusiasm. At the same time the fear of another contraction in prosperity spurred the industrial nations to overseas expansion. Many commercial and industrial groups hoped that colonies and huge international markets would maintain a continuous boom. An unprecedented scramble took place for every advantage which an alert nation could obtain in any quarter of the globe. Germany was perhaps more aggressive than the other states because she entered the colonial field late. For her it was not, as in the case of England or even of France, a question of securing and developing what she had or of reaching out by " peaceful penetration " from one colonial base to new spheres of influence. She must begin very nearly at the beginning.[9] During the depression and before

[7] Alfred Vagts, *op. cit.*; William L. Langer, *The Diplomacy of Imperialism, 1890-1902* (New York, 1935). Professor Langer has noted this correlation only very generally, however; his chapters on navalism, for example, are isolated from those dealing with diplomatic tensions.

[8] The term " business cycle " and the concept of periodic boom and depression were relatively new in Germany in the 'nineties. Developed by the English economists in the nineteenth century, they were elaborated by German economists, especially at the time of the brief depression of 1900-1. The term " business cycle " is a twentieth century rechristening of a nineteenth century discovery (" Business Cycle." *Encyclopedia of the Social Sciences*, III).

[9] Germany had her African colonies; but they were almost totally undeveloped and as yet neither a source of raw materials nor suitable for

2

1894 she could not decide to do this. Industry was not strong
enough or the government wealthy enough to be expansive.[10]   A
return of prosperity provided the material and psychological impetus to place Germany among the imperialistic nations. Nationalistic endeavour coincided as in Germany in the 'sixties with an
industrial and commercial search for new markets.

Particularly important to imperialism was the element of Power,
Machtpolitik. The ethical justification of Power was repeatedly
advanced. Behind this justification lay the conviction that modern
imperialism could not achieve its ends without the instruments of
Macht. England, the imperialist nation *par excellence*, regarded
her great navy as essential to the maintenance of her Empire.
France and Russia were rapidly increasing this weapon of their
alliance. It seemed imperative to German nationalists that their
country should back with a navy its efforts for colonies and
markets. Their navy was not to be a fleet of cruisers stationed in
overseas waters for legitimate protection of German interests abroad,
but a war navy powerful enough to present a risk, that is, to
threaten subtly foreign opponents of the German programme. Bismarck had connected the idea of *Machtpolitik* so closely with the
new Reich that it was not difficult for later German statesmen and
industrialists to link *Weltpolitik* and *Machtpolitik*. The emphasis upon *Macht,* perhaps not greater in practice than elsewhere
but certainly more often asserted in words, made German imperialism particularly unpleasant the world over.

The protective tariff constituted a second weapon of imperialism.
Economic liberalism had so far waned throughout the world as to
allow the steady erection of new tariff barriers. These barriers,
whatever their original size and purpose, were often formidable by
1900. The valuable Russian and American markets were growing
more inaccessible, and there was constant danger that Imperial
Federation might close off the British and British colonial markets

markets. A part of Germany's new imperialistic programme was to develop
these with state aid.

[10] It is not without significance that in 1896 and 1897 plans for a new
navy could not be put through but that in 1898, the date of the First
Naval Law, after three years of prosperity, the surplus in the Treasury was
sufficient to assure the Reichstag that no new taxes need be levied for naval
construction. This assurance had much to do with the passage of the law.

to outsiders. In this situation nationalists regarded the protective tariff both as a potential aid to national industry and as a means of constantly threatening with retaliation other national economic units. It became a political *Machtfaktor*. In Germany the creation of an autonomous tariff with high maximum and minimum duties, paralleling the tariffs of the United States as the navy did the British navy, became of paramount importance as a factor in *Weltpolitik*. The arguments used in the Reichstag for the navy and for the tariff were strikingly similar and the theory underlying each was the same.

Modern industrialization raised the problem of the fate of agriculture. In England agriculture had been sacrificed to industry. England's vast colonial Empire allowed her easily to adjust herself to the change, while France had solved the problem by maintaining the balance between agriculture and industry. In the United States the opening of new agriculture lands at first kept pace with the industrialization of the East. But even in the United States agriculture in the 'eighties and 'nineties suffered sufficiently to demand " free silver." In Germany by 1900 considerably more than half the population was engaged in or dependent on industry and more than half the national wealth was invested therein; but agriculture was not willing to go down to defeat through the further expansion of industry. This attitude particularly characterized the large grain producers of the East Elbian area, who entirely opposed the breaking up of their estates for intensive cultivation. Although they were unable to supply the country with the entire amount of bread-stuffs and fodder needed, they demanded strict control of imports so that the prices of their products would not fall. Unlike the American farmers, these East Elbian Agrarians belonged to or were aligned with the most powerful caste in the Prussian state, the old aristocracy. They easily commanded the support of the smaller farmers and peasants in their struggle to secure state aid, at first against industry but later even in alliance with industry. One can readily see that the agricultural question in Germany became more acute than in most other countries. No government was able to embark on a programme of imperialism without coming to terms with the Agrarians. The nature of the agricultural party and of its demands forms part of the background of German imperialism; for the agricultural struggle occupied the political stage during the entire period under survey.

In addition to their position and experience the Agrarians had another hold upon the country. Their ruin would spell the breakup of the old social order as well as of the economic, an eventuality against which all authority set its face. Although Trade Unionism was no more aggressive in Germany after 1890 than it was in the democratic countries, Social Democracy aroused more fear in autocratic and aristocratic Germany than it did in western Europe. If it had been possible after Bismarck's retirement to insure parliamentary government and ministerial responsibility, it might have been possible to reduce the friction arising out of political and social inequalities. Largely as a result of failure to make this change, the class struggle became more bitter in Germany than elsewhere and affected every important decision. Agriculture and industry gradually allied their forces against the Left, while imperialism aimed to content the workers with continued material prosperity. Even *Machtpolitik* received impetus from this motive.[11] Since England was the country in which Trade Unionism was powerful and well organized, the ruling groups found further cause for opposition to her.

Thus, just as the international affairs of the years 1890 to 1902 constitute roughly a unit for study, so the same period forms a unit in German domestic history. During this time, in addition to taking part in the world movement of expansion, Germany went through the bitterest phase of her agricultural conflict. The worst period of this struggle ended after five years of open strife with the new tariff of 1902. During the decade each step of the government's programme was bitterly opposed by the Social Democratic representatives.[12] As a result their opponents introduced

---

[11] The *Preussische Jahrbücher* in commenting on a work of Max Lorenz, *Der nationale Kampf gegen die Sozialdemokratie* (Leipzig, 1897), said: " It shows the increase of the navy as an important means for solving the internal social problems " (*Preussische Jahrbücher*, XC [1897], 569). See also Hans Delbrück, *ibid.*, LXXIX, 365-368, 373; LXXX, 388; LXXXIII, 593; XCI, 582. Other references to this idea will be found in the text of this study.

[12] Not only the Social Democrats opposed; there were Left Liberal opponents and " each step " had also other opponents, who were not, how-

several bills directed against them and brought about two changes of government personnel toward the Right. It was a period in which the country, at least up to the time of the formation of the *Sammlung*, sought to find its course first in one direction and then in another. Party feeling ran high, intrigues abounded, the new Emperor gave cause for grave concern. There was at first depression, then phenomenal industrial activity; finally, an aggressive nationalism took possession of the press and lent an almost pathological intensity to every discussion.

As has been suggested, imperialism is a manifestation of nationalism. Before Germany could embark on an expansionist movement she had to have some coördination of her disparate forces at home. Without popular belief in Germany's cultural mission abroad and in her demand for equality with all nations it would not have been possible for commerce and industry, those interests with a direct stake in new markets, to secure money and armaments for expansion. Because Germany was not socially integrated, because her people, according to Bülow, the Pan-Germans, and many journalists, were not conscious of their mission, a vast propaganda became a necessary adjunct to the imperialistic programme. Similar propaganda was of course fostered in other countries; but in Germany it served both an internal and an international purpose and assumed an unusual vehemence because it sought to obliterate many acute social disharmonies. Since it never succeeded in eliminating the cause of these disharmonies, the occasion for it persisted. The propaganda machinery was prone to set up enemies in order to arouse the country to action. It became a power in itself. It attempted through a programme of *Weltpolitik* to unify the German people, to give them a new interest in a state unlikely to solve its constitutional or social problems. It helped to turn internal enmities outward, to carry the economic and social struggles into the field of imperialism.

In the following chapters many of the questions connected with the imperialistic age in Germany—colonies, a navy, a new protective

ever, always the same. The Social Democrats formed the largest continuously opposing group, especially after the Catholic Center became more pro-government.

tariff, agriculture *versus* industry, employer *versus* labor, Germany against England—are treated in relation to the various parliamentary groups and to the press of each group. The analysis of the special problems of the several groups and of the attitudes of each toward the questions of the day provides a background for attempting to estimate more accurately the true nature of anti-English feeling.

PART I

THE GOVERNMENT, PARLIAMENTARY AND PRO-
PAGANDA GROUPS IN GERMANY AND THEIR
ATTITUDES TOWARD DOMESTIC PROB-
LEMS AND IMPERIALISM

CHAPTER I

THE GOVERNMENT GROUP

When I came back from abroad after many, many years, I found much which thoroughly displeased me, and much still does so. There is everywhere too slow a tempo. In every sense we have too much sand about us and in us, and where there is too much sand, things don't move forward as they should; we must always be saying, 'move on.' But this sandy land is still fertile, not remarkably so but sufficiently so. It needs only the right weather, especially the right moral climate, that is, at the right time sunshine and rain. And I think the Emperor Frederick would have brought it the right weather.

Fontane, *Der Stechlin*, pp. 357-8.

A study of public opinion even in a very recent period has to be confined to the vocal and literate parts of society. How the silent members reacted to the new imperialism, what they thought of England must remain obscure. The organized groups to which they belonged and the men for whom they voted presumably represented them satisfactorily. Germany was honeycombed with organizations and if one could appraise each of them, from singing societies to the Navy League, an approximation to the popular feeling might be reached. The result would be of interest, although it would not be important. The superior organization and the overwhelming influence of certain groups in German political and economic life reduced most of the others to insignificance and silenced their voice of protest before it was heard. Attention to these powerful groups is therefore a necessary preliminary to the understanding of their attitude toward imperialism and England.

The views on imperialism of the Emperor, the leading members of his Civil, Military, and Naval Cabinets,[1] and of the Imperial

[1] In addition to the Prussian Ministers of State there existed vestiges of the former Privy Council in the Military, Naval, and Civil Cabinets, whose chiefs were personal advisers to the King of Prussia. The Chief of the Military Cabinet, for example, was adviser to the Sovereign as head of the army. Reich ministers were called Secretaries.

1

Secretaries responsible for policy were naturally of consequence. In a state organized as the German state the bureaucracy formed the first important power group. Its members were removed from direct parliamentary control and for the most part adhered to a well-defined tradition of thinking and acting. It is of interest to determine which of these members were most responsible for the promotion of imperialism and what were the motives actuating each. That the Emperor or any one of his advisers would have renounced imperialism had he been at the head of a democratic state is in no way proved: the imperialism of Joseph Chamberlain and of Theodore Roosevelt was contemporary with that of Bernhard von Bülow. Since Bülow, however, had to act within a feudal-conservative-industrial framework, his policy was conditioned thereby. His *Weltpolitik* was designed to strengthen the existing régime, maintain the social system intact, and at the same time conduce to the general welfare as popularly understood. The intimate relationship between domestic conditions and imperialism made it necessary for Bülow to consider them together.

If Bernhard von Bülow is described before the Emperor, it is because he occupied even more than the latter the key position in these years, first as Secretary of State for Foreign Affairs from 1897 to 1900 and then as Chancellor after 1900. In his extensive writings Bülow gives no underlying reasons for his appointment in 1897 to his high office. The causes for the choice are, nevertheless, extremely important to an understanding of subsequent history as well as of Bülow's own policy in office. His transfer to Berlin from Rome, where he was Ambassador, was the dream of his friend Philipp zu Eulenburg-Hertefeld, Ambassador to Vienna and the Emperor's intimate adviser. For some years Eulenburg had been waiting until the psychological moment to suggest the appointment.

Bülow and Eulenburg certainly discussed the former's future rôle as head of the government, although they probably did not work out a detailed programme.[2] Eulenburg desired Bülow's appointment because of a serious situation in internal politics.[3] During

[2] Of great interest on this point are the letters of Eulenburg to Bülow given in Johannes Haller, *Aus dem Leben des Fürsten Philipps zu Eulenburg-Hertefeld* (Berlin, 1924), *passim*.

[3] *Ibid.*, Chaps. 3, 4. See also Otto Hammann, *Bilder aus der letzten*

the years 1894 to 1897 the Emperor came increasingly under the influence of his entourage. He fell out with his advisers and exposed himself to the charge of arbitrary rule, made both by the political parties and by the press. These attacks culminated on May 18, 1897, in a bitter speech in the Reichstag by Eugen Richter (Progressive Peoples' party). Richter had particularly in mind the disputes of the Emperor with several important public men, one between the Emperor and General von Bronsart over the reform of the military courts, another between the Emperor and his Foreign Secretary, Marschall von Bieberstein, in connection with the Lützow and Tausch cases, still another estranging William II from Boetticher, the Secretary of Interior.[4] Behind the differences between the Emperor and these men lay the grave question whether constitutional government should survive or whether the Crown would increase its governmental power at the cost of its popularity and at the risk even of its existence. Eulenburg was convinced that the Emperor could not rule as an absolute monarch;[5] but his love for his Sovereign and for the monarchy prevented his wishing for a radical reduction of royal power. Instead of devoting all his

Kaiserzeit (Berlin, 1922), pp. 11 ff.; Prince Hohenlohe-Schillingfürst, *Denkwürdigkeiten der Reichskanzlerzeit* (Stuttgart, 1931), *passim*; *Geschichte der Frankfurter Zeitung* (Frankfurt, 1911), pp. 740-750.

[4] Haller, *op. cit.*, Chaps. 4, 5. See also Kardorff, *op. cit.*, pp. 312 ff.; Hohenlohe, *op. cit.*, pp. 1-364, where the fullest account is obtainable. Bronsart's sin had been the desire to establish public oral courts for the army. Marschall had won great public favor by carrying the charges against himself into the courts and exposing there the Police Commissioner, Tausch (Hohenlohe, *op. cit.*, pp. 269, 286, note 2), while Boetticher had won the Emperor's disfavor by failing to answer Richter's speech of May 18. The crime of Hollmann, Secretary for Naval Affairs, who was also forced out, had been the failure to put through the new naval demands (Hans Hallmann, *Der Weg zum deutschen Schlachtflottenbau* [Stuttgart, 1933], Chap. 6). It may be suggested that the extremely unpleasant atmosphere of these years was due also in no small part to the machinations of Prince Bismarck behind the scenes. They are clearly revealed in Hohenlohe's papers (Hohenlohe, *op. cit.*, pp. 5 ff.). See also *Die Zukunft, passim*; Hermann Hofmann, *Fürst Bismarck 1890-1898* (Stuttgart and Berlin, 1914); J. Penzler, *Fürst Bismarck nach seiner Entlassung* (Leipzig, 1897).

[5] See Eulenburg's masterly summary of the situation on December 2, 1894, in Haller, *op. cit.*, pp. 178 ff. Also *Prince Alexander Hohenlohe to Eulenburg*, February 17, 1895, Hohenlohe, *op. cit.*, pp. 42 ff.

energy to bringing about a fundamental solution, Eulenburg saw his way clear only to dealing with governmental crises as they arose and to seeking some changes in personnel. His efforts in the crisis of 1897 resulted in the transfer of Bronsart to active service, the resignation of Marschall, who was consoled by the ambassadorial post at Constantinople, the replacement of Boetticher by Posadowsky-Wehner and, finally, the assurance given by Chancellor Hohenlohe, who had supported Bronsart, that he would remain temporarily in office. In the meantime Eulenburg won Hohenlohe, Holstein, Privy Councillor in the State Department, and the Emperor to the appointment of Bülow to the Foreign Office. Not before the autumn of 1897 could the political skies be called clear and Eulenburg rest from his exhausting labors. But the dropping of the three Secretaries, Bronsart, Marschall, Boetticher, and likewise Hollmann, Secretary for Naval Affairs, brought conviction to much of the public press that reaction had set in. The new ministers were not popular and it was feared that the Emperor would have his way unopposed.[6]

Eulenburg had not chosen Bülow to oppose the Emperor but to be the strong man through whom the Emperor and his Secretaries might be reconciled hereafter. When Bülow became Chancellor in 1900, Eulenburg wrote to him:

> Do you remember a long conversation which we had in a green meadow in Semmering when we worked out the programme? You were to be Secretary for a while in order to learn the Berlin terrain, that is, to know thoroughly internal politics. Then you were to become Imperial Chancellor at a moment when there was no crisis. All that has marvelously come to pass, although the time which you spent as Secretary was to me, I openly confess, rather long . . . How hard it will be for you, my dear Bernhard, I can see already in the newspaper comments, which emphasize clearly the strong man in you, the man able to restrain the poor, dear Emperor. To satisfy Germany and not hurt the Emperor [*Deutschland befriedigen und den Kaiser nicht verletzen*]—that is your motto.[7]

---

[6] Hohenlohe, *op. cit.*, pp. 365 ff.; Friedrich von Holstein, *Lebensbekenntnis: Briefe an eine Frau* (Berlin, 1932), p. 185, note.

[7] Haller, *op. cit.*, p. 254. Eulenburg was writing to Hohenlohe of Bülow for Marschall's place in 1895 (Hohenlohe, *op. cit.*, pp. 39-42). Hohenlohe,

Eulenburg had singled out Bülow to be the Emperor's new Bismarck, and his letters show how relieved he was to see affairs in the hands of his capable friend.

Whether or not Bülow discussed beforehand either with Eulenburg or with anyone the details of the programme which he was to carry out as Secretary for Foreign Affairs and later as Chancellor is not clear. Eulenburg, Holstein, and Bülow himself in his later writings did not touch on the point. Had it been agreed " that the decisive point lay on the Neva," [8] " that the problem which I must face would be essentially that of building a navy for our protection and security without getting into a war with England through the construction of this navy," [9] that " we do not wish to put anyone in the shadow, but we demand our place in the sun "? [10] To judge from his letters Eulenburg was not a zealous imperialist

upon the eve of his retirement, wrote the following: " It becomes clearer to me every day that my position was endangered with the exit of Marschall and Boetticher. Each of them had his faults; but neither wanted to be more than he was and hence both had the same interests as I had and were favorable to me. When Bülow came to Marschall's place, I had a rival at my side. . . . The efforts of Bülow were made slowly and cautiously, but with the goal in mind of replacing me in the Emperor's favor. There was nothing to be done about it. I could not lift him out of the saddle in the affections of the Emperor, who preferred him. Hence fate had to have its way until catastrophe came " (Hohenlohe, *op. cit.*, p. 592).

[8] Fürst von Bülow, *Denkwürdigkeiten* (Berlin, 1930-31), I, 44. Bülow is so unreliable a source that anything quoted from his later writings, such as *Deutsche Politik* (1916), or the *Denkwürdigkeiten*, must be taken as suggestion only and never as fact.

[9] *Ibid.*, p. 16. According to Hallmann, *op. cit.*, Tirpitz, the new Naval Secretary, had his first talks with Bülow over the naval question on August 19 and 21. There is no account of their conversation; but it is known that Tirpitz, fresh from the Far East, was impressed at the time with the fact that economic competition with England would increase in the next century (Hallmann, *op. cit.*, p. 289). Hallmann believes that Bülow never fully understood or accepted Tirpitz' point of view in regard to the navy; but this opinion does not belie the fact that Bülow was chosen by the Emperor because he would not seriously obstruct the naval plans already agreed upon with Tirpitz. Moreover, in his conversation with Tirpitz, January 28, 1896, the Emperor indicated that he would secure a Chancellor who would work with both of them (Hallmann, *op. cit.*, p. 183 ff.).

[10] Fürst von Bülow, *Reden* (Leipzig, 1910), I, 8. The remark is contained in his first speech to the Reichstag, December 6, 1897.

and tried to dissuade William II from a hasty and over-ambitious
policy of naval expansion and colonial acquisition. Bülow's objectives, however, at once became the winning of Russia, the building
of a navy, and the pursuit of *Weltpolitik*; and he cannot have
decided upon them without some forethought. Their inception was
logically connected with the circumstances under which he was
appointed.[11] Bülow and his associates must have seen that to
develop for Germany a programme of imperialism would serve the
threefold purpose of gratifying the Emperor in his desire to be a
"modern man," of employing his energy for increasing the
prosperity of the Empire, and of drawing his interest away from
domestic politics. In support of this interpretation there exists
one significant letter from Holstein to his friend, Frau von Stülpnagel, just at the time of Bülow's temporary appointment to the
Foreign Office, July 19, 1897. Holstein wrote:

> I have been a good friend of Bülow. For years he has had
> everything important which comes in or goes out of the
> political department [of the Foreign Office]. Still I don't
> believe I shall remain long. My eyes have something to do
> with it; but that is not all. Foreign policy is in good condi-
> tion but internal is not. The change to the right which is
> openly planned is not undertaken with sufficient strength and,
> according to my convictions, must end within a couple of years
> by a great swing to the left. I have even heard that there are
> people who in that case intend to divert the country from
> internal difficulties by means of foreign policy [*Es soll sogar
> Leute geben, die den Plan haben, dann die inneren Schwierig-
> keiten nach aussen abzuleiten*].[12]

Bülow should be included among the people who understood this

[11] Eulenburg, as has been mentioned above, did not favor imperialism.
His objection to the navy was, however, apparently due in part to his
view of the pernicious influence on the Emperor of Admiral von Senden und
Bibran, Chief of the Naval Staff. He also seems to have feared the Emperor's hasty action on behalf of imperialism rather than the policy itself.
Hence he may not have withstood Bülow's plans, since he trusted the latter.
It is also probable that neither Bülow nor Eulenburg weighed the effects
of the Tirpitz proposals on foreign policy; if Bülow had had any misgivings on that score, his vanity would have reassured him that he could
counteract the danger through a skillful use of diplomacy.

[12] Holstein, *op. cit.*, p. 185.

reckon with the given relations and with the given factors. One must act one way one time and another way another time.[27]

Bülow's handling of the Samoan Treaty illustrated his aims. In his eagerness to annex the Samoan territory, he ignored the small economic value of the Islands to German commerce, rejected the English offer of the Volta Delta, a much richer territory which the Colonial Department advised him to accept, and listened instead to Tirpitz and the navalists who wished naval bases.[28] Moreover, he pretended to England that he dare not retreat for fear of public opinion, although he was himself directing this opinion. The following quotation is from his instructions to Richthofen, Under Secretary in the Foreign Office, in regard to the press:

> The attitude of our official papers in this Samoan affair is to a steady, clear, and patriotic one. Otherwise the country will misunderstand us. The grounds which indicate that because of Samoa we must not let it come to a break with two naval Powers so very superior to us are, like all other arguments in this regard (relatively small importance of German interests in Samoa, especially in comparison to our Asiatic and even African interests, earlier anti-German attitude of Mataafa), to come out only in the non-official papers, *Weserzeitung, Tageblatt*, etc.[29]

Bülow showed here, as in other cases, that the details of economic policy were either unknown to him or that he preferred to disregard them. Roscher's teaching furnished him convenient clichés but not economic insight.

Thus the Foreign Secretary embarked upon *Weltpolitik* in the years immediately following his appointment. On the one hand he aimed at the assertion of Germany's position in world affairs, while on the other he hoped to harmonize the departments of government so as to avoid an open conflict or a *coup d'état* in internal affairs. Johannes Haller, the historian, concludes of Bülow. " It is the undeniable service of Bernhard von Bülow to have given back to the government apparatus a measure of unity which it had more and more lost after Caprivi's departure." [30] The means Bülow

[27] *Ibid.*, p. 81. [28] Vagts, *op. cit.*, I, Chap. X.

[29] *Bülow to Richthofen*, March 30, 1899, cited by Vagts, *op. cit.*, p. 852.

[30] Haller, *op. cit.*, p. 256.

took for effecting this harmony, the adoption of imperialism, were a tacit recognition, however, that the *de facto* constitution of the German state would not be democratized. Unity was to be attained by bringing the country to support new national goals, which under the existing circumstances, would be pursued only by feudal-absolutistic methods.[31]

Harmony among the branches of government was not immediately realized. The road was a long and thorny one and the Emperor was always an unpredictable factor. While Eulenburg continued to worry over " the dear Master " and the state, Count Waldersee, another of the Emperor's intimates and his Field Marshall, wrote in October 1899:

> Perhaps the unfortunate canal episode [the Canal Law providing for an inland canal system to facilitate transportation had just been defeated], which shows clearly that we have no unified government, that one minister goes right and the other left at the same time, that the Emperor takes one side and one never knows how long he will continue to do so, does have the advantage of showing all parties that matters cannot go on in this way. Already I hear the demand to construct a unified ministry which will say clearly where it is going, whether right or left. I really believe that this should be done, and have said before that it is to me quite acceptable if the Emperor once try the Liberals and then say plainly what he wants [On the supposition that the Liberals would not be successful and that a *coup d'état* would follow].[32]

The position vacated by Hollmann as Secretary of the Imperial Naval Office in the spring of 1897 fell to Tirpitz. Tirpitz had already won recognition for his handling of naval matters and his appointment at this time marked the Emperor's determination to

[31] The writer is reminded by a distinguished historian of the period that so able an observer as Max Weber thought that the *Machtstaat* was not incompatible with social and political reform (Marianne Weber, *op. cit.*, pp. 231 ff.). This is not to say, however, that Bülow believed with Weber in the need for reform before the " national state " could be realized; on the contrary, no attempt at reform was made before or after launching into imperialism.

[32] Feldmarschall Graf von Waldersee, *Denkwürdigkeiten* (Berlin, 1922), II, 437.

proceed with plans for a larger navy.[33] The incarnation of German
scientific ability and of German patriotism, although limited in
outlook by an exclusively bureaucratic training, Tirpitz became, by
reason of the content he gave through his naval propaganda to
German thinking, another central figure in the imperialistic movement. The calm and convincing nature of his memoirs, apparently
so much more reliable than Bülow's, leaves no doubt about the importance of his work in the development during the 'nineties and
after of German popular demand for a navy. Where the boasts
and ineptitudes of Cabinet Chiefs like Senden und Bibran, Chief
of the Naval Cabinet, prejudiced the nation against the Emperor
and himself, Tirpitz' work was designed to reconcile the people to
the naval scheme. His nationalism was not aggressive and bolstered
by fine phrases; nor was it a conviction like Bülow's, partly senti-
mental-historical, partly economic in origin. Tirpitz worked out
instead some of the finest of the *raisons d'état* for the navy. Although one must bear in mind that these arguments also justified
Tirpitz' personal interest in realizing his task as a technician and
as head of the Admiralty Office and as such are often pure ration-
alizations, they must be taken as representative of the best of
German imperialistic thought. Tirpitz had a high conception of
the individual's duty to the state; therefore, he was conscientious
and painstaking both in thought and execution.[34]

[33] A complete account of the development of Tirpitz' plans, including the
famous Memorandum No. 9, will be found in Hallmann, *op. cit.* Even
Hallmann, who lays great weight on refuting Eckart Kehr and who attri-
butes the navy almost entirely to Tirpitz, does not deny that the Emperor
wanted "more navy." Undoubtedly Tirpitz did the work necessary to
provide Germany with a naval plan and to put this plan through; but
Hallmann simplifies the problem of the "road to the building of battleships" more than anyone who has read the Reichstag debates can admit
to be legitimate. The naval bills, even the First Naval Law, were not just
"let through." It must also be pointed out that European and world
conditions quite naturally determined the nature of Tirpitz' naval plans and
domestic conditions the content of his propaganda.

[34] His officers called Tirpitz "the father of the lie" for the excuses which
he made up on behalf of naval building. For important facts about
Tirpitz and for the relation between army and navy, reference should be
made to Dr. Alfred Vagts' most recent book, *The History of Militarism,
Romance and Reality of a Profession* (New York, 1938), *passim*, especially

Tirpitz' innermost conviction was the greater worth of the German People compared with that of the Anglo-Saxon peoples. He accused the latter of tainting the thought of the western world by their emphasis upon the philosophy of capitalism.[35] In holding this view Tirpitz showed himself a true bureaucratic official. He was not an enemy of England in any pusillanimous sense. He did not wish to give her a lesson, to take her down a peg in the diplomatic game. On the contrary, Tirpitz was as critical of the Krüger Telegram and of the Emperor's sudden enthusiasms as were the English themselves. But he did believe that the Germans should oppose the world dominion of the Anglo-Saxons lest the evils of industrialism wipe out the virtues of other peoples. This idea gained ready acceptance in a country struggling to preserve its agriculture, the remnants of its feudalism, and its strong monarchy, giving moral support to the pursuit of German *Machtpolitik*. The expressions "Anglo-Saxon contagion" or England's "bad influence" occur elsewhere in the writings of the period.[36]

Tirpitz denied that the navy constituted the chief source of bad feeling between the two countries. There existed, he thought, a fundamental and inevitable difference between the outlook of the two nations. England, he said, was not in sympathy with German industrial and commercial development but could certainly not destroy the latter by making an issue of the navy. Hence he put no stock in negotiations for an Anglo-German alliance (1901), nor faith in the proposals of Haldane's naval mission (1912). One may quote from his *Dokumente*:

> According to the way of thinking as it existed in England at the turn of the century, I did not believe in the Fata Morgana of a *bona fide* understanding between England and Germany through which Joseph Chamberlain aroused, per-

---

Chap. X and p. 221. Haller has pointed out that Tripitz did not understand politics or how foreign policy must be carried out. He had no conception of the effect of the navy on general policy and, in fact, the navy was never coördinated with the army (Haller, *Die Aera Bülows*, pp. 84-87, 90-94). This view agrees with that of Dr. Vagts' analysis, in which he states that in a way the German navy helped to defeat the German army in the World War.

[35] Admiral von Tirpitz, *Erinnerungen* (Leipzig, 1919), *passim*.

[36] *Cf. infra*, discussion of Wilhelm von Kardorff, p. 44.

haps in himself, certainly in many Germans, boundless dreams. A close alliance according to English wishes for power would never have answered German needs. For this equality would have been a necessary preliminary.[37]

The differences between the two countries, Tirpitz thought, need not lead to war. To prevent conflict he advocated the navy and "peace between Germany and the great non-Anglo-Saxon Powers of the East," Russia and Austria.[38] Thus, for all his emphasis before the public upon the military, strategic value of the navy, he considered the navy primarily as of political importance. It was a means by which Germany might attain to that equality (*Ebenbürtigkeit*) with the Anglo-Saxon Powers which Tirpitz thought had been lost after Bismarck. Only in possession of a navy could she defend the multiplicity of her interests, which now included a large overseas trade;[39] the navy alone could "carry into the world the national strength which rests at home upon our monarchy and our strong army; it was born for the people out of this idea. . . ."[40] In addition to its possibilities in the field of alliances, the navy would preserve peace by making it risky to attack a country prepared with naval as well as with military armaments. Even England would not venture to attack if the navy were strong enough.[41] Here spoke not only a strategist but a *Machtpolitiker*.

Without a navy, thought the Secretary for Naval Affairs, Germany could hope neither to maintain her world position nor her industry, especially her maritime interests—her export industry, merchant marine, transoceanic colonies, sea fisheries, Germanism abroad; and without these interests Wilhelminian Germany would

[37] Admiral von Tirpitz, *Politische Dokumente* (Stuttgart and Berlin, 1924-26), p. 1. Tirpitz thought that Bismarck under later conditions would not have wanted England in his system of alliances.

[38] *Erinnerungen*, p. 229.

[39] *Ibid., Letter to Stosch*, December 21, 1895, pp. 83 ff.

[40] *Ibid., Letter from the Commander of the " Kaiser,"* March, 1914, pp. 110-111.

[41] Tirpitz thought the balance of power on the sea could be kept by Germany allied with others and hence approaching England's naval strength; but he did not think that Germany alone could ever build up to England. Clearly, his idea of "a certain balance of power at sea by means of a coalition with us" excluded an English alliance (*ibid.*, p. 165).

be at a great disadvantage in her struggle with the Social Democrats. Germany must act, he said, " in no small degree because there lies in this new, great, national task and the economic gain which is bound up with it a strong palliative against educated and uneducated Social Democracy." [42]

Tirpitz' disbelief in an English alliance was paralleled by his opposition to a Russian one and to provocation of England by a zealous *Kolonialpolitik*. The military value of a Russian alliance seemed negligible to him, while the alliance itself might cause a war with England. Yet Tirpitz wished friendly relations with Russia and much of his objection to the colonial policy and imperialism of his government was due to the unnecessary antagonizing of Russia in Asia Minor and Persia.[43] On the whole Tirpitz opposed *Kolonialpolitik* rather than supported it and was at no time an over-ambitious promoter of it. He felt, at least later, that it consisted largely of phrases, which, he said, left " the false impression of its being the outcome of a conscious decision and action when it should be the result of organic growth." [44] This shrewd observation showed that he knew well enough the dangers of the Pan-German League and of its journalistic sympathizers.

In Tirpitz' opinion too much time had already been lost if the country was to be aroused to the need for a navy.[45] Germany continued to exist, he thought, on the political fat accumulated under

---

[42] *Ibid.*, pp. 80-81. Hallmann believes this means only that Tirpitz, who, he says, was not at all aware socially, wanted the navy to weld the nation together, to overcome anti-stateism (Hallmann, *op. cit.*, pp. 133-4). It is better to take the remark at its face value.

[43] *Ibid.*, pp. 220-221. *Cf. supra*, p. 15.

[44] *Ibid.*, p. 161. Lack of enthusiasm for colonies did not mean that Tirpitz neglected to push hard for new naval bases.

[45] Tirpitz said at the time: " America goes magnificently ahead. We unveil statues and hold parades. In addition the Reichstag and the bureaucrats and the several governments busy themselves with *querelles allemandes* and with chauvinism where it does not belong. We always want to reap without sowing. We put more weight on words than we do upon continuous and purposeful work, upon appearance more than upon actuality. Thus Germany has come to the turning point: either forward, or backward with France, Spain, Italy " (*Family Letter of Tirpitz*, cited by Hallmann, *op. cit.*, p. 135). Tirpitz frequently indulged in great pessimism, especially over the Social Democratic danger.

Bismarck; if she did not push forward, while keeping her implements of Power commensurate with her political goals, she would retrograde. In spite of the Emperor's efforts, enthusiasm for a navy advanced too slowly under Admiral Hollmann.[46] Hohenlohe was convinced in the autumn of 1896 that "the desire for a navy is not yet ripe in the German people. In general the economic situation is not favorable, and the conviction that the building of a navy will lead to new taxes makes for anxiety."[47] A memorandum containing most of the ideas later carried out by Tirpitz had even been presented to the Emperor without convincing him of their validity.[48] If the latter did not understand the details of future building, how could the layman do so? Almost immediately, therefore, upon his return from Asiatic waters in June, 1897 Tirpitz created the Bureau for Publicity and Parliamentary Affairs. The purpose of this bureau included the following points:

> . . . to enlighten and teach the German people its maritime goals and needs and to control the press. Furthermore, to influence publicity by word and picture, wherever possible by its [*Reichsmarineamt's*] own publications; to stimulate the important scientists and politicians to independent action, to supply them with materials; to work in associations, exhibitions and lectures as well as to provide prompt information on naval questions.[49]

Through the all-inclusive work of the Bureau Tirpitz' ideas spread everywhere. Large organizations like the Colonial Society and the Pan-German League coöperated eagerly with the Bureau; smaller ones and individuals drew heavily on the materials of the new department. Interest and enthusiasm spread quickly and effectively and the naval laws of 1898 and 1900 were passed amid general

---

[46] Kehr, *Schlachtflottenbau und Parteipolitik 1894-1901* (Berlin, 1930), p. 93.

[47] Cited by Hallmann, *op. cit.*, p. 233. At this time Hohenlohe was afraid of a *coup d'état*, especially if Hollmann were dismissed. Hollmann, however, first took leave of absence; Tirpitz came later.

[48] Hallmann, *op. cit.*, p. 238. Hallmann mentions in particular Memorandum No. 9, Special Report of November 28, 1895, and the Tirpitz Report of January 3, 1896.

[49] Memorandum: "*Die Aufgaben und die Tätigkeit des Nachrichtenbüros*," summarized by Kehr, *op. cit.*, p. 95.

acclaim. Tirpitz accomplished what the Emperor and Bülow could not have done alone.

But the new propaganda did not improve relations with England. Tirpitz realized from the first that success in his naval plans would depend on a new approach to the question of naval expansion. Hence his propaganda laid great emphasis upon the economic advantages of a navy. By means of this argument he hoped to overcome the Reichstag's fear of heavy taxes. At the same time his propaganda rested on the conviction, strengthened by his recent stay in the East, that England was the real enemy [50] because she competed most strongly in the economic field. Although the navy claimed to be built to avoid war with England, the propaganda for it taught fear and hence hatred of her. Thus Tirpitz deceived himself about the true effect of the navy and misled a whole people.

Another Imperial Secretary, important because of his support of German imperialism, stood out in the person of the new Secretary of the Interior, Count Posadowsky-Wehner.[51] As holder of this office after 1897 and primarily responsible for the tariff, the Canal Law, ship-subsidies, and social legislation, he of all the Imperial Secretaries incurred the greatest hatred of the Social Democrats. He considered trade, colonial expansion, and the navy necessary for Germany if she were to satisfy the Social Democratic elements in the state with wages and benefits sufficient to prevent revolution.[52] In this way he linked domestic policy with foreign policy and spoke

[50] Hallmann, *op. cit.*, Chap. VII, " *Der Entschluss zur Schlachtflotte gegen England.*"

[51] Adolf Wermuth, *Ein Beamtenleben* (Berlin, 1922), pp. 215 ff.   A description of Posadowsky is given here by one who worked with him. Wermuth said of him: " He got away as much as possible from the influence and temperament of the Emperor."   Hence the Emperor did not care particularly for Posadowsky, as Tirpitz said that the Emperor did not for him.   Instead Posadowsky had close connections with the bureaucracy and with the Reichstag.   He also coöperated closely with Miquel, Minister of Finance in Prussia, and with the Foreign Office through Koerner, the specialist for commercial treaties (Wermuth, *op. cit.*, p. 216; also Hohenlohe, *op. cit., passim*, especially, p. 450).

[52] *Stenographische Berichte des Reichstages*, December 11, 1897, IX Leg. Per., V Sess., I, 154 ff.

whenever he could in favor of the navy and colonies.[53] The navy seemed important to him as an instrument of force in connection with the tariff. He felt keenly the growth of the protectionist movement in the world at large; [54] hence he urged the need for Germany to push her way against tariff barriers into new markets by means of the threat of naval power. To combat the increasing difficulty from closed markets and new industrial competition which German merchants met abroad they must have behind them what he called " a real Power," especially in the less civilized parts of the world.[55] Posadowsky likewise advocated peace and at times spoke of the navy as a great instrument for peace. How he reconciled the function of the navy as an instrument for both war and peace remains obscure. On the whole he preferred the concept of Power, for he always left room for war and in 1900-1902 he became a strong protectionist, thus accepting high tariffs, in commercial relations the corollary of force, and the resulting intensification of the struggle for markets.[56]

Although Posadowsky was a practical man, he frequently used the argument *ad honorem patriae*. He inserted this argument into his long technical speeches, often as the final reason why the Reichstag should grant him further subsidies for the East Africa Line or should agree to the high cost of new ships.[57] It did not befit a great state, he said, to have few foreign markets, to have no ships

[53] Tirpitz did not speak a great deal and usually only briefly and to a specific point. Posadowsky, partly because of the nature of his office, spoke extensively and often in answer to attacks upon his work by the Social Democrats. His collected speeches fill three large volumes. See Johannes Penzler, *Die Reden Posadowskys, 1882-1900* (Leipzig, 1907).

[54] *Reden, op. cit.*, I, 534; *Cf.* also II, 239-240.

[55] *Ibid.*, I, 535.

[56] Vagts, *op. cit.*, I, 141. Dr. Vagts shows how Posadowsky was not willing to rely upon force in the question of reprisals for American tariffs. He was in favor of a very careful handling of the tariff question " since it is doubtful whether one would help or harm our export to America by action against America." The American situation strengthened him in his desire for a navy and for the future autonomous tariff. He attempted to escape from the unpleasant realities of the commercial situation by putting his hope in the authority which *Machtpolitik* might give.

[57] *Cf.* his speech on " *Postdampfschiffverbindungen mit überseeischen Ländern*," February 17, 1898, in which he said: " In such a moment I

which could be sent to the aid of its citizens and merchants, to have no part of the earth reserved for the German flag. In one of his speeches he remarked: " As soon as one has colonies they become not only a part of a broader Fatherland but a part of our national honor." [58] It appeared to him a splendid thing for the youth of the country to have a national goal like that which the young men of the 'sixties and 'seventies had had; this goal was worth risks and worth the financial burden to the country. The cost of the colonies could even be considered as a great " cultural expense."

In addition to the *raisons d'état* for imperialism and to the need for it as a means of relieving the internal political tension, the imperial ministers were influenced by the wishes of the Emperor himself. No doubt exists that William II's own enthusiasm exceeded the bounds of a reasonable ambition and became at times difficult to restrain. Whence arose this dream of expansion and greatness and what were the motives underlying it?

As has been suggested previously in this chapter the Emperor was open to influence from many individuals—from those at Court, from the military attachés and the Cabinet Chiefs, and from others who had access to him. These men were neither reprobates nor was William II a degenerate. Many of these associates were, however, of questionable judgment in affairs of state and few could refrain from the flattery and subservience to which the Emperor easily succumbed.[59] Since the Emperor liked to act on his own

believe that a great nation must risk something " (*Reden*, I, 629-38). After 1900 the financial difficulties of the Empire became great. The debts mounted annually.

[58] *Ibid.*, II, 240; also pp. 294-5.

[59] In his memoirs Count Waldersee mentions the bad influence upon the Emperor of a man like Lucanus, Chief of the Civil Cabinet, while Eulenburg leaves no doubt of the evil effects of the Emperor's retinue, especially of the military aides (*Flügeladjutanten*), upon his conduct (Haller, *op. cit.*, Chap. VI). The son of the Chancellor, Alexander von Hohenlohe, also testifies to the stupidities of the court life and military surroundings to which William II submitted (Alexander von Hohenlohe, *Aus meinem Leben* [Frankfurt, 1925], pp. 363 f.). See also Tirpitz, *op. cit.*, I, 206 f.; Hohenlohe, *op. cit.*, pp. 193 ff. Hammann, too, gives vivid examples of the character of the Imperial environment. See especially Hammann, *Der neue Kurs, passim.*

initiative, it was dangerous to approve his impetuous judgment. The story is told that a certain Engelbrecht, military attaché in Rome, one of the Emperor's favorites, came to him just after the Italian defeat at Adua with a plan for Italian disarmament, which he wished to propose to King Humbert in the Emperor's name. William II immediately seized upon the scheme and ordered arrangements made for the prompt dispatch of the business. Only with difficulty did the Foreign Office prevent him from taking a step which might well have broken up the Triple Alliance.[60] Eulenburg complained even after 1897 of the intriguing interest which military men like Engelbrecht took in politics, of the political letters and memoranda which they wrote in order to show their ability, and of the frequent appointment of men like Count Wedel over the heads of the career diplomats. The three volumes of Waldersee's memoirs, containing relatively little of military and a great deal of political interest, bear out this criticism.

An examination of Count Waldersee's memoirs, does not show however, that the Count and Field Marshall inspired the Emperor's imperialistic ambitions. The comprehension which Waldersee displayed both of the Emperor and of the internal situation in Germany at the close of the century is striking.[61] Apparently no man regretted more than Waldersee the necessity of recording so depressing an outlook. Like Eulenburg, Waldersee seems to have understood the Emperor's peculiar nature, the danger of his unpremeditated acts, the selfish intrigues going on about him, and the detrimental influence upon him of dependents. He saw even more clearly than Eulenburg how little Bülow was able to reform the

[60] Haller, *op. cit.*, p. 260. Only two years before this Eulenburg had sought to warn the Emperor against the political activities of Engelbrecht, but with complete failure. The Emperor wrote of this aide: "He has my fullest confidence and is my comrade and aide-de-camp." Another instance of William's ill-considered action when he was away from Berlin with no advisers except his dangerous aides is given by Dr. Vagts. The occasion was furnished by the Spanish-American War. A telegram from Dietrichs, Admiral in charge of the German fleet at Manila, intended for the Foreign Office reached the Emperor at sea. Upon his aides persuading him that he could secure a part of the Spanish possessions with his fleet, the Emperor ordered the ships left at Manila (Vagts, *op. cit.*, II, 1337, 1350).

[61] For Waldersee's lack of military understanding and knowledge, *cf.* Vagts, *The History of Militarism*, *passim*.

monarch or improve internal conditions. Nor did he consider imperialism a solution. He favored neither the lease of Kiauchow and
the expansion of German influence in China, nor intervention in
China in 1900.[62]   He looked with extreme skepticism upon the
Emperor's trip to Constantinople,[63] spoke of the Bagdad Railroad as
the Emperor's " pet idea " and was troubled when William II asked
Henckel von Donnersmarck, who Waldersee thought of doubtful
ability, to head the Bagdad enterprise.[64]   Waldersee also opposed
the building of a large navy, not merely because he was a military
man.   As early as 1896 he saw the danger of competition with
England and wrote:

> The Emperor seems to me to have gone completely astray in
> his intention to increase the marine. We should, I think, as
> soon as possible try to acquire a few more cruisers but I cannot
> be enthusiastic about rapid and large increases of warships as
> well. To compete with England in the field of naval arma-
> ments would be presumptuous; we should only make ourselves
> ridiculous. A far-seeing, wise policy is very much needed so
> that we may avoid isolation. The Emperor should not forget
> that our prestige and the confidence in our trustworthiness have
> greatly decreased since Bismarck's exit.[65]

Waldersee did not wish the Crown to enhance its prestige by an
erratic pursuit of *Weltpolitik*.[66]   He knew the need for greater
national solidarity in Germany; but in the face of disunity he

[62] Waldersee, *op. cit.*, II, 449.

[63] Langer, *op. cit.*, protests that the journey was not motivated by imperialism, but Waldersee thought that it was and condemned it accordingly.

[64] Waldersee, *op. cit.*, II, 366, 393 f.

[65] *Ibid.*, III, 3-4, and especially p. 198. The following entry deserves to
be quoted. It is from December 25, 1903: " Much is written and spoken
over the character of the new century. I think that centuries as such do
not count, but that about the turn of this century it began to be clear
how world politics had changed, principally due to two circumstances, the
ability and the inclination of the United States to take part in world
affairs, and the completely changed position of the far East. Through our
confused colonial policy and our very tactless pronouncement of imperialism we are more involved with the constellations than is perhaps desirable.
Greater reluctance would surely not harm us; it would probably have
helped us " (*ibid.*, p. 198).

[66] *Ibid.*, III, 7.

remained more level-headed and cautious than his younger contemporaries. He believed that Anglo-German rivalry was primarily economic and that the Germans should apply themselves to improving their business rather than to building a large navy. He would have asserted the power of the state by crushing the large strikes and keeping down the Social Democrats,[67] by openly allying the government with the Conservatives instead of forcing them into the Agrarian League, of whose pernicious influence he was well aware,[68] and by repealing the universal suffrage law. Waldersee, however, did not persuade the Emperor to adopt these strenuous measures any more than he prevented imperialism. The Emperor was undoubtedly fond of his Field Marshall—at least at this time—and convinced of his military ability;[69] but Imperial policy was not laid down by Count Waldersee. The latter's fault consisted of his lack of courage to oppose his Sovereign and in not making clear to him the dangerous shoals ahead in domestic affairs.

Vice Admiral Baron von Senden und Bibran, Head of the Marine Cabinet after 1888, stood very close to the Emperor and took a thoroughly reactionary position in affairs of state. Eulenburg said of Senden that he, like others, would gladly have seen the Emperor rule without the Reichstag, that he thought every military, political, or juristic question best settled by the Emperor alone.[70] Senden

---

[67] *Ibid.*, II, 388, 404, 424; III, 198, 205, 216.

[68] *Ibid.*, III, 181.   [69] *Cf.* note 61.

[70] Haller, *op. cit.*, pp. 202-3. Dissolution of the Reichstag, change in the electoral law, *coup d'état* were all thought of " by the Emperor's following with Admiral Senden at the head " at the time of the refusal of the naval bill, March 28, 1897 (*ibid.*, p. 237. *Cf.* also Hohenlohe, *op. cit.*, *passim*, especially pp. 288-9). Hallmann, on the other hand, warns against these harsh estimates of Senden and pictures him as an uninspired but very loyal and devoted aide, who gave up his career for a place, which he never liked, at the Emperor's side (Hallmann, *op. cit.*, pp. 54 ff.). Haller said of him: " This gentleman had so little understanding of political considerations that he at one time naively said to a diplomat, who warned him of England's expected opposition. ' What does England matter to us? We can build what we want to.' In addition, and partly by his own fault, he had personal experiences which turned him against the English. It was due to his untiring, burrowing influence through his daily contact with the Emperor that the course of *Schlachtflottenpolitik* on the high seas was adopted " (Haller, *Die Aera Bülows*, p. 92).

supported the Emperor in the naval question and considered it his duty to watch over the rights of the Crown in the issue.   He argued, for example, that William II could appoint Tirpitz to the secretaryship for naval affairs without consulting the Chancellor.[71] It is impossible to separate his share from that of the Emperor's in formulating naval plans.   But if the initiative belonged to the latter, the Head of the Naval Cabinet encouraged him.[72]   He was known as the Emperor's confidential man in naval matters and his overbearing, tactless way grew repugnant to the Emperor's other friends.   On one occasion in 1896 he declared loudly in a public casino that the Reichstag must grant three hundred million marks for new ships and that by the time it had been ten times dissolved it would readily enough do so.[73]   On another day at his table in a café Senden harangued at some length against Hohenlohe and the government.   The episode led to a general discussion of internal politics in the street and later in the press.[74]   In both cases, as Eulenburg wrote, the effect produced harmed the Emperor's reputation. Although Senden was doubtless more stubborn than malicious, these remarks furnished grist for the mill of both the Social Democrats and Eugen Richter.   In short, Eulenburg believed that if Senden were transferred from his staff position to Hollmann's place as Secretary for Naval Affairs he would ruin himself.[75]   In his present position he remained safe from the public and for the Emperor's sake helped Tirpitz with his policy.   It is clear that in all the drives from 1891 to 1897 for an increase of the navy Senden stood forth as chief protagonist, urging the Emperor on to political

[71] Hallmann, *op. cit.*, p. 55.

[72] Waldersee certainly connected Senden closely with the naval plans, although without having definite information as to the origin of them. Eulenburg seems to have seen plans for a battle fleet shown him by Senden in 1891.   Haller said that he had found notes to this effect but had had no room for them in his volume.   On the other hand, Kehr left the impression that the Emperor was responsible and that no plan was adequately worked out until Tirpitz began one in 1894.   The Emperor, however, did not immediately agree with Tirpitz' proposals (*Cf.* Kehr, *op. cit.*, pp. 25 f.). See also Haller, *op. cit.*, p. 261, note 58; Hallmann, *op. cit.*, *passim*.

[73] *Letter from Eulenburg to the Emperor*, December 12, 1896, cited by Haller, *op. cit.*, pp. 262-3.

[74] *Loc. cit.*   [75] *Ibid.*, p. 226.

moves—dissolution of the Reichstag, *coup d'état*—which, if William II had adopted them, might have ruined the monarchy. But for the most part loyalty prompted Senden; even without him the Emperor would scarcely have failed to develop his plans for a great navy.[76]

Other intimates of the Emperor had little effect on his imperialism. Lucanus, Chief of the Civil Cabinet, exerted a bad influence.[77] Count Waldersee and Eulenburg both fought him and the former thought it partly Lucanus' fault that the Emperor regarded the Social Democratic danger less seriously than he did.[78] But Lucanus did not advocate imperialism and neither William nor Bülow nor the Pan-Germans received inspiration from him. Hancke, Chief of the Military Cabinet, seems also not to have been directly responsible in any way for the Emperor's imperialism.

The Emperor did not derive his imperialism so much from his entourage as from himself.[79] His exalted ideas of himself and therefore of the country which he ruled, his vanity in desiring to equal the greatest technicians in knowledge of modern methods and invention, his pride in possession contributed to his early conceived hopes for a navy and for prestige abroad.[80] It is difficult to trace the development of the Emperor's enthusiasm for either navy or colonies and to know what moved him most to these enthusiasms.

[76] Both Kehr and Tirpitz himself in his memoirs referred to the complete lack of plans for a navy before 1897 and of the resulting uncertainty in the Reichstag which made that body afraid of future demands. During this period, 1890 to 1897, Senden contributed to the general fear by his hints and ruthless vehemence. In a letter from Eulenburg to Holstein written at Karlsbad on May 10, 1897, Eulenburg intimated that the Emperor did not think Senden very competent but was grateful to him for his support. If he had been competent, it is probable that he would have formulated plans before a new secretary came on the scene. *Cf.* Haller, *op. cit.*, p. 240.

[77] *Loc. cit.*   [78] Waldersee, *op. cit.*, II, 424.

[79] For characterization of William II see Holstein, *op. cit.*, pp. 245, 316, 324; also Hohenlohe, Waldersee, Bülow, Haller. Extremely interesting is Houston Stewart Chamberlain's correspondence with the Emperor, but this begins only in 1901, *Houston Stewart Chamberlains Briefe, 1882-1924 und Briefwechsel mit Kaiser Wilhelm II* (Berlin, 1928), II, 131 ff.

[80] *Cf.* account of the Emperor's naval plans in 1889 and 1890, Sidney Lee, *King Edward VII, a Biography* (London, 1925), I, Chap. XXXV.

4

He wrote his memoirs many years afterward when he was able to use arguments possibly not thought of at the time. His mind functioned so erratically that it is often impossible to know whether the argument he used at one time held for another or decided him at any time. He has written that his interests in the navy began in his boyhood.[81] In his young manhood he went so far as to advise Bismarck of the need for a navy " capable of defending that property [colonial] against foreign rapacity." He had, he asserts, already seen the connection between colonies and a navy.[82] On the other hand, although in 1890 Hatzfeldt told Salisbury that " the Emperor lays value upon the development of our colonies," [83] William himself agreed to sacrifice colonial land to obtain the island of Helgoland; [84] he thought the latter necessary to naval protection and worth colonial territory in exchange. Almost at once upon his accession to power in 1888 he manifested interest in naval affairs. He spent the first few weeks of his reign at sea and upon his return commanded that the budget for 1889-90, then in preparation, be altered to include funds for four modern battleships. From this moment, in spite of a decade of hindrance, his determination to build a modern navy never lagged.

[81] William II, *My Early Life* (New York, 1926), pp. 27, 41, 42.

[82] *Ibid.*, p. 212. *Cf.* also *Ereignisse und Gestalten* (Berlin, 1922), pp. 7, 8. In the latter book the Emperor says: " I dutifully reminded the Prince that the merchants and capitalists were beginning energetically to develop the colonies and accordingly—as I knew from Hanse circles—reckoned on protection through a navy." At this early date, however, the Hanse cities were not favorable to a navy. Already the Emperor showed his preoccupation with England as the country which could land on German soil (*ibid.*, p. 8). Further, Germany's dependence on England, he said, had been made clear to him by the lectures of Privy Councillor Raschdau of the Foreign Office (*ibid.*, p. 10). At the same time, he holds, he intended to have England's help in securing coaling stations for his navy (*ibid.*, p. 68).

[83] *Hatzfeldt to Caprivi*, April 30, 1890, *Die Grosse Politik der europäischen Kabinette, 1871-1914. Sammlung der diplomatischen Akten des Auswärtigen Amtes* (im Auftrage des Auswärtigen Amtes herausgegeben von Johannes Lepsius, Albrecht Mendelssohn Bartholdy, Friedrich Thimme; Berlin, 1922-27), VIII, No. 1674, p. 9.

[84] The Emperor's memoirs lay great emphasis upon Helgoland (*Ereignisse*, p. 46).

In 1894 the Emperor read Alfred Mahan's book, *The Influence of Sea Power Upon History* (1890), and he cabled his friend Poultney Bigelow that he intended to learn it by heart.[85] This book and other reading encouraged his naval interest. In 1895 when perusing a report to the Foreign Office from Saurma, German Ambassador at Washington, on commercial relations with the United. States, he remarked, "Where is a strong navy to represent our interests?"[86] At the time of the Krüger Telegram and again in 1898 he spoke of a "war fleet able to strike and to command respect" as the appropriate implement for the occasion.[87] The colonies took second place in his mind, although this was not a negligible one. For example, in China in 1894 and 1895, before banking and commercial interests wished to dispense with English coöperation there, the Emperor led the movement for German markets and concessions. With the navalists he prepared the way for the lease of Kiau-chow in 1897.[88]

The reason why colonial policy assumed a lesser rôle in the Emperor's imperialism is revealed in the course of his thought. The connection between large commercial interests and a navy to protect them, between colonies as aids to import and export trade and an efficient German navy was a point made repeatedly by the Emperor, but not convincingly.[89] The fact that the Emperor loved to draw ship models and hated to read trade statistics seems clear. To him the navy had validity as a political instrument, a *Machtfaktor,* and colonies possessed attraction for him either to give the navy a cause for existence, as in the case of coaling stations, or especially to attest to Germany's power-prestige, her "Roman world Empire." He wrote in a marginal note to a memorandum of 1897:

> We shall secure the sympathy of America and of England in proportion as we strengthen our navy and accordingly make it inadvisable for these countries to maltreat or pro-

[85] Charles C. Taylor, *The Life of Admiral Mahan, Naval Philosopher* (New York, 1920), p. 131, cited by Vagts, *op. cit.*, I, 652, note 1.

[86] Vagts, *op. cit.*, p. 112.

[87] *Ibid.*, p. 150, note 1. The occasion was furnished by the passage of the Dingley Tariff Law in the United States.

[88] *Ibid.*, II, Chap. XI.

[89] William II, *The Kaiser's Speeches* (ed. Gauss, 1915), p. 169.

voke us lest they suffer harm thereby. I do not call the above-mentioned sympathy [that mentioned in the memorandum] anything other than a cool reckoning with the facts; it does not come from the heart.[90]

In the increasing number of international difficulties which arose for Germany William regretted the small size of the navy and sought a solution of them by urging its expansion rather than by mastering the specific situation and applying the rational remedy. Dr. Vagts has abundantly proved this in his study of German American relations during these years. It can be proved for Anglo-German relations by recalling that a Krüger Telegram was used to rally enthusiasm for the navy and to direct attention from internal to external affairs.[91] Of what specific use to alleged commercial interests and capital investments in the Transvaal was such a gesture as the Telegram?[92]

As internal difficulties increased William II became more attached to the idea of a larger navy. He seems to have felt that it might help him to bridge the gap between himself and his people. At one time he said that the German people remained hard to manage and still thought more of the individual states than of the Empire; but he hoped to revive patriotism by strengthening the navy.[93] By placing himself at the head of a movement which already commanded support in some circles and after 1898 did so widely, the Emperor undoubtedly expected to revive his popularity and convince the people of his greatness. When between 1894 and 1897 he gave up his programme of social reform and made his peace with the Agrarians, he resigned in effect his power in domestic affairs in favor of the coalition or *Sammlungspolitik*. His chief sphere of

[90] *Memoir of December 8, 1897*, with the Emperor's notation, cited by Vagts, *op. cit.*, II, 1274.

[91] *Cf. infra*, Chap. V of this study.

[92] *Cf.* also Hohenlohe, *op. cit.*, p. 32. William said to Hohenlohe on January 31, 1895: "If we wanted to retrieve in Samoa the vanished influence of Germany we should have appeared with many German ships; this would not be possible in the present condition of our navy." See also Vagts, I, 636 ff., 914.

[93] *American Minister in Copenhagen to Root*, April 7, 1906, cited by Vagts, *op. cit.*, I, 203, note 6.

activity henceforth lay in the new imperialism. He liked his rôle and in some respects it suited him well.

According to his speeches and memoirs William II felt attached by bonds of blood and sentiment to England as to no other land. As a child he loved his visits to his grandmother and as a young Emperor he took pride in his English Admiral's uniform. But, if this feeling was sincere, his English policy did not clearly follow its dictates; for his early fears were fears of England, and in order to be able to build a navy he later adopted the Tirpitz policy with its anti-English implications. It is significant that the Emperor's favorite plan for a grouping of the continental Powers into a Tariff Union against the United States did not include England. Even when the Foreign Office explained to him that this union would be ineffective without England, he unwillingly gave up the idea that the contingent should stand together against Anglo-Saxon competitors.[94] Furthermore, he changed the Bismarckian policy of always coöperating with England in the Far East when in 1894 he did not support the move for intervention in the Sino-Japanese controversy and, according to the English view, made the war possible.[95] His secret correspondence with the Tsar also suggests a definite interest in connections other than an English alliance. Through his hold on the Tsar he hoped to win support for the Tariff Union and bound himself to be pro-Russian in the Far East.[96] More important, however, is the fact that his activity in the field of imperialism carried the certainty of bringing him into constant friction with England, as well as with the United States, and William had neither the knowledge nor the patience sufficient to meet the problems involved. His English and American policies were secondary to his desire for a navy and *Macht*. Emotionally he loved England and would have shuddered at prophecy of war with her. He protested

[94] Vagts, *op. cit.*, I, 140 f.

[95] *Letters of Queen Victoria* (Third Series), II, 496. Also Vagts, *op. cit.*, II, 940.

[96] It is true that William II often showed a predilection for England. In 1901 he suggested to Lansdowne a grouping of England, Germany and France against the United States and Russia. Under Eckardstein's impetus he showed at times great desire for an alliance. But this does not mean that he was consistently friendly to England or that he worked hard for good relations. He blew hot and cold, as he did in most matters.

that his ambitions were legitimate ones for Germany and would insure peace with all the world.

The head of the German state was, therefore, interested in imperialism and passionately devoted to a navy. By the ministerial changes of 1897 he secured men loyal to him and his cause, who by realizing his dream of imperialism hoped to curb his and his favorites' influence in domestic politics and unify a torn nation. From varied motives the chief power group in the country, that of the Emperor and the bureaucrats, determined to pursue a policy of *Weltpolitik*. The policy was not aimed against any nation, except as enmities are implicit in a programme of national expansion. So great was their faith in the programme that even when statesmen perceived these implicit enmities, as in the case of Tirpitz' naval plans, they thought them not sufficiently serious to outweigh the expected benefits of imperialism or they hoped to smoothe them out by diplomacy.

CHAPTER II

GERMAN PARLIAMENTARY PARTIES IN THE POST-BISMARCKIAN PERIOD, 1890-1902 [1]

It is true that our fatherland is in a bad way, perhaps worse off than ever before in history. The long-sought new grouping of parties has been achieved. The erstwhile Conservatives now openly call themselves Agrarians and the Liberals are more a reminiscence than a political factor. The existing parties operate under the banner of hatred and envy . . . . Envy or the so-called parties of material interests are the true bases of our present party system, at the moment overwhelmingly represented by the two groups which exploit or intend to exploit the nation to the advantage of the large landowners or to that of the workers. It is also true that through its own fault the Liberal party has further made more difficult a difficult situation.

Theodor Mommsen, *Reden und Aufsätze*, pp. 473-4.

Vice-Admiral Senden advocated the ideal of a government without a Reichstag because up to 1898 the Emperor met so much opposition to his naval plans in this body. If Tirpitz after 1898 overcame this opposition, there is interest in discovering why he succeeded and in what way he won over the parties to navalism and imperialism. The questions naturally arise as to which were the leading parties and groups in the Reichstag, what their controlling interests and ideals were, what relations they had to the government, whether any among them persisted in opposing the new imperialism.

It has already been pointed out that parliamentary government had not made rapid strides in Bismarckian Germany. The Iron Chancellor had carried out the Liberal programme for unification and had set up a new state before the old Liberals had realized how exclusively he had employed Prussian methods in the work. With only a few outstanding exceptions the Liberal leaders were

---

[1] The most recent general work on this subject is Willy Kremer, *Der soziale Aufbau der Parteien des deutschen Reichstages von 1871-1918* (Emsdetten, 1936).

absorbed in the vigorous life of the Empire without fully understanding the tragedy which had befallen their principles. In the
'seventies, particularly after the economic collapse of 1873, when
they awoke to the danger of losing parliamentarism, it was too
late to recover control. They were allies of Bismarck but not his
superiors. Afterward, Bismarck's long rule coupled with the
untimely death of Frederick III excluded from active political life
the second generation of Liberals, who found outlets for their
energy in economic and scientific rather than in parliamentary
activity. By 1890 the third generation, grandsons of Liberals and
reformers, were voting either with the Conservatives or with the
extreme left parties because they found the middle or erstwhile
Liberal parties so weak and devoid of objectives.[2] The government
offices were filled with bureaucrats who had learned to obey Bismarckian orders and had accepted or acquiesced in feudal-Conser-
vative ideology. Their patriotism was unquestioned; but they were
incapable of suggesting other solutions to the problems of the
Empire and the monarchy than a further use of Bismarckian
methods.[3] After 1890 they showed even less Liberalism than before.

Glaring inconsistencies existed everywhere in the new Empire.
Universal suffrage for the Reichstag—Bismarck had granted it in
the expectation that the masses would vote Conservative—[4] contrasted with the three-class system of voting in Prussia. Similar
restrictions on suffrage existed in other states. They prevented

[2] For an example one may turn to Max Weber's search for a party to
which he could honestly belong, Marianne Weber, *Max Weber: Ein Lebensbild* (Tübingen, 1926), pp. 231 ff. Note also Friedrich Naumann's turning
away from his Conservative background to social reform programmes and
his complete lack of knowledge of Liberalism until he was well along in
public life. Theodor Heuss, *Friedrich Naumann, Der Mann, Das Werk,
Die Zeit* (Stuttgart and Berlin, 1937), esp. p. 228.

[3] The German-Social Representative Liebermann von Sonnenberg (1848-
1911) said at one time in the Reichstag: " It is unfortunately true that an
ever-growing estrangement is taking place between the German bureaucracy and the German people. It is true that the man at the green table
no longer has the needed sympathy with the soul of the people " (*Sten.
Ber. d. Reich.*, IX Leg. Per., IV Sess., IV, 2693). *Cf.* Hohenlohe's bad
opinion of the Prussian bureaucracy (Hohenlohe, *op. cit.*, pp. 290).

[4] Meinecke, *Weltbürgertum und Nationalstaat* (Munich and Berlin,
1919), p. 518 and note.

men who legally participated in national elections from taking part
in those of the states or the communities. They deprived them of
the training which would have educated them to exercise intelli-
gently their national franchise. Bismarck had so effectively controlled electoral machinery and the organs of government that a
vote did not constitute practical participation in governing. When
his spell was withdrawn, even the Conservatives found Bismarckian
methods unbearable. They wished to share in the direction of
affairs and their effort to do so led to bitter strife during the
'nineties. In these years they violently denounced the government
at times on foreign as well as on domestic policy.[5]

Bismarck had never succeeded in bringing about a happy relationship between Prussia and the Reich. Prussia, with her reactionary constitution almost intact, continued to control the Empire.[6]
When Caprivi tried to correct this, he failed completely; only a
thoroughgoing change in the *de facto* constitution could have
emancipated the nation from Prussian influence. The change never
occurred before 1914 because the Prussian Conservatives were too
strong;[7] even during the World War they resisted to the last a
change in the Prussian electoral system.

William II's accession to the throne revived Liberal hopes for a

[5] Friedrich Naumann, *Demokratie und Kaisertum* (Berlin, 1900), Pt.
II, pp. 81 ff. The part of the Conservatives in politics is described later
in this chapter. Discussion of the Reich constitution and governmental
machinery may be found in: Fritz Hartung, *Deutsche Verfassungsgeschichte
vom 15. Jahrhundert bis zur Gegenwart* (Leipzig and Berlin, 1922);
Johannes Ziekursch, *Politische Geschichte im neuen deutschen Kaiserreich*
(Frankfurt, 1930); especially, Hans Goldschmidt, *Das Reich und Preussen
im Kampf um die Führung* (Berlin, 1931).

[6] Goldschmidt, *op. cit., passim.*

[7] The actual constitution of the Empire would have allowed for a more
liberal and parliamentary system. This fact became evident enough during
the World War; but the system as it had crystallized under Bismarck
was retained. Many attempts were made to withdraw universal suffrage
in Reichstag elections, and *coup d'état* plans abounded as the Social Democrats became more powerful. See especially Egmont Zechlin, *Staats-
streichpläne unter Bismarck und Wilhelm II, 1890-1894* (Stuttgart and
Berlin, 1929); Fritz Hellwig, *Carl Freiherr von Stumm-Halberg* (Saarbrücken, 1936). This recent biography abounds in evidence of *coup d'état*
plans.

few months, especially at the time of the dismissal of Bismarck. But these hopes died when the young Emperor gave up one by one his early plans for social reform; his erratic personality and sudden interference in internal affairs increased the feeling of uncertainty.[8] Caprivi took some important steps toward a more liberal régime, particularly in new commercial and Polish policies, while the appointment of Hohenlohe preserved the appearance of liberal sympathies; but actually fewer and fewer liberal measures were given effect. William's interest changed to imperialism and, as has been noted, the shifts in administrative personnel in 1897 made the position of the Prussian Conservatives more secure.

If moderate Liberalism suffered the same fate under William II as under Bismarck, it is clear that the Progressives *(Freisinnige)* and the Social Democrats fared even worse. Although the Social Democrats emancipated themselves from the Socialist Laws and eventually secured (1899) the right of free association and certain improvements in the social security laws, they played no political part beyond that of opposition. They fought the few surviving Liberals who had aided them to obtain these privileges, as they did the other bourgeois or aristocratic parties. Their opposition was all the more ruthless because they knew that they could not hope to acquire power themselves.

By 1890 the lack of influence of the Liberal parties stood out clearly. The history of Liberalism in the 'nineties is one of further emasculation. It is not surprising, therefore, to find in the Reichstag only a faint echo of the English tradition to which the old Liberals were so devoted. The middle parties accepted imperialism, which after the passage of almost thirty aimless years meant to them the setting of new national goals.

A. *The Conservatives*

The most important single fact in the party history of the 'nineties was the return of the Conservatives to the leading rôle in German politics. Although much of the Conservative tradition had

---

[8] The biography of Friedrich Naumann illustrates the sympathy with which the young Emperor was received and the gradual disillusionment he brought his admirers (Heuss, *op. cit.*, pp. 76, 129, 176-7, 341, 344, 474, 571).

been kept alive after 1870 by William I and Bismarck as well as by the Junkers east of the Elbe, the Prussian Conservative party itself had suffered. Hammerstein, editor of the *Kreuzzeitung,* once wrote in this Prussian-Conservative organ that, like the monk in the fable who returned to his cloister after a hundred years of wandering, the old Conservatives seemed in the 'seventies in danger of wandering about among the parties without finding a resting place.[9] The creation of the new Reich had not been offensive to all Conservatives. The formation of the Free-Conservative party in 1866 to support Bismarck in foreign and internal policies early gave the latter important Conservative connections.[9a] In the elections of 1867 to the North German Confederation this party won thirty-four seats. During the first years of the new Empire (1871 to

[9] Walther Frank, *Hofprediger Adolf Stoecker und die christlich-soziale Bewegung* (Berlin, 1928), p. 139.

[9a] The Free Conservatives were more important in politics than their numbers indicated since they included high bureaucrats and men like Wilhelm von Kardorff, landowner, speculator, and founder of the Central Union of German Industrialists, and Stumm, a large industrialist of the Saar. Kardorff's own words tell something about the purpose of the founding of the Free-Conservative party. In 1907 he said: " It was not exactly easy for me. I had entered the ranks of the old Conservative party at that time, and, since I dared for the first time to express myself in the Conservative group at the time of the pending choice of President for the Landtag, it seemed to me desirable to vote for Herr von Forckenbeck of the National Liberal party, which had been founded in the meantime, in order to bring about a reconciliation with this part of the Liberal party which had decided for the national point of view. Thereupon I and a friend of mine, who was one of the founders of our party, Herr von Hagenmeister, the later President of Westphalia, were overwhelmed with ridicule and scorn, although there was no chance that a Conservative would be chosen for president. We were accusingly asked how we could do a thing like that. The result was that on the same day we left the Conservative party and went over to the Free-Conservative group " (Siegfried von Kardorff, *Wilhelm von Kardorff: Ein nationaler Parlamentarier im Zeitalter Bismarcks und Wilhelms II, 1828-1907,* Berlin, 1936, p. 31). (The National Liberal party was not founded until November 17, 1866, and the above vote took place on September 6. Forckenbeck, therefore, was still a Progressive [*Fortschrittler*]. Kardorff's son says that Kardorff probably did not join the Free Conservatives until the vacation at Christmas. This error, however, does not alter the reason why Kardorff left the Conservatives.) *Cf.* also Hellwig, *op. cit.,* pp. 73 ff., 573.

1878), however, the National Liberals held control of the Reichstag by majorities which they were able to form with help from the Free-Conservative party on their right or the Progressive party on their left. Unable to adjust themselves, the old Prussian Conservatives remained inactive.[10] Their strong religious sentiment even led them during the *Kulturkampf* into direct opposition to Bismarck lest the evangelical church suffer with the Catholic through the school and marriage laws and the dominant state control.[11] Only by 1876 did another Bismarckian group take form from among the Conservatives, that of Helldorf-Bedra's German Conservative party. For the first time the Conservatives through this new group began to seek support outside Prussia in the hope of building up a national party.[12]

During the first years of the decade 1870 to 1880 Germany had enjoyed unprecedented prosperity and industrial activity, which helped to cement Bismarck's political alliance with the Liberals. Both Liberals and Conservatives were staunch adherents of free-trade. In 1873, however, a serious economic crisis set in and lasted for several years. At the same time that industrial activity fell off and the home market for grain declined, the Agrarians came to realize that they no longer had surplus grain for export and that they faced the danger of competition within the home market from Russian and American wheat and rye. The check to industrial development and to agricultural prosperity weakened faith in the free-trade system. As early as 1876 in the founding of the German Conservative party economic issues received first place on the agenda. The continuance of unlimited free-trade was questioned, although as yet without an express declaration of protectionist sympathies.[13] In the same year Kardorff of the Free Conservatives founded the Central Union of German Industrialists to further a protectionist movement. It aimed to repeal the law, passed in 1873

[10] Ludwig Bergsträsser, *Geschichte der politischen Parteien in Deutschland* (Berlin, 1928), pp. 74 f.; Hermann von Petersdorff, *Hermann von Kleist-Retzow* (Berlin, 1907), pp. 308 ff.

[11] Petersdorff, *op. cit.*, pp. 410 f.

[12] *Ibid.*, pp. 463 f. The most famous opposition of the old Conservatives found voice in the *Aeraartikel* of the *Kreuzzeitung* in 1875.

[13] Adalbert Wahl, *Deutsche Geschichte* (Leipzig, 1930), I, 463.

and effective January 1, 1877, abolishing the tariff on iron. Although it failed for the moment, the movement gained ground and soon won over the Chancellor himself. Through an alliance of the Conservatives with Bismarck to secure a protective tariff on grain the way opened for a return of the Conservatives to influence, while Bismarck was not averse to the alliance in order to break the power of the National Liberals.

The new German Conservative party found sympathy among many of the leading Prussian Agrarians, Kanitz-Podangen, Mirbach-Sorquitten, Kleist-Retzow, Bismarck's former opponent, and others. In conditionally accepting the call to arms which the organization issued, Mirbach suggested that the new party should emphasize the Agrarian question. " Nothing can be done with the Conservative programme and a Conservative propaganda as such "; he wrote, " we must undertake an offensive in favor of the Agrarians."[14] At the time the full importance of this suggestion remained obscure. Kleist-Retzow thought that " the Conservative party has the necessary spice and toughness only when it rests upon the principles of the *Kreuzzeitung*," namely, the principles of the old Conservatives; but the words of Mirbach represented the concern with which many Conservatives regarded the change of Germany from a grain-exporting to a grain-importing land. The Agrarian cause would induce these men to join a Conservative group in support of Bismarck. Thus in order to secure state aid to meet their difficulties as landowners the Conservatives drew closer to the government of the Reich. In the election of 1877 both the new German Conservative party and the Free Conservatives gained seats in the Reichstag at the expense of the National Liberals and the Progressives. In the following years with the aid of the Center they helped to pass the tariff and financial reforms which split the National Liberals.[15] In accepting the Bismarckian Reich the Helldorf Conservatives accepted also a measure of industrialism which marked their alliance with other protectionist groups. Helldorf expressed this in 1885 in the following words, " Since the development of German industry, trade and commerce, the interests of

[14] *Mirbach to Kleist-Retzow*, cited by Petersdorff, *op. cit.*, p. 464.
[15] Poschinger, *Fürst Bismarck und die Parlamentarier* (Breslau, 1895), Hölder's Papers, II, 224 ff., 225 f., 285 f., 335 ff.

agriculture are no longer separable from those of industry and commerce."[16]

In spite of its early success the new Conservative party did not obtain a majority. Even after common interests brought it closer to the Free Conservatives and National Liberals, it could not form a parliamentary majority without the support of the Center and its dependents. With Centrist help in 1885 it secured an increase in the protective tariffs on agricultural products. It supported in time Bismarck's colonial policy, his social security laws, and in 1887 the Septennate Law, receiving in exchange a further increase in agricultural tariffs.[17]

Still another group of Conservatives led by Adolf Stoecker, the Court preacher, sought in Berlin to make the Conservative cause acceptable to the city populace. A popular appeal through a man of low birth like Stoecker was rare in the annals of Prussian Conservatism; like the turn to Agrarianism, it signified a new age. The movement aimed to create, through the Christian-Social Movement, a workers' party based on demand for social reform and to give Conservatism the wide numerical basis which a great party needed to oppose the Center and the Social Democratic party. Violently anti-Semitic and anti-Progressive, it denounced the bankers and capitalists, who formed the ranks of the so-called Liberal and Progressive parties.[18] The lower middle-classes and those workers who did not yet dare to join Social Democracy rallied to Stoecker. In the early 'eighties when the party reached its height, Stoecker was called the "uncrowned king" of Berlin.[19] But his

[16] Helldorf: *Sten. Ber. d. Reich.*, January 20, 1885, VI Leg. Per., I Sess., II, 746.

[17] For a consideration of the political agreement which was formed in 1887-8 to put through the Septennate Law and which won a majority in the Reichstag for the three parties of the Right see Heffter, *Die Opposition der Kreuzzeitungspartei gegen die Bismarcksche Kartellpolitik in den Jahren 1887 bis 1890* (Leipzig, 1927), *passim*.

[18] Frank, *op. cit.*, Chap. III. The biography of Naumann, *op. cit.*, also contains valuable pages on the Stoecker movement.

[19] Frank has shown that the movement was not so much dependent on a religious awakening, as Stoecker wished it to be, as on a socio-political interest, which drove the small people to an anti-capitalistic, anti-Semitic preacher (Frank, *op. cit.*, p. 160 f.)

attempt, like that of the Helldorf Conservatives, failed to restore Conservatism. The anti-Semitic agitation spread into the provinces and lost connection with Stoecker, while Stoecker himself later broke with the Conservatives over the social programme and was read out of the party.[19a]

For several years Stoecker worked in close alliance with Baron von Hammerstein, Junker editor of the *Kreuzzeitung*. The Conservatives associated with this newspaper held more firmly than those of the Helldorf group to the principles of old Prussian Conservatism and fundamentally lacked sympathy with the political alliance of 1887. Since they feared any concessions to Liberalism, they preferred as allies the Center to the National Liberals. The Hammerstein group wished to embrace members of both the evangelical and Catholic religions; formerly a Prussian party it sought now to expand into a national one; and it hoped to achieve if possible "Christian" social reform, not Liberal or Marxian reform. Hammerstein was a striking example of Junkerism. He was the son of a Mecklenburg owner of a knight's holding and has been described in the following words:

> A fox head on the neck of a steer, mighty muscles and small, crafty eyes, short, broad-shouldered figure. He was of a centuries old family, no great stylist and not a good speaker. His education could hardly be called broad, his appearance seemed often hard and sharp. He could want more and want it harder, more untiringly than other men and so others followed him. He manifested through and through a dual nature, which produced an inward joyous scoffing in order to play its part before the outer world.[20]

The Hammerstein group endeavored to exert in the Empire the influence which it had had in Prussia. Mutual lack of sympathy between it and Bismarck, however, created an obstacle to success. The extreme Conservatives, therefore, as a part of their programme

[19a] *Die Hilfe*, Naumann's journal, wrote over this break: "Stoecker no longer belongs to the Conservative party. At last! It is at least well that the false relation between Conservatives and Christian-Social is at an end" (*Die Hilfe*, No. 6, February 9, 1896, p. 7, also No. 7, Feb. 16, editorial).

[20] *Kieler Zeitung*, October 12, 1895, cited by Heffter, *op. cit.*; also Petersdorff, *op. cit.*, pp. 133 f.

sought to win over the young Prince William, whose succession to
the throne was assured by the serious illness of his father. They
carried on their struggle against Bismarck through their efforts to
separate William from his father's circle and from Bismarck's own,
and the *Kreuzzeitung* undertook an eager campaign for the "monarchical feeling" which, it claimed, the extreme Conservatives
alone still cherished.

In the course of the struggle between Bismarck and the *Kreuzzeitung* Stoecker gave up his place as leader of the popular Christian Social Movement in favor of his work as a leader of the
extreme Conservatives at Court.[20a] The failure of the Stoecker
group weakened the *Kreuzzeitung* party and strengthened the moderate or Helldorf Conservatives. The decisions of Waldersee and
the Emperor in 1888 to maintain the parliamentary alliance of
1887 contributed to the further isolation of the rightwing or *Kreuzzeitung* Conservatives. Such was their position in the election of
February 1890: "true Conservatism" stood without the door while
the German Conservative party and the Free Conservatives were
within the *Kartell* working with the National Liberals for Bismarckian policies.

Upon the dismissal of Bismarck the whole situation changed.
Though a Prussian and a Conservative, Caprivi favored industry
and, in order to keep the emigrating masses at home for the army,
inclined to promote Germany's evolution into a state predominantly
industrial. Any significant move in this direction was destined to
arouse Agrarian opposition and strain to the breaking point its
relations with the rightwing Conservatives and with a part of the
government-supporting Conservatives. At the same time the world
depression of the early 'nineties reduced sharply the price of grain
and forced the Agrarians to halt technical improvements. The new
grains areas opening up all over the world flooded European markets
with supplies; prices fell to a point which became alarming, especi-

---

[20a] Naumann, long a supporter of Stoecker in the 'eighties, wrote in *Die
Hilfe*, February 2, 1896: "The Court Preacher Stoecker is in a difficult
position. The Conservatives want only to hold him if he separates entirely
from 'Volk,' the only journal which has remained true to him. Will he
actually repay this loyalty by casting off 'Volk'? . . . The more he gives
in the less the Conservatives will respect him" (*Die Hilfe*, No. 5).

ally to the large grain producers east of the Elbe, who had grain to sell and could or would not turn to more intensive agriculture.[20b] National pride could hardly induce German industry to buy German wheat and rye at the former prices when these grains could be imported at much lower ones from Russia, the United States or the Argentine. It became clear to the Agrarians among the Conservatives that for the sake of German agriculture they must enter the political arena. As Mirbach had suggested, the Conservatives would definitely have to emphasize Agrarian problems if they were to preserve their class. The extreme Conservatives, as has been indicated, had made no serious effort to work with the government or with Liberals and capitalists; hence they were in a position to take up the new approach without renouncing former allies. Because the *Kreuzzeitung* party had remained a *Weltanschauung* group, while the moderate or Helldorf Conservatives represented economic and social interests in the Bismarckian alliance, the adoption of Agrarian interests marked a complete change in point of view. This change, however, the *Kreuzzeitung* group made. In the beginning it dominated the Helldorf group in the same party only in the end to be dominated itself by the Agrarian movement.[21] But by means of the Agrarian movement the Conservative party gained new vigor in parliamentary life and through the Agrarian League *(Bund der Landwirte)* popular support outside.[22]

The reason for the struggle of the Agrarian elements is evident. Although in Germany the large estates were steadily being divided into smaller holdings, the process was far from general.[23] There remained, especially in Mecklenburg and Prussia, many large grain-growing estates, whose twenty-four thousand owners faced ruin in a market of low corn prices. These owners had in many cases over-capitalized their land in order to modernize their methods and to meet the demands of a higher standard of living.[23a] With even a

[20b] Some landowners did turn to the raising of sugar beets and to the manufacture on their estates of sugar and brandy. Accordingly, they asked aid also for these agriculturally derived industries. *Cf. infra*, p. 59.

[21] Heffter, *op. cit.*, p. 45.

[22] The Agrarian League will be treated in detail in the following chapter.

[23] Theodor A. L. G. von der Goltz, *Geschichte der deutschen Landwirtschaft* (Jena, 1899), I.

[23a] Although Freytag wrote long before the 'nineties, his novel *Soll und*

slight but continued price depression, they could not meet the interest charges on their loans and mortgages. This group had been in danger since the 'seventies when Germany had ceased to export grain; but so long as prices held up in the world market the danger remained only potential. During the early 'nineties it became acute because of worldwide depression prices. Since the Agrarian aristocrats had always been closely identified with the Prussian state, it was natural for them to connect their welfare with that of the state.[24] If they were to be ruined, they argued, the Prussian state and the Empire would be ruined. Hence they were prepared to seek aid for themselves from the state; for it was clear to them that, while the times favored industry with a minimum of effort on industry's part, the times were against agriculture, especially large-scale agriculture in an old country.

Although big industrialists like Baron Stumm-Halberg had been attached to the Free Conservatives, the Prussian Junkers had always been and remained the heart of the Conservative party. In addition to the Junkers the party included many peasants, but not the small agriculturalists in the Rhineland and Bavaria, who belonged to the Center, many craftsmen, and others of the lower middle-class. After the rise of the Agrarian movement still other peasants and small holders, who were dependent for markets on the brandy and liqueur factories, flour mills and sugar refineries of the large estates, threw in their lot with the Conservatives. Finally, the upper bureaucracy contributed important members like Adolf Wermuth, an official in the Department of the Interior under Bismarck and later Secretary of the Treasury.[25]

Haben gives a vivid picture of the landowner eager to increase his income and to partake of the benefits of the industrial era. The situation of the Baron von Rothsattel, although exaggerated, parallels that of many Agrarians in the 'nineties. Immermann's *Die Epigonen* holds other parallels.

[24] Kehr, *op. cit.*, pp. 247 ff. Kehr has brought out this point in respect to the navy; but it is just as true in other connections, as any debate in the Reichstag showed.

[25] Wermuth's memoirs, *Ein Beamtenleben*, has already been cited. He wrote: "I took to heart the needs of agriculture with warmth and the desire to be helpful." In the struggle for the tariff law of 1902 he showed his willingness to work for the Agrarians.

An understanding of the Agrarian struggle is not possible without some realization of the character of the Conservative leaders to whom the cause was in part entrusted. Kleist-Retzow, who had been the outstanding leader of the Prussian Conservatives in the 'seventies and 'eighties, died in 1892.[25a] Member of an old Pomeranian family, strongly religious and monarchical, he embodied the best in the Junkerdom of his day. He had made few concessions to modern parliamentary tactics and would not have been suitable to lead the new Agrarian-Conservative movement. Hammerstein, the editor of the *Neue Preussiche Zeitung* (earlier the *Kreuzzeitung*), who has already been described, placed his paper at the service of the new movement and made it the organ of the East Elbian Junkers.[25b] Both Hammerstein and Stoecker disappeared ignominiously about 1896 from the Conservative stage and other men took their rôles. Among these Count Kanitz stood out. Kanitz was an East Prussian, owner of a knightly holding, and a member of the Reichstag and Prussian Landtag continuously during the 'nineties. Since he had been a Helldorf Conservative, he was accustomed to parliamentary opportunism and his old Prussian principles had already been somewhat modernized. Kanitz opened the Agrarian fight early in the 'nineties by a plan to keep up the price of grain through a governmental monopoly system for storing grain. The plan was proposed from time to time during the entire decade; but it so openly favored special interests, seemed so impracticable and so dangerous from the point of view of precedent that it never secured a majority. Other of the Conservative leaders were Baron Wangenheim, head of the Agrarian League and owner of a knightly holding in Farther Pomerania, Count Stolberg-Wernigerode of Silesia and East Prussia, Count Limburg-Stirum of East Prussia, Count Mirbach-Sorquitten of East Prussia, and Count Schwerin-Löwitz. All were large landowners. Kanitz, Wangenheim, Limburg-Stirum, and Schwerin-Löwitz held seats in the Prussian Lower House, Stolberg and Mirbach in the Upper House. All were at the same time members of the Reichstag. They came predominately from the East Provinces where Conservatism was traditionally strong. Farther Pomerania, for example, in its eight

[25a] Petersdorff, *op. cit.*
[25b] Hans Leuss, *Wilhelm Freiherr von Hammerstein* (Berlin, 1905).

districts elected between 1867 and 1914 only seven non-Conservatives. The leaders mentioned were ruthless in political life, willing to use any means known to politics for achieving their ends. They proved themselves the most astute, courageous and untiring of political organizers, equalled by none in Germany except perhaps by certain Social Democrats and by some of the professional propagandists like Hasse of the Pan-German League.

Two active parliamentary leaders of the Free Conservatives were Wilhelm von Kardorff and Baron Stumm-Halberg. Kardorff represented the connection between Agrarian and industrial interests, a connection which existed in spite of the hatred of many Conservatives for industry and later helped to make possible the alliance of the Agrarians with the National Liberals. As a landowner and in straightened circumstances throughout his parliamentary life Kardorff understood and urged the needs of the Agrarians. As a director of the Königs- und Laura Hütte, Incorporated, he knew industry and was one of the first to demand protection for it.[26] He also founded in 1876 the Central Union of German Industrialists, the outstanding protectionist organization in Germany before 1914, and he won over Bismarck to protection in 1878-9. For many years Kardorff strove to bring about international bimetallism; but failing in this he turned with double vigor to the promotion of the autonomous tariff bill planned for 1902, which can in part be regarded as his personal triumph. During its passage, however, he broke with the Agrarians and withdrew from the Agarian League, whose extreme measures he, as a nationalist, could not condone.[27] His inability to do so reflected his sympathy with industry and his realistic approach to the problems of government. Although Kardorff was in outward appearance and in much of his thinking a typical Prussian aristocrat, his early appreciation of Bismarck and of unification, of the need for tariffs and a navy show him to have been a man of his age. He always upheld

---

[26] Kardorff gave up this position in 1884 when he was elected *Landrat*. He had also been connected with the Posen-Kreuzberg Railroad and the Central Land Credit Company. For the unsavory details of Kardorff's connections see Otto Glagan, *Der Börsen- und Gründungsschwindel in Berlin* (Leipzig, 1876).

[27] Kardorff, *op. cit., passim.*

what he considered the "national interest" and this included a lively sympathy with the colonial movement and with the desire for a naval increase. In these matters he differed from the Agrarian-Conservatives, who supported colonies and the navy only with reservations and in return for direct concessions to their own interests. Kardorff also belonged to the Pan-German League but he criticized it for opposing Bülow during the Boer War.[28] Like other imperialists he seems to have thought English influence dangerous, though in just what way he does not explain.[29]

Kardorff clung more closely to the Prussian tradition in the domestic affairs of his country than he did in foreign policy. Always a great friend of Bismarck, he bitterly opposed Caprivi and was intransigent where any change of what he regarded as Bismarckian policy was concerned.[30] He objected to the increase of power for the Reichstag which the National Liberals wanted in the 'seventies because he thought the party strife too great, and he came more and more to regret the universal suffrage law.[31] Since he considered industry and labor, like agriculture and industry, to be

[28] At the time of the deputation to Krüger in December 1900 Kardorff wrote to Arnim-Muskau, another large landowner: "The result of the tremendous agitation of the Pan-German League against Bülow will be that the Chancellor will be forced toward the Left and the six marks' tariff [the new tariff proposed for wheat and rye] will be lost" (cited by Kardorff, *op. cit.*, p. 344).

[29] In 1893 in the course of praising Minister Miquel Kardorff wrote: "I hope that he will gradually have a useful influence upon foreign policy; at least I find him already familiar with the idea that England exerts a dangerous influence on us, and in like manner the handling of the Polish question will bring us to an estrangement with Russia and in the end will redound only to the good of Austria and the Vatican" (*ibid.*, p. 284).

[30] It is of great interest that Kardorff was one of those most eager for a reconciliation between the Emperor and the Bismarcks. He hoped to ruin Caprivi and restore the old Chancellor, possibly abolishing universal suffrage. Hohenlohe also disappointed Kardorff's expectations; but with Bülow he stood in closer relations (*ibid.*, pp. 304, 334).

[31] Kardorff wrote to his wife in December 1902: "In the turbulent Reichstag sessions where we have to be from ten in the morning until ten at night I had actually no time to write because there are constant conferences for the purpose of laying out our strategy. These wild scenes are indeed good in that they show clearly the need for discontinuing universal direct suffrage" (*ibid.*, p. 353).

closely dependent on one another, he resented the growth of Trade Unionism and hated Social Democracy. In this matter Kardorff and Stumm stood shoulder to shoulder.

Even a brief acquaintance with Kardorff affords some explanation of the persistence of Conservatism in modern Germany. With superb ability he championed monarchy, agrarianism and the authority of the state. He was an untiring parliamentary worker, a good speaker, an able writer and a vigorous antagonist. Anyone who had his support could have able coaching and advice and he readily broke with those whom he considered dangerous to the state. A member of the Social Democratic party, Lily Braun, who was herself an aristocrat, has written an account of his last speech which bears repeating:

> Quietly with the whole self-command of an old aristocrat [she wrote] von Kardorff began to speak. . . . He did not take the trouble to convince; in his manner there lay a sovereign disdain of his opponents. Deafening noise interrupted him. From the packed crowds which pressed nearer and nearer to the tribune clenched first were raised. ' Robber '! ' Thief '! ' Traitor to the people '! like blows of a whip whistled and hummed through the air. The members of the Right rose and took possession of the other side of the steps like a guard. Von Kardorff spoke further. His face had become a shade paler and his small hands gripped the desk spasmodically. Here stood no longer the individual who fought for a temporary advantage; in this man stood forth rather the old world against the new; it surrounded his sharply cut aristocrat's head with the shadowy glimmer of a tragic greatness.[32]

Carl Ferdinand Stumm, later Baron von Stumm-Halberg, coöperated closely with Kardorff in directing the affairs of the Free-Conservative party.[33] Stumm, whose factories stood in the Saar, manufactured iron and steel plates; he supplied the navy as Krupp did the army. Since his family had long been in the business, he inherited with the iron works pride in the bourgeois tradition of

---

[32] *Ibid.*, p. 352, cited from Lily Braun, *Memoiren einer Sozialistin* (Munich, 1909), II, 449.

[33] Hellwig, *op. cit.*, is the standard biography for Stumm. The following account is based upon this book and upon Stumm's speeches in the Reichstag and Landtag.

endeavour in industrial fields. When the young Carl Ferdinand was only twelve, his father died (1848), leaving the son to begin at this early age his business training. At twenty-two young Stumm took over the direction of the Neunkirche iron mills, whose affairs he personally controlled all his life. During the first year of his administration he excluded women from working in his mills and instituted a rigid system of discipline for the workers. Like the Krupps he ruled over his men as a patriarch and insisted upon controlling their social and moral life outside as well as inside the mills.[34]

The Saar district differed from the Rhineland in being pro-Prussian, although like the Rhineland the Saar had felt strongly the French revolutionary ideas and in 1848 had produced good Liberals. Fear of annexation by France drove the region into the arms of Bismarck; and Stumm declared among the first that only the strengthening of Prussia and ultimately of the Reich could deliver the Saar from its fear. Thus he early became devoted to the authority of the state. Years later in 1892 when Bismarck had been forced out of office and feeling between him and the Emperor and Caprivi, the new Chancellor, ran high, Stumm wrote to Caprivi, whom personally he did not greatly admire:

> I am of the opinion [he said] that since we have universal suffrage with its consequences all the elements of the nation which stand for preserving the state must stand doubly firmly together in order to support authority everywhere where it exists in state and church. I think that those parties which believe in the monarchy should stand together not only for the monarch but also for those who are called to lead the government in his name. According to my understanding of Conservative thought every indication of personal animus against such men and all personal differences of opinion must be avoided.[35]

In the 'sixties he was the leader of the anti-Liberals in the Saar; and as a result of his political activity one of his first trips to Ber-

---

[34] Hellwig, *op. cit.*, p. 27; Chap. X. For further evidence of the patriarchal system see *Rheinisch-Westfälische Wirtschaftsbiographien* (Münster, 1934), e. g., "Gustav Selve," II, 92, 93-8. The Selve works were not incorporated until after 1919; Stumm's were not during his lifetime.

[35] Hellwig, *op. cit.*, p. 451.

lin (1866) had as its purpose an appeal to Bismarck to retain at all costs the state coal monopoly of the Saar region.[36] Because of his interest in this question Stumm actively campaigned in 1866 as a Conservative. He suffered defeat through the election of the Liberal candidate, ran again in the following year for the new Reichstag, and overwhelmingly gained the election to it. Therewith began Stumm's political career. Like Kardorff he early became outstanding. Because he supported Bismarck and at the same time was an anti-National Liberal, he joined the Free-Conservative group to which Kardorff belonged and associated with men of influence in the industrial and political worlds.

In his long career as a Reichstag member Stumm particularly interested himself in the tariff and in social questions. It was his conviction that iron tariffs especially must not be abolished because the lower costs of production of English and Belgian iron would enable these countries to flood the German market. He maintained this conviction even in the face of the abolition of the iron tariffs in 1873. With Kardorff he continued to work for protection and with ultimate success. Stumm also recognized early the demands of the Agrarians for state aid and for higher agricultural tariffs. Like a good Free Conservative he at times favored the Agrarians to the disadvantage of his own electoral district and to the advantage of the so-termed " national welfare." [37] But Stumm's reputation rests on his social policy. As a supporter of the authority of the state he looked upon the state as the rightful protector of the workers, supplementing the efforts of the employers. It is significant that he never proposed that the state should adopt any measure for social welfare which he had not already made proof of in his own factories. While willing to see everything done for his own

[36] *Ibid.*, p. 54. When as a result of widespread rumors it was feared that the state intended to sell the mines or convert the holdings into a stock company, the Saar region became greatly disturbed. The Liberals had always wanted the state mines given over to private hands; but now, for fear of French capital, many of them were as eager as Stumm to have Prussia retain them. Stumm and the Conservatives, however, were willing that Bismarck should sell the mines if there should be no other way of getting money to carry on the wars of unification. The question furnishes an interesting study of Liberal and Conservative material interests.

[37] *Ibid.*, pp. 127, 153, 453.

and the nation's workers, Stumm wished even more ardently that they should do nothing for themselves. His entire active life was spent in providing for the needs of the under-privileged classes and in bitter battle with Social Democracy. Against the workers who organized and presumed to send their representatives to oppose the ministers of state he made his most vehement speeches. The period from about 1893 to 1896 has been called the "Stumm Era" since it was a period of bitter war against Social Democracy and rang with Stumm's denunciation. He refused to believe that the Social Democrats were no longer a revolutionary party, as Auer (Social Democrat) had recently asserted in the Reichstag, and maintained that outside that body they had no party and were only a group opposed to the foundations of society. " Marriage, family, country and monarchy, religion and tradition," he said, " are all attacked and denounced by them in the crudest language." [38] When the so-called *coup d'état* bill for strengthening the penal and press laws was introduced in December 1894, Stumm advocated the law with amendments to deprive the lower-classes of the right to vote. He held that the state encouraged Social Democracy by doing too much for the workers; even worse it allowed the Socialists of the Chair *(Kathedersozialisten)* to exist and to coquette with Social Democracy.[39] He hated this university socialism as he detested the activities of social reformers like Stoecker and Friedrich Naumann. That the Emperor should allow a play like Hauptmann's *The Weavers* to be produced he found incomprehensible.

After the strike of 1892 it seemed more and more evident that Stumm influenced the Chancellor, the Imperial Secretaries and the Emperor in their social policy. In correspondence with Caprivi over the proposed socialist law in 1894 he expressed his belief that a *coup d'état* could not be avoided.[40] He became convinced of the need for doing away with the Reichstag, but particularly for de-

[38] *Sten. Ber. d. Reich.*, IX Leg. Per., III Sess., I, 206.

[39] These were persons connected with the Society for Social Policy *(Verein für Sozialpolitik)*. In early years Stumm professed great interest in this organization; only later when the Society became, as he said, more theoretical in its interests did he become a bitter opponent of it (Hellwig, *op. cit.*, p. 380).

[40] *Ibid.*, p. 503.

priving the enemy, the Social Democrats, of the ballot. These ideas held danger for the Emperor and the government in case any attempt should be made to put them into execution. Apparently Stumm kept in touch with all of the leading personalities of the day, and his stubborn, factual mind impressed many of them likewise disposed to attempt a settlement of internal problems by resorting to a final struggle. Kardorff did not wish to go so far, nor did Caprivi or Hohenlohe.

As an industrialist Stumm approved of the Caprivi Commercial Treaties but as a Free Conservative deplored the reduction of agricultural tariffs which they incorporated. Differences of opinion over the treaties and over Caprivi separated Stumm and Kardorff for some time. Stumm supported Caprivi, with whose policy his interests were in accord, while Kardorff continued to support Bismarck. At this time Stumm placed *Die Post,* the Free-Conservative organ, at the service of the Emperor and Caprivi for upholding " the monarchical feeling." Stumm's paper also opposed the Agrarian League and, as the Agrarians increased their power over the Emperor, Stumm's influence declined. Hohenlohe's Chancellorship contributed to the fall of Stumm's political popularity; [41] the Emperor turned to other interests than *coups d'état,* while the Reichstag became indifferent. Stumm died politically isolated and defeated in the main lines of his social policy.

In both Kardorff and Stumm, perhaps more clearly in Stumm, who was neither a Prussian nor an aristocrat by birth, the Conservative tradition is apparent adapting itself to new conditions. Both accepted Bismarck, who, they rightly surmised, was no Liberal, and both looked upon the new Reich as a means of defeating for all times German Liberalism. Their leadership did much to make this possible. Both played the rôle of intermediary between the Secretaries and the Emperor and the Reichstag, both admired

---

[41] This political change lends credence to the argument, advanced earlier, that the policy of imperialism was encouraged to keep the Emperor engaged. The *coup d'état* plans which had been put before him by Stumm and which busied him for some months were not favored by the higher bureaucracy. They expected Hohenlohe to discourage them. It was generally believed that the less William II interfered with domestic policy the less difficult it would be to maintain a policy of compromise.

the monarchy, both feared and sincerely hated Social Democracy. "King Stumm," whose name will go down in all German history as the opponent *par excellence* of the trade union, typified a pre-war industrialist with his many good qualities and his political intransigence. Kardorff embodied the aristocrat-industrialist, representative of the two interests for which the Free Conservatives stood.

Stumm bought the journal, *Die Post,* in 1874 for about thirty thousand dollars and conducted it as an organ of the Free Conservatives. It naturally reflected his views, especially after 1894. At this time Kardorff and two-thirds of the party turned away from *Die Post* to the *Berliner Neuste Nachrichten.*[42] These two papers formed the backbone of the Free-Conservative press. They will be quoted often in subsequent pages.[43] Both organs were pro-navy and

[42] Hammann, *Der Neue Kurs* (Berlin, 1918), p. 8.

[43] In summing up the differences between Stumm and Kardorff and the point of view of the Free Conservatives, it is appropriate to cite from a letter of Kardorff to Stumm, December 25, 1892: "Your letter of the 23rd instant received and I can only answer as follows:

1. Agreed that economic interests in themselves are second to great patriotic and monarchical interests; but I call your attention to the fact that the present economic policy [i. e., Caprivi's] seriously endangers the latter. Not the industrial regions, not the large cities, which as a rule vote Social Democratic or Progressive, constitute the backbone of the monarchical régime, but the land, and, apparently, government circles know well the opinion of all classes of the population in this matter and do not dream to what degree anti-monarchical tendencies have grown here [in the country] under the feeling that twenty millions of agricultural population are sacrificed to perdition and that this is regarded with indifference as an inevitable development. . . .

4. Do not forget that the majority of the German Conservatives [Helldorf Conservatives] are protectionists only so far as they expect aid for their Agrarian interests. Already there are proposals under consideration for a reduction of the iron duties and without my forceful intervention suggestions would have been made in the Reichstag in this direction.

I am as sick of politics as possible. When I see how an attempt is made in social policy, in economic policy, in short, in all branches of public life to pursue roads other than those of Bismarck, when I see among broad classes of the population the lessening of respect for monarchy, it seems to me we are driving toward a revolution which will be worse than

the connection expounded between the workers and naval expansion found expression in the following quotation:

> Germany must develop her colonial possessions if she is to give work to and nourish her growing population, and for this purpose she needs a larger navy. Whoever has world power possesses the world market, from which the weak will be ruthlessly forced out. This fact is particularly true of German policy, since this has no end other than the extension of a higher civilization and the expansion of economic life. If a nation increases its market or its navy, continued work will be possible for the worker as well as higher wages and a better standard of living. Without the navy we cannot insure them.[44]

Both papers supported the *Sammlung*.[45] Both also alleged friendship for England and protested that the anti-English agitation was not connected with the naval agitation. But neither desired so close a connection with England as an alliance.[46]

The commercial treaties negotiated under Caprivi have already been mentioned as a spur to Agrarian endeavour. Caprivi had decided not to remake the general tariff but to reduce rates and stimulate trade by relying upon bilateral treaties with other countries.[47] Since the bad harvests of 1891 had temporarily raised grain prices all over Europe, even some of the German Agrarians thought

that of 1848. In this situation I would think it cowardly to leave my post even though I am more and more convinced that we are steering straight for a fearful catastrophe (Kardorff, *op. cit.*, pp. 275-6; also 311).

[44] *Berliner Neueste Nachrichten*, No. 8, January 6, 1900.

[45] *Die Post*, No. 294, October 25, 1899; *B. N. N.*, No. 56, February 3, 1900. That *Die Post* also appreciated the "American danger" was clear from an article in No. 296, October 27, 1899.

[46] The *B. N. N.* objected strenuously to an article in the *Hamburger Nachrichten* entitled "Los von England," but said with satisfaction that Germany had no close ties with England (No. 42, January 26, 1900).

[47] Walter Lotz, *Die Handelspolitik Caprivis und Hohenlohes, Schriften des Vereins für Sozialpolitik*, 90. Lotz thought that it was very dubious whether the Bismarckian commercial policy could have been continued. If France had decided not to renew her most-favored-nation treaties in 1892 or if an economic crisis had raised prices to the point where the workers had felt them seriously, a change would have had to be made, he argued. Since prices did rise, he concluded that circumstances helped Caprivi to change policies.

he was justified in lowering the five marks tariff on grain in return for treaty concessions.[48] The first treaties, those with Austria, Italy and Belgium, were made in December, 1891, and were followed in January 1892 by one with Switzerland. They reduced tariffs on wheat and rye from five marks to three and one-half marks the hundredweight (in kilograms). The government defended the concessions as made in consideration of the international price and market situation and in consideration of the German working classes. It maintained that a war of all against all would result from international tariff wars and that laborers would leave Germany because of high prices.[49]

In addition to these arguments Caprivi used an economico-political one. He pointed out that the Triple Alliance must strengthen itself economically rather than drain itself of its life blood through

[48] In the summer and autumn of 1891 Kanitz himself thought so. Since the government did not want to lower schedules through an autonomous tariff, it eased the situation temporarily by lowered freight rates to the industrial regions. Research was demonstrating that the East Elbian producers were not really gaining all they hoped to from the higher tariffs; prices were lower in the 'eighties than in the 'seventies (Lotz, *op. cit.*, pp. 72 ff.). A governmental investigation of agriculture, as suggested by the Left, should have been undertaken at this crucial time. The argument of the Agrarians was and continued to be that prices had fallen below those compatible with solvency; but the fact was that with the increased cost of living efforts had been made to increase the sale price of holdings above any possible return. The Social Democrats repeatedly pointed out that this was the kernel of the problem; but no one listened to them and the real difficulty was neither acknowledged nor corrected. Hence the struggle of the Agrarians was a bitter one because they had everything at stake. See von der Goltz, *Die Agrarischen Aufgaben der Gegenwart* (Jena, 1894); *idem, Geschichte der deutschen Landwirtschaft*, II, 354, 405 f.; Mentor Bouniatian, *Wirtschaftskrisen und Überkapitalisation: Eine Untersuchung über die Erscheinungsformen und Ursachen der periodischen Wirtschaftskrisen* (Munich, 1908), pp. 147 ff. The author of the last volume points out that when the land is held by a few large holders, a small increase in productivity may quickly lead to over-capitalization (pp. 180-1). All post-war German governments have likewise had to deal with this same agricultural question.

[49] *Sten. Ber. d. Reich.*, December 10, 1891, VIII Leg. Per., I Sess., V, 3301 ff.

tariff wars and unfavorable trade balances.[50]   A tariff union was, he said, a necessary adjunct to political alliance. He wished, likewise, to keep Belgium and Switzerland as loyal to the Triple Alliance as tariff treaties could make them. His plan would have initiated a European tariff union, though possibly one different in kind from that urgently desired by the German Agrarians after 1894 and again after 1897 (the years of the new American tariff laws) against the United States, and, with the inclusion of Russia, would have offered a counterpart to the much feared British Empire Tariff Union.[51]   At the same time the treaties represented an attempt, at the expense of the German Agrarians, to secure cheaper food for German labor and hence to maintain or increase Germany's competitive industrial ability in world markets. Caprivi saw that the comparative comfort of an agricultural economy had passed, that if Germany was henceforth to participate advantageously in world trade, she must strengthen her industrial structure. " Either we export goods," he said, " or we export men." [52]

At first the Agrarians did not fully appreciate the step Caprivi was taking. The vote on the early treaties of 1891 and 1892 stood at 243 to 48. Only a few Conservatives protested. Among them were to be found the leader of the moderates, Kardorff, and the anti-Semite, Liebermann von Sonnenberg. The National Liberals supported the government, giving no indication of their subsequent sympathy with Agrarian-Conservative demands or of their own later wrath against the treaties. Within the next few months, however, the Agrarians within the Reichstag became alarmed. An independent agricultural journal published an article containing the astounding words, " I propose nothing more or less than that we go over to the Social Democrats and seriously make common cause against the government." [53]   The *Kreuzzeitung* reprinted the proposal. In the Prussian Landtag the Agrarians attacked the agri-

---

[50] For a very succinct statement of this see Kehr, *op. cit.*, pp. 249 f. Also Lotz, *op. cit.*, pp. 87 ff.; Francke, *Zollpolitische Bestrebungen in Mitteleuropa, Schriften des Vereins für Sozialpolitik*, 90.

[51] Francke, *op. cit.*, p. 210.   Also Caprivi's opening speech in the Reichstag, December 6, 1897.

[52] *Sten. Ber. d. Reich.*, December 11, 1891, VIII Leg. Per., I Sess., V, 3308.

[53] Barth (Progressive) referred to this in the Reichstag on January 26, 1893. *Cf.* also Chapter III. " Agrarian League."

cultural Minister, von Heyden, and in February and March, 1893, a great debate took place in the Reichstag on agricultural questions. During these debates the Agrarian-Conservatives indicated that they would bitterly oppose the proposed commercial treaty with Russia. At the same time the landowners formed the Agrarian League.

Caprivi tried to defend his policy against what he immediately designated as *Interessenpolitik* on the part of the Agrarian League and the Conservatives; but he needed Conservative support for the new army law, which the left parties with the help of most of the Center had defeated. Caprivi felt that the army law must be passed because he feared a war on two fronts in the near future.[54] The Agrarian-Conservatives, however, replied that if Germany were to be dependent on grain imports which could be cut off by a blockade, such a war would be a triple danger. They argued especially that Germany must be self-sufficient in bread-stuffs. Caprivi, on the other hand, probably intended in view of the non-renewal of the Russian alliance to cultivate closer relations with England and in case of blockade to depend on the help of the English navy.[54a] By proposing to eliminate the possible need for importing grain, the Conservatives implicitly denied the need for an English alliance. In the subsequent election, with the help of the League and of the Prussian government, the Conservatives returned to the new Reichstag stronger than before.[55] Soon after the army law was passed by a vote of 201 to 185.

In the election of 1893 the Conservative power increased decidedly. The League provided a better organization for the

[54] Tirpitz, *Erinnerungen*, pp. 25 f. Also Kehr, *op. cit.*, pp. 247 f.

[54a] Caprivi is supposed to have said to a friend in 1899: "With your colonial and naval policies you weaken our territorial defense and bring us in the end to enmity with England, our only natural ally in the war which we cannot avoid and which will be decisive for Germany's future. For Germany today and for the near future the only question can be how small and not how large our navy ought to be" (cited by Hallmann, *op. cit.*, p. 100).

[55] Lotz, *op. cit.*, pp. 106 ff. Lotz has gone through the findings of the Commission for Proving Election Returns and found that this aid on the part of the Prussian government was a fact. Since it is well known that such aid was given later, there is no reason to doubt that it was in 1893.

Agrarians and raised their morale. They were ready for a vigorous campaign against further commercial treaties. The bountiful harvest abroad in 1893 sent world grain prices to a new low at the same time that drought struck Germany. The smaller farmers joined the League, contributing support and adding vehemence to the cause. Confusion grew from day to day. While Mirbach and Hammerstein in the *Kreuzzeitung* campaigned against the Russian treaty, the industrialists, to whom the tariff war with Russia brought disaster, clamored for a treaty at any price.[56] In the end the Russian treaty and one with Roumania passed the Reichstag with the aid of most of the Agrarian-Conservatives. Their support for these and for the army law had to be rewarded, however, by abolition of the *Identitätsnachweis* and by the grant of special freight rates for grain shipments to the west.[57] The victory gained

[56] The German industrialists desired the Russian treaty in the hope of gaining a larger Russian market. For the Upper Silesian coal fields and smelting works, for example, the Russo-German tariff war presented insuperable obstacles (Stumm: *Sten. Ber. d. Reich.*, 1893-4, II, 1496-7). It was also frightening to industry to find that England was gaining Russian trade.

[57] Caprivi had already planned this in 1891 but waited until after the Russian treaty to carry it through (Miquel: *Sten. Ber. d. Reich.*, 1893-4, III, 1655). *Identitätsnachweis* is a term meaning a receipt for exports deposited in the tariff treasury and used to stimulate the export of grain, meal, meat, etc. If a miller exported meal made from domestic grain, he could import a corresponding amount later free of duty. If grain, unmilled, was exported, the amount of the tariff duty was not so remitted. After 1894 exports of grain, whether of German origin or mixed with foreign grain, were allowed an export premium of about thirty-five marks a ton (metric) of bread corn. This was not paid in cash but the exporter was allowed so much rebate on tariffs and the export receipts were taken by the government instead of money. They held good for six months after the export and did not require, as was the case previously, that exactly the same kind of grain be imported as had been exported. The exporter could sell abroad when the market favored his product and buy when convenient to him, and he could do this at the expense of the state, which forfeited the tariff income from the imports. The measure operated to raise the price of grain for the East Elbians above the world price. It also happened that Germany might be short of supplies for a time before the new imports became available. If the World War had broken out a few months later than it did, this would have been the case in 1914 and new imports could not have come at all.

by Caprivi in 1894 was a Pyrrhic one, nevertheless. Within a few months the Conservatives launched their campaign for state aid and adopted measures sponsored by the Agrarian League. Caprivi resigned in 1894 and his essentially anti-Agrarian policy gradually suffered modification.[58] When in 1894-5 an upswing in the business cycle began, Germany abandoned the defensive strategy of clinging to a middle European or continental tariff union. Although the Agrarians from time to time revived the principle of a central European tariff union,[59] the country turned seaward to colonies and a navy, objectives in which Caprivi had had no interest.

In a very real sense Caprivi's defeat marked another milestone in the advance of the Conservatives. It marked also the domination by the Agrarians of all the Conservative groups. The strength which the Agrarians had won in and out of the Reichstag and in the Prussian and other *Landtäge,* the adoption by them of new tactics, the determination to wage unremitting battle for state assistance had changed the character of the old Conservative party and given it the opportunity to bid for greater power than it had yet exercised in the Empire. The fact that, despite the new treaties, agriculture increased its output through technical improvements helped the Agrarians to protest that they could supply Germany

---

[58] On the subject of Caprivi's fall see Haller, *op. cit.;* Hammann, *Der Neue Kurs,* Chap. VII; Hohenlohe, *op. cit.,* p. 3. The differences between Caprivi and the Prussian Ministry, between him and the Agrarians grew daily, and the desire for a new law against the Social Democrats led to irreconcilable breaches. The Emperor, too, was growing more conservative. Hohenlohe also hated the Agrarians and did not have much use for the Prussian Conservatives. At one time he wrote: " When I consort so with Prussian Excellencies I see clearly the difference between North and South Germany. South German Liberalism does not get a chance with the Junkers. They are too numerous, too powerful, and have the monarchy and the army on their side. Also the Center coöperates with them. All I have experienced in these four years is explicable on the grounds of this difference. The Germans are right when they think of my presence in Berlin as a guarantee of unity. I must strive to keep Prussia in the Reich as I strove in 1866 to 1870 for the federation of North and South; for all these gentlemen look down upon (*pfeifen auf*) the Empire and would rather give it up today than tomorrow, Miquel included " (Hohenlohe, *op. cit.,* p. 474, cited from Hohenlohe's journal, December 5, 1898).

[59] *Cf.* also Francke, *op. cit.;* Vagts, *op. cit.,* I.

6

with most of the grain she needed and increased their efforts to obtain the exclusive right to do so.[60] The control of the Conservatives by the Agrarians and the bitter fight waged by the group colours the entire decade of the 'nineties. The struggle intensified the *Interessenpolitik;* it prevented the industrialization of the East Provinces, thus contributing to the need of German industry to seek outlets abroad in new colonies and markets; it helped to keep in power feudal ideals and a bureaucracy more conservative than ever before; and it greatly heightened the social disharmony by lending support to the struggle against Social Democracy and the proletariat of the cities.[61] The success of the Agrarian League in winning over many peasants and craftsmen made the conflict also one of the old order against the new. Shortly after Caprivi's fall Wilhelm Liebknecht, a leader of the Social Democrats, spoke in the Reichstag on the change which he felt about him.

> Since the end of the last session [he said] a change has taken place, a complete—I may almost say, since this word is so prevalent now—revolution [*Umsturz*] in the upper regions, a disconcerting change in the personnel of the higher bureaucracy; in short, a change in the government and administration. If events only half so significant and far-reaching were to occur in other countries, immediately upon the meeting of the parliament the most extensive explanations would be given . . . . But we have received no explanations and I am convinced that every Representative—I think that I may include the Right here—feels that the position of the Reichstag is an unworthy one, that there is a failure to consider the representation of the people.[62]

---

[60] During the decade 1880 to 1890 the increase was from seven and two-tenths million tons to eight and seven-tenths million tons; from 1890 to 1900 it was from eight and seven-tenths to twelve and a half million tons, although in the latter decade the lower tariff rate of three and one half marks prevailed. The Agrarians admitted that they could not supply Germany with all the grain she needed; but they contended that they could continue to increase output. Since their position in this respect was always weak, they had recourse to many other arguments as to why they should not be abandoned by the state.

[61] This last was not reflected, however, in new anti-socialist laws. It gave rise to bitter propaganda which aroused intense feeling. *Cf.* Chapter III, " Central Union of German Industrialists."

[62] *Sten. Ber. d. Reich.,* IX Leg. Per., III Sess., I, 67. The word revolution

These strictures referred to important victories which the Agrarians had won: Heyden, Minister of Agriculture, gave way to Hammerstein-Loxten, who was more acceptable to the Agrarians; Köller, an Agrarian-Conservative, became Prussian Minister of the Interior; and Posadowsky-Wehner, then Minister of Finance, began to indicate by his support of increased tariffs wherever the laws permitted them, his tendency away from Liberal to Agrarian sympathies.[63]

The first months of the Hohenlohe Ministry were not so favorable to the Agrarians as they had expected. In the summer of 1895, therefore, the Conservatives and the League launched a further campaign of agitation. This activity was accompanied by an almost worldwide improvement in business, a condition which encouraged the Agrarians to proceed with their demand for favors. They themselves had been economically strengthened and could finance their movement more easily; the government, they argued, obtained more revenue, which made it less dependent on industry for its income and placed it in a position to subsidize agriculture.[64] During the following months the Conservatives received a variety of concessions—the abolition of grain speculation on the Exchange, a new tax on foreign sugar, changes in the brandy tax, a margarine law restricting competition with butter, and sanitary laws aiming at the exclusion of foreign meats.[65] In 1897 the government began preparations for a new tariff law and the Agrarians concentrated upon carrying through their demands in connection with the law. The

or *Umsturz* is a reference to the *Umsturzvorlage*, which the Right wished to have passed against the Social Democrats in 1894.

[63] For an attack on Hammerstein-Loxten see *Sten. Ber. d. Reich.*, IX Leg. Per., III Sess., I, 133; on Posadowsky, Oertel: *Ibid.*, Jan. 26, 1899, X Leg. Per., I Sess., I, 459. For an account of the laws in the Reich and Prussia favoring the agricultural population see *Jahrbuch des Handelsvertragsverein*, 1902, pp. 147-167. The list includes the Prussian tax reform of 1893, the Liqueur Tax, 1887 and 1895, Sugar Tax, 1861, 1892, 1896, 1902, Meat Inspection Laws, 1894, 1900, etc.

[64] It is known that Caprivi favored industry because he realized that agriculture could not support the demands of modern armaments. After 1895 the Reich for several years had a surplus in the Treasury.

[65] The programme of the Agrarians included large and small aids (*Mittel*). The Exchange Law was "large," the others above mentioned "small," favoring their various manufacturing enterprises or the farm enterprises of their supporters, such as dairying.

tariff struggle lasted until 1902. It ended with capitulation by the government and by the National Liberals to a modified version of most of the requests of the Agrarians. The Social Democrat Singer has humorously pictured the alliance which brought about the tariff as follows:

> The little comedy of 1879, the alliance of the Conservatives and National Liberals on behalf of Bismarck's first protectionist measures, has recently been repeated. The Agrarians and the big industrialists, referring always to the gentlemen without this House, form a Company of Unlimited Exploitation [*Gesellschaft mit unbeschränkter Raffgier*].[66] These gentlemen call themselves the state-protecting parties. Yes, indeed, they are state-protecting just so long as they are getting something from the state; not a minute longer; and not too little. Otherwise, it is all over with monarchism and patriotism, which with the Agrarians is according to *per centum* and the price of which rises and falls exactly as prices on the Exchange.[67]

The same Social Democratic representative pointed out that under the new tariff a few things were left free, lobster, caviar, oysters and champagne, all of them food and drink for the Agrarian. As for the laborer, he must work twelve more days a year to pay for the higher cost of his food occasioned by the tariff schedules on grain. The vote on the law in 1902 stood 201 to 100. Theodor Mommsen, the Liberal historian, wrote at the time of its passage:

> We do not stand at the end but at the beginning of a *coup d'état,* not a *coup d'état* of crowned heads, but one on the part of the alliance of interests of the reactionary parties to which, unfortunately, the National Liberal party has given its blessing.[68]

The Conservative party did not depend alone on the influence which it exerted in the Reichstag. There the support of the National

---

[66] This is a play upon the words "Gesellschaft mit unbeschränkter Haftung," our limited liability company.

[67] *Sten. Ber. d. Reich.*, December 11, 1901, X Leg. Per., II Sess., IV, 3128. See Appendix I for a chart of the largest Agrarians and the estimated financial benefit of the law to them.

[68] In *Die Nation,* cited by Roesicke, *Sten. Ber. d. Reich.*, December 13-14, 1902, X Leg. Per., II Sess., VIII, 7181.

Liberals and of at least a part of the Center was necessary to pass both governmental and Conservative measures. In Prussia, however, by virtue of the three-class voting system the party could command a majority with help from either the National Liberals or the Center. In Saxony and Bavaria the Agrarian representation bulked large in the Landtag. Hence three important states could use their bureaucracies and their power in the Bundesrat for assisting Agrarian interests. At the same time the failure to redistrict the Reich according to population accrued to the advantage of the Conservatives.[68a] In these ways the Conservatives came to be influential to a far greater degree than their numbers warranted and, the more this power was used for obtaining aid for special interests, the more it was misused in relation to the interests of the body politic. Even when the National Liberals and the Center supported Conservative measures, they usually did so for political or religious reasons rather than because the interests of the Conservatives clearly coincided with their own.[69] Such help made the return to power of the Conservatives of dubious value to the country, quite apart from the social and moral conflicts which it engendered or embittered.

Some conception of the preponderance of Agrarian interests within the Conservative party may be gained from the following figures. Out of forty-nine Conservative members in the Reichstag, twenty-nine held knights' estates or other large holdings, six were squires *(Landräte)*,[70] only ten held small estates or functioned as publicists or business men, while one was a professor and a few others were ex-officers or Court functionaries. In the Prussian Landtag of one hundred and forty-two Conservative members, fifty-one held knights' estates, twenty to twenty-five owned other types of

[68a] *Cf. infra*, p. 89, note 135.

[69] It is of interest to note here that after the World War the Catholics who did not vote with the Center party did not vote Conservative but with the Left, often with the Social Democrats. See Johannes Schauff, *Die deutschen Katholiken und die Zentrumspartei* (Cologne, 1920), pp. 108 ff. This does not alter the fact that the Center party as a whole often supported the measures of the Right.

[70] The *Landräte* were local officers and were chosen or confirmed locally, usually from among the larger landowners of a district. " Squire " is a translation sometimes given the word *Landrat*, but the two are not synonymous.

estates, twenty were squires, many of them also large holders, only two were peasant holders, one was a professor and a few were officers or officials.

The Free Conservatives in the Reichstag were also composed overwhelmingly of Agrarians, who coöperated with the industrial-ists of the party. Kardorff at one time said, " Our group consists of a lot of Agrarians plus four mine owners and iron manufacturers [Stumm, Krupp, Marbach, and Engels] and one jurist." [71]   It has been noted above that the views of the leaders of the Free Conser-vatives, Stumm and Kardorff, did not always coincide with those of extreme agrarianism; but the Free Conservatives supported Agrarian protection and the principle of the close interdependence of industry and agriculture. The programme drawn up for the new Free-Conservative press undertaking in 1891 illustrated what a majority of the group stood for: [72]

1. A national policy along Bismarckian lines;
2. An economic policy based upon the interdependence of Agrarian and industrial interests;
3. No more coquetting with the workers but a steady advance against Social Democracy;
4. A good colonial policy.

Although never a large party, the Free Conservatives exercised power because of their distinguished membership and strategic position. They sought to consolidate the middle parties against both right and left radicalism, being especially appreciative of the power of the Center and of the need for coöperating with it. Their alli-ance with industry and with agrarianism made them supporters in the front rank of imperialism, which they regarded as a means of uniting the two groups. They stood always in close coöperation with Helldorf's German Conservative party.

In conclusion it may not be amiss to consider in a general way the ideology of the typical Conservative in order to understand his approach to his problem. The Conservative belonged to a feudal so-ciety surviving in a capitalistic state, to which he had to adjust him-self in order to play any rôle in this state. He was both a feudal

---

[71] *Kardorff to his wife*, July 7, 1893, cited by Kardorff, *op. cit.*, p. 282.
[72] *Ibid.*, p. 237.

landowner and at times a capitalistic producer, especially when he had rationalized his methods and undertaken manufacturing enterprises on his own land. He worked his estates with an agricultural proletariat drawn from Russian and Austrian Poland, the living conditions of which were comparable with or worse than those of the most unfortunate town workers.[73] The state allowed him to import these workers, just as it allowed him to exclude shipments of grain. The Agrarian-Conservative maintained that his estates should be preserved because with its high birthrate and strong physique a rural population provided an army for the defense of the East. Actually, a prompt division of the estates into small peasant holdings would have formed a better military safeguard, while the seasonal employment of foreigners belied the professed intense patriotism of the Junkers. In 1893 Max Weber begged that the state rectify the conditions which he had recently uncovered among the agricultural proletariat. He wrote in a report on the subject:

> The use of the Poles weakens the German laborer in his wage struggle with the large landowner in a way more serious than one can imagine. All in all the big estate in the East is rapidly becoming Polonized. It is a matter of time until the moment comes when it must make common cause with the Poles. It will not be possible for the estate owner in the future to represent the national cause if his workers are Poles.[74]

The Conservative still disliked parliamentary government. In his antagonism to the government during the 'nineties he did not oppose the Emperor but the secretaries and ministers, who, he thought, yielded to Liberal demands.[75] Nor did he change funda-

---

[73] Max Weber, " Die ländliche Arbeiterverfassung," *Gesammelte Aufsätze zur Sozial- und Wirtschaftsgeschichte* (Tübingen, 1924), pp. 450 f.

[74] *Ibid.*, p. 454. Between 1895 and 1900 ninety-four thousand more workers came into Germany than went out, although Germany had been losing from one-third million to one-million men annually before the upswing in business in 1895 (W. Sombart, *Die Störungen im deutschen Wirtschaftsleben während des Jahres 1900, Schriften des Vereins für Sozialpolitik*, 113).

[75] Baron and Count Limburg-Stirum, *Aus der konservativen Politik der Jahren 1890-1915* (Berlin, 1921). Limburg wrote that the desire of the party to save the government from weakness, " and the government was

mentally when he adopted parliamentary tactics and methods of popular propaganda. Although compelled by the nature of the age to proceed into the market place and mix with the crowd, he did not intend to be democratic when home again in the security of his state-protected manor. In appealing to the peasant and craftsman for support he acted not from a feeling of democratic equality but from a belief that they constituted part of the old social order which was menaced. He maintained that the state rested upon the Conservative virtues and that without the Agrarian economy to nurture them German morality and idealism would suffer.[76] In this he was supported by the tradition of the army and of the bureaucracy in drawing the " best," that is, the most submissive recruits from the regions where the Prussian Junkers dominated. Whether he felt the surge of a new nationalistic enthusiasm is doubtful; but he was enough attuned to the age to recognize this enthusiasm about him and to use it ably for his purpose. The emphasis on national welfare and national development, national work and national honor now became striking features of his speeches and writings. Since he struggled to reserve the German grain market for himself, his national-mindedness had a selfish basis. He realized that it became more than ever necessary for him to proclaim the identity of his interests with those of the nation and to emphasize his importance to the state.

In the Germany of the late 'nineties the new nationalism took the form of imperialism and it was not originally a part of the Conservative tradition to support this capitalistic development. The Conservative did not easily acquiesce in the demands for a navy, for colonies, and for expensive enterprises abroad financed by German capital; he objected to imperialism as not being in accord with

weak under Hohenlohe," he added, made him and others oppose it. He wished the government to show itself vigorous against Social Democracy (pp. 16-19), urged Prussian thrift upon it so that the government might be financially strong, and often spoke on the power of the Crown. He considered strength of the Crown synonymous with feudal-aristocratic-Conservative power.

[76] Constant reference could be made here to Conservative speeches and writings. See also Naumann, *op. cit.*, Max Weber, and von der Goltz. Also Karl Mannheim, " Das konservative Denken," *Archiv für Sozialwissenschaft und Sozialpolitik,* v. 57 (1927), pt. I, p. 68; pt. II, p. 470.

Agrarian interests. But in addition he opposed the government on these matters because in doing so he saw an opportunity to bargain for advantages to agriculture. From the latter motive, therefore, the Conservatives frequently attacked the government for weakness and urged upon it a more aggressive and self-assertive policy in foreign affairs than the government or industry dared adopt. In their effort to urge the government to action they appeared, paradoxically, more imperialistic than the imperialists. This applied to both American and English relations, since Agrarian interests were deeply involved in both relationships; English markets for sugar were valuable to German agriculturalists, while American produce threatened the existence of German farmers unless safeguards were provided. Hence the Agrarians did not wish to approve governmental policy as regards these countries until they had assured themselves of safeguards. They often showed themselves intensely imperialistic in another respect, namely, in their desire for the use of Power in carrying out all ventures abroad. This striking feature of German imperialism, *Machtpolitik,* owes much to the teaching of the old Prussian Conservatives, from whom Bismarck had learned his methods. Once they agreed to the navy, they regarded it as but an extension of the army, to be used as the latter had been, to force recognition and prestige. If the navy could not march into enemy territory, it could make a brave show and extort concessions from those who opposed German expansion.

By their return to life and power after 1890 the Agrarian-Conservatives laid down conditions under which Germany subsequently developed. These representatives of the feudal system now participated actively in the new state, controlled much of the bureaucracy and were powerful enough to make political alliances which drew big business closer to the Right and crushed the last remnants of Liberalism. The Agrarians carried their domestic crisis over into foreign policy and forced the German government to consider the two together, making their support, now necessary to the government, dependent upon some payment in exchange. By preventing rapid industrialization of the German East after 1895 and excluding free imports of food supplies, they increased the cost of food and therewith of production. Finally, they intensified the *Machtpolitik* aspect of imperialism. Such were the results of the triumph of the

Agrarians over the old Conservatives. In referring to this triumph Vollmar, the Bavarian Social Democratic leader, said:

> Is not Junkerdom the center of all reaction in Prussia and therewith in Germany, which at the moment is only a dependency of Prussia? Does it not work ill to our whole development, does it not lie like a poisonous mildew on the whole German nation? Are these not the men who exercise the most unhealthy influence on decisive circles, who rejoice at every phase of personal politics and seek to sharpen as much as possible the opposing forces? They are everywhere where absolutism and Cæsarism are to be advanced. Indeed, cannot one go so far as to predict civil war? What else can it mean when a Conservative member of this house, Count Mirbach, in another parliamentary body quite openly urged the government to break the law and the constitution, forcibly to abolish the electoral right for the Empire, which is the foundation of our constitution? That is a proclamation of revolution by the government. And that could happen without one of the Secretaries feeling called upon to oppose this suggestion, without one of them noticing that this sword is a two-edged weapon which can turn upon them also! [77]

Vollmar's bitterness, not without justification, indicated the feeling which the return to power of the Agrarian-Conservatives evoked in the group which more than any other understood the implications of Agrarian control.

B. *National Liberals*

Economic and technical developments of the nineteenth century laid the foundations for German unification. The Liberals carried through these changes in Germany, while Bismarck recognized the justice or expediency of their demands for a new political order and in 1871 presented to the Liberal business men a united German market. That with a strong state he imposed upon them an increasingly conservative régime was less palatable to them. In any case, in 1884 the National Liberal party, which had been split by the issues of the tariff and the Socialist Laws and had been reorganized by Miquel, came over to Bismarck. The confirmed free-traders and left Liberals formed or joined other parties. The

[77] *Sten. Ber. d. Reich.*, March 30, 1895, IX Leg. Per., III Sess., III, 1812.

National Liberals declared for a strong army, protection, Socialist Laws, and agricultural assistance, making possible the *Kartellpolitik* of 1887. These National Liberals were dominated by the big industrialists, just as their allies were by the big agriculturalists.[78] They came particularly from the ranks of heavy industry which benefited most directly from protective tariffs. As employers they favored the laws against socialists. Formerly they had approved of a strong state and an army only in case they controlled them; now they readily accepted them under Bismarckian control in order to insure their own position against new dangers. Because the Conservative state had had time to strengthen its régime and had no fears of being " liberalized," Bismarck and the Conservatives were willing to coöperate with the Liberals. The state had gradually converted or eliminated most of the Liberal bureaucrats;[79] and a real affinity of interests between Conservatives and National Liberals had grown up.

Apart from the dependence of Conservatives and National Liberals alike on the new Reich, other factors drew these parties together. In emphasizing the parliamentary trading between the Conservatives and National Liberals, for example, in respect to the navy and agricultural tariffs, the fact is too often lost sight of that

[78] *Die Post* wrote in 1899: " If there are short-sighted politicians in the National Liberal party who think they can spare without harm the still important group of employers in the party, they will presently see how much they have been mistaken. To whom do they owe the majority of their seats and in what sections do they have their strongest support? If the industrialists were to turn their backs on the party, it would soon sink to the level of a small, noisy, but absolutely unimportant group like the National Socialists [Naumann's party] and the like; since not only the large industrialists but still more quickly the smaller ones, who feel especially the ever-increasing strength of the workers as their courage is whipped up by heated speeches, would turn their backs on the party as soon as it showed a tendency to secure political influence by giving in to the exaggerated demands of the lower classes " (No. 295, October 26, 1899. The journal showed the usual Stumm-like antagonism to the workers). When the law to protect strike-breakers split the National Liberal party in 1899, the industrialists threatened to withdraw their support from the party.

[79] Practically the same situation existed in 1848. See E. Kehr, "Das soziale System der Reaktion in Preussen unter dem Ministerium Puttkamer," *Die Gesellschaft*, II (1929), pp. 263 ff.

close ties of an economic and social nature existed between Agrarians and industrialists. Although mentioned previously, this should be emphasized. The Conservatives in the Free-Conservative and German-Conservative parties had at the outset openly acknowledged these ties; but in their eagerness to press their needs the Agrarian-Conservatives long stood out against industrialization and capitalism.

Actually the Agrarians had not remained completely outside Germany's industrial development. They owned stock in industrial enterprises, just as National Liberals owned estates. Kardorff's interlocking interests have been discussed.[80] Heyl zu Herrnsheim, one of the outstanding National Liberals and a leather manufacturer, possessed large holdings in land. Prince Hohenlohe-Oehringen, member of the Silesian branch of the Hohenlohe family, Count Henckel zu Donnersmarck, and Prince Pless held in Upper Silesia enormous properties in lands, mines, and factories, which gave them and those on their properties interests in both camps.[81] The opera-

[80] *Vide supra*, pp. 44 ff. Intermarriage, as in the United States between North and South, also helped to give members of the aristocratic and burgher families interests in both camps. An example would be Kardorff's mother's second marriage, when she allied herself and her lands with a burgher bureaucrat. Baron Gamp, whose name appears in these pages, a bureaucrat and member of the Reichstag and Landtag during this period, was the son of a *Rittergutsbesitzer* and married the daughter of an industrialist. Gamp put his own money into lands and belonged to the Free-Conservative party. For other such relationships see R. E. Martin, *Deutsche Machthaber* (Berlin, Leipzig, 1910). For an expression of the fear felt to be inherent in the union of interests see *Count Solms-Lanbach to Hohenlohe*, September 29, 1897, cited by Hohenlohe, *op. cit.*, p. 386. The Agrarian League claimed supporters from among National Liberals, and it is to be noted that Count Oriola (National Liberal) figured very often in the pages of both the *Deutsche Tageszeitung* and the *Korrespondenz des Bundes der Landwirte*, both Agrarian journals.

[81] Carl Fürstenberg, *Die Lebensgeschichte eines deutschen Bankiers* (Berlin, 1930), pp. 445, 495 f. Georg von Siemens had interests in both land and banking but remained true to his banking, the difference between him and the others mentioned being that he did not want high industrial tariffs in return for support of agricultural tariffs. Had he been an industrialist rather than a banker, he would have wanted them. For discussion of Siemens see Chapter III, " Progressive Union." The Silesian nobility particularly took advantage of industrialism, while the aristocracy

tion of this natural alliance is seen when Heyl zu Herrnsheim introduced in 1895 the measure to terminate the commercial treaty with the Argentine because of the increasing danger to German agriculture from South American imports, and when Paasche, a National Liberal but not a landowner, interpellated the government on its intended action in favor of the sugar industry.[82] The *Kreuzzeitung* wrote of the latter action at the time, " All that is quite according to our wishes; we don't mind in the least if the National Liberals save us the trouble and we are in no way jealous." [83] The economic interdependence of industry and agriculture in the Rhineland was well recognized. The General Assembly for Rhenish and Westphalian Industry meeting in Düsseldorf in 1901 resolved that if agriculture considered a higher tariff on grain necessary, Rhenish-Westphalian industry would support it.[84] When the *Correspondenz,* an organ of the Commercial Treaties Association, attacked the Central Union of German Industrialists for supporting the agricultural tariffs without the backing of all German industry, the Central Union replied that the interests of the various branches of national business did not differ essentially, that many smaller industries had coöperated with heavy industry and textiles to bring about the agricultural tariff.[85] As one industrial journal wrote:

> There [in the Rhineland and Westphalia] agriculture stands with industry in the closest give and take relationship; it prospers; it needs no League. It has even refused the erection of a state Agricultural Bureau because in its industrialized management there is no need for such artificial aid.[86]

---

of the Rhineland held more aloof (Schnabel, *op. cit.,* III, 277). See also Ernst Kohn-Bramstedt, *Aristocracy and the Middle-Classes in Germany* (London, 1937), p. 122.

[82] *Sten. Ber. d. Reich.,* IX Leg. Per., II Sess., II, 1447-9.

[83] *Kreuzzeitung,* December 13, 1894.

[84] *Industriezeitung,* No. 6, February 7, 1901. Also the General Assembly of the Central Union in Berlin, February 5, 1901 (*ibid.*).

[85] *Ibid.,* No. 9, February 28, 1901.

[86] *Hand in Hand,* No. 11, September 1, 1899. It should be noted that agriculture in this district consisted largely of that on small farms which could not supply the industrial areas with sufficient foodstuffs. Hence grain had to be imported. *Cf.* also *Industriezeitung,* No. 8, February 21, 1902. *Hand in Hand* believed firmly, however, that Germany would become

The common cause against labor formed a far more tangible bond of union. As the industrial order drew the population into the cities agricultural labor became scarce and wages high. Only by using seasonal Polish labor could the large agriculturalists meet this problem. Once in the cities the workers gravitated toward Social Democracy and were lost to Conservatism. The organized power of labor after 1890 in the Reichstag and in the country at large alarmed both Conservatives and National Liberals. They regarded " democratization " as their greatest menace, whether in economic, social or political spheres, and they dared not relent in their struggle against it. They rejected the claim that under Bernstein's influence Social Democracy had changed its stripes, and they declared war against " these enemies of all that was dear to the German nation." They considered the most pressing duty of the present to be " the preventing of the entire proletariat from becoming Social Democratic." [87] Their characteristic arguments in favor of any proposal advantageous to agriculture or industry took the form of praising its value to the worker. The laborer, they said, must be appeased and made to feel his community of interests with his employer. Cartels, said an article in the *Industriezeitung,* " strengthen the employer as against the worker. Not only the entrepreneurs of the cartel industries derive advantages from these cartels. Other circles," it continued, " do likewise and above all the workers in the industries, who prosper when their employers prosper. For them the most important effect of the cartels is to guarantee steady work." [88] The building of a navy, they argued, would furnish employment at the shipyards,[89] colonies would give

---

an industrial country and that the League would not succeed in turning back the economic clock. (*Hand in Hand* was a journal of small industry, while the *Industriezeitung* represented the Central Union.)

[87] *Industriezeitung*, No. 47, November 23, 1899, cited from the report of the Assembly, November 17. Those who repudiate emphasis on the class struggle in pre-war Germany do not sufficiently differentiate between the social struggle, which Stumm, for example, did not like to recognize, and the political struggle with Social Democracy, which he pressed. As at present the employers protested that they did not believe that the workers wanted to be Social Democrats but that they were forced to join the party.

[88] *Ibid.*, No. 51, December 19, 1902.

[89] At a meeting of the directors and in the General Assembly of the

the workers new markets for the products of their hands or a place to which to emigrate without being lost to the fatherland. During the parliamentary fight which took place in 1895 over the proposed law against the socialists the hatred of employers against organized labor came into the open. Stumm led the attack with the slogan " Social Democracy can and must be suppressed," and he asked for measures which would take away its vote and exile its agitators.[90] Bennigsen, a leader of the old Liberals, expressed the same sentiments but with more moderation and unction.

> It often seems to me that the meaning of these deep antipathies between the present bourgeois parties and the masses of the workers is not rightly understood. Here we have a matter of strife and antagonism which cannot be settled in our time but which will last through the next century . . . . It is a question of new phenomena . . . . It must be the responsibility of the government and the bourgeoisie to draw off the water from Social Democracy and to strengthen among the workers, of whom millions have not yet fallen prey to Social Democracy, the feeling that they also are in a position by working together with the government and the middle-classes to attain to the condition of felicity which comes to workers as to other classes.[91]

Bennigsen pleaded with the parties to give up their petty strife and unite with the government against the common enemy.

The antipathy of Agrarians and industrialists to the proletariat hardly needs elaboration. It is apparent enough from the very fact of *Interessenpolitik*. The big interests in the German state of the 'nineties thought they must strengthen themselves wherever they saw an opportunity. From the point of view of the ruling classes a navy, desirable in itself as an addition to the army, and new markets were useful to bolster their position against the social enemy. " Every successful imperialistic policy of force abroad [so Max Weber wrote] normally strengthens likewise, at least at first, at

Navy League, January, 1900, Count Dürckheim-Montmartin declared that the employees particularly had an interest in the expansion of the navy. He said that a questionnaire to all the large shipyards had shown at least 75%, perhaps 80%, of the money spent for warships going into wages (*Die Flotte*, No. 1, January, 1900, p. 15).

[90] *Sten. Ber. d. Reich.*, IX Leg. Per., III Sess., I, 240.
[91] *Ibid.*, p. 250.

home the prestige and consequently the power and the influence of
those classes, castes and parties under whose leadership the success
has been obtained." [92]   The interdependence of the Junkers and
industrialists and the dependence of both upon the government grew
with the fear of Social Democracy. Hence it is no exaggeration to
say that the Social Democratic danger constituted a decisive factor
in bringing together the two groups of the Right. In 1903 Eulenburg gave a partial explanation of this condition when he wrote the
following to Chancellor Bülow:

> These castes, to which even the aristocrat must be added,
> separate the population into those who give satisfaction and
> those who cannot give it. The foreigner cannot understand
> this classification and would not be in the least able, even if he
> could understand it, to measure the enormous importance of it.
> He would never grasp the fact that, for example, certain castes
> are forced to deny entrance to a man of genius merely because
> he belongs to another caste; that the marriage of a clever man
> with a woman below him destroys his career, etc. The foreigner
> would shout, ' China.'
>
> We have, however, not the courage to break the spell which
> surrounds our noblest, our best powers like a chain. [93]

Conservatives and National Liberals coöperated officially in 1897

[92] Max Weber, *Wirtschaft und Gesellschaft* in *Grundriss der Sozialökon-
omik*, III, 2, 626. *Cf.* also N. Lenin, *Imperialism* (1917). Lenin brought
out the same point by reference to English imperialism. He quoted from
Rhodes: " Yesterday I was in the East End at an unemployed meeting. I
heard inflammatory speeches; but they all echoed only one cry: ' We want
bread! We want bread! ' I thought about this on the way home, and I
became more and more convinced of the importance of imperialism. My
cherished idea provides a solution for the social problem. In order to
save forty million inhabitants of the United Kingdom from a bloody civil
war, we colonial statesmen must take possession of new lands suitable
for peopling by the surplus population of this country, where we shall be
able to find new markets for the goods produced in our factories and
mines. . . . If you want to avoid civil war, you must become an imperialist " (*State and Revolution* [Vanguard Press edition, New York,
1929], p. 63).

[93] Haller, *op. cit.*, p. 324. Eulenburg assigned the cause to the devastating
tradition of Prussian army and bureaucracy. If his statement is not
without exception, even in pre-war Germany, it remains true that no one
dared to compromise with Social Democracy. See also Kohn-Bramstedt,
op. cit.

through the efforts of Miquel, Prussian Finance Minister. This log-rolling union was known as the *Sammlung* and its political activity as *Sammlungspolitik*. In reality it was not more of an alliance than had existed in 1887 under Bismarck, although it represented a more open and lasting arrangement. Miquel's speech in behalf of the *Sammlung* principle contained the following explanation:

> Clearly the concern for the state has its roots not merely in the latter's power to exercise a decisive influence on economic relations, but also in the principle that a one-sided considera-tion of the interests of one branch should not endanger the life of another branch. In general the interests of all workers and earning classes are essentially the same; in some questions they run opposite enough but all producing classes strive for the protection of their work over against the foreigner. Agricul-ture and industry stand in mutual relation of producer and consumer; the more able to buy both are, the better it will be for both, and the solid trade of the middleman can live by means of both. . . . This great commonalty of interests should not be forgotten in the struggles and differences of the present and should be considered by all parts of the commonwealth. Every sacrifice which any one branch of business makes is not lost; it comes eventually to the good of all.[94]

The strength of the National Liberals did not lie in the Reichs-tag, although the party had usually one or two powerful represent-atives there. Bassermann, the leader of the group in the Reichs-tag, was a lawyer, and neither Bennigsen nor Miquel, the old lead-ers, was an industrialist. The majority of the Reichstag National Liberals consisted of small factory owners, lawyers and professors, just as had the Liberals of the Frankfurt Parliament in 1848. The National Liberals in the Prussian Landtag represented more nearly the power of industry. In this body the Rhenish-Westphalian group exercised great influence and was closely allied with the Con-servatives.[95] The demands of industry, however, largely determined the programme of the entire party.

Typical of the National Liberals was Friedrich Hammacher

[94] Miquel, *Reden* (Berlin, 1914), III, 278. The occasion was that of the opening of a railroad bridge, August 15, 1897.

[95] Theodor Eschenburg, *Das Kaiserreich am Scheidewege: Bassermann, Bülow und der Block* (Berlin, 1929), p. 13.

7

(1824-1904). He began his career as a democrat with socialist leanings. After expressing these views in 1848, he was ousted from governmental service and was barred from his profession as a lawyer. Thereafter he threw in his lot with big business in the Ruhr and became especially interested in the organization of industrial concerns. During the crisis of 1857 he was active in proposing measures for combatting it. In 1863 he was elected to the Prussian Landtag, where he joined forces with the Progressive party. Although eager for national unification and ready to support the wars of unification after Germany's honor became engaged in open conflict, he opposed on principle Bismarck's method. After having helped to found the National Liberal party he became a member in 1869 of the Diet of the North German Confederation. He never went over to protection so completely as to sympathize with the Central Union of German Industrialists, although he advocated the abolition of the iron tariff in the early 'seventies and although his own Mining Union (*Bergbaulicher Verein*) became affiliated with this high protectionist organization.[96] On the whole Hammacher was a government man and he gradually drew away from the old Liberal principles. He recognized that party members disagreed fundamentally, that their only bond of union was support of the existing régime, and he knew that if the party broke up it would be long " before the Liberal elements of the country recover consciousness." [97]

Hammacher's views on the important questions of the day paralleled his material interests and he was in a position to work actively for them. He supported the coöperation of National Liberals and Conservatives in the elections of 1884 and 1887 because he saw the need for stronger military measures. He did not believe in the higher grain tariff of 1887, however, since it would increase food prices for the wage-earners, although he agreed in 1894 to aid agriculture by abolishing the *Identitätsnachweis*.[98] He sat in the Reichstag almost continuously and, especially after 1890, became the speaker for the party on most measures. The government Secretaries often consulted him before introducing important bills. His many connections fitted him for this work; for he associated with

[96] Alex Bein, *Friedrich Hammacher* (Berlin, 1932), pp. 75 ff.
[97] *Ibid.*, p. 80.   [98] *Vide supra*, p. 56.

the iron, steel and coal interests in the Ruhr and held the presidency of the Mining Union. In addition to these posts he was a member of the Colonial Society, Vice-President of the Navy League Abroad, and after 1898 Chairman of the central executive committee of the National Liberal party. Together with others of similar connections, Eduard Arnold, Ernst von Mendelssohn Bartholdy, Oechelhäuser, Gneist, A. Buhl, von Eynern, and others in 1890 he formed the *Nationalzeitung Companie,* Incorporated, in order to keep alive this journal and to exercise his influence through it. He also made possible the publication of the *Nationalliberale Korrespondenz.*[99]

Because of the anti-socialist laws Hammacher was unfriendly to Bismarck and rather welcomed the accession of William II. At the same time he mistrusted him. He wrote in 1890:

> The workers think they have the Emperor on their side even when they come forward with the most foolish demands. I am convinced that that will have no good end and that shooting will begin. It is probable that the Emperor will proceed mercilessly against the masses.[100]

Hammacher disapproved of merciless opposition to the workers. He differed from Bueck and the Central Union during the strike of 1889 and used his entire influence with the Mining Union to bring about conciliation. At that time Bueck, Secretary to the Central Union, wrote: " The German employers will never, never negotiate with the representatives of the workers on the basis of equality (*Gleichberechtigkeit*)." Hammacher's distaste for reaction was expressed in his own words:

> I have watched for a long time the all-powerful success of the intriguing efforts of the Court and Junker parties to secure influence over the political views of the Emperor. The Emperor is in economic affairs through and through a modern and unprejudiced statesman and not designed for the *coup d'état* ideas of the Agrarians. For years they have tried to change this in him. If they succeed in convincing him that only in the old Prussian reaction resides that power which can serve him in the active pursuit of his political goals, we shall find

---

[99] Bein, *op. cit.,* p. 141.
[100] *Hammacher to his Wife,* 1890, cited by Bein, *op. cit.,* p. 129.

ourselves with a ministry *à la* Mirbach and the deluge will be here.[101]

At the same time he thought it very dangerous to inspire the workers from above with impossible hopes, which he called Siren songs.[102] The employers should care for them and welfare in abundance should be forthcoming; but political power—universal suffrage and trade unions—should not be given them lest the "dark clouds of the workers' movement not blow over without considerable harm being done to our industry."[103] During the 'nineties, like Kardorff and Stumm, he came definitely to the view that universal suffrage was the curse of the Empire, for it was, he held, strengthening the hands of both extreme Right and extreme Left in the Reichstag. Do away with it, he said, and if this should fail, "Let General Waldersee come on the scene."[104]

Hammacher approved the Caprivi Commercial Treaties, the income and inheritance taxes of Miquel's financial reforms in Prussia, and the canal scheme which the Agrarians rejected in the Landtag in 1899. In these matters he exemplified the natural opposition of the National Liberal to the Agrarian. He became much interested in colonial policy and thought that Germany must not neglect an opportunity to secure a foothold in Africa similar to that which she had had in the 'eighties. At that time he had affiliated with colonial interests and had helped to found in 1884 the German Colonial Union, of which he had become Vice-President, and in 1885 the German Colonial Society for South West Africa. But Hammacher had caution; he believed that no hasty steps should be taken abroad and that public opinion should be carefully prepared for a colonial policy. His interest in colonies entailed an interest in naval protection. He worked with Tirpitz after 1897 and won over the National Liberals to the naval bill.

> I quite admit [he said in summing up the reasons for supporting an expansion of the navy] that the strong national feeling which has controlled the National Liberals as a party since its inception and which will never leave it has made it

---

[101] Cited by Bein, *op. cit.*, p. 139.

[102] *Hammacher to Haniel, ibid.*, p. 129.

[103] *Ibid.*, p. 83.   [104] *Vide supra*, pp. 21 ff.

easier for us to neglect the budget and financial difficulties inherent in this law.

Hammacher understood that the prosperity of the Empire depended upon industry and thought that export trade was therefore a primary consideration. When he pointed out that German trade with the United States and the English colonies would be endangered in the future by their protective tariffs, the American press accused him of wishing to acquire new markets by force. He denied this charge; but at the same time he thought that Germany was in a slough of despondency and that she stood in need of a revival of patriotism and nationalism to arouse her. He thought also that only common action on the part of all European states could hope to curb the danger of American competition.[105] Thus his view resembled that of the power and prestige political theory of many of his contemporaries. He approved of the government's attitude in the Transvaal affair and of the Krüger Telegram, which he called " an expression of the consciousness of historical responsibility." If trouble with England should result over the Transvaal, Germany, he maintained, could not be blamed. By way of a similar process of reasoning he concluded that German naval power should be sufficient to protect the country in an emergency.

Hammacher's most important service to German industry doubtless was his organization of the coal syndicate in 1893.[106] The cartel policy to which he subscribed through necessity formed a corollary to protective tariffs. Hammacher and the National Liberals in so far as they sympathized with big industry had no alternative once they had given up free-trade but to look to a state strong enough to afford them tariff protection, to support their cartels, to reduce freight rates and to provide a navy for furthering their export trade. They needed a *Machtstaat*. Hammacher maintained that the coal syndicate did not resemble Kanitz's plan for agriculture because it did not ask the state to perform a service for one group; it was self-help. His adherence to Liberalism in this one respect was illogical because industry, if it were to increase its markets abroad, could no longer exist without state help of one kind or another.

[105] Bein, *op. cit.*, p. 135.   [106] *Ibid.*, pp. 98 ff.

Hammacher seems to have felt, as Eulenburg did, the menace of internal strife in Germany. " Not only the lower classes," he said, " but also those favored by birth and wealth are prey to a dissatisfaction which has weakened the foundations of our common life." [107] Hence he saw in the army, the navy and colonies the only hope of strengthening society and the state. New goals and continued prosperity would buttress " the foundations of our common life."

Two other men may be mentioned as representing types among the National Liberals. One of these was Ernst Bassermann, a native of Mannheim and long leader of the party. He is important to this study because, as Stresemann, Foreign Minister under the Republic, has said, " Bassermann was one of the few men in the Reichstag who regularly took a stand on foreign policy." [108] Bassermann came of a traditionally Liberal bourgeois family. Born in 1854 he belonged to a younger generation than Hammacher and one less trained in political problems. As has often happened in German history a South German became an admirer of Prussia. All his life Bassermann displayed an enthusiasm for the army, in which he held the rank of Major of the Reserve, and for the navy. As a lawyer for the South German *Diskonto-Gesellschaft* he came into relation with various economic and commercial organizations on the Rhine. From 1887 he belonged also to the City Council of Mannheim, in which he served his political apprenticeship. In Bassermann's homeland, Baden, a Liberal who admired the Reich could hardly do otherwise than join the National Liberals, since no Conservative party of importance existed there. In 1893 Bassermann was elected to the Reichstag in preference to the Social Democratic candidate and at the request of Bennigsen, who retired in 1897, he became leader of the National Liberals in that body. His biographer states that Bassermann wrote very sparingly for the *Mannheimer Generalanzeiger,* which, however, was close to him; supposedly he used the party organ, the *Nationalzeitung* of Hammacher.

Bassermann did not greatly sympathize with the conservative group of National Liberals led by Friedberg and Hobrecht in the Prussian Landtag. He tried to promote, as did Hammacher, the

[107] *Ibid.*, p. 137.   [108] Eschenburg, *op. cit.*, p. vii.

efforts of the young National Liberals in the *Reichsverband* in their struggle to revive the party.[109] His function consisted in harmonizing his own group with these other two wings of the party. It was in great part due to him that the National Liberals held together at all; for their union could only continue through constant compromise. Though he was undoubtedly one of the greatest pre-war parliamentarians, it is difficult to know Bassermann's real views because he had so often to advocate what his party would sanction. It was characteristic of the times that a party neglected its *Weltanschauung*. This neglect became evident in Bassermann. He was an opportunist.

On the whole Bassermann remained Liberal in internal politics by opposing the anti-socialist laws and advocating the right of association; but he never objected to the existing constitutional order.[110] In foreign policy he advocated *Machtpolitik,* arguing for a navy by citing the four hundred and fifty million marks of German capital (these are his figures) invested abroad, which might easily arouse jealousy. Germany could not dispense with greater protective measures. The Spanish-American and Boer Wars, he declared, had shown him that the points of friction in the struggle for world markets had greatly increased; Germany must reckon with the fact that war might develop in which she would become involved; she must be prepared with Power, which at persent she did not have.[111] He maintained that in this view he followed Bismarck; but he also spoke for heavy industry and the nationalists; he swam with the imperialist tide.

[109] This organization was one of the younger men who professed a stronger patriotism and more national outlook than the older generation. It was founded in 1900 and endeavoured in domestic politics to create a more liberal programme and draw the left Liberals over to the National Liberals (Eschenberg, *op. cit.*, pp. 11 ff.). The group often increased the internal dissension within the party.

[110] Bassermann's daughter said of him later: " He came up against the walls of the ruling system without having the desire to tear down these walls; hence his influence remained limited " (cited by Eschenburg, *op. cit.*, p. 21).

[111] *Sten. Ber. d. Reich.*, February 8, 1900, X Leg. Per. I Sess., V, 3969; June 6, 1900, VII, 5824.

So Bassermann [his biographer wrote] was in his spiritual attitude, in his political view of things, in his social position, and in his entire appearance a type of burgher from the days of the Empire, a man who found fault and might have liked to improve but never could change or wished to change things.[112]

Another type was represented by Dr. Ernst Hasse, a member of the National Liberal party in the Reichstag and one of the leaders of the Pan-German League. Hasse, the son of a Saxon preacher, had in his youth studied for the ministry. During the wars of unification he became an officer. Like Bassermann he greatly admired Prussia and resigned from the Saxon army because he found in it too much anti-Prussianism. He turned to academic life, became a professor and in 1890 secured election to the Reichstag from Leipzig as a National Liberal. He soon manifested interest in the colonial movement and was asked to become president of the Pan-German League.[113] This group, organized first under Karl Peters in 1886, owed its success to Hasse, who gave it the name it bore and established its journal, the *Alldeutsche Blätter*.[114] Hasse personified the nationalism and imperialism characteristic of this period.

We want our right recognized [he wrote], not in a country of foreign domination, but the equality of our rights with those of other great Powers in the possession of colonial domains which are to be ours exclusively; we wish elbow room, expansion, land.[115]

The kind of *Machtpolitik* and *Weltpolitik* for which Hasse stood should not be identified with the usual *Interessenpolitik*. Hasse was a professional nationalist whose vested interest lay in the propaganda which he spread. He seems to have thought that Germany had launched upon the imperialistic sea, whether by or against her

[112] Eschenburg, *op. cit.*, p. 26.

[113] Heinrich Class, *Wider den Strom* (Leipzig, 1932), pp. 43 ff.

[114] *Cf. infra*, Chapter III, "Pan-German League." Also Andler, *Collection de Documents sur le Pan-Germanisme* (Paris, 1915), II, 253 ff.

[115] Hasse, "Weltpolitik, Imperialismus, Kolonialpolitik" in *Deutsche Politik* (Munich, 1908), II, No. 1, p. 67.

will no longer mattered, and that she must make the most of it.[116]
Hasse's friend, Dr. Lehr, General Secretary to the League, also sat
in the Reichstag as a member of the National Liberal party. He
defended the same point of view. The two men were more national-
imperialistic than the industrialists whose cause they advanced,[117]
and in some respects were more reactionary than the Conservatives.[118] Hasse and his associates must be counted as an important
element of the National Liberals; they had the popular organization
with which to fight for imperialism.[119]

Several National Liberal journals have been mentioned. The
Nationalzeitung represented the leftwing group and stood close to
Hammacher. It was considered the party organ but frequently
opposed the rightwing party periodicals, the *Rheinisch-Westfälische
Zeitung,* the *Leipziger Neueste Nachrichten,* the *Münchener
Neueste Nachrichten,* and the *Süddeutsche Nationalliberale Korrespondenz.* The names of the last four indicate clearly the area
which each served and represented. The *Rheinisch-Westfälische
Zeitung* was owned by Reismann-Grone, a nationalist who regarded
the fall of Bismarck as a calamity. He made his paper a leading
opponent against the new government. Reismann-Grone served as a
very active member of the executive committee of the Pan-German
League. He received Krüger in Cologne in December, 1900, and

---

[116] *Cf. infra,* Chapter III. Also *Sten. Ber. d. Reich.,* X Leg. Per., I
Sess., X, 8724, and above quoted essay. "For us [he wrote] the new imperialism is nothing other than one form of the expansionist efforts of
great peoples and states. Whether imperialism and colonialism are independent movements or whether imperialism comprehends both is not agreed
upon yet. But in any case imperialism acts outside the boundaries of the
mother country; it is a system of foreign policy which obtains in all forms
of governments, democracies as well as in constitutional or absolute
monarchies (*ibid.,* p. 11).

[117] Hasse once cited approvingly an article in a recent paper which
accused the Pan-Germans of being those " who shook the mailed fist in the
face of the world."

[118] On one occasion Class tried to win over Heyderbrand von der Lasa
(Conservative) to allow the East Provinces to be organized by the Pan-
Germans. Heyderbrand asked Class why he did not join the Conservative
party. To this question Class replied that it was too liberal for him: it
had accepted universal suffrage! (Class, *op. cit.,* p. 267).

[119] *Vide infra,* Chapter III for the work of the League and of Hasse.

made the speech of welcome. Although a Catholic and eager to keep the Catholic nationalists attached to the Empire, he became greatly interested in Schemann, the German expounder of Count Gobineau's racial theories, deriving from him a passion for "pure Germanism" *(reines Deutschtum)*.[120] Reismann-Grone early advocated a large navy and opposed England. With his newspaper he served an industrial area Catholic in population but with Protestant leaders, Jewish industrialists being few in the Ruhr. He allied himself closely with the Central Union of German Industrialists and the propaganda organization *par excellence* of nationalism, the Pan-German League. He expressed effectively the desires of industry by appealing to nationalism rather than to vested interests.[121]

The *Nationalzeitung,* which was in a bad financial condition when Hammacher and his friends rescued it, had behind it significant interests. Hammacher's own connections have already been described. Another of the board of directors, Wilhelm Oechelhäuser, held a directorship in the Continental Gas Company of Dessau. He sat in the Reichstag as a member of the National Liberal party and was a member of the German National Chamber of Commerce *(Handelstag),* the central organization of the chambers of commerce of the Empire. Oechelhäuser helped to found the German East Africa Company and had investments in plantations in Kamerun. In connection with these interests in things colonial he joined the Colonial Society and frequently contributed articles to the *Kolonialzeitung* on the need for state aid in colonial development.[122]

The *Nationalzeitung* regarded the age, rather than the industrialists, as the true source of imperialism. The journal wrote in 1901:

> The premise that certain interests drove the Americans into the war with Spain or the English into the war against the South African Republic, that Chamberlain and McKinley alone

---

[120] Class, *op. cit.*, p. 88. On Reismann-Grone see the memoirs of Class, who later became head of the Pan-German League.

[121] Dr. Heinrich Pohl, a philologist closely connected with the Pan-German League as one of its most effective organizers in and about Essen, edited the *Rheinisch-Westfälische Zeitung.* He left this paper to become editor of *Die Post*, Stumm's journal.

[122] *Kolonialzeitung, passim,* during the 1890's. Reference to Oechelhäuser also in Fürstenberg, *op. cit.*, pp. 143, 350.

bear the blame for these wars, when quietly considered, will not hold. Imperialism is not the new discovery of certain ambitious men but the necessary result of the building of great national states and the economic movements which have done away with geographic boundaries and sought to make the world a unified whole.[123]

This historical point of view helped to make the *Nationalzeitung* support eagerly the imperialistic Germany. It differed from the *Rheinisch-Westfälische Zeitung* in being less anti-governmental in its foreign policy.[124]

The *Industriezeitung,* which became after 1897 the organ of the Central Union, will be discussed more fully in connection with the Union. It was the mouthpiece of industry. It went further afield than a technical journal like *Stahl und Eisen* and freely gave the views of the Central Union on the questions of the day.[125]

From the foregoing discussion some conception of the National Liberal party may be formed. It was a small party, not comparable in size with the Center and Social Democratic parties. Its strength lay in the support of a few representatives of heavy industry, especially in the Ruhr and the Saar (Silesian industry was always more Conservative) and in that of the South Germans, who cherished the Liberal tradition without being willing to go over to the left.[126] The professional element, which agreed with the imperialistic demands of industry and devoted itself to realizing these

[123] *Nationalzeitung,* "Demokratie und Imperialismus," No. 26, January 13, 1901.

[124] *Ibid.,* No. 6, January 4, 1901. *Cf.* article against the Agrarian, Pan-German and Social Democratic journals, which worked, said the *Nationalzeitung,* with the general premise that the government was always stupid.

[125] The writer must omit discussion of the provincial journals since she lacks knowledge of their backing and editing. Their opinions did not greatly differ from those of the conservative group among the National Liberals, although some, like the *Frankfurter Zeitung,* were outspokenly democratic. The *Generalanzeigerpresse* organized by Scherl and others to a great extent served the provinces. Although supposed to be non-partisan and to print only factual news, it relied on sensationalism and cheapness to obtain a large public. See Emil Dovifat, *Die Zeitungen* in *Die deutsche Wirtschaft und Ihre Führer,* III (Gotha, 1925), pp. 90 f.

[126] The Reichstag list for the party during the 1890's will indicate this at a glance.

demands, made up an important part of the National Liberals. This element, however, never completely identified itself with the industrialists as the Agrarian League did with the Conservatives; it was filled with patriotic and nationalistic zeal above selfish interest and sought to educate the people to the needs of the new era. But the programme of all elements offered only an extension of the former order into new fields, not a new order such as the old Liberals had stood for in 1848 or 1860. Moreover, because the old Liberal principle of freedom was gone, the programme emphasized Power as a means of holding the state together.

Because of their small numbers the National Liberals had to become opportunistic.[127] They allied themselves now with the Conservatives, now with the Centrists, now with both, seeking to maintain their identity as a party by refraining from permanent alliances. But every compromise weakened their power. Their agreement with the Conservatives, especially the alliance of 1897-8, did much to bring the Conservatives back to their former position of influence. Although they would have liked to form a great middle party,[127a] they were never able to effect this union because they had no *Weltanschauung* which could command popular support. The National Liberals held a peculiar position. Liberalism had exhausted its public idealism with the foundation of the Empire and the old Liberals had been forced to look on while new Liberals, those of the Center and of Social Democracy, pursued the struggle for rights. Furthermore, the National Liberals saw the Social Democrats fighting the state which they had helped to create and

---

[127] Counting representatives of all liberal parties and all National Liberals as Liberals there were said to be in 1898 one hundred liberal members in the Reichstag with a supporting vote of two millions. Between 1893 and 1898 Liberal votes diminished by about 20%. The loss, especially the loss of the left Liberals, brought gain to Social Democracy. The Progressive Peoples' party lost about one hundred and sixty thousand votes, the Progressive Union lost about seventy thousand, that is, the Liberals more to the left lost more votes. If one considers that Social Democracy adopted a part of the old Liberal programme, one realizes that Liberalism itself lost supporters the more it made its way into the country (*Die Nation*, No. 42, July 16, 1898, pp. 596-7).

[127a] Eschenburg, *op. cit.*, Chap. II, *passim. Cf.* also the efforts of Friedrich Naumann in this direction in Heuss, *op. cit.*, pp. 228 ff.

with which their existence was bound up. They could not sympathize with the programme of the new Left, and they gradually sought Conservative help against it. On the one hand this move lost for them all claim to being a Liberal party with popular appeal. On the other hand their alliance with the Agrarians pervented them from regaining the ascendancy which they had enjoyed in the 1870's; they had no weapons to use against Conservative control of the government and they had to be content with the power which they could command in alliance with the Conservatives. As in 1879 and 1887 they allied themselves with Prussianism and militarism. The National Liberals had nothing left but their interests. They could fight for these but they could not hope to popularize their party through them.[128]

The enormous activity which began in 1895 restored a degree of self-confidence to the National Liberals and to the industrialists. Economic prosperity created a situation somewhat akin to that of the 'fifties when increasing industrialism and population demanded wider markets. Industrialists feared that Germany and the European continent alone would not constitute in the future a sufficiently large market. To be sure, they did not neglect to cultivate both European and home markets as much as possible and German trade with the continent of Europe steadily increased. At the same time an effort was made to draw the people of the state closer together into a new nationalism, which sought to reconcile the home

[128] The writer is indebted to Dr. Vagts for one example of the way in which the National Liberals failed to function effectively. The nineteenth electoral district of Hanover during the 'eighties was National Liberal, although its political passions did not, apparently, run high. Then came the founding of the Agrarian League. Hahn, the subsequent director of the League, was a son of this district and persuaded the peasants and farmers that their interests lay with the League, although such was not the case; for there were no large estates and the district was naturally fitted for dairying and pork raising. The National Liberals, however, instead of strenuously combatting Hahn, put up as candidtae Hugo Böttger, a corporation lawyer who was not a native and had no connection with the local population. In case of a tie, the League or the National Liberals, as the case required, supported each other in the run-off elections in order to check the Social Democrats. The nature of the National Liberal candidate did much to turn the peasants against the National Liberals and toward the candidate of the League, Hahn.

market to the hardship of higher prices and to find compensation for the burden in a programme of imperialism. Since after 1895 Germany could not secure new colonies, her main recourse lay in acquiring through diplomacy equal rights with others in all markets. Furthermore, industry saw no other way of gaining these rights than through a show of Power, without necessarily being aggressive. In advancing this programme the industrialists and their allies wished to maintain the prosperity and prestige of their country by insuring their own future.

It would be difficult to say how aware the industrialists were of all of these motives. Their arguments for expansion clung rather closely to "economic necessity" and "national labor" or "prestige." [128a] It is certain that the feeling of insecurity and futility which the National Liberals felt as a result of their weakened position in the Empire contributed greatly to the eagerness with which they engaged in the pursuit of the new objectives. Out of the new national imperialism they made for themselves spiritual and political, as well as economic, aims such as they had not had since 1870.

C. *The Center*

During the period from 1895 to 1906 the Center or Catholic party held the balance of power in the Reichstag. A Centrist was President of the Reichstag, and both there and in the Prussian Landtag Centrist support was sought by the Conservatives and was necessary for the enactment of any important measure. This strategic position encouraged the party to preserve its power by adapting itself to the needs of the situation. Other considerations also contributed to obliterate the memory of the *Kulturkampf* and to transform the Center from a party of opposition into one supporting government measures.[129] The Centrists, unlike the Con-

---

[128a] Max Weber, *Wirtschaft und Gesellschaft*, Pt. II, 626. Also Kehr, *op. cit.*, and Meinecke, *Staat und Persönlichkeit*. For a discussion of the relation between peace and war in the mind of industry and the state see F. Lenz, *Macht und Wirtschaft* (Munich, 1915), pp. 105-ff.

[129] Georg Hertling, *Erinnerungen aus meinem Leben* (Munich, 1920), II, p. 16. This fact was already true in 1883 when Hertling noticed a decided change in attitude since 1879 on the part of the Reichstag group of the Center. But support of government measures was not a matter of

servatives and National Liberals, lacked homogeneity in caste or class and their programme was not dictated by one group of economic or social interests. Catholicism itself bound them together, and Catholicism professed to teach its adherents transcendental values rather than the pursuit of material interests. Absence of a controlling economic group gave the party mobility. When it saw an opportunity for achieving power, it was in a position to place the objective of party advantage above special interests.[130] Moreover, the Centrist leaders retained, together with the nationalism and patriotism of the German Catholic, much of the political instinct and ability acquired through centuries of conflict. Catholic leaders developed an ideology flexible enough to embrace a navy, imperialism, or other national objectives. Their ideology has sometimes been called the philosophy of the mission (*Missionsideologie*). One member of the party formulated it in 1900 as follows:

> Upon every Christian people lies the blessing of a heavenly mission and therewith the right of God to preserve and care for its existence and effectiveness in the world. Attacks upon the holy faith, upon freedom and country, hindrance of the justifiable use of the means upon which the material existence of a people depends compel and make it the duty of a people to arm and to offer all its strength against the enemy.[131]

---

principle; the Center decided on each question according to its merits. Bachem, the historian of the Center, has written that the Center was not elected as a government party but could often allow itself the privilege of being so (Karl Bachem, *Vorgeschichte, Geschichte und Politik der deutschen Zentrumspartei* [Cologne, 1927-32], V, 16). Opposition ended definitely with the election of von Levetzow as President of the Reichstag.

[130] Eckart Kehr believed the Center free to negotiate politically, that is, realistically, as no other party was because it lacked the rigid bonds of mundane ethics. The means meant nothing to transcendentalists (Kehr, *op. cit.*, pp. 365 f.). *Cf.* also Naumann, *op. cit.*, p. 122. The government preferred to make friends with the Center because it was a monarchical party, as Hohenlohe made clear (Hohenlohe, *op. cit.*, p. 453). *Cf.* also *Die Nation*, No. 20, February 12, 1898. This Progressive organ well appreciated the Center's power.

[131] W. P. Englert, *Speech in Bonn* (Paderborn, 1900), p. 9. At this time the Center made much use of religious theses. Only later did it deny economic interests and seek to replace these with purely political motives (Kehr, *op. cit.*, p. 367). In the Prussian Landtag the Center concerned

The diverse character of the Center constituted perhaps the best guarantee for maintaining its political mobility. The professions were well represented. Spahn, Buol, Porsch, Gröber, all leaders of the Center in the 'nineties, were lawyers, as Windhorst had been.[132] Only in Bavaria were the leaders seldom jurists. Hertling, another of the leaders, was a professor of philosophy. Many priests and theologians always secured election, although the party did not allow church interests to direct its political activity. "Nothing lies further from the mind of the Center," said Ernst Lieber, successor to Windhorst as leader of the party, "than the desire to attend to the affairs of the Catholic church."[133] Count Ballestrem, President of the Reichstag group of Centrists and later President of the Reichstag, was an industrialist from Silesia. As a Silesian he understood the Russian menace and favored the Military Law of 1893. When the party opposed the measure, he withdrew from the elections and stayed out of the Reichstag from 1893 to 1898. Heeremann, President of the Centrists in the Prussian Landtag, owned a knight's estate and stood close to agricultural interests.[134] At one time he supported his colleague Schorlemer in an attempt to organize the Westphalian peasants into a union outside the Center party for furthering peasant interests. The attempt failed because party ideals and the party bond proved stronger than economic interests. There existed among the Centrists a large Agrarian group, including beside Heeremann, Prince Karl zu Löwenstein, Baron von Huene, Count Hompesch, Baron zu Franckenstein, and others. After 1893, however, Bavaria and Silesia elected no more aristocrats to the Reichstag. The number of ecclesiastics also decreased. Gradually the party democratized itself, electing more workers, peasants and small merchants as the nature of the national problems changed. In 1898 the party had one hundred and two members in the Reichs-

itself more with religious questions, while in the Reichstag religious matters were less and less discussed. Here after 1890 economic questions threatened to disrupt the Center; but it was able to withstand the pressure. *Cf.* Hertling, *op. cit.*, II, 99. Ability to withstand it was owing to the fact that before 1914 economic interests asserted themselves in the Center only slowly and vaguely (Bachem, *op. cit.*, V, 31 f.).

[132] Bachem, *op. cit.*, V, 27 ff.

[133] *Ibid.*, p. 293.   [134] *Ibid.*, p. 21-2.

tag and one hundred and one members in the Prussian Landtag and constituted the largest party in the Reich.[135]

With such a background it is not surprising to find the Center supporting a variety of ideals and measures not always strictly compatible with one another. The most important compromise was that between church and state. The Center accepted the Reich as a *fait accompli* and German Catholics became loyal citizens. The state was considered as a second " *gottgewollte Ordnung* " and the burgher's duties to his state were put on an equal basis with those to his church. The Centrists perceived clearly that if the state had no importance for the party and if political life should be considered as unnecessary or below church life in value, the Center as a party would cease to exist and Catholic interests would lose all weight. On political matters Catholic views, especially the views of Rome, were discouraged and each Centrist considered himself a free agent. The Center wanted no formal alliance with the Con-

---

[135] In the Prussian House of Representatives the party had in 1907 one hundred seats out of four hundred and forty-three; in Bavaria, ninety out of one hundred and fifty-two; in Baden, twenty-six to twenty-eight out of seventy-three; in Württemberg, twenty-five out of ninety-three; in Hesse, five to eight out of fifty (Erzberger, *Das deutsche Zentrum* [Amsterdam, 1910]). The figure of one hundred and two members in 1898 in the Reichstag represented 25.2% of that body. This percentage reached 26.4% in 1907 but fell to 22.9% in 1912 (Johannes Schauff, *op. cit.*, p. 11). In the case of the Center in this period the mandate strength of the party was greater than the popular strength, due to the old electoral system. If the proportional representation of 1919 had obtained, the Center's one hundred and six mandates of 1890 would have been only seventy-four. Under the system in force the land districts held the advantage over the city districts. Bavaria, for example, in 1890 had thirty-three out of the one hundred and six mandates; under proportional representation she would have held only twenty-seven (*ibid.*, pp. 20-22). Furthermore, the Centrist vote was decreasing in proportion to the total vote as the population increased. The Center won no new groups or classes after 1890. (After 1884 the Conservatives likewise had more mandates than their popular strength warranted. The concentration of the party districts helped to achieve this condition. The National Liberals, who were scattered, had fewer mandates than popular strength. The Social Democrats suffered most, however, for not only was there no proportional representation but the electoral districts had not been revised on the basis of population growth, and city districts had grown most.)

8

servatives, but in respect to ideals it acknowledged many similarities with them. Both wished to protect religion and the Christian basis of the state and both wished confessional schools; both defended monarchy as against revolution and acknowledged the authority of tradition; and the Centrists wished to support agriculture.[136] On the other hand, the Centrists held many views similar to those of the democrats and old Liberals. They guarded jealously the rights of the Reichstag, especially those rights pertaining to the budget, with which the poor were to be protected. They had no anti-capitalistic or anti-industrial prejudices,[137] and they ardently supported social reform.[138] The Centrists detested Social Democracy, partly for its hatred of the church and the monarchy, but quite as much because they feared that the Social Democrats would join with the Liberals and one day upset the balance of power which the Center held.[139] Because of this fear the Centrists dreaded revisionism, which they thought would offer to the liberal bourgeoisie more chance of coöperation with socialism.

The Center ascended to its position of 1895 fairly rapidly. In 1893 it threw off the influence of its rightwing members, the group of Prussians under the Silesian representative Huene, by voting against the new army bill. The Ballestrem-Huene group wished to

---

[136] Erzberger, *op. cit.*, pp. 106 ff. Mr. Erzberger's book contains the election programmes (*Wahlrufe*). For the agricultural question in the Centrist ranks see also Joseph André, *Zentrum und Landwirtschaft* (Stuttgart, 1918) ; Dr. F. Pichler, *Zur Agrarfrage der Gegenwart* (Berlin, 1897).

[137] Several writers maintain that the Center did not oppose capitalism. Franz Schnabel, the greatest present-day Catholic historian, points out that industrialism in its very inception, however, was not Catholic; it was even introduced into Catholic regions in Germany by Protestants, as, for example, in the Ruhr. No one seems to think that the Catholic industrialists ever controlled the Center party and the writer has no evidence that their influence was great (Franz Schnabel, *op. cit.*, III, 428). Englert, a writer quoted above, accepted the theory of "the industrial state."

[138] Franziska Vincke, *Die Arbeitnehmer Sozialpolitik des Zentrums* in *Münsterer Wirtschafts- und Sozialwissenschaftliche Abhandlungen* (Münster, 1933), XVII. The attitude mentioned obtained in spite of the fact that the Center knew the danger of increasing the power of the state (Hertling, *op. cit.*, II, 21). Hertling always opposed state socialism.

[139] Bachem, *Zentrum, Katholische Weltanschauung und allgemeine politische Lage*, Speech, October 20, 1913, pp. 7-8.

support the measure and sought the advice of the Pope. Lieber, too, would like to have voted for the bill if he could have seen his way clear; but he knew that the Catholics in the country were overwhelmingly opposed to it. For the sake of the future of the party he did not dare accept the Pope's advice, which favored the law. By freeing the party from the conservative-aristocratic element and from whatever connection this group might have with Rome Lieber obtained more scope for action within the party.[140] At the same time he demonstrated his intention of remaining free of entangling alliances with parties to the right or left. When in 1894 Miquel tried to ally the Conservatives, National Liberals, and Centrists against Social Democracy, the Center proved unwilling. By its opposition to the Exceptional Laws proposed against the Social Democrats after the murder of President Carnot of France, it demonstrated its lack of sympathy with what the right parties would demand from an alliance such as Miquel proposed. Miquel's plan therefore failed. In 1895 the party voted with the Left to defeat the Conservative proposal to send a congratulatory telegram from the Reichstag to Bismarck on his eightieth birthday. To offset this vote with the Left the Center made clear that it did not intend to support the Left regularly.[141] Of great importance to the position of the party was its help, particularly Spahn's, in aiding Hohenlohe's government in 1896 to complete the codification of the civil law. Coöperation with the National Liberals and Free Conservatives in this enterprise continued until 1906.

Pursuing the independent road thus taken the Center did not join the *Sammlung*. It showed its attitude toward the log-rolling agreement in its election programme of 1898 in remarking, " The policy of the *Sammlung* has for its purpose the expulsion of the Center from its decisive position in the Reichstag. As previously, we stand alone and will have to maintain our position by our own wits." [142] Over every law of the *Sammlungspolitik* hung the " Da-

[140] Hertling, *op. cit.*, II, 171: " That two opposing groups existed within the party—a Right and a Left—could no longer be denied; and now in the new elections after the dissolution of the Reichstag over the military law a complete change had taken place in the composition of the group. The aristocrat with a few exceptions had disappeared from it."

[141] Bergsträsser, *op. cit.*, pp. 125 ff.

[142] Cited by Bachem, *Vorgeschichte*, etc. V, 485.

mocles sword of rejection " [143] by the Catholic party. Although this
way of control was a negative one—the Center seldom took the
initiative in legislation—, it proved effective. If the Center had
chosen to refuse the outstanding laws of this group, the history of
pre-war Germany would have been quite different. In accordance
with its conception of national welfare, however, the Center voted
for the navy and for colonies.[144] The history of the party after
1893 explains this acquiescence. The fact that it had become a large,
powerful party gave it in turn certain responsibilities to the country and to popular feeling. Friedrich Meinecke has pointed out
that, as Bismarck supposed in 1887, on questions of international
import the country would follow the government and not a political
party.[145] With the same premise in mind Eckart Kehr has worked
out the thought doubtless in the minds of Centrist leaders as regards
the vote on the naval laws. He held that, had the Centrist party
rejected the laws and the Reichstag been dissolved, parliamentary
history in 1887 and 1893 would only have been repeated,[146] that is,
even if some members had split from the party—twelve did in 1893
vote for the army bill—the bill, because it was a bill for national
defense, would have been passed without the vote of the Center.
The outcome would have weakened the strategic position of the
party. It is also clear that this outcome would have diminished
Centrist prestige; a mass party like the Center found it difficult to
resist the growing popular demand for national assertion similar

---

[143] Eschenburg, *op. cit.*, p. 30.

[144] " We have neither thought of, wished, nor provoked the war of all
against all [wrote Englert] and its resulting armament, so to speak, up to
the hilt. God has allowed it. It brings with it, I grant, heavy sacrifices,
greater tests for our country today than ever before. But we fulfill them
obediently and patriotically, truly because of our great love of country.
As St. Augustine well says, our country is our father and mother, and
disloyalty to her is a kind of parricide, while it is a virtue to live for her.
He who serves his country well will have his good reward in Heaven "
(Englert, *op. cit.*, pp. 10-11). The same writer referred to the navy as
" an educational device " (*ibid.*, pp. 17-8).

[145] Meinecke, *Staat und Persönlichkeit*, p. 177.

[146] Kehr, *op. cit.*, pp. 375 f. The same view is expressed by the newspaper
comment of 1897 and 1898 when the Center's ultimate stand on the navy
was being discussed. *Cf. Vossische Zeitung*, March 17, 1898.

in form to that of other nations. "There is so much arming everywhere that Germany cannot remain behind . . . .; in France even
the Social Democrats want more ships," said one of the Centrist
deputies.[147] Thus the government obtained support from the Center for the most crucial measures of the 'nineties.[148]

If the Centrists could have refused the programme of imperialism, they would have done so on most counts. There were among
them ardent colonialists, navalists, and nationalists, as there were
everywhere; but the majority feared William II and his imperialism. The Center appreciated the danger of the naval agitation and
opposed the propaganda of the Pan-Germans.[149] It disliked especially the theory of *Macht* and based its colonial policy on the desire
to bring Christianity to backward peoples. Centrists were also not
anti-English. If they had acted more as Catholics in politics, they
might have resented English treatment of Ireland; but they preferred a neutral attitude and *Germania,* the official journal, regularly opposed the anti-English outbursts of the Pan-Germans.
Bachem has tried to exonerate the Centrists from any blame in
arousing anti-English feeling and the historian of the party, no

---

[147] *Cf.* also Hertling, *op. cit.*, II, 202. Hertling was the only Bavarian
Catholic representative who at first voted for the navy. He wrote: "Aggressive or imperialistic tendencies were foreign to us; on the basis of the
material before us we had come to the conclusion that Germany's rising
position in the world demanded naval protection. Even later provocative
utterances which went beyond this found no echo in the Center." Bachem
said that the Center really had no one who understood foreign policy;
hence it could not combat the government effectively had it wanted to do
so. It was eager to restrain imperialism but could not. It confined its
work to doing naval building as cheaply as possible (Bachem, *op. cit.*,
VI, 33 ff.).

[148] In 1906 the Center and the Social Democrats defeated the government
demands for South West Africa, a move which led to the dissolution of
the Reichstag for the first time since 1893 and led to the formation of the
Bülow *bloc.* The Center did not lose seats as the Social Democrats did;
but its position was no longer so powerful as at the turn of the century.
Lieber had expected that this would be the case in the event that imperialism was not supported. The Center's opposition to the government
was never so great again, however, as in the 'eighties (Meinecke, *op. cit.*, p.
187).

[149] Bachem, *op. cit.*, VI, 50.

doubt sincerely, wished that Germany had accommodated naval building to English proposals. But the fact remains that before 1906 the all-powerful Center did not resist the imperialists' programme.

The period of greatest power for the Center coincided largely with that of Ernst Lieber's leadership. Some knowledge of Lieber's life and point of view is significant for understanding the decade of Centrist history from 1893 to 1903. After the death of Windhorst, March 14, 1891, the question arose as to what would become of the Center without the wise and omnipresent personality which had made it strong. At that time Count Ballestrem wrote to his friend Hertling:

> The Catholics in the German Empire are a born minority; only through their unity as opposed to the split ranks of their opponents can they exercise decisive influence. This unity is expressed and exercised through the Centrist party. On the day when the Center ceases to exist or becomes powerless, the Catholics in the German Empire in all the aforementioned spheres of life will be enslaved by their opponents.[150]

The need for an able leader becomes clear from this remark. Dr. Ernst Lieber finally secured general recognition in consequence of his part in the fight over the Military Law of 1893. Years of experience in the Reichstag had given him a taste for politics and enthusiasm for the cause of the Center.[151] He belonged to the left wing of the party and sympathized with the German Empire.[152] He was clever, sensitive, and a brilliant orator, although not equal to Windhorst in intellectual force.[153]

Lieber was born in 1838 in Nassau and had entered the Reichstag at the time of its first election.[154] His romantic, national, and

[150] *Ballestrem to Hertling*, 1891, Hertling, *op. cit.*, II, 139.

[151] Bachem, *op. cit.*, V, 328-332; IV, 92.

[152] The left wing of the party was made up of younger men drawn largely from the representatives of the workers and middle class of the common schools in place of the older generation of priests, professors and aristocrats (Vincke, *op. cit.*, p. 56).

[153] Kehr suggested that Lieber's extreme sensitiveness made it almost impossible for him to oppose a man like Tirpitz, by whom he was frankly influenced (Kehr, *op. cit.*, p. 377).

[154] Bachem, *op. cit.*, IV, 92 f.

democratic tendencies doubtless came from his middle German origin, but he added to these an understanding of Prussia and of the Conservative tradition. He had travelled a great deal, especially in North America, and was well acquainted with the Catholic world at large. "He was not only a parliamentarian, but an able agitator and leader of the Catholic movement," said Bachem.[155] In the Reichstag he specialized in social and constitutional questions and later in naval affairs. He had coöperated well with Windhorst and Hertling for the social laws of the 'eighties, believing that these laws were rightfully due the workers.[156] Unlike the older leaders he did not fear an extension of the powers of the state.[157] Lieber had belonged to the Commission of 1887 for discussing the Septennate Law and his determination to preserve the powers of the Reichstag made it impossible for him to accept the seven-year proposal of this law. When in 1889 after the *Kulturkampf* part of the Center became reconciled to the state, Lieber did not approve of the Center becoming a party committed to the support of governmental measure and warned Windhorst against the new turn. But after Lieber acceded to leadership, he also saw the expediency of working with the government.[158] He never admired Bismarck, however, and rejoiced over his downfall; hence he might not have given up his oppositional tactics if he had had to coöperate with the old Chancellor instead of with Hohenlohe or Bülow.

In 1893 the new army law came up for discussion. Lieber had discovered from his frequent contact with the provinces that Catholic Germany did not sympathize with the competitive arming in which Europe had engaged. Opposition seemed especially strong in Bavaria, less strong in Silesia, where there was always fear of Russia. Since Lieber sided with the view of the Bavarian group,[159]

[155] *Loc. cit.*

[156] *Ibid.*, IV, 95, 105, 107, 115-6, 118, 121.

[157] *Ibid.*, V, 75-6. Hertling also saw that the state must take up social matters.

[158] Bachem regarded Bismarck with affection, forgiving the latter the *Kulturkampf*. His interest in and emphasis upon nationalism in his great history of the Centrist party were typical of many German Catholics.

[159] Bachem, *op. cit.*, V, 273. His position at this time is of special interest because of the change, noticeable by 1900, in the point of view of Lieber and of much of his party.

the right section of the Center led by Huene voted against him, and the dissolution of the Reichstag placed the Center in a dangerous position. Would Lieber's tactics of opposition wreck his party as he had thought Windhorst's support of the government would do? This was the test of Lieber's fitness for leadership and he proved equal to withstand it. Except for the rightwing, the party held together and emerged from the election with small numerical loss. But the law passed without Centrist support and Lieber realized that he could not continue his policy. He recognized the futility, at least in questions of national defense, of opposing the government.[160] What facts and reflections decided him? Did he feel the economic pulse? Did he take greater interest in foreign affairs? Did his nationalism speak to him in words of *Machtpolitik?* Or was he thinking alone of increasing the power of his party and of the use he could make of the power once he had it? One can only suppose that all these considerations affected his decision. With the change Lieber also redoubled his efforts to augment the power of the Reichstag so that this body might achieve more for the good of the whole people. If the authority of the Center and the Reichstag were simultaneously increased, he argued, Centrist Liberalism might carry through some of its own demands.

Thus Lieber hoped to use Centrist power for a more democratic government within Germany, a plan which he might have carried out had he allied his party with the left parties, but which he could not realize through his frequent support of *Sammlungspolitik.*

Dr. Martin Spahn, who was to become one of the leaders of the Centrist group in the Reichstag after Lieber's death in 1902, represented the party in the tariff discussions.[161] He took the stand that economic success lay in Germany's being able to keep the city and country populations in much the relation in which they then stood.

---

[160] *Ibid.*, V, 308. *Cf.* also Hertling, *op. cit.*, pp. 188 f. Hertling says that Hammacher told Lieber during the negotiations on the first naval bill that if the law did not go through Hohenlohe, Marschall, and others would retire, the Reichstag would be dissolved and a *coup d'état* carried out. Hertling did not believe in this threat. The writer does not know whether or not Lieber did, but neither he nor the Center deserted the government, as Bismarck had predicted.

[161] *Ibid.*, IV, V, VI, VII, *passim.*

To this end he thought agriculture should be sufficiently aided to prevent its decline. He wished particularly to benefit the small farmers within the Catholic party. At the same time he stipulated that the proceeds from higher tariffs should be used to help the lower classes to overcome the effects of higher tariffs, namely, to reduce taxes and prices. His aid sufficed to pass the tariffs.[162] The Center disapproved of the exorbitant tariff rates demanded by the Agrarian League, however. and attacked this organization for its unscrupulous tactics.[163] Spahn was equally moderate in his view of imperialism, pointing out that Germany had no cause for hostility against any country on economic grounds and urging that the feeling against England be not artificially excited. One should think, he argued, of the great value of the open-door in China and realize that the German trade with England stood at many times the value of that with China.[164] Spahn believed that economic interests should be subordinated to affairs of state.

The chief organs of the Center were the Berlin *Germania* and the *Kölnische Volkszeitung.* Windhorst had not written for the press but had long maintained close connections with Julius Bachem, the editor of the *Volkszeitung,* and with Theodor Stahl, the chief editorial writer of the *Germania.*[165] He also secretly admitted to his office Stein, Berlin representative of the *Frankfurter Zeitung.* Lieber doubtless kept up the relations established by his predecessor with the Catholic journals and may have done some writing for them. Julius Bachem, a member of the Reichstag and an extremely able man, wrote of his party:

> The Center party has up until now always withstood the severest test which the modern party must meet, that of the diversity of interests in its own camp. Almost all other parties in Germany represent primarily a certain group in the population. More than any other party the Center embraces within its ranks the most diverse circles and castes whose material interests are often sharply opposed and yet the Center has succeeded in overcoming this. . . . More than once have special Agrarian circles become difficult; also workers have now and

[162] *Sten. Ber. d. Reich.*, 1900-1902, IV, 2013-19.
[163] Heim: *Ibid.*, VI, 5795-6.
[164] Spahn: *Ibid.*, X, 8837.   [165] Bachem, *op. cit.*, V, 198.

again shown themselves dissatisfied; but the early coöperation
of the party as a whole has never been destroyed.[166]

One can readily see that the objective of the *Volkszeitung* coincided
with Lieber's aim.   In 1896 the *Rheinische Volksstimme* was
founded to represent the Rhenish Peasant Union.   This paper,
which soon supported the Kanitz proposal and other Agrarian demands, attacked the Jews, and favored a Catholic social programme,
was opposed by the majority of the Center.[167]   Opposition sprang
from the fact that the new journal favored a special interest, and
the Centrists discountenanced such a press.   " Not the press but the
party makes Centrist policy," writes the historian of the *Volkszeitung,* " even if the party press is not without some influence."
Through the Augustinus Union the press of the party worked with
the Reichstag members to insure unity between press and party.[168]

Many of the political and social changes of the 'nineties, the
weakening of the free-trade doctrine, the desire for political influence, and the change to imperialism, found reflection in the attitude
of the Center.   By following these trends the Catholic party made
good its strategic position and held the balance of power in the
Reichstag.   One more group went over to *Weltpolitik.*

D.   *The Progressive Union*

More liberal than the National Liberals was a small party known
as the Progressive Union (*Freisinnige Vereinigung*).   Even in 1900
it counted only twelve representatives in the Reichstag.   The group
which constituted this party separated from the Progressive party
(*Freisinnige Partei)* in 1893 during Caprivi's struggle for the new
military law.   At that time six members of the Progressives voted
for the law because they feared and resented the advantage of
France and Russia over Germany in armaments.   Eugen Richter,
leader of the Progressives, denounced this treachery and ordered the

[166] Bergsträsser, *Der Politische Katholizismus: Dokumente seiner Entwickelung,* 1871-1914 (Munich, 1923), p. 333, citing from *Historische-
politische Blätter,* " We Must Leave our Ivory Tower."

[167] Hermann Cardanus, *Fünfzig Jahre Kölnische Volkszeitung* (Cologne,
1910), pp. 71-2.

[168] Wilhelm Kisky, *Der Augustinus Verein: Zur Pflege der Katholischen
Presse, 1878-1928* (Düsseldorf, 1928).

six renegades out of the party. When the Reichstag went to the country, two parties campaigned in place of one. Georg von Siemens, one of the directors of the *Deutsche Bank,* led the new group while Theodor Barth and two former leaders of the old Liberals, Bamberger and Rickert, joined it.[169] The kernel of the new party consisted of the Secessionists, a left-wing group of the National Liberals which had separated from them in 1880, and the Schleswig-Holstein Progressives under von Hänel, professor of law at the University of Kiel. In the ensuing elections of 1893 the new Union secured thirteen seats in the Reichstag, six in the Landtag.

Until after Richter's death in 1906 the left Liberals remained divided. The split further weakened the Liberalism of the old school. The Progressive Union now coöperated with the government, thus withdrawing support from the opposition. It refused to relinquish its political tradition and to follow the government on every score; but, sensing the demands of the age, it was unwilling to mark time to the beat of Richter's dogmatism. This small party illustrates the tremendous force turning the world toward imperialism. Its members, lawyers, small factory owners, merchants, bankers, university men, even agriculturalists, many elected from seaport towns and other commercial areas, seem to have come over to imperialism through the logic of events.[170]

The new party appealed primarily to the middle class and aimed to revive Liberalism by arousing this class to a sense of the dangers threatening it. It feared that the activity of the feudal-agrarian element of society on the one hand and of Social Democracy on the other would engulf both the burgher and his Liberalism.[171] The

---

[169] *Letter to a Party Colleague,* May 24, 1893, cited by Karl Helfferich, *Georg von Siemens* (Berlin, 1923), III, 194-5. See also Rachfahl, " Eugen Richter und der Linksliberalismus im neuen Reiche," *Zeitschrift für Politik,* V (1912), 359 f.

[170] Rickert and Siemens both owned landed estates. Mommsen and Max Weber stood with the party on certain questions, for example, in agreeing with it on the need for naval expansion. Mommsen often wrote for *Die Nation,* the journal which supported the party and which Dr. Barth edited.

[171] *Die Nation,* No. 30, April 24, 1897. *Cf.* also the works of Ludwig Bamberger, in which the same thought was expressed. " What is the reason [asked *Die Nation*] that Social Democracy plays a so much larger

party denounced vehemently the Agrarian League, urged the coöperation of the left bourgeois parties against this organization, and criticized the National Liberals for supporting the agricultural tariffs.[172]   In 1900 its leaders, especially Siemens, organized the Commercial Treaties Association to oppose these tariffs and the *Sammlungspolitik*.   Siemens and his associates scorned " the ' log-rolling ' carried on by the alliance of interests of the reactionary parties," in which industry, they thought, had sold out to the Junkers.[173]   *Die Nation* believed firmly that the Agrarians did not really favor a navy, would welcome a dissolution of the Reichstag in the hope of defeating the naval law, and were voting for it only as a form of blackmail.   The party tried to consider the effects of domestic policy on Germany's position in the international market.   It concluded that agricultural tariffs, by raising the cost of production at home, would injure Germany's competitive power abroad.   It thought the government helpless before the Agrarians when industry and commerce would not unite to oppose them.   At the same time it thought all groups too eager to look to government for a solution of their ills and found the government too yielding.[174]   It wished a return to individual endeavour.

part here than in other civilized countries, even in those in which capitalistic development is further along than here?   In the last analysis it is the continuation of backward political and social conditions through the power of and in favor of the Junkers . . . Social Democracy is simply the strongest negation of feudal survival and the more lax Liberalism is in the natural struggle against this cultural lag the more Social Democracy feels called upon to inscribe the war on its banners " (*Die Nation*, No. 34, May, 1897, article by Hugo Preuss, author of *Die Junkerfrage*).

[172] *Ibid.*, 1897-1902, *passim*, especially No. 37, June 16, 1900.

[173] An article by Lujo Brentano, the economist, showed his scorn of the Junkers in pointing out that those who now talked of their service to the state were not those landowners who had actually rendered service.   The land had changed hands many times.   In Stein's day, he continued, they did not talk of their service to the state because they knew that they were responsible for Jena.   Nor did they, when times were good for them in the latter part of the eighteenth century, interest themselves in the least in the cause of the small farmers, as they now professed to do (*Die Nation*, " Die Agrarreform in Preussen," No. 24, March 13, 1897).

[174] *Cf.* series of articles by Schulze-Gaevernitz, " Handelspolitik und Flotte," *Die Nation*, Nos. 22, 23, 24, February 26, March 5, 12, 1898.

The Progressives believed in *Machtpolitik* but did not wish Germany to be chauvinistic. When the First Naval Law was presented to the Budget Commission, *Die Nation* stated its point of view as follows:

> Do we want a navy for demonstrating a policy of Power, one might almost say a policy of bluff, so that wherever there is something doing in the world Germany will be there with her navy? In this sort of thing we see the chief danger, the danger of increased political complications and then increased disturbance to German commerce.[175]

Yet Progressives saw the dawn of imperialism and wanted to share in what it might usher in. The Spanish-American and Boer Wars decided for them the question of the need for a navy. A navy was probably a necessity, they said, for maintaining peace in disturbed quarters of the globe. The Transvaal War, wrote Barth in *Die Nation,* seemed to be demonstrating that peace could more easily be kept if opponents appeared formidable.[176] Although the Progressives vied with the most Anglophil in appreciation of Britain, they thought European navies necessary to keep world markets open where England would otherwise close them and warned that, if a day of reckoning should come because of economic competition, Germany would be powerless without this weapon.[177]

The Progressives did not accept imperialism and naval power in the hope of distracting attention from the needs or interests of the workers. They wished the new programme to be accompanied by expansion of liberal democracy in Germany and by the achievement of internal harmony. Their goal on one occasion found expression in *Die Nation* as follows:

> The important work which it is the duty of the bourgeoisie to perform lies in two directions. The vestiges of feudalism must be done away with and the bearers of this system must be made

---

[175] *Ibid.*, No. 24, March 13, 1897.

[176] *Ibid.*, No. 4, October 28, 1899. The remark was made in spite of the obvious fact that the Boers had not respected England's might. Barth, however, thought Europe did respect it and that a European war would probably not come, perhaps never again, because the presence of such large armies would make it too horrible to be endured.

[177] *Cf.* Schulze-Gaevernitz, *op. cit.*, March 5.

politically harmless. That is the battle which Liberalism has to wage on the one hand. But it has still another struggle: it must prevent the modern workers' movement from remaining, because of false political measures, in bitter opposition to our social order; it must secure to the workers through spiritual freedom and free discussion the possibility of learning to distinguish between the politically possible and the politically impossible in the hope that thereby the time will be advanced in which the bourgeoisie, together with a proletariat better able to appreciate the attainable, can in common and consequently victoriously undertake to complete the construction of a modern state. Measured by these goals, which are the great goals of our time, every division of the powers of the Left will amount to an aid to the continued existence of reactionary feudalism, and measured by these goals every symptom of an inner development of the modern workers' movement gains decisive importance.[178]

It is perhaps most easily possible to understand the character of the Progressive Union by referring to an outstanding member of the party. Georg von Siemens was director of foreign investments for the *Deutsche Bank*.[179] His enormous interests and activities abroad led him to believe in international coöperation and interdependence and in world peace, to which Germany freed from the shackles of traditional Conservatism would contribute. He early decided to forsake the career of a state official in favor of that of a business man; for in this field he saw untold possibilities. He also decided that the new Reich needed technical men in its parliaments. In spite of the active disapproval of von der Heydt, head of the *Deutsche Bank,* in 1873 he stood for election to the Prussian Landtag and in 1874 to the Reichstag, and except for short intervals remained in the Reichstag until his death in 1902.[180] Siemens' specialized in the Reichstag in questions of finance. In early years he

---

[178] *Die Nation*, No. 19, February 5, 1898. See also No. 10, December 4, 1897, article by Dr. Barth in which he said: "The government continues by sensational acts; but it cannot be successful until the internal situation is satisfactory."

[179] Karl Helfferich, *Georg Siemens: Ein Lebensbild aus Deutschlands grosser Zeit* (Berlin, 1923) is the chief biography of Siemens.

[180] Helfferich, *op. cit.*, III, 153. In this volume of Siemens' life Helfferich gives a summary of the former's activity as a parliamentarian.

seldom spoke on matters of general policy, since the National Liberals, to whom he attached himself, had Lasker, Bennigsen, Bamberger, and others to discuss these subjects. The Exchange became his special care and he sought to answer the attacks of the Agrarian-Conservatives upon it by presenting its purpose, its work, and its political importance. In 1885 and again in 1893 and 1900 he argued that taxes on the business of the Exchange would lead to greater concentration of industry and would impose greater obstacles upon the sale of goods abroad. In his practical nationalism he always regretted that the government placed hurdles in the path of German interests, finding it undesirable to prohibit stock issues in small denominations so that German capital abroad was compelled to organize under English or Dutch law.[181] He opposed the bills proposed on these matters, presenting carefully worked out technical data, but with no great success.

Siemens understood the situation in Germany. He observed the control exercised by the Agrarian-Conservatives over the Prussian bureaucracy, the favor shown by the government to these Conservatives, the alliance of the latter with the rightwing of the old National Liberals, and the fatal effects to industry of the high grain tariffs. He appreciated likewise the cost to the German worker of the protectionist policy. He regretted this, although he did not approve of Social Democracy, and he defended the Liberal view in these words:

> To develop individuality, to build up the people in the school and in the church to their highest mark, to bring them together in the family, in the municipality and in the state to coöperation in the community administration and council for the common good of the municipality and the state is our aim. In

---

[181] The Agrarians, National Liberals, Pan-Germans, and colonialists opposed as un-German and anti-nationalistic the investment by Germans of money in foreign concerns or in companies organized abroad. Yet before this time they had never been ready to do anything in the direction Siemens indicated to facilitate investment in German companies. The laws against the Exchange did do a great deal to concentrate capital further. See Loeb, *Die Berliner Grossbanken in den Jahren 1895-1902* in *Schriften des Vereins für Sozialpolitik*, 110, pp. 100 ff.

short we have proceeded from the view that the first law for
the progress of man is not help from without but personal excellence, and that personal excellence suffers from the moment
when the aid of the state is invoked.[182]

He regarded social legislation as a " sop to Cerberus," expensive
and unnecessary if the interests of the workers were considered in
the formulating of tariff policy, taxation policy and the like.   He
never ceased to blame the National Liberals for their surrender to
protectionism, especially agricultural protection, in the *Kartellpolitik* of 1887 and in the *Sammlungspolitik* of 1897.

After many years of criticising Richter's doctrinaire and partisan
point of view Siemens broke with the Progressive party on the occasion of the passage of the Military Law of 1893.   At that time he
said, " Richter seeks to center his policy on opposition.   He would
be completely embarrassed if it were proposed to him to take over
the government." [183]   Siemens resented Richter's opposition to this
measure because he was convinced of the necessity for it.   He
thought that Germany could not remain behind other nations in
arming, that the two-year term of service (rather than three) was so
important a concession on the part of the government that the
party must not refuse at least to negotiate.   Siemens voted for the
law through fear " that France and Russia would take new courage
if the bill was refused." [184]   He favored staunch support of Caprivi
because he thought the commercial policy of the latter important.
Insufficient as they were, he found the commercial treaties a benefit
to German industry in international competition and a step toward
making politics and economics coincide.   " The theory of Bismarck," Siemens said, " that one can be a political friend and an
economic enemy has simply fallen to the ground."

Siemens seems to have broken with Richter primarily because he
felt convinced that the latter's point of view was antiquated.   On
the basis of his experience and observation he came to believe that a
state must have Power to maintain itself; otherwise economic measures would fail and better armed states would take advantage of the

---

[182] Cited by Helfferich, *op. cit.*, p. 78.
[183] *Ibid.*, p. 80.
[184] *Siemens to his Daughter*, May 10, 1893, cited by Helfferich, III, **192 f.**

weaker.[185] While he did not wish war, he despised peace at any price. He no longer believed, if he ever had, that free-trade alone would lead to that happy concourse of nations claimed for it by Richter and his friends. For several years Siemens had wanted a definite colonial policy. Now he advocated railroads in the colonies, subsidized steamer lines, and a navy to protect these and German financial interest throughout the world. Although he opposed paying for the navy by more taxes on the Exchange and on industry, he voted for naval expansion. In both views he was consistent and the Right inconsistent; for if the navy was to protect German industry, other measures such as high taxes should not handicap this same industry.

Siemens' last activity resulted in the formation of the Commercial Treaties Association in 1900. He had always worked in this direction and for the sake of his own interests should have organized the opposition earlier; but the forces favoring lower tariffs were divided. By 1900 the protectionist movement had advanced too far for him to do more than wage a losing campaign. Most manufactures, he wrote, did not comprehend that protection would not solve the problems of a country manufacturing for export.[186] Eminently a banker he was always influenced by considerations making for world trade.

In reading through the life and speeches of Georg von Siemens one is impressed by the striking harmony between him and his age. Having contributed as much as any one person to Germany's rise in the world, his life and *Weltanschauung* were inextricably bound up with this rise. He saw clearly the pitfalls of reaction, the need for further democratization and for the welding together of the elements in the German state, and the wisdom of a well-considered

[185] *Cf.* Friedrich Lenz, *Macht und Wirtschaft* (Munich, 1915), p. 155. Lenz believed that a separation of economics and politics was not possible. He wrote: " Our imperialism heretofore without Power could not preserve this inmost unity of politics and economics as it existed in our past and in the structure of the modern state. With the renunciation of this we were relegated to the second class nations." See also Rudolf Ibbeken, *Das Aussenpolitische Problem in Staat und Wirtschaft in der deutschen Reichspolitik* (Schleswig, 1928).

[186] *Letter to Adolf Woermann*, September 9, 1901, cited by Helfferich, *op. cit.*, III, 220 f.

9

imperialism able to protect itself and yet not jealous or unduly competitive.[187]   It may easily be said that this likewise constituted only *Interessenpolitik.* True; but it contained a broader conception of the world and of Germany's place in it than that of the majority of Reichstag members.   Siemens and his party did not perceive, however, that, if they feared and sought to change the régime in Germany, they should not give it new weapons before they actually had effected this change.   Their handful of votes would have been better cast with the Social Democrats than in support of an imperialism which they could never control.   This was the tragedy of the Progressive Union.   The Hohenlohe and Bülow governments won another group of Liberals to their policies without making any concessions to liberal democracy.

E.   *The Progressive Peoples' Party*

The story of the Progressive Peoples' party *(Freisinnige Volkspartei)* has been touched upon in connection with its rival, the Progressive Union.   In a sense this party was the sole one in the new Reich to remain uninfluenced by the work of Bismarck; it never became reconciled to him nor to his method of unifying Germany. Its history helps to explain the decline of Liberalism.   Social Democracy and the handful of men in this party offered the only opposition to the policies of those in power.   Neither group attracted new elements (that is, in the case of the Social Democrats, elements outside the proletariat), neither showed willingness to coöperate with the other unless here and there in an election trade, and both dwelt in an unreal world, the Social Democrats in the future, the Progressives in the past.   Since neither group could hope to attain power, the rôle of each was confined to bitter protest.

Practically speaking Eugen Richter made up the Progressive Peoples' party.   For years, especially after 1893, he not only led it

---

[187] *Cf.* Siemens' desire to coöperate with other countries abroad, for example, with England in the Bagdad Railroad enterprise.   The National Socialists, who were anti-capitalistic, wrote in 1900 in their organ *Die Hilfe:* " He who does not recognize a nation must have the Bank of England as the center of the universe, since this is the center of capital " (*Die Hilfe,* No. 14, April 8, 1900).   The Progressives could not be fairly accused of such disloyalty, although they were eager for international coöperation.

but wrote and spoke for and represented it almost to the exclusion of his associates. A change was possible only with his death.[188] Born in 1838, Richter grew up in the Rhineland during the time when the ultra-Conservative Kleist-Retzow presided over the bureaucracy in that province. From his school days he opposed, as a Liberal, the existing order. Though he studied for the law, he became greatly interested in economics, especially in the classical theory of economics. This interest and his acquaintance with Schulze-Delitzsch decided the course of his politics. He joined the Progressives, who took their stand against the indemnity for Bismarck. In 1870 Richter secured election to the Prussian Landtag and in 1871 to the Reichstag, where he remained with only short interruptions until his death in 1906. In 1875 at the death of von Hoverbeck he and Hänel assumed leadership of the party. Because of Richter's Liberalism the Prussian government had gone out of its way in the early 'sixties to close local municipal offices to him. Bismarck afterward said this move had been a mistake; it only enhanced Richter's eagerness to get to Berlin crying, "Away with Bismarck." In the 'seventies the Progressives with their forty-four seats formed a significant element in the Reichstag and Richter was not a nonentity. He specialized in financial questions and soon found his work in defending the budgetary rights of the Reichstag against Bismarck's specious constitutionalism.[189]

It is not difficult to imagine the stand taken by Richter towards the important questions of the next few years. First and foremost he opposed the Septennate Law of 1874-5 and the *Kulturkampf*. He spoke vehemently against the tariff changes of 1878-9 and against the anti-socialist laws. This latter battle weakened irretrievably the left-Liberal cause and cost Richter his seat in the Landtag. The bitter opposition characteristic of Richter in the

[188] Rachfahl, *op. cit.*, Pt. I. The writer knows of no good discussion of the party other than that in the life of Richter. Kehr has a brief summary of the effect produced by the tactics of Richter (*op. cit.*, 219 ff.). The discussion of Richter which follows is based on that in Rachfahl and on his numerous speeches in the Reichstag during the 'nineties. Some knowledge of his earlier life may be obtained from Hermann Oncken, *Rudolf von Bennigsen* (Stuttgart and Leipzig, 1910).

[189] In 1869 he published his first book, *Die preussischen Staatsschulden und die preussischen Staatspapiere*.

following decades dates from 1879, although at that time he did not give up all hope of liberal reform. When in 1880 the National Liberal party split, Richter could not agree with the left-wing seceders and neglected the opportunity to strengthen the Liberalism of the Left. Further efforts to draw all the Liberals together also shattered on the rocks of Richter's determined stand; he would not budge an inch from his principles.[190]

It seems unlikely, however, that without a new programme Liberalism could have revived. Bismarck had triumphed and even Richter realized the decline of popular interest in a purely negative cause. In the election of 1890 he might have formulated new ideals for Liberalism; but he made no use of the opportunity and proceeded against Caprivi as against Bismarck. His autocratic way in a democratic party, especially in his use of the *Freisinnige Zeitung,* antagonized his associates until they refused to elect him chairman of an important inner committee of the party. Though Richter survived this reverse, he could not prevent the split of 1893. The formation of the Progressive Union left Richter with a handful of disciples to pursue his undeviating way. The loss of these members delivered the *coup de grace* to the left-Liberals; even the Progressives themselves blamed Richter for precipitating the death of their party, while the democratic papers, the *Frankfurter Zeitung* and the *Berliner Tageblatt,* deplored his misrule; his day, they said, had passed.

Richter paid no heed to the criticism. He drew the remnants of his followers more closely about him, issued a fresh party programme, which contained nothing new, and continued his way. The progress of events in the 'nineties confirmed in Richter's mind every reason for his opposition. He considered the fall of Caprivi as proof of the Emperor's personal rule, thought the new tariffs

---

[190] In 1884 the Progressives and Secessionists after careful negotiations among their leaders allied under the title Progressive party. The result in the country was not hopeful; their mandates suffered a reduction from 105 to 67 seats. This definite stand of the Secessionists, moreover, drove the National Liberal party further to the right. The dissolution of the Reichstag in 1887 reduced the Progressives to 32. The Secessionists complained of Richter's rule, and the party divided its loyalty. The Liberal cause received little strengthening.

ruinous, and denounced the rise of Social Democracy. Colonial and naval proposals were especially distasteful to him and he spoke against them hour after hour. He ruthlessly exposed the expense of colonies, from which, he declared, no returns could be expected.[191] He laid bare the logical contradiction in a tariff made to cut off imports and a navy built to protect them.[192] He raged at the government for taking advantage of incidents like the seizure of German ships during the Boer War in order to carry through its naval programme [193] and he denounced the Agrarians and their League, which, he thought, Bülow encouraged.[194] His last speech dealt with the " neglect of pressing needs in domestic policy in favor of a colonial policy." [195]

After Richter's death the party disintegrated. Only his personal force had held it loyal to the old principles. Was it better that these last disciples of 1848 should go over to *Welt-* and *Machtpolitik* and acknowledge the advent of a new age? The tragedy of German Liberalism is embodied in Richter's life. Clever as he was, it is to his lasting discredit that he did not see the writing on the wall and

[191] *Sten. Ber. d. Reich.*, 1896 to 1902, *passim*. In almost every colonial debate, especially in those connected with the budget for colonies, Richter's voice came forth in protest.

[192] *Ibid.*, December 3, 1901, X Leg. Per., II Sess., IV, 2919-2930. Richter did not deny that some ships were needed. In his *Flotte und Flottengesetz* (Berlin, 1898), he pointed out that all the left-Liberals had agreed on the need for a navy and that his own party had voted in 1897 in the Commission to reduce the naval budget from 70 to 58 millions but not to destroy the appropriations. He opposed Tirpitz, however, and the battle fleet, which, he maintained, was not needed to protect overseas trade (*ibid.*, p. 69). He believed that Germany did need a strong army; so much he was willing to accept. In his *Zur Flottenfrage: ein kritisches ABC Büchlein* (Berlin, 1900), Richter again pointed out that there existed no actual connection between overseas trade and a battle-fleet. Germany's overseas trade was growing faster, relatively, than England's, although England's navy was so large. Furthermore, England's enormous overseas trade had the protection of a comparatively small number of battleships. These observations contained much truth but no one seemed ready to heed them.

[193] *Ibid.*, February 7, 1902, p. 3995.

[194] *Ibid.*, March 5, 1901, X Leg. Per., II Sess., II, 1704; December 3, 1901, *ibid.*, IV, 2919.

[195] On July 15, 1904.

throw in his talents with the Social Democrats.[196]   After 1893 at the latest left-Liberalism exerted no influence on the Reich. All forces conspired to strengthen and extend the Bismarckian policy of Power; and for all his wisdom, wit, and knowledge of facts Richter knew no way out. · The man who thought himself first and always a Progressive lived the last thirty years of his life as an irreconcilable. As historian contemplating the fatal results of the policies and ideals which Richter never accepted is forced to pay some tribute, however, to his stand. He at least never surrendered to that "new spirit" of nationalism; in place of the existing federation of interests he at least with those few thousands who elected his party still wished to see a democratic Empire, a true "nation." [197]

The *Freisinnige Zeitung* was the party organ. Richter largely directed its policy. In 1893 the *Frankfurter Zeitung* wrote of it:

> Every party needs its press . . . . A regulating press which tries to secure followers is indispensable; but a party press such as the Progressive party possesses in the organ which Richter conducts and still owns is always harmful . . . . Let us overlook the embittering effect which the sharp personal polemics of the *Freisinnige Zeitung* have had for years and the way they have heightened the differences which a party leader ought to try to reconcile . . . . The personal conduct of a great party and of a newspaper cannot go together; the purposes of the two are of entirely different kinds." [198]

It was not in Richter's nature to give the reins out of his own hand. The great democratic papers fortunately stood outside Richter's control; but neither did they keep to the old Liberal road. The

[196] The year before his death Theodor Mommsen in an article in *Die Nation*, No. 11, December 13, 1902, entitled "Was uns retten kann " asked for an alliance between Liberals and Social Democrats against the " federation of interests of the Junkers and priests " (*Interessenbund des Junkertums und der Kaplanokratie*). "We stand [he wrote] not at the end but at the beginning of a *coup d'état* through which the German Empire and the representation of the German people are to be subjected to the absolutism of a Junker-priest combination of interests."

[197] Richter objected to the navy as not built by the nation in its entirety but by the state (Kehr, *op. cit.*, p. 293).

[198] Rachfahl, citing the *Frankfurter Zeitung*, Rachfahl, *op. cit.*, p. 362.

usual story was repeated in their pages: "The majority of the nation must be educated and made to realize its material interest in the development of colonies." [199] Only in this way, they said, could the enthusiasm for the navy be built up. In the press world, as in the parliamentary, the Progressives stood alone.

F. *The Social Democratic Party* [200]

The second important group in opposition was the Social Democratic party (SPD). Like the Progressive Peoples' party it had principles, a dogma; but unlike the latter it represented class interests. Because of both characteristics the SPD exercised a great indirect influence on political life; although it could not control, it inspired fear.

Post-Bismarckian governments perceived only half-truths and manifested only half-courage. The Emperor never carefully planned a social reform programme. He started with greater toleration and freedom for the Social Democrats, sought to retract this toleration when he sensed antagonism, and dared not complete the retraction.[200a] Social Democracy continued to grow unhindered, and hatred of it among the bourgeois parties increased proportionately. The discussion of each measure introduced to restrict Social Democracy nourished the hatred and, since these measures largely failed, the ruling groups sought to accomplish their end by indirect means. These indirect means, however, differed entirely from those so ardently urged by a person like Max Weber, the broadening of the democratic basis within the Reich. Instead they called for an extension of the policy of Power abroad. Through the acquisition of new markets the imperialists believed that they could compensate the masses for high prices by steady work and thus reconcile them to the state and to imperialism.[201]

[199] *Berliner Tageblatt*, No. 14, January 9, 1900.

[200] The fact cannot be overlooked that, in spite of oppression, there existed enough toleration in the Wilhelminian era to give the SPD a chance to grow and to raise up in support of its ideals writers and artists like Julius Bab, Kathé Kollwitz, Adele Gerhard, and others.

[200a] *Cf.* Heuss, *op. cit.*, p. 129: "William II has now become Stumm's man."

[201] Hohenlohe indicated that the very change to realism, the turn from Utopian dreams on the part of Social Democracy, increased the fear felt

The question arises, as in the case of Liberalism, why German Social Democracy, representing so large a percentage of the public, endured quietly the rule of the *Sammlung*.

In view of the reactionary régime in Germany, German Social Democracy was never so thoroughly revolutionary a party as was to be expected, and it became less so as its numbers grew.[202]   It retained always a strange mixture of democratic and Marxian ideology.[203]   This came to light in the way in which the party supported the Liberal ideals of a United States of Europe, harmony of all nations through international trade, an international court of justice, and a militia, while believing at the same time that the classless society would make these bourgeois instruments superfluous. One explanation of the contradiction lay in the fact that the organization of German Social Democracy had begun with small industries whose workers formed part of the bourgeoisie.   This condition was true of the Lasallean and Eisenach groups, neither of which in the early period understood Marxian teaching.[204]   Both fed upon all manner of democratic and middle-class ideas.   Even after 1875 true Marxism made slow headway.   The party had no Lenin and the Socialist Laws of 1878 and 1883, by destroying the Social Democratic press and forbidding meetings, deprived it of most of the means of clarifying and spreading its doctrine.   The Reichstag group alone could legally express party opinion; thus the entire party became more dependent on parliamentary tactics than would

of it.   " The SPD loses with time the intensity of its devotion to dreamgoals but wins continually in scope the more it stands on a basis of facts and changes to a radical workers' party " (Hohenlohe, *op. cit.*, p. 451).

[202] Lenin scores German Social Democracy for this.   See his attack on Kautsky's definition of imperialism in Lenin's *Imperialism, op. cit.*, pp. 73 f.

[203] Friedrich Lenz, *Staat und Marxismus* (Stuttgart and Berlin, 1922), Pt. II.   Lenz finds even Marx's own teaching on state and foreign policy not completely consistent.   The democratic ideology resulted partly from Lasallean tradition, which had been excluded in the Gotha programme (1875) and in that of Erfurt (1891) but persisted.

[204] Paul Fröhlich, Introduction to Rosa Luxemburg's *Gesammelte Werke*, III, 5.   An amusing picture of the reverence for and ignorance of Marx in the first generation of Socialists is to be found in Felix Riemkasten's novel *Der Bonze* (Berlin, 1930).

otherwise have been the case. Although conflicting interests not yet subject to party theory and discipline divided it on important issues,[205] the party did not like criticism.[206] Marx and Engels tried to help by expounding their teachings through correspondence, but without much success. When in 1882 Kautsky established the *Neue Zeit,* it was thought that he would provide an organ for explaining Marxian theory. But Kautsky's limitations and point of view were such that he did not always elucidate the true character of revolutionary socialism. Hence up to 1890 German Social Democracy had no thorough theoretical training. It was trying to digest a mixture of Utopian, Liberal, and socialist teaching.[207]

Bismarckian social policy during the 'eighties may also have had some of the effect which its sponsors desired. It is difficult to measure the influence which the patriarchal attitude of the state and of so many of the industrialists and economists exerted upon the socialist movement. Naturally enough the Social Democratic leaders understood Bismarck's purpose and denounced it. But the trade unionists can easily have been lulled into a quieter mood by the benefits which they enjoyed without the necessity of fighting for them. It is reasonable also to suppose that the academic socialists *(Kathedersozialisten)* did not expend in vain their efforts to draw the Social Democrats closer to the state, although their influence was fundamentally small.

In 1890 the party faced a change of tactics on the part of the government, compelling it to reconsider its own tactics. Vollmar, for example, previously a radical leader in the Bavarian group of the party, was impressed by the new policy of leniency and declared immediately for *Realpolitik* and for negotiations with the bourgeois leaders.

> There are two ways open to the Socialists [so Vollmar declared], the road of revolutionary tactics which is above every pettiness of shallow reality and takes no less than the whole,

---

[205] This state did not last. It existed, however, in 1878 in so important a matter as the tariff.

[206] Fröhlich, *op. cit.,* p. 6, note 1.

[207] Even a group of younger men who sought to oppose opportunism and the hegemony of the parliamentary group had unclear views. It could put up no real fight and was promptly cut off from the party.

and the road of political compromise which seeks to reach the
goal in the only possible way, by practicable, partial successes.
The latter moves in a sphere of reality which is broader but all
the surer, while the former draws an ideal line through the air
and is surely shorter and more perfect but all the more impossible.[208]

The programme which Vollmar advanced comprised a law for the
right of association, laws against the intervention of the state in
favor of the employer in wage disputes, laws against trusts, and
measures for the abolition of high food tariffs. It did not contain
anything which could not be achieved within the capitalistic state.
When brought to bay afterward in the party, Vollmar admitted
that his state socialism and Marxian Social Democracy were not
compatible. He affirmed his loyalty to the workers, however, by
asserting that even state socialism came about through fear of them.
In this way certain Socialists subscribed to reforms within the existing state and Vollmar's adherents coöperated in the Bavarian
Landtag with the Liberal parties.

After 1895, the year of Engel's death, Eduard Bernstein joined
the ranks of the reformists. Through editing the *Geschichte der
französischen Revolution von 1848* by Louis Heritier he drew the
conclusion that forcible conquest of political power by the proletariat was a crime. At the same time the more considerate policy
of the government weakened his belief in Marxian teaching. His
stay in England may also have contributed to convincing him that
the need for revolution did not press.[209] At first the party seemed
not to notice the importance of revisionism; but at the party convention in Stuttgart in 1898 the great revisionist controversy began.
Vollmar, Gradnauer, Auer, Frohme, and others supported Bern-

[208] *Vollmar's Speech in Munich*, July 6, 1891. It is known as Vollmar's
Eldorado Speech. The quotation refers to Vollmar's view and is cited by
Fröhlich, *op. cit.*, p. 10.

[209] E. Bernstein, " Probleme des Sozialismus," *Neue Zeit*, XV (1898),
164 ff., 204 f., 303 f., 772 f. In conclusion he wrote: " I admit openly that
I have very little feeling indeed or interest for that which is commonly
understood by the ' aim of socialism.' This goal, whatever it is, is nothing
to me; the movement is everything, and by movement I mean not only
the general movement of society, that is, social progress, but also political
and economic agitation and organization to effect this progress."

stein while Bebel, Kautsky, and Rosa Luxemburg rejected their premises. After the debate Bernstein set down his ideas in his book, *Die Voraussetzungen des Sozialismus und die Aufgaben der Sozial-demokratie.*[210]   It was a critique of Marxian teaching, ending with the view that revolutionary tactics must be given up, that with demo-cratization of society the opposition of classes had grown fainter, not sharper, as Marx said it would.   In consequence German Social Democracy must aim to obtain a parliamentary majority and must strive " to emancipate itself from a phraseology which has actually outlived its day and to appear what today it is, a democratic-social-istic reform party." [211]

Bernstein's position afforded an opportunity for the German Social Democratic party to acquaint itself more thoroughly than before with Marxian theory.   But the chance was lost, partly it would seem because Bernstein resorted to so many easily disprovable arguments that Marxists paid him little heed.   Several refutations found their way into print; [212] but the bulk of the party did not clarify its thinking.[213]   The reformists continued in the party and held their seats in the Reichstag.   Another battle between the re-formers and the radicals at the Dresden meeting in 1903 ended with no more decisive results, although in this year the Russian Socialists split over the same question.   Apparently the lack of immediate need for action in western Europe obscured the vision of Social Democrats.

The party now had three groups, the reformists led by Bernstein and the *Sozialistische Monatshefte,* the old party under Bebel, and the Left.   The Left in turn split in several directions, following Mehring, Kautsky, Luxemburg, to mention only three who did not agree on important questions.   The Right and Center had the sup-

---

[210] Stuttgart, 1899.   [211] Cited by Fröhlich, *op. cit.*, p. 19.

[212] Rosa Luxemburg, *Sozialreform oder Revolution* (second series), Kautsky, *Bernstein und das Sozialdemokratische Programm,* and several articles published during these years in *Neue Zeit* give some idea of the literature.

[213] Bebel's resolution, introduced at the meeting in Hanover in 1899 and adopted by reformists and die-hards alike, did not go beyond the Erfurt programme in essentials.   Bernstein said he could, with a grain of salt, easily subscribe to it.   Luxemburg, who did understand Marx and wished a swing to the left, represented a small group only.

port of the aristocracy of the proletariat, that is, of the trade unions and guilds with the hierarchy of their officials. As these organizations grew in size and importance they left behind all thought of revolution and tacitly accepted the existing state.[214]   In South Germany, where the revisionists were strong, the Social Democrats voted frequently for the budget. Even in the Reich before 1914 they occasionally supported the government. The Left looked upon this group as ridiculous and after the Russian Revolution of 1905 as dangerous. But the Left had no mass support. War between radicals and revisionists continued. The Center held the strategic position and, since it did not aid the Left, it actually benefited the Right.[215]   Much the same process went on in the Social Democratic parties of other European countries.

It is not possible to show whether revisionism made it easier for the government and its supporters to carry out a policy of imperialism. Even though imperialism was directed in part against Social Democracy, Social Democrats disagreed among themselves on the proper theoretical and material defenses against it and may be said to have drifted with the tide. On the other hand, between 1895 and 1900 revisionism had only begun and had certainly not gained the strength it had in 1914. It seems more likely that the inherent weaknesses in German Social Democracy, which the revolution of 1918-19 revealed, allowed Germany to stumble from crisis to crisis. If the Social Democrats as a party had taken a more united and aggressive stand during the Boer War, in the controversy over the naval laws, the first Moroccan crisis, the *Daily Telegraph* affair, they might possibly have compelled the state to reform the constitution. They might, however, only have led to the strong union against them of all the bourgeois parties, with the resulting destruction of parliamentary government. Had this happened, one can only surmise that the revolution of 1918-19 would have been more

---

[214] Today the unemployed look upon the trade unions as offering them no hope. Even erstwhile officers in them in England will have nothing further to do with them because they realize that the organization and bureaucracy have rendered them sterile. *Cf. Memoirs of the Unemployed* (London, 1934).

[215] *Cf.* Alfred Rosenberg, *Die Entstehung der deutschen Republik* (Berlin, 1928), p. 49 f.; also Luxemburg, *op. cit.*, III, 92 f.; against Bernstein, p. 408 ff.; against South German Social Democracy, pp. 410 ff.

thoroughgoing, although the immediate effect would have been disastrous.

It is well known that Marx took his start from Hegelian philosophy and that Hegel's theory of the state as well as Marxian social theory both rest on the concept of Power.[216] Although Marx believed in the ultimate evolution of the socialist order, he believed in assisting this evolution by revolution. Since Power must be exercised at opportune moments, two things were necessary, means of action and an understanding of the political situation. In this way Marx arrived at his interest in foreign affairs and followed very closely the events of the years 1848 to 1871.

After 1871 Europe settled down to a needed peace and as the possibility for revolution receded German Social Democracy saw diminished urgency for active study of foreign policy. One German historian offers the interesting theory that the dangerous political situation of Germany in the center of Europe narrowed the outlook of German Social Democrats from that wide view of which Marx was master to one approximating that of a bourgeois German.[217] Whatever the explanation, Social Democratic foreign policy either did not exist—Liebknecht said, "The best foreign policy is none "—, or in varying degrees and for many reasons the Social Democrats accepted a foreign policy formulated by others, thus strengthening the hands of the bureaucrats of the Foreign Office.[218]

The Social Democrats began by accepting the state itself. Marx and Engels had wanted a strong centralized Germany as a means of uniting the workers' movement and placing Germany at the head of the International. But Marx had criticized the idea of the " free state " in the Gotha programme of 1875 " as an independent thing which possesses its own spiritual, traditional and free basis instead of treating society as the basis of the existing state." [219] Yet the

---

[216] F. Lenz, *op. cit.*; Hans Rothfels, " Marxismus und auswärtige Politik " in *Deutscher Staat und deutsche Parteien* (Munich and Berlin, 1922), pp. 308-341.

[217] Rothfels, *op. cit.*, p. 341.

[218] Max Victor, " Stellung der deutschen Sozialdemokratie zu den Fragen der auswärtigen Politik," *Archiv für Sozialwissenschaft und Sozialpolitik*, LX (1928), p. 153. *Cf.* also Lenz, *op. cit.*, pp. 95 f.

[219] *Neue Zeit*, 1890-1.

party did not give up the recognition expressed by Motteler in 1874, "We are not opponents of the Reich as such, as a national state entity, but of those institutions under which we suffer."[220] This view persisted. The proletariat made up the German people and felt itself coëxtensive with the nation whose outward form was the German state.[221] It seemed impossible to break away from the fact of a German party working within German territory.[222] Further-more, the party accepted the German state as a means of securing immediate benefits and insuring economic and political stability. This view made Bebel and Liebknecht, as it did the Conservatives, adopt the tactics and the premises upon which other parties worked. The more opportunism developed the more the existing state was looked to as the source of reform. It seemed understood that the state existed fundamentally for the ruling classes and that it func-tioned to protect them; but the Social Democrats consoled them-selves as follows:

> The stronger the military power of the state, just so much the stronger is the political pressure on the exploited classes; the more this pressure grows, the more quickly comes the moment when a weakening of the state through a war becomes the pre-condition for its freer development.[223]

Although the Social Democrats disliked war, like the bourgeois parties they considered a defensive war legitimate to perserve the state, and they never undertook to prevent a war by appeal to the strike and to the aid of a foreign proletariat.[224] Perhaps, as Kaut-

[220] Motteler: *Sten. Ber. d. Reich.*, April 20, 1874, II Leg. Per., I Sess., p. 961.

[221] Victor, *op. cit.*, p. 154, citing Kautsky, *Neue Zeit*, 1887, and the election programme of 1884. See also, Kautsky, "Nationalität und Internationalität," *Ergänzungshefte zur Neue Zeit*, 1907-8. In this article he said that the feeling for the greatness of the nation had increased with the rise of the modern state just as the necessity for a national language, culture, etc. had increased with the rise of the capitalistic market. Kautsky also criticized Otto Bauer, Austrian Socialist, for underestimating the strength of the pressure (*Drang*) toward a national state because Bauer, as an Austrian, he maintained, had more interest in the state of multiple nationalities.

[222] Rothfels, *op. cit.*   [223] *Vorwärts*, April 8, 1907.

[224] Appeal to the general strike was refused in 1870 and in 1878 by Liebknecht and time and time again turned down by the German party.

sky suggested in 1915,[225] the idea of an "international proletariat" had only a psychological and moral value. If so, German Social Democracy was thrown back, whether for geo-political reasons or because of its own inertia, upon the German proletariat, and hence upon the vicissitudes of the German state.[226]

> German Social Democracy [Victor has written recently], avoided a conflict between state reality and revolutionary ideal. As is easily understood, therefore, it would emerge from this middle position to a point where it would acknowledge the state in its temporary existence—in order to be just national enough—and would withdraw into passivity—in order not to be too national—. This means that the SPD simply went the way of the Liberal opposition.[227]

Along with its acquiescence in the German state Social Democracy developed a social ideal, a belief in the spiritual and intellectual power of man. "Man's best human weapon is his head, not his fist," wrote one member.[228] The glorification of the individual and of reason meant the development of respect for the cultural achievements of the age.[229] Hence Social Democrats could tolerate imperialism and Power because they were confident that these must eventually give way before culture.[230] So long as Social Democracy did not intend to hasten by revolution the day of retribution, it could ignore imperialism and concentrate on internal matters. In this way it came to accept the *status quo* in external affairs. It recognized the principle of "saturation" and of the "balance of power," defended the sanctity of international agreements and

---

After 1905 a small left-wing group under Rosa Luxemburg did propagate the principle of a mass strike, but Bebel opposed it.

[225] *Neue Zeit*, 1915-16, I, 34.

[226] It contented itself with renouncing the "responsibility" for the results of imperialism (in 1914), but voted the appropriations.

[227] Victor, *op. cit.*, p. 158.

[228] Wilhelm Liebknecht, *Der Hochverratsprozess*, p. 261, cited by Victor, *op. cit.*, p. 159, note 3.

[229] "Never before has the civilization of the world reached so high a point as today" (*Vorwärts*, December 31, 1899).

[230] This does not mean that Social Democracy took no stand on these matters. But it did not agitate to overthrow the social order. It did not oppose Bismarck's policy, especially the Russian alliance, but hoped that western culture would be able to defeat Russian barbarism.

adopted the principle of plebiscite in place of the principle of nationality. In 1899 Bebel brought forward the proposal to stabilize
armaments through international treaty.[231] The Social Democrats
denounced war as a catastrophe which harmed all humanity and
regarded intervention as justifiable only in special cases.[232] The
similarity of their point of view in many of these questions to that
of the Liberal bourgeoisie does not seem to have troubled the leaders
of Social Democracy. So long as they were opposing specific bourgeois *mores,* they were content with their position. Their attacks on
governmental foreign policy frequently lacked any definitely socialistic character. When Kiauchow was taken, they emphasized, for
example, the future competition of Chinese labor with German labor
more than the unethical nature of the seizure of the province.[233]

In general Social Democracy did not favor political expansion
and bitterly opposed the colonial policy of the Reich.[234] The social
question, it said, could not be exported.[235] Imperialism, Bebel
maintained, " is the spirit of a former century, the spirit of absolutism; it is the spirit of imperialism as it ruled in its day in the old
Roman Empire," or, as Bernstein said, " Imperialism equals Cæsar-
ism, Bysantianism, Bonapartism." [236] Social Democratic imperial-

---

[231] *Sten. Ber. d. Reich.,* January 13, 1899.

[232] *Cf.* Victor, *op. cit.,* p. 162; also *infra,* Chapter VI.

[233] Bebel: *Sten. Ber. d. Reich.,* February 8, 1899, IX Leg. Per., V Sess.,
II, 902-3, and Kautsky, " Chinas Eisenbahnen und das europäische Proletariat," *Neue Zeit,* 1886. Even if this emphasis were only a matter of
tactics, it shows a change in point of view. *Cf.* with an article by H.
Cannon, " Unsere Interessen in Ostasien," *Neue Zeit,* XV, 805 f., in which
the author desires an opening of Asia in order to keep German export
industries going and because the more quickly the industrialization of
Asia proceeds, the better for socialism. Kautsky began in 1883 to argue
against the need for colonies for over-production and over-population
purposes. He wished these problems solved at home.

[234] *Neue Zeit,* 1883, and afterward. The expense and lack of returns from
colonies were always favorite arguments of the opposition. In addition
the argument suggested above, that the problems which colonies were to
help solve should be solved at home, carried some weight with Social
Democrats.

[235] Liebknecht: *Sten. Ber. d. Reich.,* March 4, 1885, VI Leg. Per., I Sess.,
III, 1539.

[236] Bernstein, " Sozialdemocratie und Imperialismus," *Sozialistische
Monatshefte,* 1900.

ism would consist in educating the backward peoples rather than exploiting them, and in the end this method, they said, would bring greater economic results.[237] The Social Democrats preferred to the German kind of imperialism the English and American kind based on freedom at home; they always criticized in the German its bureaucratic character, which made of colonies an extension of Germany and not a free land. If American competition must be fought, they argued, let a central European tariff union be formed.[238] When Rosa Luxemburg in her *Akkumulation des Kapitals* [239] called attention to the inevitability of a political struggle when all foreign markets should be exhausted, she received small hearing. On the other hand the views of the more moderate Socialist, Rudolf Hilferding in his *Finanzkapital*,[240] which left open the question of the effect of continuous accumulation of capital and emphasized the value of international trusts for the preservation of peace, won popularity with the party. " All this," writes one critic, " throws light upon the liberal-ethical position of the party." [241] That the Social Democrats did not entirely reject imperialism *per se* is seen in the fact that they admired English imperialism, which corresponded more closely to the socio-ethical ideal of Social Democracy, and desired English friendship above all others. Social Democracy inherited from Marx its fear of Russia and its belief that a Franco-Russian alliance would come. It rejoiced in the Anglo-French entente as a " victory of civilization." Even when Germany found herself completely surrounded, Social Democrats did not despair because they believed that England had no evil intentions.[242] They were also reassured by confidence in Germany's military power [243] and in the final triumph of western European civilization.

[237] The Liberal theory of Cobden and Bright, good-will through free-trade, was revived here (Frohme: *Sten. Ber. d. Reich.*, X Leg. Per., II Sess., IV, 3967).

[238] Ledebour: *ibid.*, April 3, 1911, v. 266, 6199 f.

[239] Volume I first published in 1913.

[240] Berlin, 1910.   [241] Victor, *op. cit.*, p. 67.

[242] *Vorwärts*, July 29, 1908, and Roesicke: *Sten. Ber. d. Reich.*, October 21, 1902, X Leg. Per., II Sess., VII, 5817. As early as the time of the Second Naval Law Bebel said that Germany need fear no one if she would only maintain her friendship with England.

[243] *Sten. Ber. d. Reich.*, March 30, 1911, and April 24, 1912, v. 266, 5971 f., v. 284, 1355 ff.

10

Social Democrats recognized that the navy, as the army, was an instrument of capitalism; but not all of them felt alike about it. Franz Mehring, who belonged to the left wing, opposed the navy on the ground that the commerce which it was to insure and foster would be of no permanent value to German labor, and, if not to German labor, then not the German nation. He wrote:

> If Germany wishes to excel richer nations, she has only one way to do so, the way of a socialist revolution, which so long as there is still time itself changes production and transportation methods according to the needs arising out of the modern forces of production; and this makes possible the creation of new forces of production, which erase the disadvantages of geographical position.[244]

Mehring lumped the navy, grain tariffs, anti-socialist laws together as an effort of decadent capitalism to prevent emancipation of the proletariat.[245] He saw that more and more ships would be needed before the aim could be attained. " This is," he said, " to conquer the world market at the expense of world collapse." [246] The same attitude was taken by Rosa Luxemburg in 1899 at the party meeting in Hanover.[247] At the same assembly Schippel, a South German Social Democratic writer and editor, and Heine, Vollmar and Auer defended a standing army. These four thought that without an army and navy Germany would be at a disadvantage in the world. " The possession of a strong navy," they said, " is of as much value

[244] Mehring, "Weltpolitik," *Neue Zeit*, XV, 801, following Marx in substance.

[245] *Idem, Weltkrach und Weltmarkt* (Berlin, 1900), cited by Kehr, *op. cit.*, p. 335. *Cf.* also Bernstein: " The protective tariff policy is the policy of the external putting on the screws just like military policy or naval policy. All three stand, as I believe I have pointed out in this House, in the closest relationship with one another. Why does the protective tariff of the German Empire find so much support from those who should be its opponents? Quite simply because higher tariffs bring in high revenues to the Treasury. In Committee that has been clearly enough pointed out to us. Why are they in the financial position they are? Because of the growing demands of the military state, the naval budget, etc. And these demands will increase the more the protectionist policy comes into its own, the more the threat to other nations gains ground and becomes a reality " (*Sten. Ber. d. Reich.*, January 15, 1903, VIII, 7316).

[246] Mehring, *loc. cit.*   [247] Luxemburg, *op. cit.*, III, 193.

for present-day decisions in questions of imperialism as the possession of a central bank with a strong gold reserve is of value in the world market." [248] But no members of the party actually voted for the naval or military or colonial laws because they believed that such laws would only serve capitalistic interests and not the interests of the German nation as a whole.

After Caprivi's fall the government coöperated with the Right to try to restrict the growth of Social Democracy. By the so-called Revolution Bill of 1894 they sought to sharpen the teeth of the penal code, the military code and the press law against the Social Democrats. Every suggestion of revolution and every attack on the fundamental institutions of the state was to be punished by imprisonment.[249] Even the Liberals denounced the severity of the measure, and with the help of the Center decisively defeated it. Th defeat discouraged the government from introducing further anti-socialist bills until the increase of strikes during the economic upswing after 1895.[250] Then the desire for some check upon the movement revived; but in 1897 another bill, the Little Socialist Law, failed to pass by a vote of 209 to 205. The setback aroused the Emperor to try to injure unions by a bill to protect strikebreakers. The government and the Emperor had been recently defeated by the Right in Prussia over the canal project, and the Emperor's disappointment in this matter may account for the energy which he put behind the new bill; he did not wish a second defeat. Bülow said in his memoirs that the Emperor while on a yachting trip during the summer of 1899 (July) was aroused by news of labor unrest.[251] A long conversation with Eulenburg on the internal danger convinced him that "the government must act or all will be lost. If a serious external conflict arises and half the army must be kept at home by a general strike, we are lost." A bill "For the Protection of Working Conditions" had gone to the Reichstag in May, 1899, and had been rejected at the first reading,

[248] Calwer, *Sozialistische Monatshefte*, 1905, pp. 919 f., cited by Kehr, *op. cit.*, p. 338.

[249] *Sten. Ber. d. Reich.*, 1894, Appendix I.

[250] Georg Frey, *Die Streikbewegung in Deutschland, 1900 bis 1910* (Bamberg Dissertation, 1927).

[251] Bülow, I, 348 f., citing largely from a letter from Eulenburg.

June 26, 1899. The Emperor had already made efforts to aid the passage of the bill and on July 12, a telegram to this effect from him to Hinzpeter made its way into the papers and increased the fear of a dissolution of Reichstag.[252] His Majesty felt great concern over the entire affair. The bill was reintroduced in the autumn and after a two-day debate fell through again. Even amendments lessening the severity of the proposed measures failed to bring about a third reading. The Emperor again experienced great disappointment; but for the time no further efforts were made to crush the Social Democrats. Hohenlohe liquidated the government's defeat graciously by allowing the abolition of the law against association. William II now gave up an active policy and called Social Democracy "a temporary phenomenon." Bülow, too, prepared to turn to other affairs. He told William that if he wished an antisocialist policy he should have kept Bismarck.[253]

The failure of the anti-socialist laws, the concessions made in the law of association, the rise in wages, and the economic boom of the late 'nineties undoubtedly helped to moderate the revolutionary character of the Social Democratic party. In spite of revisionism, however, wide circles of the German public from the Emperor down remained troubled by the menace of Social Democracy. It is difficult to know how convinced the upper classes actually were of this menace, how far they simulated or exaggerated it. In 1903 Bülow wrote:

> The question of if, how, and why measures are to be taken against Social Democracy controls the situation behind the scenes more than in the open. Behind the *Hamburger Nachrichten, Die Post,* and others stand powerful circles.[255]

The social question continued to provide one of the most important

[252] Haller, *op. cit.*, p. 264. The occasion of the presentation of a picture of the Great Elector to the city of Bielefeld led the Emperor to announce that it signified that he, like his ancestor, would sweep opposition out of his way. People thought that this absolutist statement could only refer to the unpopular anti-socialist bill. Eulenburg said that the Emperor kept silence for some days after the popular reaction to the public telegram became known (Haller, p. 267).

[253] Bülow, *Denkwürdigkeiten,* I, 367. The frequent proposal of *coup d'état* measures has been discussed in previous pages.

[255] Ziekursch, *op. cit.*, II, 174.

problems which industry faced, the Agrarians dreaded the effects of organized labor, the government feared the bitter parliamentary attacks of the Social Democratic members, while the ranks of the Center and of left Liberalism saw without being able to prevent the flow of support to Social Democracy.

The evidence is overwhelming that influential groups feared the Social Democrats. Reference has already been made to the uncompromising and bitter attitude of Baron Stumm-Halberg towards them. Although his associates expressed their views less violently, Count Limburg-Stirum pledged the support of the Conservatives to Bülow in 1900 as follows:

> We are convinced that the Chancellor, as a statesman who has come up out of the school of the great Prince Bismarck, after his apprentice and journeyman years, will uphold the two great principles, that a strong government must act energetically against the forces of revolution, and secondly that a government which recognizes the value of the agricultural population for our country will keep in mind in formulating its measures the burning question of agriculture.[256]

Even Prince Schönaich-Carolath, who had left the Free Conservatives because of their support of the anti-socialist laws and who remained opposed to the use of force against Social Democracy, grew fearful with time. His biographer writes that he too paid little attention to the rise of revisionism in the trade unions, that he became impatient because of the growth of the SPD. He believed that the years of effort to win over Social Democracy had borne no fruit, and his biographer says, " The Prince, too, was surprised by the nationalism of the socialists in the August days of 1914." [257] The *Industriezeitung* wrote in 1903:

> That which separates the individual groups of industry is as nothing in comparison with the great dangers which threaten German industry as a whole and the great common danger of

---

[256] *Sten. Ber. d. Reich.*, December 10, 1900, X Leg. Per., I Sess., X, I, 413.

[257] Ludwig Maenner, *Prinz Heinrich zu Schönaich-Carolath: ein parlamentarisches Leben der wilhelminischen Zeit, 1852-1920* (Stuttgart and Berlin, 1931), p. 97 and Chap. V. Also *Industriezeitung*, No. 40, October 4, 1901 for an article by Bueck pointing out that Social Democracy would not lose its stripes.

democratization, not only of industry but of the whole of public life. The race of the parties to bring socio-political measures into the Reichstag in their enmity to industry and in their desire to win votes is not only a danger for industry; it is a public danger for the German people because through these the already strong influence of democracy in the organs of public administration and social legislation, as well as the self-confidence of Social Democracy, is fed.[258]

The industrialists feared that the powerful organization of Social Democracy would win converts willy-nilly until quite legally it would be beyond control.[259] The increasing votes were constantly cited and mention made of the growing representation of all large cities solely through Social Democratic candidates.[260] Industrialists considered that they had an organization (the Central Union of German Industrialists) " by which the war against Social Democracy can be conducted with all the means at its disposal. This war is directed toward ameliorating the danger threatening the state and society and if possible toward eliminating it completely." [261] The fight must be merciless; but at the same time the workers must be given property, an interest in the existing order, so that their reconciliation with it might be possible.[262] The industrialists thought that their allies, the Conservatives, underestimated the power of the Social Democratic organization and did not realize that it was separating employers from employees, sharpening the class war, and carrying it into regions where it had never before been noticeable. The attempts of the government to set up an obligatory organization of employer and employee, they said, could come to nothing; such an organization could only aid the laborers

---

[258] *Industriezeitung*, No. 9, February 27, 1903. Also as early as March 8, 1899 in No. 10 an article entitled " Die drohende Demokratisierung der Industrie."

[259] *Ibid.*, No. 22, May, 31, 1900, cited from the *Jahresbericht der Handelskammer zu Ruhrort*, 1899.

[260] *Ibid.*, No. 25, June 19, 1903.

[261] *Ibid.*, No. 28, July 11, 1901. The pertinent article is entitled " Die Nationalzeitung und der Zentralverband." It continued, " The movement which is so joyfully and hopefully greeted by the *Nationalzeitung* can only heighten the danger against which the Central Union considers it its duty to fight with every possible means."

[262] *Ibid.*, No. 22, May 31, 1900, " Soziale Bewegung."

by making them more effective against their employers rather than more reconciled to them. Clinics, sick bureaus, they thought, became merely centers for Social Democratic propaganda.[263] Industrialists believed that because of the need for appealing to the masses the National Liberal party had weakened in its stand toward Social Democracy. If this trend were not counteracted, the party would split up; the elements which stood for " the greatest possible extension and increase of production as one of the foundations of economic advance " would break away.[264] The industrialists left little doubt of their point of view.

> The number of Social Democratic voters [wrote the journal of the Central Union] has increased since 1893 from one and seven-tenths millions to two and one-tenth millions. It is expected to go up even more quickly from now on. Bourgeois society will have to stand on its head. The Social Democratic party meeting declares it is a question of force. Good! State and society will also know how to answer this question with force.[265]

Strikes, said Bueck, were no longer undertaken merely for economic reasons but for power; they were intended to compel recognition of the unions.[266]

[263] *Ibid.*, No. 12, March 22, 1899, article by Bueck, General Secretary of the Central Union.

[264] *Ibid.*, No. 1, January 4, 1899; No. 45, November 9, 1899; No. 52, December 28, 1899.

[265] *Ibid.*, No. 20, October, 1898. The quotation closed a very bitter article entitled " Zeil und Taktik der Sozialdemokratie." *Cf.* also *Die Post*, No. 274, October 5, 1899: " Social Democracy cannot forsake its goal because it would immediately lose the greatest part of its supporters, especially the most radical. Moreover, it is of importance that it use a more passionate and fiery language than the radicals among the Liberals. Its agitation is of such a kind now that it can only be surpassed by direct reference to revolution and *coup d'état*. . . . But it is clear that Social Democracy could wish for nothing worse than to come into power. The clever ' diplomats ' of the party, who look down so superiorly on the trade unionist politics, would be like lost children and could neither advise nor help. . . . All clear cut and practicable ends are lacking to them."

[266] *Ibid.*, No. 40, October 4, 1901, p. 482. The increase of strikes, especially in those taking part in strikes, furnished great cause for alarm. In 1896 there were four hundred and eighty-three strikes with over one

The question arises as to the influence of social problems and of Social Democracy in furthering a policy of imperialism. The Emperor once said:

> When one sees the strife of the people at home, one can lose all desire to rule. The only way out is not to take any notice of it. The colossal discrediting, the collapse of parliamentarism makes public opinion sick, just as Russia is internally sick. There they escape into foreign policy. With us the illness is aired in unsteadiness and dissatisfaction. These hinder the aims of the government and put obstacles in the way wherever they can.[267]

Did prestige politics likewise provide a supposed remedy for Germany's internal ills? The historian Ziekursch believes that Bülow hoped to satisfy Social Democracy with *Weltpolitik* and distract interest from domestic tension. Bülow may easily have entertained this hope without undertaking his foreign policy for any such initial purpose. Kehr has burrowed more deeply into the subject by showing that the *Sammlungspolitik,* which was directed against Social Democracy in internal policy, bore the responsibility for foreign policy as well. " The *Sammlungspolitik*," he wrote, " meant the end of the diplomacy of the old school which thought it could isolate foreign policy. It inaugurated the subservience of diplomacy to the behest of the combined Agrarian and industrial interests." [268] In this way the internal situation, which lay uppermost for the *Sammlung,* could not but make itself felt in foreign policy. At the same time, the burden of Social Democratic Trade Unionism and of the social levies for insurance, old-age pensions, and the like rested heavily on an industry trying to compete in a world market; and this pressure from within made imperialism necessary so that German industry might continue to expand. Imperialism was intended as a means of avoiding discontent and strikes by maintaining employment and keeping up wages. Furthermore, an army and navy sufficient for the day of reckoning were deemed indispensable; for

hundred and twenty thousand men engaged; in 1901 there were almost fifteen hundred strikes and half a million men. *Cf.* Frey, *op. cit.,* for confirmation of the fear of strikes.

[267] *Eulenburg to Bülow,* July 27, 1899, cited by Haller, *op. cit.,* p. 267.

[268] Kehr, *op. cit.,* p. 265.

in the case of foreign conflict the existing order in Germany could not be preserved except by Germany's triumph in that conflict. It is impossible to deny that the logic of the situation, whether wholly conscious or not, was to create a powerful and successful Germany as the surest means of preserving the social and institutional *status quo*.[269] The Social Democrats and the Max Webers preferred the alternative of not preserving it; but their opinion did not seriously count.[270]

A survey of German parties and politics in the 'nineties shows that responsibility for imperialism does not lie at the door of the class struggle alone; but the importance of the latter as a factor in its growth must not be overlooked. If imperialism flourished in countries where the class struggle was less acute than in Germany, yet even in England Rhodes saw the possibility of solving social problems by a vigorous colonial policy. Along with the problems raised by the organization and education of the masses are to be placed other factors equally contributory to the rise of imperialism. Such were the persistence in Germany of absolutism, the specious nature of parliamentary government, the collapse of Liberalism,[271] the rise of new social and economic problems which the Right was

[269] Dr. Vagts has kindly called the attention of the writer to the fact that the Prussian War Ministry did not want a *maximum* development of power. Before the World War it turned down the demand of the General Staff for three new army corps because, in its opinion, the " right " kind of officers were no longer available. The *status quo* was considered safest under a slow increase of forces which would maintain the correct tradition intact. This shows how carefully the social fabric was guarded.

[270] This was especially true after the fall of Caprivi. The question may be said to have arisen again after the *Daily Telegraph* affair; but with no greater success. For Caprivi's social views see Ziekursch, *op. cit.*, II, 46 ff.

[271] Theodor Barth once wrote that the Liberal press had more readers than any party press in Germany, but that still Liberalism was politically unimportant. He ascribed this situation to the fact that not the press but complicated interests determined political opinion (*Die Nation*, No. 15, January 8, 1898). It is interesting to note how often a speaker in the general assembly of the Agrarian League announced that his district was formerly National Liberal (*Korrespondenz des Bundes der Landwirte*, *passim*).

unwilling to solve by new methods, the struggle of agrarianism
with industrialism and finance capitalism—all these created a total
condition which, if it did not give rise to, greatly encouraged the
adoption of imperialism.[272]   In addition to the complicated domestic problems, the national psychological state contributed to general
approval of imperialism.   Just as the country grew to believe in
the Agrarian crisis, it soon accepted as truth the reiterated statement of Germany's need to embark on an imperialistic policy and
became readily convinced of the moral justice of *Machtpolitik*.   The
present-day belief in Germany that National Socialism has saved
Germany from Communist revolution represents the same easy
acceptance of nationalistic propaganda.   Party leaders and the
ranks of their followers soon accepted the new creed, hoping from
it internal harmony and external glory.

[272] Reference may well be made here to an article in *Die Post*.   In
summing up the year this organ found that bourgeois society did not have
the courage to fight the social revolution and that in the near future
there was no hope of more energetic measures against Social Democracy.
" Therefore," concluded the article, " the second of our tasks, the strengthening of our navy, becomes all the more the middle point of Imperial
policy " (*Die Post*, No. 2, January 3, 1900).

CHAPTER III

LARGE PROPAGANDA ORGANIZATIONS IN THE GERMAN EMPIRE, 1890-1902

> I don't know whether my contemporaries feel it in the same measure as I do at this moment. It is the heavy curse of being epigone which burdens the nation from the broad masses to the highest circles. We cannot revive the naïve enthusiastic activity of a generation ago because we are faced with tasks of another kind than those of our fathers . . . . We cannot appeal to the great feelings common to the entire nation, as was the case when we were occupied with the creation of national unity and a free constitution.
>
> Marianne Weber, *Max Weber,* p. 138.

From political parties it is appropriate to turn to the important propaganda organizations outside the parliaments. These groups were in almost every case connected through personnel with the parties in the Reichstag and Landtag and exercised influence in three directions: on public opinion in the country, on deputies in the parliaments, and on the government. In some cases they initiated policy, in other cases they became propagandists for policies proposed by others or by the government; in all cases they had their own organs of publicity and exercised a wide influence throughout Germany and even among Germans abroad. All of them took a keen interest in German foreign policy, especially in colonial policy, the navy and alliances. Although the influence of these organizations cannot be measured, the size and importance of their membership indicate clearly their significance.

The activity of many of the propaganda organizations was closely connected with the tariff question, the most crucial problem of the Bülow era. This problem dominated the political stage and evoked political hatreds and alliances which determined the history of the period in various fields, especially in that of foreign policy. A brief history of the tariff is therefore sketched in the following account of the Agrarian League *(Bund der Landwirte).*

A. *Agrarian League*

It remains one of the most striking peculiarities of German history that the Junkers have been able to maintain themselves through all the dangers which have threatened them in modern life. They recovered from the attempted inroads upon their power in the Stein-Hardenberg period; they recovered from 1848; and they did not succumb to the greatest menace of all, the industrial revolution. During the decade from 1890 to 1900 when economic signs pointed to their downfall, they strengthened themselves politically. In this decade few in the nation failed to recognize the anomalous position occupied by the Agrarians or were ignorant of the methods used by them to maintain it. All parties in the Reichstag attacked them, especially the Social Democrats and the left Liberals, as did prominent writers like Hugo Preuss *(Die Junkerfrage)* Naumann *(Demokratie und Kaisertum)*, von Polenz *(Die Grabenhäger)*, Max Weber, Lujo Brentano, as well as members of the Association for Social Policy *(Verein für Sozialpolitik)* and of the Association for Commercial Treaties *(Handelsvertragsverein)*.[1] In spite of onslaughts the Agrarians persisted, as they do to the present day.[2] Sieveking, an economic historian, has recently written:

> Happy that land whose agriculture during the present-day changes already rests, as in South Germany, upon the broad basis of peasant settlement. How different it would be in eastern Germany if timely reform had fostered more actively German peasant settlement and if that which the land law offered with ample means had not been more than counteracted on the one hand by favoring in trade and especially in domain policy a large-scale production dependent on foreign labor. A Germany of free peasants would have been in the East a firmer stronghold and it is, wherever it exists, the most fortunate victory . . . . A similar agricultural constitution would be the strongest tie for the Germans and one which would not allow separatism to be thought of.[3]

---

[1] Hugo Preuss, *Die Junkerfrage* (Berlin, 1900); F. Naumann, *op. cit.*; Max Weber, *op. cit.*; Lujo Brentano, *Mein Leben im Kampf um die soziale Entwickelung Deutschlands* (Jena, 1931). Each of the above was a constant contributor to periodicals and newspapers.

[2] *Cf.* Kosok, *op. cit.*, Chap. IV, "The Landed Aristocracy."

[3] Heinrich Sieveking, "Zur süddeutschen Agrarentwickelung," *Erinnerungsgabe für Max Weber* (Munich and Leipzig, 1923), II, 337.

A stronghold of feudal power thus persisted in the midst of a rapidly industrialized economy. One of the means for continuing this power in the 'nineties was the Agrarian League, an organization established in 1893 during the Caprivi era and before the conclusion of the Russo-German commercial treaty. In 1892 the *Landwirtschaftliche Tierzucht,* an agricultural paper, published a call to arms by Rupprecht-Ransern, lease holder of a large estate.

> We must carry on *Interessenpolitik* [he wrote]. If we have the courage to bear the name ' Agrarian,' which the anti-Agrarian press so often gives us unjustly, and bear it with justice, we must cease to vote as Liberals, ultramontanes, or Conservatives and rather band together in a great Agrarian party and through it seek to secure greater influence over parliament and legislation. . . . We must shout out until the whole people hears, we must shout until our voices penetrate into the offices of the parliaments and the ministers, until they reach the foot of the Throne.[4]

In answer to the plea a small meeting took place on January 28, 1893, under the direction of Baron von Wangenheim-Spiegel, who later became president of the League. Through the activities of those present a large meeting was called in Berlin on February 18-19 to found the organization. The opening speech of this meeting gave the keynote: " We cannot go on like this; we demand aid and protection for German agriculture or it will go to ruin." Rupprecht declared that, when it was a question of life or death to the Agrarians, the old Conservative loyalty to King and state could be changed into energetic opposition.[5] The speeches made at this early gathering showed the vigorous egoism of the leaders and presaged the vehemence of their campaign.[6]

Although at the first and at subsequent meetings representatives from all Germany registered, the organization spread particularly among the large landowners in East Prussia. Since these lacked the numerical strength to constitute a popular movement, they appealed to the farmers of middle-sized and small holdings on the

---

[4] Cited by J. Croner, *Geschichte der agrarischen Bewegung* (Berlin, 1909), pp. 131 f.

[5] *Ibid.,* p. 134.

[6] Several of these speeches are cited in part by Croner, *op. cit.,* pp. 134 ff.

basis of common interests. The appeal could not have succeeded before Germany ceased to be a grain-exporting country because up to that point the interests of the large producers demanded an extension of their holdings at the expense of the peasants. After the 'seventies when Germany imported grain, they did not demand more land.[7] On the contrary, the number of smaller holdings, especially of the middle-sized holdings, was in the 'nineties slowly increasing.[8] The change did not create commonalty of interests between large and small holders; but the League was able to persuade many thousands of peasants that their interests were best served within the organization. The success of the large landowners in winning many of their traditional enemies to this view constituted their greatest propaganda achievement.

The long history of agricultural organization assisted in bringing the peasants into the fold. Although this history goes back to the eighteenth century, new agricultural organizations arising out of the reforms of the Stein-Hardenberg period became general in the early nineteenth century. The independent possession of land by the peasants as well as the effects of emancipation upon the estates threw each owner more on his own resources and made the enterprising eager to learn new methods. These organizations, which the state through its bureaucracy encouraged in Prussia, existed primarily for imparting technical information. They spread rapidly and led to the foundation in 1842 of the Prussian *Landes-Oekonomie-Kollegium* as a central point of reference.[9] To these groups belong much of the credit of the progress of German agriculture during the nineteenth century; but they were not founded or equipped for political activity. Since they were partly official, political discussion in them was legally restricted. As an adjunct, Christian Peasant Unions sprang up in the 'sixties and 'seventies; but these likewise did not serve agriculture in the political field.

[7] Naumann, *op. cit.*, p. 100. Rationalization of agriculture also played a part in this question of land extension; the large owners introduced better methods.

[8] Von der Goltz, *Vorlesungen*, etc., pp. 82 ff.

[9] Willy Kreb, " Die öffentliche Ernährungswirtschaft und die Organisation der Landwirtschaft," *Hildebrands Jahrbuch*, 110 (Third Series, 55), 38-9.

In addition to such groups and more important in the history of the League stood the credit organizations known as *Landschaften*.[10] These organizations of the eighteenth and early nineteenth centuries, to which the Junkers and wealthier farmers belonged, gave to the big estates a feeling of solidarity and mutual interest. Through the *Landschaften* money was lent by the many to the one in need, and each member knew the resources, character, and ability of the others. Nothing could have trained the landowners more effectively to coöperate in any enterprise for bettering the conditions of the landed proprietors than these mutual aid societies. Through them the big landowners had kept the peasants in control and dependent on their favor.

The League spread rapidly to all parts of Germany. In 1899 it had 188,000 members; [11] in 1901 membership reached 232,000 with an increase of 26,000 in 1900 and 1901. In 1902, however, the increase amounted only to 18,000, and in 1903, after the passage of the Bülow tariff, it ceased.[12] Of the 232,000 members in 1901, 110,000 lived east of the Elbe, 122,000 in west and south Germany. Only two-thirds of one per cent or 1,480 members possessed large estates *(Grossgrundbesitzer)*; 28,000 or 12½% belonged to the group of the middle-sized farmers, and 202,000 or 87% to the small holders.[13] About 18,000 were craftsmen. The League endeavoured, just as the Conservatives had long done, to ally with the guilds in common cause against industrialism.[14] 8,000 persons at-

---

[10] M. Tcherkirsky, *The Landschaften and their Mortgage Credit Operation in Germany, 1770-1920* (Rome, 1922).

[11] *Korrespondenz des Bundes der Landwirte*, No. 12, February 13, 1899. The *Korrespondenz* reported that the increase from 1898 was only 1000 members because the League had been too busy campaigning for the Reichstag to get members. For the election the League issued 4,000,000 pamphlets, had 2804 meetings, and received 550,000 marks to expend (*loc. cit.*).

[12] Dix, *Der Bund der Landwirte, Entstehung, Wesen und politische Tätigkeit* (Berlin, 1909), p. 27; also *Korrespondenz*, Nos. 10 and 11, February 9-11, 1903. The dues had been doubled for 1902; hence the League felt proud to have held its own. The fact that the percentage of large landowners in the League decreased only means that more small owners were persuaded to throw in their lot with the League.

[13] *Korrespondenz*, No. 12, February 11, 1901.

[14] " The handworkers know that the Agrarians are always ready to

tended the eighth annual meeting in February 1901. In 1900 the League held nine thousand meetings and its approximate income from dues reached 107,423 marks.[15]

The executive head of the League consisted of a committee of eleven members made up of two presidents, a director, and eight Reichstag members; but the organization was essentially decentralized. Every state of the Empire had its own president and vice-president, who with others formed an executive committee. Every electoral district for the Reichstag likewise had a president, and every subdivision of the electoral district had its leader. In regions of special activity the League maintained headquarters with paid officials. These existed for East Prussia, West Prussia, Pomerania, Schleswig-Holstein, Bavaria, Saxony, Württemberg, South West Germany (Hesse, Baden, Rheinpfalz) and for Thuringia-Brunswick.[16] According to its constitution the League aimed "to embrace all agricultural interests without consideration of political party and size of holding in order to protect the influence which agriculture should have over legislation, in order to secure for agriculture representation in the parliamentary bodies equal to its importance."[17] Hahn's statement of purpose in February 1899, at the sixth general assembly may also be cited. It showed the manner in which the purpose should be achieved.

> The activity of the League [he said] does not consist alone in injecting its ideas into political parties and in being helpful to the candidates who stand on its platform in order to get

---

support all their efforts to recover the 'golden ground' which they have lost through modern development and the liberal era in legislation" (*Korrespondenz*, No. 8, January 29, 1901).

[15] The opponents of the League said five hundred thousand marks (Bräsicke: *Sten. Ber. d. Reich.*, December 7, 1901, 1901, 3056). This may be nearer the correct total, since in 1897, 492,000 marks were taken in. The League, like the Social Democrats depended on dues. Whatever else it had was added to the dues income and was not enough to equal a separate fund. The by-laws provided for the dues to be at the rate of 4½% of the Prussian land tax or 15 pfg. a hectare of cultivated land. Three marks annually were the minimum dues per member. *Cf.* Kehr, "Grundlagen der Tirpitzschen Flottenpropaganda," *Gesellschaft*, 1928, p. 211.

[16] Dix, *op. cit.*, pp. 8 f.

[17] *Ibid.*, pp. 12-3, citing the entire constitution.

these men elected. At times when there is no election it pursues its great goal, that of making clear the situation and the interests of agriculture and of making sure that they are always represented to the public, both through the parliaments and by means of the press and public gatherings.[18]

A glance at the table in the footnote indicates that the League rallied the various agricultural sections of the country to its support and gave them representation in the Directory.[19] It is also clear that the members of the Directory were rather large landowners with important parliamentary connections. Count Limburg-Stirum expressed the intimacy, already referred to, between the League and the Conservative party as follows:

Most of the members of the Conservative party are members of the League because the tendency of the League opposes in no way that of the party. Every member of the Conservative

---

[18] *Korrespondenz*, No. 12, February 13, 1899.

[19] The Directorate of the League follows. It is taken from the *Jahrbuch des Handelsvertragsverein*, 1901, p. 140.

President, Baron von Wangenheim, Farther Pomerania, owner of a knight's holding, Member of the Reichstag, Member of the Prussian House of Representatives.

Vice-President, Dr. Roesicke (Gustav), Brandenburg, Owner of a knight's holding, Member of the Reichstag.

Director, Dr. Hahn, Hanover and Berlin, Officer of the Reserve (?), Member of the Reichstag, Member of the Prussian House of Representatives.

Vice-Director, von Plaskunda,   ?

Count von Mirbach, East Prussia, Owner of knight's holding, Member of the Reichstag, Member of the Prussian Upper House.

Rupprecht in Ilnisch, Silesia, Owner (lease-holder?) of a knight's estate.

Otto Baron von Manteuffel, Brandenburg, Owner of a knight's holding, Member of the Reichstag, Member of the Prussian House, *Landrat*.

Pfahler, Holstein, Farmer.

Wrede, Hanover, Knight's estate.

Baron von Kettler-Harkotten und Schwarzenraben,   ?

E. König, Saxony, *Amtmann*.

Friederic Beckh, Bavaria, Farmer, Member of the Bavarian House of Representatives.

Frege Weltzien, Saxony, Knight, Member of the Saxon Upper House.

Haug, Württemberg, Member of the Württemberg House of Representatives, Magistrate.

Lücke, Offenbach, Renter, Member of the Reichstag.

11

party can be a member of the League without being untrue to his position as a loyal subject of the Crown and the state. And when an article is written which does not please him and perhaps many of us, that does not mean the impossibility of belonging to the League. The question is whether the League's aims are at variance with our own principles and that, I affirm, is not the case. Therefore, gentlemen, all speculations about the League are superfluous.[20]

In 1893 the new League returned only one representative to the Reichstag, von Ploetz, its first president. Ploetz, however, succeeded in building within that body an economic union of one hundred and forty members, including Poles and anti-Semites, with which to fight the commercial treaties. By 1898 the League had organized its electoral machinery more efficiently and secured over 250,000 votes, electing, together with the Bavarian Peasant Alliance, eleven representatives to the Reichstag and thirteen to the Prussian Landtag.[21] The chief promoters of the League, Baron Wangenheim, Dr. Gustav Roesicke, and Dr. Dietrich Hahn, sat in the Reichstag, Wangenheim as a Conservative, Roesicke and Hahn officially without party affiliation. Hahn also belonged to the Prussian Landtag. His frequent speeches, as well as those of Roesicke and the Conservative members, adequately represented the League's views.

Dr. Dietrich Hahn, director of the League after 1897, came from Hanover.[22] He was in no way a large landowner, but was the son of a

[20] *Sten. Ber. d. Reich.*, December 2, 1896, IX Leg. Per., IV Sess., V, 3672. *Cf.* also Werner Sombart, *Die deutsche Volkswirtschaft im 19. Jahrhundert* (Berlin, 1912), pp. 469 f. Sombart says that the natural leadership of the aristocracy was such that the League easily fell under its control. The way was opened for the domination, mentioned in the foregoing chapter, of the Conservatives by the Agrarians. See also *Korrespondenz*, No. 30, May 1, 1900: "League and Conservative party belong together; a separation is absolutely unthinkable." Also note the satisfaction with which the League welcomed the formation of the new Conservative Union in Hanover—formerly a stronghold of National Liberalism—and its declaration of sympathy with the League (*ibid.*, No. 16, February 28, 1899).

[21] *Cf.* Naumann, *op. cit.*, p. 104. Naumann reckoned ten mandates and Wahl, *op. cit.*, III, 559, gives eleven with the Peasant Alliance. The *Korrespondenz* counted ten in the Reichstag.

[22] The writer is indebted to notes of Dr. Vagts for the material on Hahn.

lock builder *(Schleusenbauer)*. He had attended the university, studied history, and become (1886-93) an archivist of the *Deutsche Bank*. In this position he quarreled with his superiors and found that he disagreed on principle with high finance, a fact which made him readily sympathetic with the anti-finance-capital attitude of the Agrarians. The district from which Hahn came, the area around Hamburg and Bremen primarly engaged in manufacturing and shipping, was not one of large-scale agriculture and, so far as agriculture went at all, was by nature more fitted to dairying and cattle-raising. In spite of this and because Hahn was a native son of the district, it elected him to the Reichstag and under his tutelage supported the League in other ways. Apparently his secret desire to own land and the possibility of his achieving a political position by adhering to a new cause led Hahn to become active in the League. That he was either stupid or thoroughly convinced of the justice of the League's cause was illustrated by the following attitude. The most enterprising of the peasant sons and daughters of his home district emigrated steadily to America. Hahn regretted this loss, but, like the Junkers, opposed settling them on new peasant farms, preferring that they become mere agricultural workers or that they drift to the cities rather than that the large estates be broken up. His opportunism was illustrated by the fact that during the World War he bought up at very low prices all the heath and uncultivated moor land in his home area and with the aid of Russian prisoners of war put it into cultivation. He thus created a large estate in an area which had never known one. Only his early death prevented his subsequently receiving governmental aid *(Osthilfe)*.

Though privately referring to " the hideous navy," Hahn accepted imperialism outwardly and introduced it into his electoral district. He also made his district anti-English when, apparently, it might as easily have been made pro-English. He accomplished these things by holding great old-home celebrations at which he aroused patriotic fervor in support of the measures he put forward. No one at the meetings seriously challenged his views and those who stayed away had little political influence. He occasionally stirred up opposition to the government in order to bring pressure to bear for governmental aid to agriculture and did so both in the Reichstag and at home. In short, as in the case of the bourgeois Tirpitz, Hahn served his adopted cause with the fervor of a convert.

The weekly journal, *Bund der Landwirte* and later *Korrespondenz des Bundes der Landwirte,* had a circulation of 130,000 copies, but many more than the original subscribers read it. In 1902 the League gave out 7,766,000 copies. The *Korrespondenz* showed clearly the concern of the League over Social Democracy, emphasized the national as against the international point of view, reaffirmed loyalty to the Emperor and the state, encouraged Centrist agriculture to support the League, and generally voiced League ideals. It did not indulge in such unpleasant vehemence as the speakers in the general assemblies of the League or in the Reichstag.

With this modern organization the Agrarians prepared to meet the demands of a new age. They adopted the tactics of the democratic parties. Even so biased an historian as Adalbert Wahl admits that the violence of their campaigns introduced a new tone into parliamentary debate.[23] Barth, the Progressive editor of *Die Nation,* said in the Reichstag in 1895: " The League is founded for the express purpose of continually complaining and it carries out this programme to the last dot of the ' i.' It is constantly trying to discover new troubles, to come forward with new demands on the state, to say, ' State, help us.' " [24]

The programme of the organization announced several lines of attack. It aimed immediately in 1893 at the defeat of the Russian commercial treaty. In this case it fell short of success. In addition it hoped to bring about the rejection of all treaties with low tariffs on grain. Its primary endeavour centered always around adequate import duties, which should rise above the three and one-half marks tariff of Caprivi and be secured by a new autonomous tariff law with minimum duties below which the government in treaty bargaining could not go. Further aims included the reduction of meat imports by means of sanitary laws against cattle diseases, fewer taxes on agriculture, especially on rural industries, more advantageous arrangements for loans, cheaper administration of workers' social insurance, further safeguards for landowners against violation of contracts by agricultural workers, bimetallism,

[23] Wahl, *op. cit.,* III, 560.
[24] *Sten. Ber. d. Reich.,* January 10, 1895, IX Leg. Per., III Sess., I, 252.

and abolition of the Produce Exchange. In view of the extensive scope of the programme, the League could emphasize one or more of the points of its programme as occasion demanded. It has already been indicated in the foregoing chapter how the Conservatives battered away at the Reichstag during the decade after 1893 with proposals for the amelioration of agricultural conditions. Their campaign coincided exactly with the organization and growth of the League.[25]

The Agrarians professed a body of principles as a basis for their programme. However serious their condition, however much they needed governmental aid in their difficulties, they did not argue solely in terms of interests. They refused to consider Germany as preponderantly industrial; a percentage of industry, they maintained, produced for the agricultural population and hence depended on agriculture. As agricultural needs increased, this part of industry would benefit, said the Agrarians; to neglect agriculture would ruin industry as well. The Agrarians reckoned also that agriculture accounted for one half, that is, they estimated, for 73.70 billions out of 150 billions, of the national wealth; hence they refused to be relegated to an inferior position.[26] They believed, moreover, that Germany should maintain her agricultural basis because " all states," they argued, " have sacrified their defense forces in the measure in which they have gone over to commerce and industry." To the Junkers Germany's future continued to depend on the army, and the securest basis for an army was the agricultural population, which showed itself physically more fit for service and more appreciative of the military tradition than the city proletariat could ever be.[27] The Agrarians never wearied of emphasizing this point and eagerly supported it with statistics of the rejection of recruits from

[25] *Cf. Korrespondenz, passim.*

[26] The writer has not seen a detailed statement of the basis on which this estimate rested; but since land values were over-capitalized, the figure is probably too high. For the above see *Agrarisches Handbuch* (2nd. ed., 1903), pp. 15 ff., and *Korrespondenz*, No. 7, January 24, 1902. For discussion of over-capitalization see Lujo Brentano, *Agrarpolitik* (Berlin, 1925, 2nd. ed.), pp. 235 ff. The controversy over land values was a long and bitter one.

[27] *Agrarisches Handbuch, op. cit.*, article " Armée," pp. 68-74. Also *Korrespondenz, passim.*

the cities and by comparisons with the fate of ancient Rome, Holland, and England, where the army had fallen prey to commercialism and industrialism. Though the League eventually consented to support the navy,[28] it continued to prefer the army. As Conservatives the Agrarians believed that army discipline and education were desirable for the lower classes, both in themselves and as a bulwark against Social Democracy. One of the chief sources of anti-English feeling among the Agrarians lay in the fact that England had allowed her army to decay at the same time that she had sacrificed her agriculture, and England's early experiences in the Boer War confirmed this observation.[29] Wangenheim said in 1901:

> It is not only that our sense of justice is outraged, it is not only that we see a kindred folk barbarously treated; no, we feel deeply that the struggle which is being fought out there is only another form of the struggle we are carrying on. [Stormy applause] There [South Africa] likewise naked Mammon driven to the final consequences, there the struggle with fire and sword; here the struggle with the more refined weapon, economic exploitation and law! The results the same, ruined peasant farms, ruined peasants.[33]

The landowners of Prussia had always had sympathy and support from the state. When in a time of steadily declining prices for agricultural products the state passed social legislation in favor of another class, thus entailing an increase in the tax burden, the resentful Agrarians felt justified in seeking state relief for them-

---

[28] According to the *Berliner Neueste Nachrichten*, 849 members of the League belonged to the Navy League and still others supported the naval laws (No. 64, February 8, 1900). The *Korrespondenz* did not subscribe to the laws. The *Tageszeitung* made it perfectly clear that it did not approve of the expansion of the navy on any grounds but " national " ones. It bitterly attacked the idea that economic reasons for the navy existed; exports had developed too far already, said the journal (*Deutsche Tageszeitung*, No. 21, January 13, 1900). When accused of " *Schacherpolitik* " for voting naval expansion, Agrarians said that they were only pointing out that sound agriculture was as necessary to *Grossmachtstellung* as a navy.

[29] E. Kehr, " Englandhass und Weltpolitik," *Zeitschrift für Politik*, XVII (1928), 505 f. The same idea is also brought out by speeches in the Reichstag.

[30] *Korrespondenz*, No. 12, February 11, 1901.

selves.[31]   One of the League writers, Gustav Ruhland an economist, said of social legislation:

> The Agrarian movement of the present thinks and feels quite differently.   For Agrarians the usual treatment in present-day science of the ' social ' as a question of the wage-earner recalls impossible English conditions.   And English industrial development does not seem to it an exemplary one but an example to be avoided.   Only by strengthening and advancing the independent middle-class can the day-laborer be helped.[32]

The dissatisfaction of the Agrarians with the new tariff of 1902 was heightened by the thought that in the various adjustments made in the social laws after 1897 the government so little regarded Agrarian interests.[33]   Although the Agrarians denied that they opposed all commercial treaties, they rejected every vestige of the theory of laissez-faire and favored complete protection of trade and agriculture.[34]   Their theorists even said that if the state did not assist agriculture, it might as well take over and administer the land.   They held that because output could never be reckoned and because psychological factors inherent in land possession were peculiar the state should regard agriculture differently from other branches of national economy.[35]

As is to be expected the theorists of the Agrarians and of the League criticized classical economic theory.   One of them wrote:

> So much is perfectly clear to us, that in that moment in which old Europe, Russia excepted, did not know how definitely to free itself from the curse of English economic theory

---

[31] Dix, *op. cit.*, p. 5.   See also *Agrarisches Handbuch*, Preface to 2nd. ed., 1903.

[32] Gustav Ruhland, " Professor Schmoller und sein Agrarprogramm," *Ausgewählte Abhandlungen, Aufsätze und Vorträge* (Berlin, 1900, edited by *Bund der Landwirte*), p. 143. Ruhland is the theorist of the Agrarian movement.   An account of him can be found in Joseph Kyrion, *Gustav Ruhlands Volkswirtschaftliche Anschauungen* (Giessen Dissertation, 1930), and in Friedrich Bülow, " Gustav Ruhland als Nationalökonom," *Weltwirtschaftliches Archiv*, January, 1937.

[33] *Agrarisches Handbuch, op. cit.*, Preface.

[34] *Korrespondenz*, No. 14, February 22, 1899.

[35] W. Skarzynski, *Die Agrarkrisis und die Mittel zu ihrer Abhilfe* (Berlin, 1894), p. 120.

under the firm of Adam Smith, Ricardo, Malthus, Stuart Mill, Cobden its fate was sealed. It is true that Germany endeavoured under Bismarck in 1879 to 1887 to break away, but did not go over completely to the List-Carey-Dühring ground. One does not need to be a prophet but only to look about him with his own eyes and without English glasses.[36]

The theorists felt that Russia and America, the two nationalistic, protectionist states, would not be able alone to hold out economically and politically against England and that a policy of laissez-faire would prevail, to the utter ruin of German agriculture. When prices fell, they blamed laissez-faire speculation in grain on the Exchange.[37] Their programme included a law to prohibit this speculation.

The economics of the Agrarian League, at least so far as the large landowners were concerned, foreshadowed in Germany the present National Socialistic theory of autarchy. The Agrarians believed that the less Germany entered into world trade and the more she developed a home market, the less dependent she would be on England and the better off she would be. If this argument merely rationalized agricultural interests, as it largely although not entirely did, it appealed to a nationalistic age. But imperialism created a rather difficult problem. To oppose it on economic grounds proved simpler than to overlook the political aspect. The League did not wish to encourage German export industry to the point to which its ships would bring home foreign meat and grain in exchange; it did not want agricultural colonies which would compete with German products; but it desired Germany's political power to equal that of her peers. With respect to colonies the Agrarians therefore compromised. They posed two conditions: that German colonial policy should harmonize with the entire economic and political system; that the creation for commerce and industry of a future market in the colonies should not be made the basis of future German economic life or allowed slowly to diminish

[36] *Ibid.*, p. 12. Here as so often the contempt of the Agrarians for England and Manchesterism is evident. See also *Agrarisches Handbuch, op. cit.*, pp. 583-87.

[37] Ruhland, *op. cit.*, Ruhland advocated the speculation theory of price decline and was responsible for the acceptance of this principle by the League.

interest in other problems, for example, protection of home agriculture. If these two conditions were kept in mind, the League,
said its *Handbuch*, would support "an extensive increase of our
own overseas possessions" as plantation colonies where non-com-
petitive products could be raised for the home market.[38]   At the
same time the *Handbuch* continued:

> The League would oppose definitely any effort in connection
> with the German acquisition of colonies to locate abroad the
> political center of gravity and the economic power of Ger-
> many. The strength of the German people should and will
> always remain at home in the national labor, in agriculture,
> and in the middle-class. Through a wise policy which under-
> stands how to bring these factors to flower, that is, through a
> national domestic policy, our industry will be assured of a
> rising internal market.[39]

The League eventually voted also for a navy, but it opposed the
Canal Law of 1902 and an extension of the railroad network because it considered these measures beneficial to industry at the
expense of agriculture and unnecessary to "national prestige."[40]

Mindful of its own interests as opposed to those of industry the
League did not wholeheartedly support Miquel's *Sammlungspolitik*.
After Miquel's first attempt "to reconcile opposing opinion and at
least to destroy an artificial increase in real or supposed differences,"
the League in its general assembly on February 14, 1898 declared:

> In opposition to announcements which propose a policy of
> coöperation without setting up clear and distinct goals the
> League stands for a policy of *Sammlung* which seeks to
> strengthen Germany abroad as well as at home, to protect the
> entire national production against foreign competition. It
> demands the recapture of a competitive position for German
> agriculture as over against foreign countries and the re-creation

---

[38] *Agrarisches Handbuch*, p. 511. The reason given here is that "it
would be a severe blow to the prestige of the German name if we did not
keep pace with other countries in our colonial efforts so that we alone
would be left out of consideration in international questions."

[39] *Ibid.*, pp. 513 ff. See also *Die nationale Seite der deutschen Agrarfrage*,
in *Materialien zum Zolltarif*, No. 12.

[40] *Ibid.*, p. 292. The same thought is often expressed in Reichstag
speeches.

of an assured existence for the middle-class threatened equally in its existence in agriculture, trade, and commerce.[41]

This declaration was generally interpreted as indicating opposition to the *Sammlungspolitik* and the commercial treaties. The League thus challenged the industrial state and devoted itself to maintaining Germany at least half agricultural. It felt no responsibility for supporting the government, spoke of the " empty promises and mistaken policy of the Chancellor," [42] and if necessary to obtain its ends, showed no reluctance to sharpen the domestic political crisis.[43]

Critics accused the League of picturing the agricultural crisis as blacker and more widespread than it really was in order to win the support of the small farmers. The local League officials held meetings in their districts to " educate " the peasants to a realization of the dangers which beset them, making it appear as if peasant interests were identical with those of the large landholders.[44] Representative Bräsicke, who, although himself a landowner in East Prussia, opposed the League, declared that it over-emphasized the agricultural crisis and that by its agitation it was destroying the unity of the country. He maintained that too large farms were taken up on too little capital, that difficulties of individual management caused much of the trouble in agriculture.[45] He urged that

[41] *Jahrbuch des Handelsvertragsvereins*, 1901, p. 29, cited from the General Assembly of the League for 1898.

[42] *Korrespondenz*, No. 2, January 9, 1900 is an article which supported the utterances of some of the members of the League, Höningen and Roesicke, against the tariff of 1902.

[43] *Korrespondenz*, No. 2, January 8, 1901.

[44] Rickert: *Sten. Ber. d. Reich.*, December 14, 1895, IX Leg. Per., III Sess., I, 208-9; IX Leg. Per., IV Sess., V, 3662-3.

[45] There are no figures which give the debts of agriculture for the whole of Germany before the War. In Prussia statistics were worked out for 1902 (F. Kühnert, *Die ländliche Verschuldung in Preussen*. Preussisches statistisches Landesamt in Berlin, V [Berlin, 1905]). The average debt was 26.4% of the entire wealth or 7.5 billion marks; for the Empire at the same rate this would have made 13 to 14 billion marks. Before the War the causes of debt varied with the individual farm; after the War the cause became more uniform due to the general economic situation. Before 1914 30% had no debts, while later almost all had some (Erich Conrad, *Die gegenwärtige Verschuldung der deutschen Landwirtschaft und ihre*

less military duty would aid the peasants more than higher grain prices, which would in the end only increase the cost of production for other agricultural products.[46] In other words, he said, the League was making every effort to popularize with all groups on the land higher grain tariffs irrespective of whether or not these duties best served their real interests. The League answered his charges by citing the enormous percentage of peasants in its membership, although it must have known that the programme of the League did not aid all peasants.[47] The care with which the Reichstag Agrarian representatives emphasized the similarity of interests between their own and peasant problems shows that they were conscious of having to prove the point rather than secure in taking it for granted.

It is true that the Association of Peasants of the Northeast, founded in 1896, another peasant association in Mecklenburg founded in the same year, and two other groups founded by peasants in Bavaria organized against the League, the first two in favor of the Caprivi treaties and the two Bavarian groups against the large estates.[48] But these peasant associations proved ineffective as propaganda organizations and remained regional in scope. Even then the League claimed in the case of the Peasant Union of Lower Bavaria that the demands of the Union coincided with those of the League but that the tariff demands were too low.[49]

Bekämpfung unter besonderer Berücksichtigung der Provinz Pommern [Griefswald, 1927], pp. 92 ff.). According to the *Agrarisches Handbuch, op. cit.*, pp. 384-89, Prussian agriculture alone had a debt of three and one-half billion marks. It considered the increase in debt during the six years between 1892 and 1898, that is, during the era of the Caprivi treaties, as 1,926 million marks.

[46] Bräsicke: *Sten. Ber. d. Reich.*, December 7, 1901, X Leg. Per., II Sess., IV, 3053 ff. Naumann in his charges agreed with this and the idea runs through all the literature of the Commercial Treaties Association.

[47] The dairy farmers, for example, who had to buy grain for feed did not profit from the higher tariffs unless they could have prices for their own products raised. This was also true of the hog-raisers.

[48] *Jahrbuch des Handelsvertragsvereins*, 1901, pp. 141-2. *Die Nation* said that the League really persecuted these organizations (No. 7, November 13, 1897).

[49] *Korrespondenz*, No. 4, January 15, 1901. The ease with which a peasant district could be won over to the League was illustrated by Hahn's success in his electoral district (*cf.* above, p. 85).

The League was also accused of making political advances to the craftsmen, especially after the failure of the Kanitz proposal (1894), when it needed popular support.[50] The Conservatives had lately secured influence in the guilds and the League found these fertile ground in which to sow seed. The guilds, it thought, could, since they were opposed to industry, produce their share of propaganda against industrialism. The *Korrespondenz* published numerous promises of League support to the "middle-class" in its struggle against capitalism.

Dr. Borgius, one of the officials of the Commercial Treaties Association, who watched critically every move of the League, said that League agitators had succeeded in impressing even the educated public. The right and middle-class presses, the bureaucracy of the central and provincial governments, and most industry, he said, acknowledged the existence of a crisis in agriculture and the need for assistance to it. The two groups which might be supposed to oppose the League, the Central Union of German Industrialists, and the National Chamber of Commerce, had largely given up active propaganda against it. The members of the Central Union, Borgius stated, "on the basis of their tariff policy and not less on socio-political grounds agreed with the Agrarians," while the National Chamber of Commerce, intimately connected with the Central Union and the Rhenish-Westphalian Chamber of Commerce, dared not take other than a moderate position.[51] If the League could succeed in better educated society, it had excellent chances to succeed with peasants.

The most important source of power for the League lay in its control over the local governments. It influenced local officials (*Amtsvorsteher* and *Landräte*) to act in its favor, especially to give it the right to hold meetings from village to village, often without satisfying the police regulations which were enforced against the Social Democrats and the Center.[52] Protection of the

---

[50] Pachnicke: *Sten. Ber. d. Reich.*, December 17, 1895, IX Leg. Per., IV Sess., I, 184-5.

[51] Borgius, *Der Handelsvertragsverein, ein Rückblick auf die ersten drei Jahren ihrer Tätigkeit* (Berlin, 1903), pp. 6 f. *Cf.* Stumm's attitude as previously given.

[52] Rickert: *Sten. Ber. d. Reich.*, IX Leg. Per., IV Sess., I, 369-702; December 2, 1896, V, 3662-3. The League also controlled the *Kreisblätter*

League by local authorities allowed propaganda to attain un-precedented vehemence; under the eyes of state officials it even reached the extreme of treasonable utterances against the province or state.[53] The provincial and central governments alike responded to this agitation. In Mecklenburg, a stronghold of large estates, one of the local officials of the League became a minister; in Prussia the lower government officials, the squires (*Landräte*), usually landowners themselves, had identical economic interests with the League.[54] The central government of the Empire, how-ever, felt from the first greatly embarrassed by it. It attacked Caprivi and Marschall at the time of the treaties so bitterly that one of its own members resigned with the public statement: " From whatever angle I view the measures of the executive com-mittee of the League, I see only blunders, destruction and con-fusion." [55] The exaggerated demands of the League committees in regard to the new tariff troubled Bülow and occasioned some of the most bitter party strife of these embittered years.

The League fulfilled its purpose of arousing the country to the agricultural problem. Nothing is more striking in the debates of

(Hohenlohe, *op. cit.*, pp. 522, 565). The *Korrespondenz* was always re-pudiating a charge of this kind, but the evidence seems against the League. There was really very close contact on the part of the League with all local organizations so that a local leader, who allowed the Reichstag or Landtag representative from his district to vote against the League's measures, was removed. When the government occasionally displaced some of the *Landräte* as a result of complaints of their connivance with the League, it frequently put them later into higher administrative offices (*Die Nation*, No. 14, January 6, 1900, p. 185).

[53] Bebel: *Ibid.*, December 5, 1901, X Leg. Per., II Sess., IV, 2978, 2993.

[54] Rickert: *Ibid.*, December 14, 1897, VIII Leg. Per., IV Sess., I, 208 f. On one occasion in the place where Rickert was speaking the squire had ordered the *Gemeindevorsteher* to appear and to oppose Rickert's speech by one of his own in the interests of the League. After Rickert charged this in the Reichstag, Hahn said that the League had done everything possible to convince the farmers and peasants that the free-traders like Rickert were in the wrong. See also Steinhauer: *Ibid.*, January 21, 1900, X Leg. Per., II Sess., IV, 3637-9. Since information about the tactics of the League is not easily obtainable, such evidence from the opposition is of great interest, especially in view of the fact that the opposition was in agreement about these tactics.

[55] Cited by Croner, *op. cit.*, p. 130. The dissentient was Schulz-Lupitz.

the Reichstag or Landtag than the way in which it used every opportunity to bring up the subject. Budget debates, army, navy, and colonial debates, debates over aid to industry, protection to employees, new commercial treaties, new taxes, all led the Agrarian representatives to proclaim their cause and the League organ to launch its propaganda. One doubts if the Agrarians in the Reichstag could have so effectively carried out their task without the stimulus of the League organization. In the debate over the Roumanian treaty, the first opportunity after the formation of the League, the agricultural crisis monopolized the discussion. The Conservatives and the League representative, Ploetz, engaged in a bitter dispute with Caprivi and Marschall.[56] The latter declared that if the League persisted in linking the five marks tariff with loyalty to the Sovereign as the *Kreuzzeitung* did, this would be the most exaggerated propaganda which Germany had yet known. When the treaty with Roumania and others with Spain and with Serbia were accepted, the vehemence of the League rose to new heat. In *Der Reichsbote, Das Volk,* and the *Kreuzzeitung* attacks on Caprivi multiplied.[57] The parties of the Left answered this agitation with attacks on the League and the long years of recrimination began.[58]

The struggle over the Russian treaty in February and March of 1894 ended with a setback for the League. Shortly afterwards, however, the government aided agriculture by abolishing the *Identitätsnachweis*[59] and setting up agricultural chambers. These

---

[56] *Sten. Ber. d. Reich.*, November 24, 1893, IX Leg. Per., II Sess., I, 44 f. In the general assembly of the League in 1900 Oertel spoke on the treaties as follows: " The Commercial Treaties are for me a shameful sign of the fact that we were (1891-4) under the influence of foreign forces and could not assert that strong, energetic and, if necessary, ruthless independence needed to maintain our economic life. The Treaties are in our economic history what Olmütz was in our political history. Such an Olmütz must never come again " (*Tageszeitung*, No. 72, February 13, 1900).

[57] Citations from these in Croner, *op. cit.*, pp. 140 ff. The *Kreuzzeitung* said that his acts had created " an unbridgeable gulf " between the government and the Right.

[58] Discussion of the League in the Social Democratic meeting at Frankfurt, 1894, and in Lieber's speech in Frankfurt on January 4, 1894.

[59] *Cf. supra*, Chapter II, p. 56.

chambers, like the chambers of commerce, were intended to give agriculture a legal means of representing all agricultural interests,[60] but never fulfilled their purpose. The chambers remained technical bureaus like the old *Landes-Oekonomie-Kollegium,* while the League and the peasant associations functioned outside. In fact many chambers elected as officers men known to be Agrarians. In Westphalia about one-half of the members of the chamber consisted of League members; in Hanover thirty-eight out of sixty-nine members belonged to the League.[61] The failure of the chambers left agriculture without any organization which actually represented the entire body of farmers, large and small. Rapidly as the League grew, it never embraced more than one-fifth to one-fourth of those engaged in agriculture. The Conservatives and the League disliked the chambers because they suspected that the government had set them up only to compete with the League and ultimately to replace it. Apparently they feared the diminution of the influence of the estate owners through the equal representation in the new bodies of all agricultural interests. If this condemnation seems severe, one must recall that the estate owners were, so they thought, battling for existence. " In truth," they said, " the Agrarians represent the just and righteous demands of independent German labor in city and country." [62] The League withheld its approval of the government's attempt to create the chambers.[63]

To recapitulate the struggle of the Agrarians during the next few years is unnecessary. It is sufficient to indicate here that the Kanitz plan, the effort to suppress the Grain Exchange, the fight for the double standard, these so-called " big aids," stood in the original programme of the League. Just before the fall of Caprivi the Emperor received on October 20, 1894, a delegation of the League in East Prussia. The League thought that this sign of favor to

[60] Dr. Wittig, *Die Landwirtschaftskammern nach dem Gesetz vom 30. Juni 1894* (Berlin, 1895); also Wygodzinski, *Schmollers Jahrbuch,* XL, No. 3, 308. According to Wittig the agricultural chambers had their source " in the recognition of the great importance of domestic agriculture " (p. 1).

[61] *Korrespondenz,* Nos. 25, April 6, 1899, 36, May 18, 1899, and 40, June 10, 1899.

[62] *Agrarisches Handbuch, op. cit.,* article " Agrarier," pp. 7 ff.

[63] *Sten. Ber. d. Reich.,* February 6, 1894, IX Leg. Per., II Sess., II, 1025 f.

agricultural interests on the part of the Emperor hastened Caprivi's resignation.[64]   Hence the Agrarians entered their struggle with increased hope of success.[65] At the time of the second introduction of the Kanitz plan they secured ninety-seven votes instead of the previous thirty. But at the third general assembly in 1896 the members of the League revealed themselves as dissatisfied with their accomplishments; they criticised the government's continued unwillingness to content them and expressed doubt about the value of the " small aids." [66] By 1897, however, the League obtained an Exchange law to its liking, one abolishing trading in grain futures. Its assembly that year was jubilant.

The greatest achievement and likewise the greatest disappointment of the League was the Bülow tariff of 1902. In the course of its agitation it had brought the government to acknowledge the crisis in agriculture and the need for higher grain schedules. It secured the adoption of the principle of the double tariff, that is, of a maximum and minimum rate for grains. The specific demands of the League for the grain schedules, however, amounted to far more than the government dared to accept, including as they did a seven and one-half marks' tariff on wheat and rye. In the general assembly of 1902 the League threatened to oppose the bill if the government disregarded its demands. In the final debate on the tariff, December 13-4, 1902 Wangenheim declared:

> However moderate the demands of the League have been, they have unfortunately not received the approval of the federated governments. Agriculture has been denied the most necessary protection. The government has refused our proposals as well for raising agricultural duties as for lowering industrial duties. . . . In this way one cannot in the long run hope to fight Social Democracy; for this a powerful agricul-

---

[64] Croner, *op. cit.*, p. 156.

[65] The League was pleased over the change in government policy, but completely ignored the Emperor's warning that they had gone too far in the previous year and his advice to them to avoid sensational agitation (Croner, p. 157, citing from the *Korrespondenz*). Dix pointed out that the League had an excellent chance here to change its tactics and stand for scientific investigation of its problem; but it preferred to continue as it had begun.

[66] Croner, *op. cit.*, p. 182.

ture is necessary. Through this law agriculture is severely injured. Therefore, we reject it.[67]

Although the Reichstag regularly voted down the amendments of League members, the law benefited landowners. Nonetheless the League bitterly attacked the Conservatives who voted for the compromise clauses. Kardorff's withdrawal from it over this issue has' been referred to earlier. Its stand in regard to the tariff probably harmed it more than any previous action. In 1903 its membership dropped and three of its principal candidates were not returned to the Reichstag. The extreme League enthusiasts, Oertel, Hahn, Oldenburg, Roesicke, Lücke, and Schrempf had actually made good the threat thrown out by Rupprecht-Ransern in 1892: in voting against the government's tariff law and the Kardorff compromise, they had kept company with the Social Democrats. During the campaign over the tariff the League and the *Tageszeitung* had shown themselves in their true light. Kanitz had demanded a new anti-socialist bill before he would vote for the tariff and Heyderbrand und der Lasa had refused to support the Canal Law. This open blackmail was more than usually crude and, when in 1903 the *Agrarisches Handbuch* proposed another campaign for the Kanitz plan, the League fell into further disrepute with all governmental circles.[68]

The general attitude of the League toward England has been indicated in mentioning its dislike of English example in allowing the decline of agriculture, in upholding free-trade, and in promoting cosmopolitanism rather than autarchy. The *Korrespondenz* was wont to call the *Kölnische Zeitung* an English or Manchester journal, indicating its disdain of both a Liberal paper and of England. Sympathy with the Boers was a matter of course; they, too, were persecuted by money capital.[69] Actual fear of England, however, did not compare with that of America. The League shot its most venomous arrows against the American competition. Higher grain tariffs, the Meat Inspection Laws, the Sugar Tax

---

[67] *Sten. Ber. d. Reich.*, December 13, 1902, X Leg. Per., II Sess., VIII, 7146 ff.

[68] Dix, *op. cit.*, pp. 24 f. The *Deutsche Tageszeitung*, founded in 1894, was the Berlin daily which supported the League.

[69] *Korrespondenz*, No. 12, February 10, 1902.

12

Laws were aimed at the United States and were wrested from a yielding government at the expense of German-American relations. Germany, wrote the *Korrespondenz* on more than one occasion, ran the danger of becoming a satrapy of America. When during the Boer War English ships seized and searched German steamers, the League compared this breach of international law with the breach of economic contract made by the United States in differentiating against German sugar and concluded that the German Foreign Office would take no firmer stand in the former case than it had in the latter.[70] Hence the League contributed further to drive a perplexed government into *Machtpolitik.*

Such was a decade of League history. Much of the bitterness in the internal politics of the Empire during the period resulted directly from the propaganda of this organization. With the founding of the League the East-Elbian Junkers created an organ of expression similar to those which they had used at other periods of crisis but never on this scale. Through it they entered into politics on a popular basis and sought to impose their demands upon the government. Not even dynastic and state loyalties deterred them; the League placed *Interessenpolitik* first and foremost. That the demands of the League were often excessive and its tactics vicious is shown by the criticism of them from some of the Conservatives themselves. It is clear that an organization with a definite interest, with paid directors, with its own public press, and moved by the necessity for maintaining itself proved more effective than a parliamentary group or party which needs to be oriented on a greater variety of subjects. The League could undertake propaganda and work out measures and arguments in a way which the Conservative-Agrarians in the Reichstag could not do. It could supplement the Conservative electoral machinery. It

---

[70] *Korrespondenz,* No. 1, January 5, 1900. Opposed to England and menaced by America, the Agrarians should have clung to the Austrian and Russian autocracies. The *Deutsche Tageszeitung* may be said to have done so; but the Agrarians, especially in the *Korrespondenz* of the League, argued against making any economic concessions to hold the Triple Alliance together and constantly complained of Russian imports of foodstuffs, maintaining among other things that the Russian market for German industrial exports was not so good as industry claimed. It judged even foreign policy on the basis of self-interest.

could appeal with a definite programme of reform to elements of the agricultural population. Yet the League really remained small in size in comparison with the numbers engaged in agriculture. Since the large producers controlled it, it helped effectively to keep the Agrarians in power. It saved large-scale agriculture at a crucial moment, but in the process it embittered other groups and accentuated domestic enmity. It has been called the Agrarian parallel to the trade union; and it made use of the equivalent of the bitterest Social Democratic propaganda. The following words about the League are taken from the Liberal *Welt am Montag*:

> First of all, one must be clear about the fact that the League is actually a political force of the first order; it is next to the Center and to Social Democracy the greatest power in Germany. That a membership of 200,000 is paraded before us at the general assemblies does not mean much, certainly. . . . But in addition there is an organization ready to go into the smallest detail, a far-reaching and very clever press, a well-filled treasury, and a staff of zealous agitators. All these taken together represent a political factor with which every politician must reckon. Here is the nucleus of a new Conservative party, which is bound together by the strongest bond of union the modern world knows, that of economic interest.[70a]

B. *Commercial Treaties Association*

The Commercial Treaties Association (*Handelsvertragsverein*) provided the only outspoken economic opponent of the League within the bourgeoisie. This organization belonged, however, only to the period after 1900. Its late start and comparative insignificance prove further the weakness of Liberal tradition. The defense of the classical economic theory against the Agrarian League up to this time devolved largely upon the academic socialists and the powerless Liberals of the Richter group. These lacked influence with the public at large and even with the few business men of their own persuasion, although the League and the Central Union of German Industrialists saw fit frequently to denounce them. Economic Liberalism needed a counter propaganda organization and a group of men, who came forward during the preparations for the tariff of 1902, eventually furnished it. The group was not

[70a] Cited by *Korrespondenz*, No. 13, February 18, 1899.

strictly free-trade but wished to preserve the system of tariff treaties which Caprivi had established and, through an extension of it, to secure from foreign countries lower tariff rates. It wished like-wise to secure as low schedules as possible, especially for agricultural products, in the autonomous tariff then under preparation. It is almost superfluous to add that the group represented commercial services and export industries.

Adherents to low-tariffs had been indignant for some time with the policy of the Central Union and of the National Chamber of Commerce, whose efforts to found a central committee for preparing new tariff treaties proved lukewarm and unsuccessful. Yet in 1903 the Caprivi Treaties would run out and many economic circles regarded their renewal as vital. In 1897 the government set up with the approval of Posadowsky, Minister of Finance, and Boetticher, Secretary of Interior, an Economic Committee on Preparation of the Commercial Treaties. The opponents of the Central Union roundly condemned the efforts of that organiza-tion to secure a majority on this committee. According to Borgius, business manager of the Commercial Treaties Association, the Central Union secretly negotiated with the government and with agriculture to obtain equal representation for commerce, agricul-ture, and industry on the final committee. Borgius charged further that industry and the Central Union actually controlled three-fifths of the National Chamber of Commerce. Because of this fact, he said, industry and agriculture would control the committee.[71] The Economic Committee on Preparation of Commercial Treaties was therefore considered to be overwhelmingly protectionist. Of the ten representatives of agriculture all but two belonged to the League and one of the two was Count Kanitz, perhaps the most active of the Agrarian-Conservatives. Hence there were nine Agrarian protectionists. At least ten of the fifteen representatives of industry favored high tariffs and belonged to the Central Union. Only five possibly sympathized with low tariffs and desired renewal of the treaties. Of the six representatives of commerce and banking two, although members of the directorate of the National Chamber of Commerce, nonetheless opposed the treaties. The total added up to twenty-one high tariff men as against at most ten who could be

---

[71] Borgius, *Jahrbuch des Handelsvertragsvereins*, 1901, pp. 20-24.

counted on to defend lower tariffs and the system of commercial treaties.[72]

All signs pointed toward higher protection under an autonomous tariff, possibly with maximum and minimum schedules. As a result the demand grew for an organization to popularize the renewal of the commercial treaties. Bremen and Hamburg, cities entirely dependent on overseas trade, gave the impetus and secured the services of the Reichstag member and railroad director, Schrader, to initiate action. On October 24, 1900, a small meeting was held in Berlin. Those attending recognized that a really effective agitation must include the entire Empire. They hoped to exercise some influence on the Center and National Liberals, " who marched along completely," they said scornfully, " in the train of the Agrarians." The meeting recommended that a large general assembly be held which it directed Georg von Siemens to call and to preside over. This assembly founded the new organization in November 1900.

The first meeting illustrated how difficult it would be to bring together the diverse elements concerned. Siemens wished the association kept non-political and united only by common economic interest; but the Progressive Peoples' party protested that it could not recognize " a purely economic " organization in a question which must be politically decided. Further dispute among the delegates ensued over the grain tariffs and a real difficulty arose as to how and by whom propaganda could be carried on.

Everyone agreed on the purpose of the Association and regretted that the body had not come together sooner, since the National Chamber of Commerce, the only organization including advocates of low tariffs, could not carry on propaganda because of its quasi-official status. The new society aimed primarily to counteract some of the influence of the Agrarian League. Siemens expressed this as follows:

[72] *Ibid.*, p. 24. The writer has checked the analysis as carefully as possible and kept the figures conservative. Of the ten " treaty men " some may have been protectionists but there is no evidence that they were. Four of them definitely favored treaties because they were later members of the Commercial Treaties Association. The Social Democrats and the left Liberals were angry that they had not representation for the workers and the lower middle-classes on the Committee. The Reichstag debates reflected clearly this shortcoming.

The main end pursued by the Commercial Treaties Association is long term commercial treaties, since only through these
can a sound basis for our industrial life be laid. One of the
means to this end is the abolition of the hindrances which
stand in the way of reaching the goal. One of these hindrances—and not the only one—is the effort of the Agrarians
to raise tariffs on food products. The Association opposes
this with all its force, because it sees in this effort a danger
for carrying through its own programme. The steps already
taken admit in my opinion of no doubt on this subject.[73]

In so far as the Central Union had allied itself with Agrarian
demands the Association also opposed it. The Association appealed
to the lower middle-class and the craftsmen as that part of public
opinion whose interests coincided with its own programme.

The Association believed world trade desirable and healthy.
Since Germany could no longer supply her population with sufficient breadstuffs, to say nothing of meat and raw materials, she had
become an industrial country in need of this trade. Agricultural
subsidies would penalize the industrial population. The Association stated that the Agrarians refused to admit how far world production controlled grain prices and regretted this narrow view. In
order to have prices reduced it wished to see German agriculture
unsubsidized and forced to face world competition.[74] The Association criticized the League particularly for defending exclusively the
grain growers and ignoring the cattle-raisers. The latter needed, it
said, a low tariff on grain in order to buy cheap fodder. The Association blamed the League for trying to suppress knowledge of this
divergence of interests and urged the small farmers to join its
organization.

The Association argued that the treaty system should be retained
rather than an autonomous tariff erected because Germany exported

[73] *Georg von Siemens to the Nürnberg-Fürther Verein*, June, 1901, cited
by Borgius, *Handelsvertragsverein*, p. 40. See also Vosberg-Rekow, *Die
Politik der Handelsverträge* in *Schriften der Zentralstelle für die Vorbe-
reitung der Handelsverträge*, No. III, pp. 68 ff. Also *Jahrbuch des Handelsvertragsvereins*, 1901, p. 4.

[74] "*Die deutsche Volkswirtschaft und der Weltmarkt*," in *Handelspolitische Flugschiften*, No. 1 (Berlin, 1901), and Hans Kurella, "*Der
neue Zolltarif und die Lebenshaltung des Arbeiters*," ibid., No. III (Berlin,
1902).

the greatest amount of her goods to the so-called civilized nations—nine-tenths according to the Association—with whom Germany had such commercial treaties. She should certainly continue them in order to preserve and improve these markets.[75] Although the Association did not use this argument to refute the anti-English feeling of the time, it might well have done so; for its members, or more certainly its workers like Borgius or Schultze-Gaevernitz, understood that in England Germany possessed her best customer, one far more important than any number of German colonies, and that she should cultivate her rather than antagonize her. Hence it was tragic that the Association, like the Liberals in the Reichstag, proved weaker than its opponents.[76]

In November 1900, the Association organized with only one hundred and one members. This number grew to four hundred and thirty by December, nine hundred and thirty-one by January 1901, over ten thousand by August 1901, fourteen thousand six hundred and eighty-five by January 1902, and almost seventeen thousand by July 1902.[77] It established a decentralized scheme of organization so that each section of the country could work out its own programme in conformity with its interests. It maintained secretaries in seventeen of the leading industrial cities.

The Association consisted, not of great names, but of men connected almost entirely with banking, transportation, especially shipping, and with small and light industry. In this respect the list contrasted sharply with that of the Central Union. The members of the executive committee lived in Berlin, home of finishing industries, in port cities of commercial importance, and in South German towns, centers of light industry. The textile centers of Elberfeld and Breslau, even though located in areas of heavy industry, had representatives on the committee. The Association in

---

[75] *Die Wirkung der Handelsverträge von 1892-4* in *Handelspolitische Flugschriften*, No. II. The same idea is constantly expressed in Borgius, *op. cit.*

[76] In the publications of the Association the navy, colonies and imperialism in general are considered only briefly. The tone is one of earnest interest in the world-trade opportunities of Germany. *Cf.* especially Vosberg-Rekow, *Das britische Weltreich und der deutsche Wettbewerb* in *Schriften der Zentralstelle*, No. I (Berlin, 1898).

[77] Borgius, *op. cit.*, p. 70.

the main affiliated with the left-wing of the National Liberals, with the Progressive Union, and with the Progressive Peoples' party. Members from each of these parties sat in its privy council and the *Tägliche Rundschau* asserted accurately, " The Association can in the future quite rightly be regarded as a general representative of Liberalism." Georg von Siemens was first president of the Association. When he resigned because of ill-health, Wilhelm Herz, president of the Berlin Chamber of Commerce, became head for a time. Gothein, a member of the Progressive Union, a member of the Reichstag and of the Prussian House of Representatives, held the vice-presidency. He had been head of the Breslau Chamber of Commerce and had written at the instigation of the Society for Protection against Agrarian Attack, an organization opposed to the League, a work entitled *Der deutsche Aussenhandel*. Through this book Gothein became widely known for his interest in export trade and low tariffs. Another leader was Richard Roesicke, general director of the Schultheiss Brewery and a Reichstag representative for the Progressive Peoples' party, from which in 1902 he brought in other supporters for the Association. Borgius, a confirmed proponent of tariff treaties, served as business executive of the Association, assisted later by Dr. Hjalmar Schacht and by Schultze-Gaevernitz, then a young lecturer at Freiburg, who undertook the first series of public talks. His topics show the trend of the Association's endeavour:

1. Connection between National Policy and Economic Policy.
2. The Commercial Policy of the Agrarians and Criticism of It.
3. The " Neo-Merchantilism on a Broader Basis " and Criticism of it.
4. The Programme of the Commercial, Industrial, and Agrarian Policy friendly to Trade.

The other members of the Association, including those who made up the larger committee of eighty-five, chiefly represented chambers of commerce. They included Dr. Goslich of Stettin, director of the Portland Cement Works of Stettin, Emil Rathenau, director of the great electrical corporation, A. E. G., H. C. Koch of Rostock, president of the silk manufacturers, B. Gutmann of Göppingen, president of the South German Cotton Thread Consumers, G. Marwitz, president of the same industry in Dresden, Max Kraus of

Berlin, president of the paper manufacturers, F. Achelis, consul in Bremen and president of the Bremen Chamber of Commerce, Hans Jordan, bank director of Elberfeld, Adolf Woermann, shipper and President of the Hamburg Chamber of Commerce, and many others. The textile and machine industries furnished the largest group of members.[78]   The Association tried at first to obtain money rather than members, but it needed both for any measure of success.

Not until the autumn of 1902 with the establishment of the *Deutsche Wirtschaftspolitik,* a Liberal journal, did the Association possess a press organ of its own.[79]   In 1902 it established a central committee to prepare for the renewal of commercial treaties.   It planned courses of lectures open to the public and a series of brochures under the title, " The Interest of German Industry in the Commercial Treaties."   It published twelve volumes of this series, each volume dealing with an industry in a way suitable for propaganda.[80]   The Association also published eight special works like Soetbier's *Zolltarif-Handbuch,* miscellaneous articles and speeches, technical and statistical studies based on questionnaires to members of the Reichstag and other works of research.   Until 1903 this list grew slowly.   The late start handicapped the Association. In places like East Frisia, Mecklenburg, Pomerania, Schleswig-Holstein, Bavaria, Württemberg, and Oldenburg some little agitation against high tariffs went on, but the Association found the League so firmly entrenched that it could not succeed without a long, carefully planned campaign.[81]   Since it lacked time, the Association made little headway in those provinces which most needed anti-League propaganda.

From the beginning the Association blundered in its tactics. Instead of declaring for definite treaties, it proposed to wait until foreign countries had made offers which Germany could discuss. Apart from the difficulties of explaining the advantages of this method to the ordinary audience, the proposal lacked the precision

---

[78] *Jahrbuch, op. cit.,* p. 13.

[79] There is no indication in Borgius as to what the circulation of this journal was by 1903 and the writer has not had access to the *Jahrbuch* for 1903.   One can always count on a large circulation relative to membership because free copies of the journals of all organizations were widely circulated.

[80] Borgius, *op. cit.,* pp. 98-100.   [81] *Ibid.,* p. 91.

and the nationalistic appeal so characteristic of the propaganda of the League and of the colonial and Pan-German groups. The inexperienced Association at first overlooked this defect. When in 1901 it demanded the renewal of all commercial treaties, it had already lost the initial chance to arouse enthusiasm. Moreover, the League had discovered the weakness and taken advantage of it.[82]

Although the organization influenced the few Reichstag members belonging to it, it seems to have had no very close connections with the government or the Reichstag as a whole.[83] Its influence upon the chambers of commerce seems likewise to have been small. Those chambers whose reports before 1900 advocated low tariffs and renewal of treaties joined the Association. Those chambers which defended the tariff policy of the Central Union remained impervious to its arguments. Others presumably went on as before. The attitude of the chambers toward tariffs can be ascertained through the votes on the new tariff in the National Chamber. After the publication in the *Reichsanzeiger,* July 26, 1901, of the governmental tariff bill, the National Chamber in its general meeting voted down the recommendation of the representatives of the Dortmund-Essen Chambers to accept the higher rates by 244 to 65. It supported a proposal to reject the bill and adhere to the system of commercial treaties by a vote of 151 to 145. It accepted a resolution against higher tariffs on food-stuffs by 288 votes, thirty-four members, largely those of the Central Union, abstaining. The speakers of this assembly stated correctly that the Central Union of German Industrialists favored the law on political grounds.[84] The government, therefore, in the matter of an autonomous tariff

[82] *Ibid.,* pp. 37 ff.

[83] The Association never achieved one of its most desired goals, an official investigation of agriculture (*Jahrbuch des HVV,* 1902, pp. 21-25).

[84] *Stenographische Berichte der 28. Vollversammlung des deutschen Handelstags,* September 30, 1901, pp. 45 f. This vote indicates that the assertion of the Association that the National Chamber was dominated by the Central Union was not true, although it was not entirely untrue. For example, the vote of the Rhine Province on the July tariff law was 12 to 21; more than half the representation from that area supported the bill; it was 4 to 9 for Silesia, and 4 to 10 for Westphalia. In the large industrial centers the interests of the National Chamber and the Central Union naturally coincided.

and higher food tariffs took other advice than that of the chambers of commerce. But the Association and the National Chamber had at least one wish fulfilled. Against the bitter and persistent opposition of the Agrarians between 1903 and 1906 the government renewed the commercial treaties. Bülow says in his memoirs that he had determined upon a combination of autonomous tariff law and treaties and before the bill was published had agreed upon this arrangement in a secret conference with the Bavarian Minister Reidel.[85] Whether this statement is true or not is difficult to say. If it was true, one cannot say how much the Association or the sentiment it represented contributed to his decision. No doubt both economic facts, such as the increased market for German goods in Europe, and consideration of foreign relations determined Bülow more than did the stand of the Association. As the treaties ran out, they were accordingly renewed for another decade.[86] The Association felt, however, some justification for its labor, although it continued to deplore the minimum rates on grains established by the new autonomous tariff law.

The Association may have contributed to modifying the plan for a complete double tariff schedule. The principle of double schedules was being generally discussed in 1900. Soon after its formation the Association sent a circular letter (December 1900) to potentially interested groups urging that they oppose it. Early in 1901 the plan apparently died; but in the summer it revived in the form of a double schedule of duties for grains alone. In this form the government incorporated it in the bill of 1902.[87] Again, one cannot say definitely how much the Association had to do with the outcome; but it rallied opinion against a plan which would certainly have endangered the negotiation of commercial treaties. The Association also claimed some credit for the defeat of the League representatives in the Reichstag, Oertel, Hahn, and Gustav Roesicke, in the election of 1903. According to the League's

[85] Bülow, *Denkwürdigkeiten*, I, 531 f.

[86] Sartorius von Walthershausen, *Wirtschaftsgeschichte Deutschlands im 19. Jahrhundert* (Jena, 1923), pp. 419 ff.

[87] Bülow, *op. cit.*, I, 531. Bülow said that he arranged in the conference of May (June?), 1901, for double tariffs on " as few wares as possible." *Cf.* Borgius, *op. cit.*, pp. 43-4.

estimate the Association spent fifty thousand marks a head in order to defeat the League candidates. It is true that in those districts in which the Association especially campaigned the anti-Agrarian vote was greater in the election of 1903 than in 1898. As the Association acknowledged, however, Liberals and Progressives did not profit but Social Democrats. This outcome is significant for the history of Liberalism; where it weakened its opponents, it seemed only to contribute to the success of the extreme Left.

The Association was the only one of the propaganda groups under review which upheld the old Liberal traditions, and it succeeded least of them all. Its short life does not alone explain this failure. Three other reasons must be added. First, the Association lacked powerful connections. Secondly, it did not appeal to the growing national desire for power and prestige. It wished to promote German commerce and industry, but proposed a thoroughly unimaginative way of doing so. In spite of its sound argument, it failed to interest a nation eager for prestige and glory. As *Die Nation* said critically, it tried to cook with lukewarm water. Thirdly, a short depression set in during the spring of 1900 which made industry desirous of assistance; it wished neither to give up the chance of being aided through the tariff nor to antagonize the government or the Agrarians more than necessary by refusing their demands. After a compromise was reached to limit to grain the double schedules and to renew the commercial treaties, the Association became almost superfluous. As things stood the struggle over the tariff between the Agrarians and the government on the one hand, between the Social Democrats and the government on the other, and the conflict over the renewal of the treaties were long and bitter. Only a longer campaign and a more far-reaching popular sympathy could have made a significant impression in favor of lower tariffs and even then success seemed doubtful. The trend toward protectionism not only in Germany but everywhere had destroyed the popular basis for free-trade. Even the Association did not thoroughly support free-trade, but its use of Liberal arguments such as emphasis on " world trade " and " international " prosperity made it suspect; they seemed too idealistic in a period of rising trade barriers. The Association had no more chance of

[88] Borgius, *op. cit.*, p. 123.

restraining the League and the Central Union than had Siemens' plan for international coöperation in the Bagdad Railroad undertaking of being accepted at this time.[89]

C. *Navy League*

Privy Councillor Holstein wrote of the Navy League in 1908:

> As long as the Keim Navy League [General Keim directed the propaganda of the League] pursues its way and exerts itself to represent to the German people that England is our archenemy, we cannot wonder at the distrust of the English. I only wonder that it isn't greater.[90]

Although this charge is exaggerated as regards the character of the Navy League in 1900, it discloses its general significance. The League resembled in character and influence the Agrarian League rather than the Pan-German League. Especially in the first year or two of its existence its propaganda appeared active far less for idealistic and nationalistic purposes than for certain economic interests. It did not attempt to conceal its purpose behind a facade of anti-English nationalism, but launched directly into an unskillful campaign to hasten the fulfillment of naval plans in order to promote industry. Unfortunately, however, information about the early history of the League and of its practical work in support of the Second Naval Law (1900) remains scant. The organization had close connections with heavy industry, but this connection cannot be traced with precision. It is known that Tirpitz, who always understood the importance of basing naval agitation on economic arguments and who welcomed all the support which he could secure for his plans, was still wary of adopting the Navy League. He realized that its propaganda in 1899, as he said, " had perhaps begun to take a direction which did not agree with the views of the government." [91] The Imperial Naval Bureau (*Reichsmarineant*) as a whole thought the same way, saying that the Navy League placed " the business interests before the objective considera-

---

[89] F. Eulenburg, " Aussenhandel und Aussenpolitik " in *Grundriss der Sozialökonomie*, VIII, Chaps. VII and VIII.

[90] *Holstein to Frau Stülpnagel*, March 15, 1908, Holstein, *op. cit.*, p. 309.

[91] *Report of the Hanse representative in the Bundesrat session*, November 2, 1899, cited by Kehr, *op. cit.*, p. 175-6, note 30.

tion " of building a navy; hence it distrusted coöperation with the organization.[92] For the same reason the Navy League was not acceptable to the Berlin professors, who likewise ardently desired a navy. They found the organization "a representation of the interests of Conservatives, big industrialists and financiers," and not a national undertaking.[93] Only by 1900 and after did the League learn the importance of becoming a popular organization and of making itself acceptable to the government.

Business had not directly campaigned in 1897-8 for the First Naval Law. In 1897 Krupp had instructed Jencke, chairman of his board of directors, to hold back.[94] Neither the *Industriezeitung* nor the *Rheinisch-Westfälische Zeitung* had carried on much agitation. But when in 1898 a group of ex-navy men and nationalists attempted to found an Imperial Naval Society in Berlin, business leaders in Essen began to stir, apparently from fear that such a group would be too idealistic and would not sufficiently represent industry.[95] The latter employed Victor Schweinburg, a journalist, to forestall the patriotic naval group by establishing an organization closer to their own interests. Schweinburg represented the close connection between the Navy League and heavy industry. He edited the *Berliner Politische Nachrichten,* a journal used up to 1897 by the Central Union. He was a friend of Miquel and of Count Zedlitz, a leader of the Free Conservatives. The democratic papers called him the confidential man of Miquel and a link between the Agrarians and heavy industry.[96] Krupp, who had recently bought the *Berliner Neueste Nachrichten*, appointed Schweinburg business manager of this paper. Schweinburg founded the Navy League on April 30, 1898. The League enjoyed the support of Krupp's paper and of *Die Post,* Stumm's journal, and chose as its president the Prince of Wied, another representative of heavy industry. Since the Prince acted largely as a decoration, in April 1901 Prince Salm-Horstmar succeeded him. Theodor von Hassler,

---

[92] *Loc. cit.*   [93] *Ibid.*, p. 171, and note 10.

[94] *Ibid.*, p. 168, cited from two private letters of Krupp to Jencke.

[95] *Ibid.*, p. 169.

[96] *Die Nation*, No. 6, November 11, 1899, p. 72. The *Deutsche Tageszeitung* partially defended him, a fact which gives some credence to Barth's assertion.

president of the Essen branch of the Central Union, and Bueck, general secretary of the Central Union, kept in close connection with the executive group of the new League.[97]

A large number of high government officials and of army and navy officers joined the Navy League.[98] The industrialists did not come to the fore, since a purely nationalistic and disinterested exterior best served their designs. There were, however, as was to be expected, representatives of heavy industry and shipping.[99]

[97] *Berichte der Handelskammer zu Essen*, 1898, I, 36: "The members of the Chamber who were present agreed to enter the Navy League and to propagate it in their districts." The purpose of the League was stated as follows: "The German Navy League which was founded in Berlin on April 30, 1898 has for its aim the arousing, cherishing, and strengthening in the German people understanding for and interest in the meaning and purpose of a navy. It has the further purpose of stepping in to be of service to the employees of the navy when the laws and administration of the Empire cannot provide sufficient protection. The Navy League considers a strong German navy a necessity, especially for securing the coasts of Germany against the danger of war, for maintaining Germany's position among the world Powers, for protecting the general interests and commercial relations of Germany as well as the honor and security of her citizens engaged in business abroad " (*Die Flotte*, No. 1, January 1900, p. 15. The ccnstitution was not passed before 1900 in order to allow time for all parts of the Empire to declare their wishes in the matter).

[98] In the general assembly of January 1900 one of the speakers, von Bressendorf (Leipzig), declared that the results of the League had been excellent up to the present. The chief purpose of the propaganda, he said, was to attract people who had definite connections with the lower classes, small bureaucrats, teachers and the like. He recommended that illustrations to aid the cause be put in the text-books of the schools (*Die Flotte*, No. 1, January 1900, p. 15).

[99] Following is a sampling list of those present at a joint meeting of the large executive committee, chief committees, and directory of the Navy League on January 24, 1901. About one-third as many more attended as are listed below (*Die Flotte*, February, 1900, No. 2, p. 17).

Toegel, Major (retired), Eisenach
Heinrich Stalling, Publisher and bookseller, Oldenburg
Kühle, Lieutenant, Brunswick
von Stabel, Lieutenant Major, Karlsruhe
Erwin von Bressendorf, Leipzig
Pfeiffer, Banker, Düsseldorf

De Cuvry, Bureaucrat, Coburg
Schlutow, Stettin, Business man (?)
Hagen, Bureaucrat, Stettin
Prince of Wied, Industrial investments, Neuwied
Dr. Hugo Sogliani, Representative of the Italian Navy League, Rome

At first the Navy League did not grow rapidly. In the winter of 1898-9 Lieber forced Tirpitz in the Reichstag to deny that he planned to introduce a new naval bill. But the Samoa crisis in the middle of 1899 increased popular enthusiasm for naval expansion. The membership of the Navy League reached one hundred thousand and after that increased rapidly. The areas with the largest number of local organizations were Baden, Brunswick, Alsace-Lorraine, Hesse, Berlin and Brandenburg, Hanover, East Prussia, Saxony, Silesia, Düsseldorf, in the main industrial areas.[100] In 1900 the League had fifty large regional organizations, one

---

Butze, Bureaucrat, Arolsen

Marx, Business man, Danzig

Count Dürckheim, Hanover

Dannenbaum, Banker, Berlin

Hermann Diez, Editor of the *Hamburger Korrespondent*, Hamburg

T. Landau, Editor of the *Börsen-Courier*, Berlin

Schmöle, Bureaucrat, Essen

Von Haeseler, Lieutenant General, Schwerin

Dr. Merck, Manufacturer, Darmstadt

Menges, Major General, Darmstadt

D. Kauffmann, Manufacturer, Silesia

Jaeger, Architect, Silesia

Elsner, Secretary, Silesia

Wasserschleben, Major, Bückeburg

Dr. Ritter, Bureaucrat, Silesia

Hohenlohe-Schillingfürst, Munich

Dr. Sering, Professor, Berlin

Von Pflaum, Consul, Lawyer, Stuttgart

Hollmann, Minister (retired), Berlin

Von Loë, Army officer, Bonn

Klein, Bureaucrat, Lawyer, Bonn

Dr. Schäfer, Professor, Heidelberg

Riedel, Army officer, Rostock

Dr. Scharlach, Lawyer, Member of the Colonial Council, Hamburg

Von Engeström und von Dahlstjerna, Army officer, Schwerin

Alfred Landt, Bureaucrat, Berlin

Niemeyer, Berlin

Krause, Silesia, Member of the Landtag

Thon, Bureaucrat, Posen

Dr. Pauli, Senator, Bremen

Von Salmuth, Army officer, Brunswick

Briegleb, Engineer, Gotha

Von Linde, Professor, Munich

Brehmer, Lawyer, Lübeck

Wilhelm Kronsbein, Editor of *Die Post*, Berlin

Robert von Mendelssohn, Banker, Berlin

Von der Planitz, Bureaucrat, Dresden

Albert Müller, Banker, Essen

The auxiliary organization, Navy League Abroad, included in its executive committee von der Heydt, Hammacher, Krupp, von Kusserow, Prussian Minister, diplomat, and son-in-law of Hansemann of the *Diskonto Gesellschaft*, General von Spitz, head of the veterans' organization, Albert Ballin, Major Wissman, Governor of West Africa, and other prominent names (*Kolonialzeitung*, no. 24, June 16, 1898).

[100] *Jahresbericht des Flottenvereins,* 1906.

thousand four hundred and seventy-nine smaller ones, and six hundred thousand members; of these about half were individuals, the rest organizations which had joined as a body.[101] *Die Flotte,* the publication of the Navy League, had at the beginning of 1901 a circulation of 270,000, and rose later to three-quarters of a million.[102] The *Allgemeine Marine-Correspondenz* was also bought up and placed under General Keim, director of propaganda after 1900.[103] For the law of 1900 the League sponsored three thousand lectures at a cost of 86,840.24 marks and more than six millions of books, brochures, and writings.[104] Ample funds, which came from industry, made it possible to carry on agitation in this grand style.[105] In 1900 membership dues brought in 348,488 marks; but even in *Die Flotte* the Navy League acknowledged the use for special purposes such as propaganda of 411,812 marks more.[106] In 1901 dues brought 225,348.75 marks and gifts an additional 168,-357 marks. The League subscribed 208,182 marks to the China Expeditionary Fund alone. At the end of 1901 the League had a surplus of 147,550.58 marks.[107] After 1902, however, with the new law passed, the Boer War over, and business conditions improved, the extraordinary budget decreased and the ordinary no longer increased so rapidly.[108] The surplus for January, 1903 amounted to

---

[101] Keim, *Erlebtes und Erstrebtes* (Hanover, 1925), pp. 98 f. The number given by Die Flotte in February, 1900, was over 320,000 members (*Die Flotte,* February 2, 1900, p. 14). By March this had passed the 400,000 mark. The growth was regarded as phenomenal.

[102] Kehr, *op. cit.,* p. 101, and *Die Flotte,* No. 1, January, 1901, p. 11.

[103] *Die Flotte,* January 2, 1901, p. 18.

[104] *Loc. cit.*   [105] Kehr, *op. cit.,* p. 101, note 30.

[106] Kehr cannot establish the origin of this 411,812 marks but says there is no doubt about the amount since the Mendelssohn Bank, whose head, Robert Mendelssohn, was treasurer of the Navy League, exercised control over the finances of the organization throughout its existence (Kehr, *op. cit.,* Appendix, II, p. 453). The figures in *Die Flotte* are from the issue of February 2, 1901, pp. 18 ff.

[107] *Die Flotte,* March 3, 1901, p. 45.

[108] It is interesting to compare these figures with the income of the Pan-German League: 1898, 51,715 marks; 1899, 78,416 marks; 1900, 88,449 marks; 1901, 93,328 marks; 1902, 105,989 marks. After this last date the amounts decrease again (Mildred Wertheimer, *The Pan-German League* [New York, 1924], opposite p. 76, citing the *Alldeutsche Blätter*). If there

13

only 72,629 marks.[109]   Even so in 1903 the League set up a reserve fund of 40,000 marks and made every effort to justify a continued existence.[110]

In the spring of 1899, the year after the founding of the Navy League and the passage of the First Naval Law, industry began to urge an increase of the navy. Months before the Boer War broke out the Pan-Germans, influenced especially by the Samoan affair of March-April, agitated against England. The inflamed state of public opinion encouraged the Navy League to press its cause. Moreover, Tirpitz had been making the rounds of the private ship-building yards, and industry interpreted these visits as a hint to it to popularize naval construction.[111]   *Die Post* began a mild agitation; but its efforts came to nothing. The Conservatives, who wished to oppose industry by blocking further naval construction, foiled them through a clever manoeuvre in the *Kreuzzeitung*. This paper dropped the hint, as if casually, that the yards were inadequate for undertaking any new building. On the next day all the newspapers hostile then to a navy reprinted the news. They thus exposed the connection between heavy industry and the propaganda of the Navy League; the incipient campaign broke up.

Toward the close of 1899 the Navy League suffered an even more discouraging setback. In November one of the Social Democratic papers published a circular letter addressed to the local branches of the Navy League by the Prince of Wied and by Schweinburg.[112] The letter urged naval expansion as a means of assisting industry. The publication of the letter by the opposition press raised a storm of feeling in the nationalistic press against the methods of the Navy League.[113]   The *Tägliche Rundschau* among others led in the con-

were gifts to the Pan-German League for special purposes, the total would still be far below that of the Navy League.

[109] *Die Flotte*, April 4, 1903, p. 70.

[110] *Cf.* the speeches made at the annual assemblies. The total assets in January, 1907, were 191,653 marks. At this time the League was expanding again and had 315,350 individuals and 591,356 corporate memberships (*Jahresbericht*, 1906).

[111] Kehr, *op. cit.*, p. 175.

[112] In the *Münchener Post*, November 4, 1899.

[113] Kehr in detailing the story cannot decide the exact cause for the campaign; whether the nationalist press was angered that the Navy League

demnation and carried articles against the League by Professor Delbrück and by Stroschein, the man who had tried to found the patriotic Imperial Naval Society. The professors at this time established a separate organization for their naval activities, and the Center also took part in the fight against the Navy League. Bueck as well as Zedlitz resigned immediately to escape contamination. Schweinburg would have gone likewise but was persuaded to hold his post. He continued on until December, when his stay had become a scandal. A new director, von Beaulieu, succeeded him.[114]

After this unsavory episode the Navy League pretended to reorganize and to purge itself of its undesirable elements. Beaulieu declared in *Die Flotte* that he would break with Schweinburg's "feudal tendencies" and base his work upon the masses. *Die Flotte* spoke of the League as a Peoples' League designed to educate and enlighten them in respect to the navy, and declared that there was to be no politics.[115] In 1900 General Keim became a member of the executive committee and assumed the propaganda and editorial work.[116] Keim, a former army officer, should have reassured the

meant to teach "from above" the meaning of imperialism when the nationalists had been active for years, or whether there was some other ground for their violent outburst is not evident. No doubt a variety of motives was present; certainly among the important ones was the exposure of the thoroughly undesirable nature of a part of the naval propaganda, although the nationalists themselves were carrying on this same propaganda on what they considered a higher level. Their cause would suffer from any seeming alliance with selfish interests and they must seek to repudiate all such connection from the outset.

[114] So great was the feeling against the League that the meeting of the executive committee set for December 16, 1899, could not be held. In explaining the reason for postponement of the meeting the Prince of Wied said at the annual meeting in January, 1900 that the League was an organization for propaganda but only in the highest sense of the word, that is, for propaganda of an unpolitical character. Hence it could not run the danger of arousing bad feeling against it and so harming the future of an organization whose purpose was so patriotic (*Die Flotte*, January, 1900, p. 14). See *Berliner Neueste Nachrichten*, No. 10, January 7, 1900, for a resumé of the attacks on the League.

[115] *Ibid., passim. Die Flotte* itself was certainly free from politics.

[116] Keim, *op. cit.*, pp. 100 f. After the change several important Berlin professors and members of the Free Association for Naval Laws joined the Navy League. They included Ernst Francke, editor of *Soziale Praxis*, Hans

public if any one could. He professed an ardent nationalism, held a prominent place in the Pan-German League, and belonged to several other patriotic organizations. " We navy people," he wrote, " by whom ' German ' is always written in capital letters have the special duty of arousing and nourishing with all our powers national feeling as well as national pride." [117] He wrote that the Navy League was completely independent and that it remained entirely apart from all party politics but that " it naturally had to take up the cause whenever national-political honor was threatened." [118] Keim may have believed his own words, although one doubts this when one reads his statement that all questions, even internal problems, were ultimately questions of Power.

Opponents of the Navy League, as *Vorwärts* remarked in December 1899, were skeptical of the sincerity of the change. " The Pan-Germans," it said, " have preached control of the seas for years. Not until big industry and Schweinburg took up the matter did it go forward. . . . The support of Krupp is more important than the assembled arguments of science." [119] The Pan-Germans charged at the time that Krupp was important to the *Reichsmarineamt* and the latter to him. Class, an active Pan-German and later leader of the Pan-German League, has written in his memoirs, " People who hoped to make money by building up the navy gave the Navy League large sums and others who grew enthusiastic over the expansion which had become the Emperor's pet idea were given orders and titles, all things which for the Pan-Germans did not come into consideration because they opposed the general policy of the government." [120]

Since Tirpitz was already being pressed by the Emperor, it is not possible to say that the revamped Krupp-Keim Navy League persuaded Tirpitz to hasten the introduction of a second naval bill. On October 18, 1899 William II had made his famous speech on the

Delbrück, editor of the *Preussische Jahrbücher*, Gustav Schmoller, Max Sering, Adolf Wagner, and others. The League soon cited proudly the remarks of these men on the need for a navy. In fact, *Die Flotte* was only too glad to cite any persons of the Left when they showed themselves in sympathy with naval plans.

[117] *Ibid.*, p. 102.   [118] *Ibid.*, p. 100.
[119] *Vorwärts*, December 2, 1899, cited by Kehr, *op. cit.*, p. 188.
[120] Class, *op. cit.*, p. 83.

"bitter need" for a strong German navy. The country had been upset by uncertainty and expectation ever since that time.[121] Industry had immediately approved an increase, but the Agrarians were at first uncertain. In January, 1900 the government brought forward a new naval bill. The Navy League participated actively in the campaign for its adoption and the May-June number of *Die Flotte* already regarded the passage of the law as a certainty.[122] It undertook an entire series of pamphlets and books, titles of some of which follow: *Die Bedeutung der Seemacht für das Aufsteigen und Sinken der Völker, Eine neue Zeit ist gekommen* by the high school teacher Dornheim, *Deutschlands Seemacht* by another teacher, Dr. Rassow, *Die Hanse* by Professor Dietrich Schäfer, *Die Bedeutung der deutschen Kriegsflotte für unsere überseeischen Interessen* by Lieutenant Captain von Veltheim-Cottenstedt, and others of similar character.[123] As in the case of the *Jahrbuch des Flottenvereins* there was no indication in these publications of other than patriotic interest in the navy. The list of authors shows that for the work of persuasion the League drew upon technicians and teachers rather than journalists and industrialists. In fact, the League endeavoured to hide the direct interest of industry in the new bill behind the modest veil of an appropriate nationalism.[124] Since, however, an economic crisis set in by the spring of 1900, the interest of industry in an expansion of naval construction un-

---

[121] The country did not know whether the speech indicated plans for further naval increases or was merely a temporary outburst. The papers at first denied an increase was planned, but changed their tune immediately. The Navy League printed 4,000,000 copies of the speech of the Emperor.

[122] *Die Flotte*, Nos. 5 and 6, May-June, 1900, p. 1.

[123] *Jahrbuch des Flottenvereins*, 1900, p. 12. The *Jahrbuch* was published to answer all important questions in regard to the navy. The contents, very carefully put together, especially after 1900, contained world trade statistics, notes on German shipyards, naval budgets in all countries, etc. The League also published *Überall*, an illustrated magazine for deepening the love of the navy, *Mitteilungen des deutschen Flottenvereins*, and *Jahresberichte des Flottenvereins*, a periodical report for the executives of the League. A few of the latter for the period after 1906 are available but they fail to yield a great deal of information because they were too general. The *Jahrbuch* openly advertised the *Berliner Neueste Nachrichten* as a pro-navy daily.

[124] *Vide supra*, pp. 171 f.

doubtedly increased. Tirpitz welcomed the League's money and propaganda as an adjunct to his efforts, and his Press Bureau certainly supplied material to it.

The Navy League did not intend to disband as soon as the law of 1900 was passed. Its rôle should be that of "a loyal Eckard, always on the watch to see that the great national enthusiasm, which has flared up so brightly, may become an eternal fire upon whose burning the future of the Empire depends."[125] Scarcely a year after the passage of the naval law of 1900 the crisis in industry led the Navy League to campaign for more ships. It either took the initiative or at the instigation of Tirpitz sounded out the country in August and again in November. Probably the initiative was its own since Tirpitz would scarcely have approached the Reichstag so soon again for ships. The *Berliner Neueste Nachrichten* inaugurated a press drive for overseas cruisers.[126] Otto Prince of Salm-Horstmar, president of the League, wrote to Tirpitz concerning the needs of industry. By way of emphasizing the persistence of the old in the new Navy League a part of his letter follows:

> I have been asked by men of different parties to initiate a movement in the Reichstag to petition the government that, in view of the depression and of the unfavorable condition of trade and the resulting unemployment of many thousands of workers, it should speed up the building of warships.
>
> If the shipbuilding provided for in the last law were hastened as quickly as the German yards could make room for it, many branches of business would receive contracts by which they would not only be kept above water but would also be in a position to employ their workers and to re-employ those they have let go. One of the most important results would be that through the contracts for new warships and the impetus these would give to trade and industry the stock market would rise, many stocks would be saved from ruin, and a consolidation of the market would set in.[127]

---

[125] *Die Flotte*, Nos. 5 and 6, May-June, 1900, p. 1.

[126] Kehr, *op. cit.*, p. 456.

[127] *Ibid.*, Appendix II, p. 457, note 17. It will be seen that the demands of the newspaper and of the letter were not identical. One wished cruisers and the other the hastening of the building programme. This discrepancy serves to illustrate that building and not policy was the important thing at this time.

As in 1899 this effort of 1901 by the Navy League ended in defeat. Tirpitz, seeing no hope of serving industry in this way, discouraged agitation. By 1902 the Navy League was again losing members.

The Navy League was almost as a matter of course imperialistic and for popular consumption used all the customary national-imperialistic arguments. Industry joined in, mentioning the share of the workers in the benefits of navalism. At the meeting of the directors and in the general assembly of January, 1900 Count Dürckheim-Montmartin declared that a questionnaire to the large shipyards had shown that at least 75%, perhaps 80%, of the money spent for battleships went into wages.[128]

The true view of the League toward the Boer War and toward England can not easily be stated. Naturally enough events during the Boer War emphasized the need for further naval building. At the time of the seizure of German ships by England (1900) *Die Flotte* wrote:

> The seizure and search of German ships represent nothing less than another demonstration of England's power, which is never weary of showing the world that 'Britannia rules the waves' . . . Moreover, we must learn from this new show of force that we can only take an energetic stand against such attacks on the part of foreign Powers when our demands can be supported in case of necessity by ships and cannon.[129]

One can well imagine that General Keim did not neglect the use of anti-English propaganda and that the thousands who flocked to the public meetings of the Navy League devoured this propaganda along with the rest. After the war *Die Flotte* seemed to take the view that general feeling toward England had changed because England had shown injustice not only to the Boers but to all.[130] The League could not overlook this change, it knew, if it were to continue to appeal to popular interest. It should be recalled, however, that industry for and by itself did not oppose England so much as its propaganda implied. The Krupp works and other firms would willingly have sold arms to England at the time, and, as is shown elsewhere,[131] the *Berliner Neueste Nachrichten* and *Die Post*

[128] *Die Flotte*, No. 1, January, 1900, p. 15.
[129] *Ibid.*, pp. 10-11.
[130] *Ibid.*, July 7, 1903, pp. 118 f.   [131] *Cf.* Chapter VI.

favored naval expansion more than they hated England. As for shipping, writers have exaggerated the harm done to it during the Boer War; it is probable that the rank and file of supporters of the Navy League took the danger to shipping more seriously than the firms themselves. The important fact, however, is that the war furnished the League with ready-made propaganda for navalism and, as usual, feeling toward England suffered both through real and assumed antagonism to her.

Notwithstanding its widespread propaganda the Navy League did not dictate naval policy. It attained its greatest membership and maximum activity in 1900 when its desires coincided with the plan Tirpitz was putting through the Reichstag. In 1902 it failed to procure aid for industry by new laws or by hastening naval building, because at that time political conditions did not favor the programme. When Keim resigned from the League in 1910, he did so because he thought the organization too much the tool of official policy. Presumably he resented the restraint which the Imperial Navy Department exercised and was disappointed in not being able to make the League more popular and more effective.[132] The League always received bitter attacks from the Pan-Germans, who called it an organization representing the plans of the Navy Department. Behind the League, they said, stood all the government officials from lowest to highest as well as Prince Henry of Prussia and scions of all the ruling houses.[133] The statement is true only to the extent that all these persons wished navalism. Industrial interests had double cause for supporting the League; in addition, they knew that a larger navy was already desired in high places and that both the Emperor and Tirpitz were pushing ahead as rapidly as they could. The League and General Keim, however, both helped to mobilize industry and public opinion for the Second Naval Law and their propaganda strengthened greatly the two arguments used widely for this law, those of the economic-industrial need for a battlefleet and of *Machtpolitik*. At the same time the League spread the doctrine of nationalism, the emotional basis needed by the government for its entire programme. In this way it cloaked the interests which it served and aided the government, but it was less the tool of the latter than of the former.

[132] Class, *op. cit.*, pp. 156-7.   [133] *Ibid.*, pp. 80 f.

D. *Colonial Society*

The Colonial Society (*Kolonialgesellschaft*) and the Pan-German League introduce a type of propaganda different from that of any foregoing organizations. Although as notorious as the Navy League, they do not deserve to be classed with it. This difference is not difficult to explain.

Maximilian von Hagen in his book on colonial policy shows that German interest in colonial expansion began as early as the 'seventies.[134] During these years the Central Association for Commercial Geography (*Centralverein für Handelsgeographie*) broke ground for the founding of German colonies; the Associations for Protection of German Interests Abroad (*Vereinigungen zum Schutz deutscher Interessen im Ausland*) were founded; Hasse established in 1879 at Leipzig the Society for Commercial Geography and Colonial Policy (*Verein für Handelsgeographie und Kolonialpolitik*) and the Düsseldorf West German Society for Colonization and Export (*Westdeutscher Verein für Kolonisation und Export*) turned its attention to colonization. Innumerable articles and pamphlets on the subject appeared. In 1882 Baron Hermann von Maltzen, an old colonial pioneer, with the aid of Prince Hohenlohe-Langenburg established at Frankfurt-on-the-Main the German Colonial Association. The organization first acquired importance, however, in the following year when Dr. Friedrich Fabri, author of one of the more famous studies showing Germany's need for colonies,[135] joined it together with more than five hundred other persons. Hagen declared that this society was founded without Bismarck's previous knowledge and " without the financial assistance of a powerful capitalistic group." [136] It appears, however, that Hohenlohe sent a circular to industrial leaders and politicians, se-

[134] Hagen, *Bismarcks Kolonialpolitik* (Stuttgart and Gotha, 1923), Chap. I. More recent works on the subject are, Mary E. Townsend, *Rise and Fall of Germany's Colonial Empire* (New York, 1930), and William O. Aydelotte, *Bismarck and British Colonial Policy: The Problem of South West Africa, 1883-1885* (Philadelphia, 1937); A. J. P. Taylor, *Germany's First Bid for Colonies 1884-5: A Move in Bismarck's European Policy* (London, 1938).

[135] F. Fabri, *Bedarf Deutschland der Kolonien?* (Gotha, 1879).

[136] Hagen, *op. cit.*, p. 37.

curing for the project the moral support of seventy-one important Free-Conservatives, among them Baron Stumm, Count Frankenburg, Count Stolberg and Baron von Varnbüler, as well as several others. Hohenlohe wrote Baron Stumm, as if counting on attracting him with the remark, that he believed colonization would prove "the best lighting-rod for the Social Democratic danger." [136a] Hohenlohe-Langenburg was president and in addition to Dr. Fabri the Association boasted as members Johannes Miquel, then burgomaster of Frankfurt, Rudolf Bennigsen, Gustav Freytag, Rolfs and Schliemann, the explorers, and many others.[137] Scientific organizations and the Chamber of Commerce of Frankfurt supported it. In 1885 the Colonial Association moved its headquarters to Berlin and shortly thereafter became one of the most active propaganda organizations in Germany.

The organization did not intend to set up a practical colonial policy for the government to execute. Being without money or capitalistic support, as Miquel pointed out, it aimed to further the interest in and understanding for a colonial policy, to establish a focus, free from party or group interest, for the various groups interested in colonial expansion. It also hoped to solve the emigration question by setting up through private means trading posts and settlements in German colonies.[138] Unlike Karl Peter's Society for German Colonization, founded in 1884, the Colonial Association preferred to educate the public to undertake immediate and visible colonial action. The Association expected also to promote commerce; but the Hanseatic cities did not sympathize with the organization, both because they divined that Bismarck would pay no attention to so general a programme, and because they were already engaged in individual efforts at colonization. Likewise West and South German protectionists shunned it because they desired a national

---

[136a] Hellwig, *op. cit.*, pp. 336-8.

[137] Thus the foundation stone of the organization was the old Liberalism and nationalism of the National Liberals, whose leaders these men then were.

[138] E. Prager, *Die deutsche Kolonialgesellschaft, 1882-1907* (Berlin, 1908), pp. 17, 20 ff. H. H. Meier of Bremen, for example, pointed out to the Colonial Union that it must avoid supporting factories in colonies and must not encourage Germans to settle where they would be less able to get on than in North America (p. 20).

movement for colonization led by the government.[139] This lack of support left the Association rather weak and made it impossible to give it a more practical programme. Fabri, who remained dissatisfied with the movement, tried to combine Peter's group with his own. When he did so in 1887 by the formation of the Colonial Society, theory and practice were united.

It has often been observed that imperialism in the first instance is not born of economic pressure.[140] The Colonial Society and also the Pan-German League were not conceived by those whose interests immediately demanded expansion, raw materials, new markets, and new capital outlets. The work of organizing these two groups— and many others like them not discussed here—was largely carried on by geographers and explorers, ex-military and naval officers, a few merchants, and a small group of theorists, to whom the emigration of German people abroad, expansion of German markets, German prestige and development represented true problems for the future. At the same time these people displayed a growing restlessness over the questions of imperialism. Lüderitz and Adolf Woermann were already active in Africa and the Hanseatic cities presented Bismarck in 1883 with a memorandum from the Hamburg Chamber of Commerce asking for protection on the Gold Coast, since " it no longer corresponds to the position of the German Empire that its subjects abroad should have to rely on the protection of foreign Powers." [141] The memorandum brought action from a government previously disinclined to mingle in colonial affairs.[141a] Some concern about England's future policy contributed. Whereas England had been friendly to Germany before, she appeared now more eager to draw her colonial lands together and to exclude or take advantage of the foreigner.[142] Great commercial and industrial

---

[139] Hermann Oncken, *Rudolf von Bennigsen* (Stuttgart and Leipzig, 1910), II, 411.

[140] *Cf.* Leonard Woolf, *Empire and Commerce in Africa* (London, 1919).

[141] Hagen, *op. cit.*, p. 159.

[141a] Recent research indicates that Bismarck was cautious rather than opposed to colonies (Townsend, *op. cit.*, pp. 60 ff.). This is borne out by Hohenlohe, who wrote to Stumm in 1882 that Maltzan had found support in Berlin for the founding of a colonial organization (Hellwig, *op. cit.*, pp. 336-7). In 1884 Stumm wrote of a colonial policy as being the " *Gemeingut* " of the government (*ibid.*, p. 339).

[142] Poschinger, *op. cit.*, I, 274. Adolph Woermann at least thought so.

interests as yet remained silent. The *Kolonialzeitung* established in 1884 featured colonial news and information more suited to missionary societies than to big business.

In the 'nineties the character of the Colonial Society changed rapidly. The few thousand members of 1887, organized into one hundred and eight local groups, had grown by 1897 to 23,500 members divided into two hundred and fifty-six local societies. The Society proved especially popular in the great industrial regions along the Rhine from Düsseldorf to Mühlhausen and in Saxony and Silesia. In the port cities, notably Hamburg and Danzig, there were large memberships.[143] Only the agricultural regions of North Germany and the eastern parts of Prussia afforded few local groups. The members of the executive committee included important industrialists like Friedrich Hammacher of the Ruhr, Wilhelm Oechelhäuser of the Continental Gas Company in Dessau, and Krupp; von der Heydt, banker, high government officials like Poehlmann, *Oberregierungsrat* at Metz, Dr. Hamm, *Oberreichsanwalt* at Leipzig, were also among them. Woermann, founder and owner of the government subsidized East Africa Line, served on the committee, as did the Prince of Wied, Ernst Hasse, and Major Wissmann, all members of other societies. Teachers, explorers, exservice men and ex-officers, professions to be found in every organization of this kind, formed the ranks.

The list of members was imposing, designed to represent most of the special interests as well as all classes and castes of the Empire. The directorate of the organization interlocked with directorates of similar groups.[144] The connections of Hasse and the Prince of

[143] *Cf.* Map, *Kolonialzeitung*, No. 41, October 9, 1897, p. 415.

[144] Class, *op. cit.*, criticizes the Colonial Society for not wishing to oppose the government and for leaving that to others, for example, to the Pan-Germans (p. 85). There follows an analysis of the membership of the directorate of the Society for the year 1898-1899. The list is taken from *Kolonialzeitung*, No. 27, July 7, 1898.

President: Albrecht Duke of Mecklenburg-Schwerin, Landowner, Member of the Pan-German League.

Vice-President: Georg Albrecht, Bremen, Scientist.

Otto Ammon, Berlin, Engineer and specialist in race questions, Member of the Directorate of the Pan-German League.

Prince von Arenberg, Aachen, Army officer, Attaché, Probably also iron and steel interests, Member of the Reichstag for the Center, Head of the

Wied are known. Prince von Arenberg and Arnim-Muskau were active in more than one propaganda society. The Duke of Mecklenburg served as honorary president and figurehead. He came from a stronghold of Junkerdom, but his support was not typical of the Junkers.

In 1895 the Colonial Society set forth its aims as follows:

1. To turn the national ardor toward German colonization and to spread in ever-growing circles the knowledge of the necessity for it;
2. To further the practical solution of colonial questions;
3. To arouse and support German national colonial undertakings;

Berlin branch of the Colonial Society until forced out by Peters in 1890 over the naval issue.

Arnhold, Berlin, Merchant.

Count von Arnim-Muskau, Silesia, Iron and coal interests (?), Member of the Reichstag, Member of the Directorate of the Pan-German League, and had an "open hand" for it (Class, p. 46).

Dr. Auler, Dortmund, School director.

Rudolf von Bennigsen, Hanover, National Liberal party leader, President of Hanover, Member of the Reichstag.

Bojunga, Hanover, Lawyer, National Liberal.

Von Bockelmann, Danzig, Teacher.

Bormann, Berlin, *Oberregierungsrat.*

Von Brandt, Wiesbaden, Diplomat, Former Minister to Peking.

Clemm, Ludwigshaven, Pfalz, Member of the Reichstag.

Douglas, Berlin, Mine owner and speculator.

Eschenburg, Lübeck, Senator.

Hamm, Leipzig, *Oberreichsanwalt.*

Hammacher, Ruhr, Iron and steel and mine interests, Member of the Reichstag, Newspaper owner.

Dr. Hasse, Berlin and Leipzig, Professor, Member of the Reichstag, Member of the Directorate of the Pan-German League.

Hespers, Cologne, High Catholic prelate.

Von der Heydt, Berlin, Banker.

Von Hofmann. ?

Baron von Höningen-Huehne, Silesia, Ex-army officer.

Haffmann, Schwerin, Bureaucrat, Director of the post.

Klupfel, Essen, Banker.

Kretzschmar, Dresden, Manufacturer.

Von Kusserow, Coblentz, Diplomat, Member of the Navy League, Son-in-

4. To work for the best solution of the questions connected with German emigration;

5. To hold and strengthen the economic and cultural dependence of the Germans abroad upon the fatherland;

6. To create a center for all the efforts, now separated, which are directed toward these goals.[145]

If these aims seem vague and show little improvement over those of the earlier period, they become clearer if one reads the editorials and articles in the *Kolonialzeitung,* journal of the Society. The opening article in 1895 regretted the lack of colonial progress dur-

---

law of Hansemann.   Bismarck said that Kusserow led him into colonial troubles. (Kusserow was an important Free-Conservative also, thus linking the Free Conservatives with colonialism.).

Liebert, Governor of German East Africa.

Livonius, Vice-Admiral.

Dr. Mehnert, Dresden, Important agrarian leader in Saxony.

Mollmann, Westphalia, Merchant (?).

Oechelhäuser, Dessau, Gas Company, Plantation owner in Kamerun, Director of the German East Africa Company, Member of the Reichstag, Member of the National Chamber of Commerce.

Pahde, Crefeld, Teacher.

Karl Peters, London, Explorer and colonist in East Africa.

Count Pfeil, Silesia, Explorer and co-worker with Peters.

Poehlmann, Metz, Bureaucrat.

Poensgen, Düsseldorf.

Prosch, Breslau, Lawyer.

Ritter, Saxony.

Sachse, Berlin, Bureaucrat, Executive Vice-President of the Colonial Society.

Schering, Vice-Admiral.

Schwabe, Consul.

Count von Schweinitz ?   Frequent speaker and writer for the Society.

Siegle, Stuttgart, Member of the Reichstag.

Simon, Bureaucrat, Later Foreign Minister and Supreme Court Justice.

O'Swald, Hamburg, Senator, Member of the Navy League.

Baron von Tucher, Nürnberg, Brewer.

Vohsen, Consul.

Prince of Wied, Rhineland, Head of the Navy League, Industrial interests.

Von Wissmann, Major, Member of the Navy League, ex-Governor of West Africa.

Woermann, Hamburg, Shipping, Member of the Navy League.

145 *Kolonialzeitung,* No. 1, January 5, 1895, p. 2.

ing the Caprivi era, but announced that more than half the Reichstag desired an active colonial party. It emphasized the need to prepare for the time when Germany must extend her colonial territory. The Society rejoiced at Hohenlohe's opening speech to the Reichstag in the fall of 1894 and hoped to make the most of his lead.[146] The *Kolonialzeitung* criticized Caprivi and welcomed Hohenlohe as follows:

> Whoever has followed the development of our Society in recent years will remember the time when the danger arose that a carefully built up unity would fall to pieces, especially when the Zanzibar Treaty in 1890 gave such a severe blow to our colonial movement. A deep-seated feeling, one can well say a bitterness, was felt by all groups of colonial friends and under Caprivi many would like to have given up the whole thing in spite of the fact that colonies are more lasting than ministers. This crisis was successfully weathered and Hohenlohe has approached the colonial question in quite another spirit.[147]

In taking this stand the Society believed that it was unreservedly furthering the highest welfare of the country. It believed that the ability to plan and execute colonial policy measured the degree of ripeness and power of a people. Germany, it held, was asleep and must be aroused to this work.[148] Her need for colonies was said to arise from the following circumstances: 1) between 1830 and 1890 her population had greatly increased, leading to an annual emigration of 600,000 persons with an estimated capital loss annually of two hundred million marks; 2) German industry had no sure markets abroad for its manufactured goods, as did the states with colonial holdings; 3) German experts and technicians had to work abroad for others because they lacked a place where their skill could accrue to German benefit alone; 4) the German people had as much energy and power as had formerly found expression in great undertakings such as national unification, but lacked an outlet for it; 5) German naval power had " necessarily increased "; but it cost much money and had little to do; 6) Germany needed " greater security

[146] *Ibid.*, No. 1, January 5, 1895, p. 1. See also Chapter IV.

[147] *Ibid.*, No. 24, June 13, 1896, p. 185.

[148] *Ibid.*, Supplement XII, May 1, 1897, " Die koloniale Bewegung Deutschlands, eine nationale."

for our trade and markets for our industry so that even a part of the eight hundred million marks which Germany pays out annually to foreign colonies for tropical products can be saved for the fatherland." [149] In other words German colonial enterprise, according to the *Kolonialzeitung,* followed historical necessity; it was not an adventure or a plaything. " We seek colonial possessions to further and consolidate our *Volksleben* and our *Volkskraft,*" it wrote. Many of these reasons could not have withstood logical analysis and did not deserve the attention of persons like Hohenlohe, Hammacher, and von der Heydt.[150] Probably these men did not take them very seriously [151] but were accustomed to repeat the argument as a means of securing aid from the government and the Reichstag in the form of subsidies for new shipping lines, railroad reductions to the ports, help in building colonial railroads, and other concessions desired by industry. The *Kolonialzeitung* with its modest circulation of 30,000 [152] tried to win from the German public support for a national undertaking. The cold logic of necessity did not move it; rather it used all available arguments to convince the country that political and cultural development, as well as economic growth, demanded colonies. It shared the attitude of the colonialists in the Radical-Socialist party in France, who were primarily moved by the idea of *" la plus grande France "* and only secondarily by economic considerations.[153]

Colonial agitators assumed that German character was inherently

[149] *Ibid.*, Supplement XV, June 12, 1897, p. 61.

[150] German emigration was negligible after the upswing of 1896-1900 set in and absorbed more workers; German capital continued to find markets abroad in other colonies than German, as did that of all growing countries. That German colonies were expensive and did not pay well was known in the Reichstag; that German investments throve in British colonies was also known.

[151] In Carl Fürstenberg's memoirs, for example, one gets very little echo of any such propaganda sentiments. As a banker he invested wherever his money made most profit, whether in German or in foreign enterprises. *Cf.* also Siemens' projects.

[152] *Kolonialzeitung,* No. 1, January 5, 1899, p. 2.

[153] Bertha Leaman, *The Radical-Socialist Party* (Unpublished dissertation in the University of Chicago Libraries, 1935). She shows that Delcassé had to bring all pressure he could to bear on French bankers to put money in Morocco.

too cautious for colonial policy, too given to rationalization and "penny wise" measures. Hence the German did not and would not act until after the golden opportunity had passed. This inertia could be overcome only by the careful cultivation, the gradual growth of national pride. The colonial journal wrote:

> This teaches us [i. e. this pride] to esteem our country and to put the good of the whole above everything. It gives us the self-confidence from which alone quick and purposeful action springs. It shows us the need for future development of the Fatherland and prevents our compatriots, whom the struggle for existence or German *Wanderlust* draws away to foreign countries, from casting off their nationality, their German souls, like a useless piece of clothing, to the disadvantage of Germany and to their own disgrace." [154]

The Society tried at first to emphasize the larger view of the question and refused to dwell on details, especially those of the diplomatic situation. It trusted to the government to protect the honor and immediate interests of the country, while it advised the public in a general way on future policy. Hence in 1899 regarding the Samoan question the *Kolonialzeitung* took no definite stand, indulged in no heated propaganda, but printed information about the islands of a sort likely to illustrate to the public the economic value of the territory.[155] In the same way its championship of railroad building in Africa, of plantation settlements, of colonization took the form of descriptive articles, often written by scientists. Beginning in 1899 the *Kolonialzeitung* added supplements to its main editions and also published *Beiträge zur Kolonialpolitik und Kolonialwirtschaft*. In these pamphlets were to be found countless detailed articles on the German colonies, their trade, their schools and missions, their economy, and the like. These articles appealed to national interest and pride. Their propaganda, like that of *Nauticus*, Tirpitz' naval journal, was more subtle than that of the Navy League, although it was designed for the petit-bourgeoisie. On the other hand, in a crisis the Society did not always adhere

[154] *Kolonialztg.*, No. 14, April 6, 1899, pp. 119-20, "Deutsches Volkstum und deutsche Kolonialpolitik."

[155] *Ibid.*, No. 22, June 1, 1899, p. 188, and *passim*. As has been indicated, the territory was not extremely valuable to Germany.

14

to its principle. For example, as early as 1894 in the Samoan affair the general assembly of the Society, as well as local groups, embarrassed Caprivi by resolutions demanding that he protect German rights " in the oldest German colony." [156] A few days later Prince Hohenlohe-Langenburg presented to the Emperor a memorandum in which he stressed the general agitation over Samoa and urged him if possible to assure to Germany possession of Samoa.[157] Similar resolutions appeared during the Boer War.

If one grants that the Society with its modest membership influenced pre-war Germany—and one must do so—,[158] it is worthwhile to pursue in more detail the recommendations of the organization to its supporters. This influence can be traced only by comparing the views of the Society's members with those expressed elsewhere and with the policies actually executed. It is also possible to check the similarity between the ideas of the press of the Society and those of the general public. Since these comparisons will be referred to later from time to time,[159] it is profitable to look more closely at the *Kolonialzeitung*.

The Society early advocated naval increase. Already in 1893 it petitioned the Reichstag for cruisers. In 1895 it asked for a station in China.[160] It had a special propaganda division which controlled and centralized its naval activity. In every city it emphasized the peculiar connection between the local situation and world trade. In this way the colonial group was " more and more forced out of its rôle as an organization sponsoring practical activity in the col-

[156] Vagts, *op. cit.*, p. 740.

[157] *Loc. cit.*

[158] Apparently Caprivi asked for information on the Society in 1894, since Kayser drew up a note for him on the day after Hohenlohe's memorandum to the Emperor in which he said that he thought the membership to be about ten thousand, including hundreds of officers (army and navy). Dr. Vagts has kindly pointed out to the writer that here exists one of the few signs of the fact that the Foreign Office paid some heed to the colonial enthusiasts.

[159] In the treatment of public opinion in the next and last chapters, as well as in many of the foregoing pages, the views of men and groups will be found in close agreement with views expressed by colonialists and the *Kolonialzeitung*.

[160] *Cf.* section on the Pan-German League *infra* and Kehr, *op. cit.*, p. 97.

onies to one carrying on propaganda." [161] In 1895 the colonialists were citing copiously from popular works to point out the need for the navy. Uhl wrote one of these studies, *Deutschlands Seemacht,* for the Bamberg branch of the Society. He drew special attention to the early activity of the Society in the matter of naval expansion.[162] On February 7, 1896, the day on which Marschall announced in the Reichstag the intention of the government to introduce a new naval bill, the Berlin branch of the Society held a large meeting under Prince von Arenberg [163] and Count Schweinitz to support naval expansion. Karl Peters talked on Germany's position as a world Power as did Eiffe, a merchant, who had lately traveled in South Africa and advocated Germany's building a navy, apparently because he would like to have seen more of the German flag there. The meeting resolved to support the popular assembly which Hasse of the Pan-German League was holding to arouse the *Volksseele*.[164] The entire programme exemplified close coöperation with the government in support of a project which the Society had much at heart. This coöperation is also manifested by the facts that Vice-Admiral Senden influenced the Duke of Mecklenburg to support the bill [165] and that, just after the Hollmann naval plans were defeated in 1897, von Kusserow offered the Chancellor the aid of the Society.[166]

With the outbreak of the South African War the *Kolonialzeitung* redoubled its efforts for the navy. The issues of the periodical during the last part of 1899 contained frequent discussions of the naval question. Almost every number contained a supplement of articles by marine technicians and reprints from *Nauticus* and from the Emperor's speeches. The arguments lacked originality. The supplements obviously tried to arouse the German people to appreciate its duty to the country. The colonialists admired Tirpitz,

[161] Kehr, *op. cit.*, p. 99, citing *Jahresbericht der Kolonialgesellschaft,* 1898, p. 5.

[162] *Kolonialzeitung,* No. 26, June 29, 1895, p. 202.

[163] It is interesting to note that there was a von Arenberg in the colonial group of the French Radical Socialist party. Apparently the family had interests in the industry of Alsace-Lorraine.

[164] *Kolonialztg.*, No. 7, February 15, 1896, p. 50.

[165] Kehr, *op. cit.*, p. 57.

[166] *Ibid.*, p. 98.

who expressed and carried out their convictions, and were eager to aid his work. And Tirpitz welcomed their support.

The propaganda for a navy did not preclude other agitation. On the contrary, events in South Africa and England had much to do with convincing the Society of the need for naval expansion. The Society had bitterly regretted the " loss " of Zanzibar to England in 1890, and early in January, 1895, it turned its attention to Delagoa Bay. The *Kolonialzeitung* cited with satisfaction an article from the *Volkstem,* a Pretoria bi-monthly newspaper, which had declared :

> The appearance of German flags and ships in Delagoa Bay is a great source of gratitude and we hope that the German government will lend a willing ear to the press and by actively supporting German interests in South Africa indirectly support those of the Transvaal . . . The increase of the German in- fluence has given English prestige a staggering blow and in- spired the sister South African Republics with new courage.[167]

This article was followed by quotations from the *African Review* of January 12, 1895, which wrote of Germany's increasing activity. The *Kolonialzeitung* concluded that Britain's acquisition of Delagoa Bay would fatally injure German interests ; the German govern- ment, it warned, must not let this happen.[168] Shortly afterward a leading article recognized that the tide of British imperialism could only be stemmed by safeguarding the independence of the Transvaal. The article urged the government to act because the Germans abroad were not likely to organize even in the Transvaal into a compact, aggressive group.[169] In the same year the Society became concerned over the English development companies. One company, the Kar- askoma Exploring and Prospecting Syndicate, Limited, had already secured large concessions in German South West Africa. The So- ciety wished to know why more was not officially published about this company, what were its actual holdings, its activities, leader- ship, its relations to German finance. The group was clearly dis- turbed over the situation in regard to the company and feared that

---

[167] *Kolonialztg.*, No. 1, January 5, 1895, p. 4.

[168] *Ibid.*, No. 5, February 2, 1895, p. 33.

[169] *Ibid.*, No. 10, March 9, 1896, pp. 73-4. An article in No. 27, July 6, 1895, p. 209 is in the same vein with even more earnest recommmenda- tions to the government that Britain be opposed in further annexations.

through the activities of the latter English interests would endeavour to secure the eastern strip of the colony. Loss of Greater Namaqualand, wrote the *Kolonialzeitung,* would hinder Germany's development of the whole.[170] Colonialists even brought the matter up in the Reichstag.

The *Kolonialzeitung* showed alarm over these troubles well before the Jameson Raid.[171] It recognized Rhodes as a menace to German interests in South Africa and called him the mortal enemy of German colonial endeavour. It feared that the de Beers Company controlled by Rhodes operating through the South West Africa Company might get control of German mines in South West Africa.[172] It widely publicized Rhodes' control over public opinion in London and South Africa and the extent of his power.[173] When the events of late 1895 and early 1896 occurred the *Kolonialzeitung* immediately sided with the Boers, as it had already hinted that it would do. It applauded the Krüger Despatch and sent a long letter to Chancellor Hohenlohe expressing approval and gratitude.[174] In their public meetings and in their press the friends of colonial expansion emphasized the present and future economic interests of Germany in the Transvaal.[175]

When excitement over the Jameson affair had died down, the *Kolonialzeitung* turned again to the Portuguese colonies, where it supposed England to be intriguing for control. If only Germany, it lamented, possessed a navy to uphold her interests here.[176] When rumors came that Germany had signed a treaty with England over

[170] *Ibid.,* No. 11, March 16, 1895, pp. 81-2. This will be referred to later. *Cf.* also Lovell, *Struggle in South Africa, 1875-1899* (New York, 1934).

[171] See article by Blind on the precarious position of the Transvaal, *ibid.,* No. 47, November 23, 1895, p. 370.

[172] *Ibid.,* No. 16, March 19, 1900, pp. 49-50.

[173] *Ibid.,* No. 21, May 24, 1900. A list of the papers he controlled was given. The articles on Rhodes were written by Dr. Passarge, who appears to have been well versed in South African affairs.

[174] *Ibid.,* No. 2, January 11, 1896, pp. 9-10. Another article in the same number emphasized that the Boers must remain independent.

[175] *Ibid.,* No. 4, January 25, 1896, pp. 25-6. Public meeting in Berlin, January 1, 1896.

[176] *Ibid.,* No. 35, August 28, 1897, p. 348.

the Portuguese colonies, it strongly disapproved,[177] especially in case England had been given a free hand in Delagoa Bay. The *Kolonialzeitung* complained that part of the German press and the English and German owners of gold mines' stock seemed to be in collusion against the Boers. This collusion, it said, indicated treasonable coöperation with Britain, of which Germans should be ashamed.[178] Were they not aware of Chamberlain's ambitions and of England's violations of treaties all over Africa? [179] Did they not know that England would terminate her trade treaty with Germany and would eventually close the British colonies to outside trade, thus initiating an economico-political struggle for markets? [180] In that case Germany would badly need a navy and a policy of Power. If Germans did not appreciate these dangers, they must be awakened to them. Germany must try to make her colonies so attractive that Germans would settle and invest in them instead of in British colonies.[181] The *Kolonialzeitung* insisted that Germany must formulate a policy which would aid colonial development and reduce dependence on British finance.[182]

Together with the fear of England, the *Kolonialzeitung* felt that Germany must " be " something, must " do " something to promote and protect Germans and German interests overseas. The supporters of a colonial policy formed the advance guard for calling the attention of economic groups to colonies, just as they did for arousing the interest of the government and the nation as a whole in them. In November 1899 the *Kolonialzeitung* cited from an article as follows:

[177] *Ibid.*, No. 36, September 8, 1898, p. 319. *Cf. infra*, Chapter V.

[178] *Ibid.*, No. 16, April 21, 1898, p. 140.

[179] *Ibid.*, No. 5, February 3, 1898, pp. 39-41.

[180] *Ibid.*, No. 33, August 14, 1897, p. 325. This is a good example of the fear felt throughout Germany over the result of the Canadian tariffs and subsequent termination of the Anglo-German commercial treaty. *Cf.* Chapter V.

[181] *Ibid.*, No. 30, July 24, 1897, p. 296. Germans recognized that many emigrants preferred to live in British colonies and that money was often safer or more unhampered under British rule than under German. There was also general recognition that English colonies were not likely to unite closely with England in tariff union, but others preferred to ignore or doubt this (*ibid.*, No. 25, June 20, 1896, Supplement, 1-2).

[182] *Ibid.*, No. 2, January 12, 1899, p. 11.

It is not very flattering to the enterprising spirit of the Germans that British capital, and capital under Rhodes' influence to boot, has been the first to bring economic life into our colony [South West Africa], while German companies, above all the German Colonial Society for South West Africa, richly endowed with munificent gifts, have up to now exercised a quite unfruitful activity.[183]

Or again:

The anxiety, not to say penny-wise foolishness of German capital, which should see further into the future, is above all to be deplored. What has our industry, which has long lived from the fleshpots, done for the development of our colonies? Apart from a few admirable exceptions, it has made no noteworthy sacrifice, if money which can be realized only at some future period can be called sacrifice. Any list of the stockholders in a German colonial company would give an idea of the small share of industry; for while industry is ready to do a certain business with the colonies, it will risk nothing. Also the great bank capital which lives on the fat of European business is not, with few exceptions, to be had for promising colonial undertakings which do not bring a large and immediate return.[184]

Although the Colonial Society was acting in an industrial and capitalistic setting and in a time of great industrial prosperity, these expressions of sentiment leave the impression of nationalistic idealism rather than of materialism. The Boer War broke out just as this feeling took root in the country.

The war heightened the fear of England and stimulated the colonialists to demand immediate action. However the war might turn out, they argued, German colonies, especially South West Africa, would be endangered. If the Boers lost, they would emigrate in large numbers into German territory. If England lost, she would endeavour to acquire other sections of South Africa. The government was urged to station more troops in South West Africa. Wherever Germans and English come in contact, warned the *Kolonialzeitung*, the English dominate; they must be turned back and

---

[183] *Ibid.*, No. 46, November 16, 1899, pp. 456-7. The *Kolonialztg.*, denied the truth of this but implied that it was worthy of consideration and was symptomatic.

[184] *Ibid.*, No. 35, August 28, 1897, p. 348.

the Boers too must be restrained from entering German territory.[185]

When conditions grew worse for the Boers, the Society showed concern for all German activity in Africa. It brought up the problem of German South West Africa again and again. There were British interests in the northern part of the colony and the Boers would pour into the southern, it said. " Germany must find a way to settle this vital question," urged the Society's journal.[186] The Society also considered British influence in German South East African trade too large. Even with an increase in the gross amount of trade with this colony, the German percentile share was decreasing in favor of Zanzibar.[187] Hence Germany, wrote the *Kolonialzeitung,* must reduce the Zanzibar trade as much as possible in favor of the mother country. The journal in 1899 redoubled its efforts in favor of railroad construction. Oechelhäuser, one of the founders of the German East Africa Company and a director of the Society, wrote many articles on railroads. He especially interested himself in the East African Central Railroad. He thought the road necessary because the English had already completed six hundred kilometers of the Mombassa-Ugandi road, which was capturing the trade from the interior of the German colony. He and other colonialists called the immediate construction of an East African railroad a " national question." [188] They also wanted new railroads and extensions in South West Africa to open up the mining regions and thought that the government could afford to guar-

---

[185] *Ibid.*, No. 2, January 11, 1900, p. 10. This is excellent evidence of the nature of the Boer championship, the wish to defend the Boers in the Transvaal, but not to desire them in German colonies if they would endanger German control. The difficulty was that there were almost no Germans in the German colony; hence it could easily become Boer or British so far as a majority was concerned.

[186] *Ibid.*, No. 37, September 13, 1900, pp. 426-7, and succeeding issues.

[187] *Ibid.*, No. 10, March 8, 1900, pp. 93-4.

[188] *Ibid.*, No. 35, August 31, 1899, p. 313 was a good example. There were many others. Oechelhäuser had secured the aid of the *Deutsche Bank* for the Central Railroad in 1894. In 1895 the Colonial Office and the East Africa Company made a treaty to prepare plans for the road and Mendelssohn and Company, Delbrück, Leo and Company, Heydt, Kersten and Company were party to this treaty. The government and the Reichstag, however, in spite of many speeches in favor of the road, hedged and the plans were not carried out.

antee the investment. The Society repeatedly blamed the government for its near-sighted neglect of this development.

From South African questions the colonialists turned their attention to events in North Africa. " The time is not far-distant, wrote the *Kolonialzeitung,* when a foothold in the Mediterranean for Germany as a point of security for her civilizing activity and commercial power will be necessary. Cyrenaica would be quite suit-' able." [189] The colonialists feared that France would control Tripoli and the caravan routes from Chad Lake and shut off German access to these areas.[190] They wished, in addition to a sphere of interest or a possession on the Mediterranean, to obtain a post on Chad Lake and freedom to use the caravan routes. Fear of France was further expressed in articles on Morocco. The German colonialists regarded German interests and prospects in Morocco as too great to allow the French to endanger them.[191]

The publicists of the colonialists were surveying the entire African scene in order to make clear the pressing need for action. They did not desire the German government merely to protect during the war what Germans had already acquired, but pleaded for a thoughtful and far-sighted regard for Germany's future. In view of subsequent history the economic value of the German colonies seems hardly to have merited all the concern displayed; for German material interests lay outside her colonies even more than in them. German investments in non-German areas in Africa, apart from Egypt, already amounted to one billion marks. Territorial acquisition had not seemed necessary to economic gain; but the colonialists complained that sufficient German money was not being invested

[189] *Ibid.,* No. 15, April 13, 1899, pp. 126 f. This took place even before the South African War.

[190] This fear existed in spite of the fact that France had been willing as early as 1890 to abandon Tripoli to Italy in return for concessions in Tunis (and eventually did so by the terms of the Tripoli-Morocco Agreement in 1900) and Italy had been given assurances about Tripoli in the Triple Alliance renewals. These details of diplomatic affairs were unknown to the Society, and if suspected, did not diminish the desire to exploit its fears.

[191] *Ibid.,* No. 22, April 31, 1900, pp. 234-5. It should be noted that the paper printed an article by Dr. Hermann denying the size of German interests in Morocco and pointing out that it would be an adventure for Germany to concern herself there; but this was only one article to many of the other tenor. *Cf.* No. 32, August 8, 1901.

in German colonies. Presumably, the publicists saw beyond to the day when Germany's place in Africa would be strong and well assured politically, culturally, and economically.[192]

It is not necessary to follow the *Kolonialzeitung* into the Moroccan crisis and the period of the Franco-English entente. An effort has been made to indicate merely the general line of approach which the large colonial group represented by this journal took from the beginning of the Hohenlohe era through the Boer War. Colonial questions assumed importance during this general period. The group's interests centered about the German colonies in Africa, which took on particular importance during these years; but they included any area where German *Kolonialpolitik* might succeed. The activities of the Society harmonized with the spirit of the times and stimulated the national interest in colonies and colonial policy. The ideas of the Society were repeated elsewhere; the government made use of its assistance in crucial times; and selfish interests welcomed as a smoke screen its sincere but exaggerated nationalism.

E. *Pan-German League*

When the Pan-German League (*Alldeutscher Verband*) published in 1910 a commemorative volume, Heinrich Class, the director, wrote a brief preface in which occur these words:

> When upon the publication of this book we look back over our work, we ask ourselves the question whether the endeavour of those who have labored in the cause of the Pan-Germans has not been in vain and whether it has found its justification in the result. The answer can be found in a comparison of the state of public opinion twenty years ago and today in those fields which we have tilled. We do not need to show in detail the changes, for example, which have taken place in the understanding of the question of our naval armament, of the defense of the East, West and North Marches, in the esteem of Germans living abroad. And we believe that our efforts have, at least, helped to bring these about. We can perhaps be said to have shown public opinion the way in two directions: we have emphasized the fateful importance of Germanism in Austria and

---

[192] For the extent of German investments abroad, *cf.* Supplement XV, pp. 46-7, and No. 12, April 12, 1900, citing a memorandum worked out for the Imperial Naval Bureau.

Hungary for Germanism in the Empire, and we have constantly demanded control of public opinion by the public. No one will deny that this education of public opinion was needed.[193]

This passage gives an indication of the work of the Pan-German League, which in the character of its membership and the nature of its propaganda resembled the Colonial Society. It remains necessary to show how and by whom the work mentioned was done and so far as possible why it needed doing.[194]

The French historian Andler has indicated in his collection of documents pertaining to Pan-Germanism the long historical background of the movement,[195] tracing it through the nineteenth century from Fichte and Hegel to de Lagarde, Bernhardi, Houston Stewart Chamberlain. This survey cannot linger over these writers, but may mention briefly the early influences upon a loyal Pan-German like Heinrich Class. " It is impossible," he writes in his memoirs, " to describe the impression which Treitschke made on my cousin and me . . ." [they were attending his lectures as university students] ; " it was as if everything noble, great and strong had taken form in this man." [196] Later Class read Paul de Lagarde,

[193] *Zwanzig Jahre alldeutscher Arbeit und Kämpfe* (edited by Heinrich Class, 1910), pp. viii f.

[194] A full treatment of the League can be found in Mildred Wertheimer, *The Pan-German League, 1890-1914* (New York, 1924). The official history of the League is by Otto Bonhard, *Geschichte des alldeutschen Verbands* (Leipzig and Berlin, 1920). The present writer has relied largely on the *Alldeutsche Blätter*, publication of the League, *Zwanzig Jahre alldeutscher Arbeit und Kämpfe*, Heinrich Class' memoirs, *Wider den Strom* (Leipzig, 1932), which Miss Wertheimer could not consult, and Andler, *Collection des documents de pangermanisme* (Paris, 1916), assembled to discredit the Pan-Germans. There is supposedly a special publication of the British Foreign Office on the history of Pan-German ideology; but the writer has found no trace of this so far. The most recent publication on the League is Lothar Werner, *Der alldeutsche Verband, 1890-1918* (Berlin, 1925), in no sense a definitive work on the subject.

[195] Andler, *op. cit. Cf.* particularly the introductory volume which gives the early extreme nationalists' thought. Though tenuous at times the line of this thought extends into the present century.

[196] Class, *op. cit.*, p. 41. Treitschke's philosophy of Power was certainly of great importance to the entire period. A short summary of this may be found in Meinecke, *Die Idee der Staatsräson* (Munich and Berlin, 1924), pp. 488-510.

Chamberlain, and Gobineau; he did not know " from which of these three great men I had profited most." At the same time he came into personal contact with Schemann, the disciple of Gobineau and a " pure German idealist." [197] Everything German appealed to Class. The ideological background of his racial nationalism should not be emphasized to the exclusion of other forces. The Pan-German League grew out of the same circumstances as the Colonial Society and reacted against the tardy progress of *Kolonialpolitik*, the Zanzibar-Helgoland Treaty, the lack of naval expansion and of prestige politics. It longed for the great age of Bismarck and desired to weld the politically united Germany into a spiritually united *Nationalstaat*.

The All-German Association, precursor of the Pan-German League, was created in April, 1891, by Karl Peters, Alfred Hugenberg, a professor, and a handful of other serious idealists similar to those who founded the Colonial Society.[198] The Association remained ineffective until Professor Ernst Hasse and his friend Dr. Adolf Lehr took it over in 1893, acting as professional publicists for the organization. Hasse was sincere, completely obsessed by the German nationalist cause, and, although not brilliant, capable of unceasing labor.[199] To aid Hasse his friend, Lehr, a professional man with some business experience, was appointed business manager and editor of the organization's journal, *Alldeutsche Blätter*.[200] From a Zürich school teacher it received the name *Alldeutsch*.[201]

---

[197] Class, pp. 87-8. These men were mystical nationalists. See Chamberlain, *op. cit.*; *Idem, Die Grundlagen des 19. Jahrhundert* (Berlin, 1899); Count Arthur Gobineau, *Essai sur l'égalité des races humaines* (Paris, 1835). In 1893 Schemann founded the Gobineau Society. See Schemann, *Gobineau: eine Biographie* (Strasburg, 1913-6). It will be noted that the '90s saw a decided revival of interest in the subjects of race and nation.

[198] *Zwanzig Jahre*, vi-vii, and Wertheimer, *op. cit.*, Chap. II, pp. 22 f.

[199] For further details of Hasse, see Class, *op. cit.*, pp. 43 ff. and *supra*, Chapter II.

[200] After 1899 the League also published *Odin*, a weekly *Kampfblatt* edited by Hans Korden, former editor of the *Münchener Neueste Nachrichten*. This appeared with special supplements on the Low-German movement and on colonial and naval policy.

[201] Miss Wertheimer distinguishes carefully between *Alldeutsch* and *Allgermanisch*, the former referring to things German, the latter to all-Germanic or Teutonic (Wertheimer, *op. cit.*, Chap. V, pp. 90 f.). The

Although Lehr died in 1902, Hasse continued as head until his death in 1908. Heinrich Class, a lawyer already trained in the ideals of the League and more of a nationalist even than Hasse had been, succeeded him. Class entered the League by way of the German Alliance (*Deutschbund*), another nationalist group organized under the inspiration of Friedrich Lange, editor of the *Tägliche Rundschau* and author of *Reines Deutschtum*.[202] This group was losing ground when Class met Lehr in Berlin and became convinced that the two organizations pursued identical aims. Through the efforts of Class the branch of the German Alliance in Mainz joined in 1897 the Pan-German League. From then on the League grew, largely by means of the absorption of branches of other nationalistic organizations whose general purpose corresponded with that of the League. Class had already turned as anti-Semitic as the League nationalists and had learned from Lange to look upon Caprivi's New Course as a betrayal of the Bismarckian tradition.

The League like the Colonial Society was founded by idealists for a vague general purpose, "the struggle for Germanism." Essentially a propaganda organization rather than a power group, it aimed to force through specific measures. In 1899 Hasse wrote:

> Wide groups of our people, even political circles, still oppose our Pan-German demands because they, in their blind formalism, cannot or will not comprehend that a Pan-German stands, on the one hand, for the development of the German Empire into a national state and therewith the restricting of the non-German population surplus, and, on the other hand, for the preservation of Germanism beyond the boundaries of our Empire, particularly where Germanism finds itself statistically in the minority.[203]

The programme and membership of the organization reveal its idealism. When in 1893 Hasse assumed direction of the League, it had only five thousand members,[204] excluding a few inactive corporate members such as singing societies. The following figures re-

former was a new word and stands for nation-istic, as will be seen subsequently.

[202] Class, *op. cit.*, pp. 30 f.

[203] *Zwanzig Jahre*, p. 69. Speech by Hasse at the annual meeting, August 29-31, 1899.

[204] Wertheimer, *op. cit.*, pp. 54-5, 65.

veal the rapid gain in membership. In the spring of 1896 there were 8,601 members; by the end of the year, 9,443; at the end of 1898, 17,364; at the end of 1900, 21,735; in 1901, 21,924. From 1901 on the rate of increase fell off at about the same number per year. These figures indicate that the 'nineties with the naval programme, the Boer War, and economic expansion awakened public interest in the propaganda of the League. Between 1898 and 1899 membership increased annually by over three thousand, more than in any other year. In 1899 subscribers to *Alldeutsche Blätter* reached 7,781. There were one hundred and fifty-nine local groups and a budget of about sixty thousand marks.[205] The organization remained, however, smaller than the Colonial Society. It included some groups abroad; but these did not contribute to the work of the League in Germany.

A cross-section analysis of the membership in Germany in 1901 shows the academic profession to have led with a total of 5,339 members; business men came next with 4,905; then the liberal professions with 3,760; industrial and crafts workers with 2,673; and farmers only 416.[206] The business men of the group consisted of small merchants or factory owners. The League attracted no Krupp, Oechelhäuser, Woermann, or Heydt; but it included some important members of the Reichstag, for example, Arnim-Muskau of the Colonial Society, Ernst Bassermann, leader of the National Liberals, Barons Gamp and Kardorff of the Free Conservatives, Dietrich Hahn, Heyl zu Herrnsheim, Liebermann von Sonnenberg, anti-Semite, and Count Udo Stolberg-Wernigerode, president of East Prussia and an Agrarian-Conservative leader. Stolberg and Arnim belonged to the executive committee of the League.[207] The business committee of twenty members, apparently more important than the executive committee, consisted of more typical Pan-Germans such as Otto Ammon, Alfred Hugenberg, Dr. Fick, Reismann-Grone, Paul Simons, Dr. Pohl, Dr. Lehmann, Professor Samassa, Dr. Petzoldt. Hugenberg had been employed by the Prussian government for some time as a specialist in questions pertaining to

---

[205] *Alldeutsche Blätter*, No. 20, May 14, 1899.

[206] The above figures represent the twenty-one thousand members whom Miss Wertheimer could trace.

[207] Class, *op. cit.*, p. 43.

East Prussia; later he became chairman of the directorate of the Krupp works in Essen and eventually head of the united chambers of commerce of the region and president of the Mining Association. When he accepted these positions, however, he gave up work in the League; hence his activity in it fell in the time of his academic rather than of his business career.[208] Reismann-Grone, owner of the *Rheinisch-Westfälische Zeitung,* has already been mentioned. An ardent Pan-German and at the same time closely connected with a large industrial region, he undoubtedly used his nationalism to cloak specific economic desires.[209] Fick was a professor living in Switzerland; Paul Simons was a small manufacturer, who fanatically hated Bismarck's successors; Lehmann was a bookseller and publisher, Ammon a physician.[210] Professor Samassa, more prominent than the foregoing, was a publicist. In 1900 he assumed the editorship of the *Alldeutsche Blätter.* Race problems, history and colonial policy particularly interested him and he enjoyed great popularity as a speaker and local organizer. He became indispensable as a publicity agent for the League. Class has written in his memoirs that each of these men impressed him by " national feeling," " idealism," hatred of the post-Bismarckian régime. The manner of thinking of these persons, if not peculiar to Germany, was often found there, especially in the professional classes. Men like the leaders of the Pan-Germans, shut out from any effective political activity, took refuge in visions of a Utopia, which under a new Bismarck *Das Deutschtum* would some day possess.[211] Hence their frequent bitter opposition to the existing régime.

[208] *Ibid.,* pp. 46-7.

[209] *Ibid.,* pp. 47-8. Miss Wertheimer finds Reismann's paper not at all given to Pan-German material (pp. 194-5); but she has apparently examined it for articles on the League, whereas the entire attitude of the owners and editors counted for more. Reismann, for example, was a very active anti-government man during the 'nineties.

[210] *Ibid.,* pp. 45 ff.

[211] The following table gives the especially active membership of the League. It is taken from Class, *op. cit., passim* and from Wertheimer, *op. cit.* Some comparison of intellectual level with that of Fascism and National Socialism is not unwarranted.

Dr. Ernest Hasse, Saxony, Professor of Economics and Politics, ex-army officer, Member of the Reichstag, Member of the Colonial Society.

The League stated its purpose in the original petition presented to Karl Peters in 1890 urging the foundation of a society. This document, the work of Professor Alfred Hugenberg, Dr. Fick, Professor Wislicenus and others, contained the following points:

> It is our wish and intent to create an independent association firmly rooted in the citizenry, a center for all the national aspirations of our people. The first aim of the organization shall be to work for a united, fundamentally patriotic view of life for all citizens in the sense of creating a *national morale*.

In detail the aims of this association shall be:

1. To bring together the nationally-minded citizens without consideration of party in the thought that the accomplished fact of the unification of the German race is only the beginning of a larger national development, that is, the development of the German people into a cultural and political world power, as the British people already are and the Russian people doubtless will become.

Dr. Adolf Lehr, Wiesbaden, Professor of Philology, Member of the Reichstag.

Count Stolberg-Wernigerode, Prussia, President of East Prussia, Member of the Reichstag and President of the Reichstag.

Count von Arnim-Muskau, Army officer, Member of the Colonial Society.

Alfred Hugenberg, Hanover, Bureaucrat.

Reismann-Grone, Essen, Newspaper owner.

Paul Simons, Elberfeld, Manufacturer.

J. F. Lehmann, Munich, Bookseller, Publisher of Pan-German literature.

Dr. von Tischer, Augsburg, Member of the Reichstag.

Dr. Arendt, Berlin, Member of the Reichstag.

Ernst Bassermann, Mannheim, Lawyer, Leader of the National Liberals in the Reichstag.

Dr. Beumer, Heavy industry, Member of the Reichstag (1901-1907).

Eugen von Brockhausen, Pomerania, Bureaucrat, Member of the Reichstag, Member of the Landtag.

Count Dohna-Schlodien, East Prussia, Member of the Reichstag.

Baron von Gamp, Berlin and Pomerania, Owner of a knight's holding, Bureaucrat, Member of the Reichstag.

Dr. Dietrich Hahn, Hanover, Member of the Reichstag and Landtag, Director of the Agrarian League.

Baron Heyl zu Herrnsheim, Hesse, Landowner and industrialist, Member of the Reichstag.

Karl Peters, Berlin and London, Explorer, Member of the Colonial Society.

Dr. Adolf Fick, Zürich, Physician, had lived in South Africa.

2. To begin an energetic colonial policy for the acquisition of wider colonial possessions and the organization of our emigration.

3. To widen interest in the overseas commercial and civilizing tasks of Germany to the fullest extent.

4. By the firm presentation of the views expressed here against indifference and indolence, against a superficial cosmopolitanism and against the widely over-rated world position of Germany today and the value of one-sided continental politics, to make our desires finally felt on the side of the parties of the government.[212]

Vague as they seem these aims became the primary ones of Pan-German endeavour. In no place do the Pan-Germans define "national-mindedness," "national morale," "superficial cosmopolitanism," "larger national development." "Germanism" and the "struggle for Germanism" lacked tangibility; they were emotional phrases. The Pan-Germans like the Colonial Society thought that the German public must be aroused to a more poignant emotion. They looked forward to a revival of spirit such as the age seemed

---

Dr. Otto Ammon, Baden, Physician.

Dr. Ludwig Wilser, Heidelberg, Ethnologist.

Dr. Paul Samassa, Heidelberg, Professor of Zoölogy.

Alfred Giser, Westphalia, Journalist, later business manager of the League.

Heinrich Class, Mainz, Lawyer, Later head of the League.

Dr. Gustav Petzoldt, Plauen, Lawyer, spoken of by Class as especially of *Grossdeutsch* sympathies (Class, p. 54).

Dr. Heinrich Pohl, Mülheim and Essen, Teacher, Journalist, Later editor of *Rheinisch-Westfälische Zeitung* and of *Die Post.*

Hermann Horn, Hanover, Manufacturer, Member of the Reichstag.

Heinrich Kramer, Coblentz, Mayor of Coblentz and Member of the Reichstag.

Louis Leinenweber, Manufacturer, Member of the Reichstag.

Philipp Lichtenberger, Pfalz, Merchant and farmer, Member of the Reichstag.

Liebermann von Sonnenberg, Brandenburg, ex-Army officer, Agrarian, Journalist, Member of the Reichstag.

Von Liebert, Army officer (General).

Count von Mirbach, Silesia, Owner of a knight's holding, Member of the Reichstag and Landtag, Member of the Agrarian League.

Oswald Zimmermann, ? Member of the Reichstag.

[212] Cited by Wertheimer, *op. cit.*, p. 35. The writer is indebted for the translation to Miss Wertheimer.

15

to call for if Germany were to take her place with other great peoples. One popular writer said:

> The German nation alone besides the Anglo-Saxons has developed to the point where it is numerous enough and internally strong enough to demand that its nationalism (*Volksgedanken*) have the right decisively to help form the coming world age.[213]

The Pan-Germans wished German emigrants to remember their country. They asked that the German colonies be reserved for peasants and craftsmen and that large land grants be denied to foreign exploiters. They wanted to strengthen the ties between Reich Germans and Austrian Germans, the Dutch, the Boers, and Germans abroad.

The Polish question represents the difficulties in pre-war Germany encountered by an organization like the League. The Committee on Agitation of the old All-German Association declared in 1891 that the Polish question constituted "above all a national question." [214] The Germanization of the East March, declared the *Alldeutsche Blätter,* was far preferable to "an unreliable Polish friendship" and the League took the Prussian government severely to task for its concessions to Polish subjects.[215] It roused the "genius of the German people" to shout out against this wrong to "national interests." At its first general assembly in 1894 the League adopted a programme to turn back the Polish tide. The programme protested against Caprivi's more liberal Polish policy and against the Polish immigration to the Prussian estates.[216]

[213] Paul Rohrbach, *Der deutsche Gedanke in der Welt* (1912), pp. 7-9, cited by Andler, *op. cit.,* II, 353. Rohrbach was a collaborator of the *Preussische Jahrbücher,* a prolific writer and traveler. He was apparently not a member of the League, but his thoughts frequently coincided with those of the nationalists.

[214] *Zwanzig Jahre,* p. 1.

[215] *Ibid.,* pp. 5-11, cited from *Alldeutsche Blätter,* Nos. 16, 34, 1895.

[216] *Cf.* also *All. Bl.* No. 11, March 12, 1899: "And Germany will never win *das Deutschtum* in the East March so long as there are Poles, this people whom Fate has unfortunately given us as the irreconcilable enemy at our side and whom we unfortunately must handle as such. . . . The struggle against the Polish people is one of the gigantic struggles which we still have to fight out if we wish to maintain our political independence as a great people. The premise that there is equality of nationality must be given up in the East March." See also No. 18, April 30, 1899.

Powerful Agrarians, however, perhaps through the Agrarian League, were able to counteract propaganda offensive to their interests. In 1899 Max Weber resigned from the Pan-German League in protest against its " consideration for the money interests of agrarian capitalism, which is represented by the numerous Conservative members." [217] In his letter of resignation he pointed out that the League had failed to rid the East March of Polish laborers, that it had silently allowed the Königsberg agricultural chamber to further the immigration of these laborers, and had permitted the Prussian Landtag to agree in this respect to the demands of the Junkers. [218] Hence *das Deutschtum* apparently came out second when it conflicted with powerful vested interests, whose money or favor a struggling, idealistic society welcomed. Open reconciliation between the League and the Agrarians, however, occurred only in 1913, when the League began to decline; [219] but money passed between the Agrarians and Pan-Germans. [220]

Pan-German interpretation of " national interest " included warm support of naval expansion. Class said in his memoirs that the part played by Pan-Germans in passing the First Naval Law convinced him that he had done rightly in leaving the German Alliance for a more active organization. [221] Immediately after the Emperor's speech of January 18, 1896, the League called for gifts for naval propaganda. [222] At the end of February, Hugenberg, a leader in the League at the time, spread the rumor that Admiral Senden had under consideration a bill providing for expenditure of two hundred million marks, that the League would agitate for it, and that the Reichstag would be dissolved if the bill failed to pass. Hasse halfheartedly denied this statement. [223] In October the *Alldeutsche Blätter* pleaded for naval expansion. The call to arms emphasized the " holy mission " of the League on behalf of the naval agitation.

> Wide circles of our people [wrote the journal] do not yet know what the naval question means and hence are indifferent

[217] Marianne Weber, *op. cit.*, pp. 237-8.

[218] *Loc. cit.*   [220] Kehr, *op. cit.*, p. 100, note 27.

[219] Class, *op. cit.*, p. 270.   [221] Class, *op. cit.*, p. 33.

[222] A. Lehr, *Warum die deutsche Flotte vergrössert werden muss*, in *Flugschriften des alldeutschen Verbandes*, No. 10 (Munich, 1899), p. 1, cited by Kehr, *op. cit.*, p. 56.

[223] Kehr, *op. cit.*, p. 59.

and prejudiced toward it. To enlighten them, to spread understanding for and interest in the meaning and present position
of our navy and to bring to the consciousness of influential
persons that the future material and political welfare of our
people is dependent on an increase in the navy is during the
next few years a task of greatest importance to the League.
Since we are independent of those above or below and belong
to no party or confession, we are in the best position to proceed
without considering any interest other than that of the
nation.[224]

In a memorandum to the Chancellor the organization pointed out
how it had been a cause of " shame to the German Empire " that
the government commanded so few ships.[225] The memorandum
demanded equality with the Russian fleet in the Baltic and an increase bringing German naval strength up to two-thirds of that
of the French navy.[226] The usual arguments for a navy included
the truly Pan-German one: " In order in the future to conquer
more and more of the earth for German intelligence " we must
send out merchants and they must be protected.[227] Like the Colonial
Society, the Pan-Germans wished to do more than maintain the
status quo; they wanted a navy sufficient to usher in a worthy future
for Germanism. The League easily fell into line with the demand
for battleships and in 1899-1900 funds given by interested persons
and groups outside the League supported its agitation.[228] Lehr,
one of the most eager Pan-German navalists, obtained in 1898 a
seat in the Reichstag and from this vantage point gradually won
favor with the government, becoming, as Class wrote later, " an
admitted confidential man of this bureau [the *Reichsmarineamt*]."

[224] *Alldeutsche Blätter*, No. 44, 1896.

[225] *Ibid.*, No. 12, 1897. The memorandum was sent March 2, 1897.

[226] *Zwanzig Jahre*, p. 41. Resolution of the annual assembly, June 8-10, 1897.

[227] *Ibid.*, p. 50. Munich assembly, September 1898.

[228] Kehr, *op. cit.*, p. 100. This fact does not appear in Wertheimer, but Kehr cites from Grell, another historian of the League, who implies it. The enormous amount of space given by the *Alldeutsche Blätter* to the naval question in 1899-1900 showed how active the League was on its behalf. Hasse argued, just as many Germans argue today as regards Nazism, that Germany had no choice. It was the same with colonies: the assumption that Germany needed colonies for raw materials was considered irrefutable.

Almost every day he had contact with it and the propaganda of the League revealed the effects. The League could say at last that it did not always oppose the government. With the development of the Navy League, however, the Pan-German League took second place as a society for naval propaganda. The Pan-Germans scorned the *Interessenpolitik* of the Navy League; they themselves gave the naval problem, they said, a broader interpretation than the majority of Germans.[230] The British, Class asserted scornfully, had already written *ceterum censeo Germaniam esse delendam* before Germans other than Pan-Germans recognized the need of a German navy. Desire for the navy undoubtedly paralleled the eagerness of the Pan-Germans that Germany assert herself in world affairs. The *Alldeutsche Blätter* expressed its devotion to the deed (*Tat*) in the words: " We don't want to hear speeches, but we want to see action and record success." [232]

The Pan-German League cherished its independent position and criticized the Navy League as well as the Colonial Society for slavish adherence to governmental policy. " For us Pan-Germans support of the colonial efforts of our people is a matter of course," they said; but the League maintained that it had its own colonial policy. Like the Colonial Society, the League regretted the Helgoland-Zanzibar Treaty of 1890. In 1894 it condemned the Franco-German Kamerun Treaty, which, it said, would close, except by way of French or English colonies, the central African Soudan to Germany. Could the Chancellor not make a treaty for once satisfying to " German national feeling? [233] The League displayed the same interest as the Colonial Society in Delagoa Bay and insisted that if Portugal proved incapable of retaining her colonies Germany should be treated on an equality with England in the subsequent partition.[234] On the Asiatic question it said proudly:

> Both prestige and interest demand that nowhere on the earth's surface shall a change occur without adequate compen-

---

[229] Class, *op. cit.*, pp. 82-4.
[230] *Ibid.*, p. 83.   [232] *Alld. Bl.*, No. 43, October 22, 1899.
[231] *Ibid.*, p. 84.   [233] *Ibid.*, No. 9, 1894.
[234] *Ibid.*, No. 40, 1894. Also No. 1, 1899: " If England should take Lorenzo Marques by force there would be no compensation sufficient to repay Germany for her lost prestige."

sation to the Empire . . . May the government for the sake of
the reputation and interests of the Empire proceed energetically and without consideration for the objections of other
states to the conquest in Chinese waters of an adequate, strong,
and secure possession, whether it be a harbor or a group of
islands.[235]

Again and again it referred to " prestige," " *Machtstellung,*" equality with others. In its discussion of the colonial question the League
manifested awareness that a new partition of the earth was under
way which, wrote the journalists of the League, " will regulate
anew the bases of our economic and political welfare in the coming
century." Germany must demand a part of this activity. The government did not act readily enough for the League and slighted
the " national interest." The Pan-Germans found England, Russia,
and other Powers recognizing Germany as a great Power and asked
why could she not take advantage of this.

> We must reiterate again and again [wrote Hasse in 1898]
> that we are nowhere for a sentimental policy. A policy of com-
> pensations seems to us thoroughly acceptable. But these com-
> pensations must also be to the point. They must bring us
> what we really need in the present and still more what we
> need for the future. They must not allow any change in the
> balance of power to our disadvantage. They must not provide
> small change for the future, but must give us guarantees in
> hand. And all treaties must not lose sight of the great mutual
> interests of the continent over against the island of Great
> Britain and the newly created overseas world Power.[236]

At the same time " a nationalistic awakening in the people " seemed
a necessary forerunner to governmental action.[237]

Although the League emphasized more than the Colonial Society
the menace of competition with America and Russia, it did not

[235] *Memorandum to Hohenlohe,* October 8, 1895, cited by *Zwanzig Jahre,*
pp. 31 f. Note the early date. The Pan-Germans boasted that they were
the first to urge this acquisition. Interest in the German colony in southern Brazil, in Morocco, etc. was also lively. *Cf. Alld. Bl.,* 1900.

[236] Hasse in *Alld. Bl.,* No. 25, June 17, 1900.

[237] *Ibid.,* No. 7, February 12, 1899: " Finally, the government for a successful representation of its interests needs a powerful nationalistic movement in the people, a movement which in all situations can subordinate
party and confessional interests to the country's welfare."

disguise its anti-British feeling. The Jameson Raid, the question of the disposal of the Portuguese colonies, the Samoan dispute and, finally, the attack on the Boers incensed it against England and made it hate her more than the other two countries. Dr. Ammon warned the League, however: " There is one thing we must not do because it is un-German, that is to arouse and encourage a wild hatred against Britain. To denounce when one cannot negotiate is not German. We must seek to learn from the British; that is German! " [238] But the League regarded only the latter part of his admonition. It was proud that increased consciousness of *das Deutschtum* made possible widespread sympathy with the Boer kinsmen. This sympathy went so far as to desire closer commercial relations with Holland and in 1900 an article in the *Blätter, Gegenwart,* and *Norddeutsche Allgemeine Zeitung* advocated a commercial arrangement with Holland similar to that between South Germany and the North German Confederation in 1866.[239] It warned England that she should realize that she had lost her monopolistic position in China and advised Germany to draw nearer to Russia before England left her in the lurch. The League likewise urged Germany to observe how firmly the British stood together in their crises. The greatest lesson it drew from the war was that of the need for a strong German navy. Had Germany had this navy, argued the Pan-Germans, a quiet word to England would have sufficed to save the Boers.[240] They hoped that the courageous defense of the Boers against England would be a lasting example to the German people of how to protect themselves. The League worked untiringly to collect money and to fit out relief units to aid the Boers and at a meeting for these purposes always spread naval and imperialistic propaganda. Since it regarded England as a hindrance to the fulfillment of an imperialistic programme, its speakers frequently coupled her name with their plans; nationalism was best aroused by naming an enemy.

In subsequent years other disturbances at home and abroad, replaced the Boer and Spanish-American wars as arguments for further naval expansion. Such was the First Moroccan Crisis.[241]

[238] *Ibid.*, No. 25, 1900. Ammon at the assembly, June 6-8, 1900.
[239] *Ibid.*, No. 7, February 11, 1900.
[240] *Zwanzig Jahre*, p. 90.　　　　[241] *Ibid.*, p. 239.

Like the Navy League, the Pan-German League eagerly seized
upon the temporary depression of prices and unemployment in 1901
as an excuse to hasten the construction of the navy.[242] Between
such occasions the League carried on agitaticn to keep alive popular
interest in the navy.

The economic policy of the Pan-Germans was one of their most
interesting objectives. This policy, growing out of the Spanish-
American and Boer wars, may serve as a final illustration of Pan-
German nationalism. "The approaching termination of the commercial treaties," wrote the *Blätter,* "lays upon the Pan-German
League the duty of clarifying the demands, which if they are to be
patriotic and not those of selfish interests are in the future desirable
for our commercial and economic policies." [243] The consideration
from the "higher patriotic standpoint" led the League to conclude
that the next commercial treaties must not allow the annual importation of Polish agricultural labor. In order to prevent this,
since a sudden change would ruin much of eastern agriculture, it
proposed extensive reforms to induce labor to remain on the land.
Furthermore, the government should break up bankrupt estates at
the rate of at least ten square miles a year, turning the land over
to peasant farmers. If agriculture had to be compensated for the
loss of seasonal immigrant labor, the League agreed that the tariff
on agricultural products be raised. Industry, continued the *Blätter,*
might be harmed in some branches if by intelligence and technical
improvements it could not meet higher prices. Such harm could
be offset by expansion of the navy beyond that provided by the laws
of 1898 and 1900. "In this way we may not only avoid humiliation
like that of Apia," [244] wrote the *Blätter* again, "but also our commercial and economic future can be assured and be brought to the
point where we need not worry about our economic existence every
time our commercial treaties expire." This statement expressed the

[242] *Ibid.*, p. 113. In the assembly of December 8, 1901.

[243] *Alld. Bl.*, No. 18, April 30, 1899. The fact that the League did not
press this programme consistently has been brought out. *Cf.* pp. 203 f.

[244] Apia was the harbor of Samoa. During bitter civil disputes there
the British (1899) supported by the American Admiral landed marines
and forced the German consul to reverse an action which he had taken.
The Germans regarded the episode as a disgrace. *Cf.* Vagts, *op. cit.*,
Chap. X.

commonly held belief in the value of the navy as a Power factor in commercial affairs. In addition Pan-Germans wished the immediate construction of canals and railroads at home, asked to have railroads built in the colonies, thereby "richly compensating industry for any loss in export." Better agricultural conditions would improve the internal market and Germany must learn to concentrate, on the expansion of this internal market as a basis for a strong national state.[245]

This point of view was intensely nationalistic. It implied that Germany's economic position should be upheld by Power. Germany, backed by force, should exact from others without reciprocity. The line of reasoning pursued here as elsewhere at the time seems to have been somewhat as follows: the world is being partitioned off by the British, American and Russian Empires; open markets will no longer exist; Germany must be strong enough to hold her own; she must in the meantime build an autarchic state. The nationalism of the Pan-Germans was in theory more consistent than that of the Agrarians, who were willing to use foreign labor but no foreign grain, or of industrialists, who were willing to use foreign foods if foreign manufactured goods could be kept out. They had also a wider horizon than groups concerned with only one subject or representing only one special interest. At the same time they could not keep themselves free from agrarian and industrial pressure; in practical politics they often compromised their teachings.

It is true that Pan-German thinking became confused, unworthy of Bismarck the *Realpolitiker,* whom Pan-Germans so devotedly honored. Although they suggested specific measures and programmes, all centering around the development of imperialism, they were also mystical nationalists. Before them flitted constantly the dream of Germany bringing civilization to other peoples. To play this rôle Germany must preserve everything German in its purest state. The League existed to arouse public opinion to the importance of this duty; it excited the emotions where and when it could. It is not surprising to find it using the Boer War, the Samoan affair, the Far East as a means for stressing the dangers with which it thought Germanism confronted.

The thesis of Miss Wertheimer's book, *The Pan-German League*

[245] *Alld. Bl.,* No. 18, 1899.

is open to criticism. Miss Wertheimer pointed to the relatively small size of the League, its meagre financial resources, it bourgeois character; to the fact that Hasse almost exclusively represented it in the Reichstag, because the other Pan-German members put party first; that it was not quoted in the newspapers; and stated that, consequently, compared with its reputation in after years, it had little importance. All these facts have weight; but it remains true that the League grew and flourished especially in the 'nineties, when its views coincided with those expressed by the overwhelming majority of the vocal public. If it helped to educate this public, as Class asserted and as seems to have been the case, its importance was indirectly large and the numbers actually within the organization are of less significance than would at first appear. Hasse always maintained in the Reichstag that untold thousands in the country at large, whether they belonged to the League or not, supported him. Moreover, the League stood in the forefront of anti-English public opinion and supported all those policies which reacted unfavorably upon English opinion toward Germany. Hence it cannot have been unimportant to the growth of Anglophobia.

F. *Central Union of German Industrialists* [246]

The creation of the Central Union (*Centralverband der deutschen Industriellen*), the powerful organization of German big industry,[247]

[246] For the Central Union there exists what there does not for any other organization surveyed in this study, a three volume work on its history and interests by its secretary, H. A. Bueck, *Der Centralverband deutscher Industrieller, 1876-1901* (Berlin, 1905). The treatment is, however, disappointing. The work is not only dull to read, but dull in thought; for it contains a careful chronicle of the attitude of the Central Union on all tariff and social legislation, but almost no analysis and little explanation. More useful is the *Industriezeitung*, the journal of the Central Union. Interesting for an understanding of the working and " spirit " of the group is Erich Reger's novel *Die Union der festen Hand* (Berlin, 1931). The organization pictured in this book is the post-war counterpart of the Central Union.

[247] " Big industry " does not mean here heavy industry alone, but rather large-scale, organized industry. A glance at the chart will show that textiles and other so-called light industries were included. Smaller industry was organized in the Industrialists' Alliance (*Bund der Industriellen*), which had less power.

antedates that of any other group studied. Organized in 1876 through the efforts of the iron and steel industry of the Rhineland and Westphalia and of the cotton textile industry of South Germany, it sought to check the free-trade movement. The tariff law of 1879 resulted partly from the first activities of the Central Union. Almost immediately after this law the problem of social legislation arose and occupied the attention of the Central Union during the 'nineties.

Unlike previous organizations discussed, the Central Union did not carry on extensive propaganda. It represented industries rather than persons. The organization united these industries in pursuit of a single course of action and functioned as a great lobbying unit. It was comprised of the industries essential to Germany's prosperity, was well established, and possessed connections among high and low. Any agitation for popular consumption could be carried on through the various propaganda organizations with which big business had personal connections; but the Central Union itself exerted direct pressure on government. Unfortunately, Bueck, long secretary of the organization and its historian, who knew precisely how this pressure was applied, has not revealed details to his readers; but it is possible to discover some lines of contact. For example, Hammacher constantly conferred with Reich Secretaries in the interest of big business.[248] The Central Union put together the material which he used at his conferences and in his speeches in the Reichstag. In the case of the commercial treaties of the early 'nineties, Beumer, head of the Economic Union of Düsseldorf, Rentzsch, manager of the German Iron and Steel Industrialists, and Bueck himself assembled the material.[249] Bueck constantly mentioned in his history memoranda drawn up by the Central Union on important questions and handed to officials. Since the memoranda came from so powerful a source, they could not have been entirely ignored. The government by no means yielded to such advice in every detail; but it endeavoured to satisfy big industry's basic needs.

In 1905 when Bueck finished the third volume of his history he added a survey of members. Since this list would not differ greatly from one of 1900, it may be used here. In 1905 sixteen industrial

[248] *Cf.* Chapter II, " National Liberals."
[249] Bueck, *op. cit.*, I, 454.

organizations,[250] twenty-eight commercial, and eight professional ones belonged to the Union. In addition there were forty-seven coal and iron organizations, seven from the metal industries, seventeen textile organizations, four paper, five food and luxury, twenty-three from the building trades, fourteen chemical and a few unclassified. In all there were one hundred and seventy-four of these. To them may be added over six hundred individual concerns, including all the heavy industry of importance, for example, three Krupp works.[251] The list clearly indicates the general nature of the Central Union, and the membership of the directorate may be added by way of further proof of its character. Vopelius, a member of the directorate after 1893, was at this time (1905) president. He was a mine-owner of Saarbrücken, president of the Glass Industrialists Association and a Free-Conservative member of the Upper House of the Prussian legislature. The first vice-president was Kirdorff, a National Liberal and general director of the Gelsenkirchen Mining Company. G. Koenig was second vice-president. He was president of the directors of the German Sugar Industry. Jencke, one of Krupp's directors, member of the Prussian State Council (*Staatsrat*) and of the Upper House of the Saxon legislature, a financial expert, was one of the most active members. Other members were A. Rieppel, director of the United Machine Manufacturers of Augsburg and of the Machine Building Factory of Nürnberg; Theodor Schlumberger, president of the Alsace-Lorraine Industrialists' Syndicate of Mülhausen; Semlinger, director of the Mechanical Cotton Thread Spinning and Weaving Association of Bamberg; Roetger, president of the directorate of Friedrich Krupp of Essen; Hilger, general director of the Königs and Laura Mines; and Stahl, general director of the Stettin Machine Building Company, "Vulcan." H. A. Bueck was active in the Union from the first. After having been general secretary of the Rhenish-Westphalian Industrialists' Association, in 1887 he became business manager and secretary of the Union. His work was prolific and vehement.

[250] Organization refers here to a group of individual enterprises of the same or allied industries organized as a whole in a locality or in the Empire for the practical purposes of the industry.

[251] Bueck, III, 701-749.

In contrast with several of the organizations surveyed here, the membership of the Central Union increased after 1900.[252] The Union estimated in 1903 in answer to an attack upon it in the *Soziale Praxis,* a liberal journal, that thirty-five thousand industrial concerns, whose output constituted seven-tenths of the total German production, maintained connections with it.

When Bueck entered upon his duties in 1887 the financial status of the Central Union was such that members of the directorate extended to it a credit of ten thousand marks. In 1889 the income and expenditure amounted to 41,710 marks;[253] in 1889 65,000 marks with an added expenditure of 15,000 more;[254] and in 1900 the budget totalled 92,000 marks.[255] This sum was less than the Agrarian League raised from its membership dues alone, but its smallness is perhaps explicable by the fact that Bueck could raise extra sums as he needed them. He subsidized the agitation of other organizations for the navy, colonies, or railroads. For example, the Navy League, whose financial sources are difficult to discover, certainly drew from the Central Union members a part of its extraordinary income.[256]

Die deutsche Industriezeitung was established in 1897. Before this time the Union used the *Berliner Politische Nachrichten* edited by Schweinburg, later secretary to the Navy League. The *Industriezeitung* fought Social Democracy bitterly and Bueck wrote many of its editorials. It was not conspicuous for anti-British propaganda, but strongly supported the navy and imperialism in every form.

According to article I of its constitution the Union aimed to " protect the industrial and economic interests of the country and to further the national work." This general aim made possible elasticity in detail. To achieve its purpose the Central Union supported the specific proposals of its members in regard to the economic legislation of the Reich and of the several states; the conclusion of favorable commercial and shipping treaties; the extension of means of communication, especially canals, the improvement of transportation on these and the simplification and favorable formu-

[252] Bueck, III.
[253] Bueck, I, 226-7.
[254] *Ibid.*, p. 275.
[255] *Ibid.*, 287.
[256] *Vide supra,* " Navy League."

lation of the general tariff; the regulation of labor relations; the opening of new sources of imports and of markets; the support and introduction of new inventions; the education of public opinion to the common interests of producer and consumer; the foundation of such arrangements as seemed justified for improving the material position of the entire German industry.[257] It goes without saying that the Central Union favored the *Industriestaat*;[258] but during the log-rolling era of the *Sammlung* it made concessions to agriculture. It also made concessions to the workers. In the 'eighties it did so willingly; but in the 'nineties it championed increasingly the rights of employers and opposed any attempt to democratize industry, so that it grew more unfavorable to social insurance and the like.[259] The Central Union considered this programme to be a defense of " national work " and national interests against international labor and special class interests. Some of the industrialists in the Union sympathized with the efforts of the academic socialists; but the great majority preferred Stumm's point of view and the Union approved his speeches.[260] Hence in its domestic policy it grew more reactionary as the strength of Social Democracy increased. This change did not prove embarrassing, especially after it embraced imperialism and could point to the benefits which the latter would bring to the workers.

The Central Union struck difficult years between 1895 and 1903. At the time when industry expected to benefit from the commercial policy of Caprivi, it faced opposition to that policy on the part of organized Agrarian interests. During the first outbreaks of the Agrarians in 1891, the Central Union tried to keep the peace by declaring that it did not insist on decrease of the grain tariffs.[261] For this attitude toward the Agrarians the government attacked

[257] Bueck, I, 139 f. *Cf.* with Kardorff proposals of 1875, which were more specific but were therefore rejected in favor of this more generalized statement.

[258] It is only necessary to compare the frequent studies made in the *Industriezeitung* of the increase of corporations and trusts, the increase of the use of iron and steel, the growth of trade, etc. Incidentally, it considered that the Agrarians got all the advantages from the *Sammlungspolitik* (*Industrieztg.*, No. 8, February 20, 1903).

[259] *Vide supra*, Chapter II, " Social Democrats."

[260] Bueck, III, 355-6.   [261] *Ibid.*, I, 253-4.

it in the *Reichsanzeiger* as opposing the treaties, and the Union had to persuade Caprivi that such was not the case.[262] The Central Union merely wished to preserve contact with the Agrarian-Conservatives, whose votes were important in the matter of industrial tariffs. The Union naturally favored the treaties. It welcomed the Russian treaty because of the ten-year period of stability given industry. It thought the Austrian treaty desirable because it believed that the central European states should set up an economic defense against Russia and the United States, the two future industrial colossi of the world.[263] But the Union also believed that the general tariff must be completely revised and precautions taken against too great lowering of tariffs. As the decade advanced the struggle sharpened. The Agrarian League grew bolder, low tariff interests attacked the Central Union, and dissension appeared within the Union's ranks as to the form of the new tariff.[264]

The bitter war going on about him determined Posadowsky to invite the parties of the Right into the *Sammlung*. The Central Union welcomed coöperation more than did agriculture. Beumer had declared in 1897 that the next election would show the need for agriculture and industry to join against the revolutionary party. He said that if the League would moderate its demands industry would support it on a variety of measures including one to assure good prices for grain.[265] Bueck also feared the Agrarian League and willingly considered coöperation with the Conservatives on condition that the influence of the League among them be curbed.[266] At the instigation of the Central Union, in 1897 an Economic Committee for Advising the Government on Preparation of the Tariff Law was set up.[267] Before the elections (1898) Vopelius of the Union and Schwerin-Löwitz representing the Agrarians called a meeting of twenty-three members of this committee—the other members were not invited—eleven of whom signed an election appeal

---

[262] *Ibid.*, pp. 255.   [263] *Ibid.*, pp. 476-7, 458.

[264] *Ibid.*, p. 274. Both the Agrarian League and the Commercial Treaties Association noticed this dissension (*Jahrbuch des Handelsvertragsvereins*, 1901, pp. 4-5, and *Industrieztg.*, No. 24, June 13, 1902).

[265] *Industrieztg.*, No. 11, June 1, 1897.

[266] *Ibid.*, No. 4, February, 1898.

[267] *Vide supra,* " Commercial Treaties Association."

recommending the *Sammlung*.[268] Although the League hated a moderate tariff as much as before, the Central Union tried to promote harmony. When the Prussian House of Representatives rejected the canals' bill in 1899, the *Industriezeitung* said in a conciliatory way, although industry had set its heart on the bill, that the rejection probably constituted only a tactical move in the tariff struggle. It anticipated with pleasure the day when industry and agriculture, with industry ranking first however, should coöperate throughout Germany as harmoniously as they did in the Rhineland-Westphalia district.[269] The failure of the canals' bill and the desire for naval expansion convinced the Union of the need for an agreement with the Conservatives. Bueck suggested in his history that fear of a political deal between Conservatives and free-traders (which would have been an act of spite on the part of the Agrarian-Conservatives) likewise contributed much to industry's friendliness toward Agrarian demands.[270] In any case, according to its own account, the Union agreed to the demands of agriculture in the commission without knowing whether its own tariff demands would subsequently be met by agriculture. Actually it was disappointed in its confidence, especially in the iron and machine tariffs;[271] but it secured support for the naval laws and ultimately for a part of the canals' project.

Two aspects of the coöperation between Conservatives and the Central Union and between government and Central Union are important. First, a tariff favorable to both industry and agriculture and acceptable to the government passed the Reichstag. Under this tariff the fears of the extreme Left in respect to retaliation from abroad did not ensue and Germany enjoyed further prosperity. The League gradually abated its vehemence and, since the free-traders also became quieter, the internal struggle after 1903 temporarily lessened. Seconly, the *Sammlungspolitik* laid the basis for bargaining between agriculture and the Central Union. Industry had many desires, especially as to canals, railroads, lowered freight

[268] *Jahrbuch des Handelsvertragsvereins*, 1901, pp. 30-1.

[269] *Hand in Hand*, No. 11, September 1, 1899, and *Industrieztg.*, No. 6, February 7, 1901.

[270] *Industrieztg.*, No. 8, February 21, 1902, articles by Bueck.

[271] *Ibid.*, No. 33, August 15, 1902.

rates, and a navy. It also needed aid in its conflict with labor. To obtain these it sought support among the powerful Agrarians, although it had to buy this support by helping to maintain large-scale agriculture.

Beumer expressed in 1897 one of the strong reasons for the sympathy of the Central Union with agriculture when he referred, to the "revolutionary party." [272] Although the Union had grudgingly helped Bismarck with his social legislation, during the 'nineties it opposed each of the government's efforts to revise and extend this legislation. The Union feared that the government yielded to the pressure of the masses, that it was intimidated by the Social Democrats into making unnecessary concessions too expensive for industry to afford.[273] The Union grew agitated over the frequent strikes and over the international connections of German Social Democracy, particularly with English trade unions.[274] In these years Bueck made many trips to England to study labor conditions and reported the disturbing power of the Socialists in the trade unions. The Union thought that strikes were becoming more widespread, were changing their character, and were political rather than economic. The belief that because of world competition industry could not bear additional expense especially perturbed it. Higher wages and insurance costs would raise prices, the Union predicted, and reduce competitive power in the world market.[275] The Union opposed all new bills concerning social insurance, using arguments like the following:

> These conclusions, shot through and through by Social Democratic spirit, and the proposals which go still further in this direction must arouse in the Central Union very serious considerations since they do not proceed from the Social Democratic members alone, as is clear from the vote, but also had the willing support of the representatives of other parties. . . . Thus the Central Union finds it better, so long as the present dangers in the makeup of the Reichstag persist, to give up entirely the effort to abolish the deficiencies in the law. The effectiveness of the law, which has been successful in the high-

---

[272] *Vide supra,* " National Liberals " for similarity of thought and point of view toward the Social Democratic question.

[273] Bueck, III, 282-3; 298 f., 341.

[274] *Ibid.,* pp. 402 ff.   [275] *Ibid.,* II, 480.

16

est degree for the insured persons, that is, for the entire German working population, has not been up to now in any way lessened.[276]

At first the remonstrances of the Central Union had their effect and the bills were dropped; but between 1898 and 1900 they failed to prevent the adoption of a number of new social laws. During these years the Left parties and press bitterly attacked the Central Union. One noteworthy exposure by *Vorwärts* in 1900 (October), the affair of the twelve thousand marks, came up in the Reichstag.[277] According to the charges in this case, the Secretary of the Interior had asked the Central Union to contribute twelve thousand marks to the cause of furthering a law for the protection of strike-breakers.[278] The Union had supposedly promised the sum to the Secretary. Whether it ever paid the full amount was not proved; but Bueck acknowledged his acceptance of a donation of at least five thousand marks for that purpose, stating that Jencke had secured this much from Krupp.[279] The Social Democrats used the admission as absolute proof of the intimacy between the Department of the Interior and the Central Union and, although the money appeared to have been actually solicited by Woedtke, an under-secretary, they condemned Posadowsky.[280] Auer (SPD) maintained that the Central Union was primarily responsible for the failure

[276] *Ibid.*, pp. 551 ff. In the case of the Accident Insurance Law of 1896.

[277] *Geschichte der Frankfurter Zeitung*, p. 779. The *Frankfurter Zeitung* at this time "threw light upon the enormous influence of the Central Union in ruling circles; but it was already in a position to indicate that in the preparation of the *Zuchthausvorlage* Posadowsky had felt rather more than less the power of big industry. At that time the government became clear for the first time that the powerful economic force of big business could in the near future disturb its sacred precincts " (p. 779).

[278] Introduced into the Reichstag, May 26, 1899.

[279] Auer: *Sten. Ber. d. Reich.*, November 24, 1900, X Leg. Per., II Sess., I, 132 f.

[280] Schoenlank: *Ibid.*, pp. 147 f. I, 149: "The intimacy between the Central Union and the Department of the Interior has, as one can see from the history of the social laws, increased from year to year. It was, indeed, slightly disturbed during the years of von Berlepsch, but he has been forced off the stage and the intimacy has grown. The office of the Central Union in Berlin is the head office for determining governmental social policy and the famous office in the *Wilhelmstrasse* only acts as an agent."

of William II in 1890 to fulfill his promises of new social legislation.[281] As for Posadowsky, he said, " He has capitulated before
the wishes and demands of the Central Union." [282] Auer also said
that the last report of the Central Union furnished twenty in-
stances of communications to the Union from the Department of
Trade and Commerce, from the Department of the Interior, and
from the Chancellor.[283] Fischer (SPD) cited from the *Berliner
Neueste Nachrichten* a list of services performed by the Union for
the Department of the Interior.[284]

These charges are not entirely confirmed. The Central Union
had certainly attempted to bring pressure on the government; but
even before the exposures of 1900 Bueck realized that his memoranda on social matters no longer had great weight with Posadowsky.[285] He wrote later that industry was so concerned over the
economic crisis of 1900 that it could not oppose the bills for social
betterment as before.[286] At the same time, although its attitude did
not change, the affair of the twelve thousand marks made the Union
wary of outspoken opposition to them.[287]

The Union found it necessary to look about for other means of
achieving its ends. In the years 1901 and 1902 it turned to the
formation of trusts. It thought the trust would strengthen the
position of the employer over against the worker and by insuring
steadier employment would benefit the worker.[288] In this way the
Union hoped to forestall the strikes, which an upturn might bring,
and to regain for industry some of the popularity lost in the recent
struggle with the government and Reichstag over social laws.

In addition the Central Union became more interested in imperialism. The group as a whole apparently did not support the
navy until 1899, when Bueck stated in his annual report that
Germany needed power on land and sea. Later he used the English
seizure of German ships during the Boer War as evidence of Germany's need for a navy. Until she had a navy, he said, Germany

---

[281] *Ibid.*, p. 134.   [282] *Ibid.*, p. 150.   [283] *Ibid.*, p. 135.
[284] *Ibid.*, January 12, 1901, X Leg. Per., II Sess., I, 629 ff.
[285] Bueck, II, 703 f.   [286] *Ibid.*, p. 730.
[287] *Cf.* speech by Bueck, October 1, 1901, *Industriezeitung*, No. 40, October
4, 1901. In it he warned the delegates against revisionism and discussed
the *Macht* nature of recent strikes.
[288] *Industrieztg.*, No. 51, December 19, 1902.

was balancing herself on only one leg (the army) and might easily topple over.[289] Bueck's open support of the navy was enthusiastically received; for as early as 1897 the *Industriezeitung* had drawn attention to the trade problems of South Africa and had called for a navy to protect commercial interests there against further English development of the field.[290] The *Berliner Neueste Nachrichten* published material given it by Bueck in favor of naval expansion.[291] Fischer of the *Kölnische Zeitung* in his discussion of the Union spoke of its " great and excellent naval agitation." In the same year the Union likewise adopted a resolution stating the motives which impelled it to action:

> The representative assembly of the Central Union recognizes that the present war strength of Germany on the sea is quite insufficient to give our country the position of world power which the high development of its interests on the sea and abroad demands. In these interests is included the whole people, especially that of considerable numbers of workers, since the existence of millions depends on the unhindered progress of work, on the continued importation of raw materials, the continued increase of our overseas market and of our entire world trade. Thus the members of the Central Union gladly welcome the new naval law and the assembly expresses the expectation that the plans will find the hearty coöperation of the Reichstag.[292]

Oechelhäuser tellingly expressed one of these motives as follows: " Shall we be silent because we are accused of *Interessenpolitik?* We are in a position to judge how necessary the protection of a strong navy is to us, since we are all in a higher sense *Seeinteressenten,* namely, for the sake of our workers." [293]

There seems little doubt that the Union's ready support of a second naval bill came in response to the fear it felt of the Social

[289] Bueck, I, 291-2.

[290] *Industrieztg.*, No. 21, November 1, 1897.

[291] *Sten. Ber. d. Reich.*, January 12, 1901, X Leg. Per., II Sess., I, 629 ff.

[292] Cited by the *Industrieztg.*, No. 7, February 15, 1900.

[293] *Loc. cit.* No doubt the stress placed on nationalism and on the workers' good resulted in part from the experiences of the Navy League with which Bueck had been connected. But it is also a result of the failure of the Union to oppose the workers through the government and the need of doing so in another direction, namely, through imperialism.

Democrats. Unable to check Social Democracy or to cut down the expense of social insurance, faced, so it thought, with the necessity for continuing the rapid advance of German industrial development, the Union visualized the navy as a means of enabling industry to expand. It offered the government an excellent chance to prove its loyalty to industry and to diminish the internal social antagonisms by putting through the naval law. At the same time, by helping to support imperialism, the Central Union threw off the onus of the charge of *Interessenpolitik* and seemed to coöperate with the government and the propaganda organizations.

The Union did not at this time approve a naval law solely as an instrument against Britain and British competition. It knew that German industry did not need a navy in order to compete successfully with Britain. The *Industriezeitung* pointed out that Germany's imports of food and luxury goods, indicating higher standards of living and greater national buying power, were increasing relatively faster than England's, that Germany's imports of raw materials for the spinning and weaving industries were increasing more rapidly than England's, that German export of consumption goods compared favorably with England's and exports of raw products more favorably. Where discrepancies occurred, as in the case of larger English exports in 1899, the Union pointed to the unusual English coal export in that year, attributing the increase to the rise of industrial enterprise abroad.[294] Although English industry continued to grow, the Union refused to feel concern. Germany's comparative increase, it wrote, was 1.7% greater than that of England. This view, often met with in the reports of the chambers of commerce, indicates that German industry sincerely believed that with the necessary political support it could continue to compete satisfactorily. For the Central Union the naval law and the tariff served much the same purpose: they assured the world that Germany could protect her industry. The Union did not expect the navy to precipitate war and hoped the government would lessen the disaster from high tariffs by commercial treaties with friendly nations. It emphasized the need for renewing the commercial treaty with England, Germany's best customer.[295]

[294] *Ibid.*, No. 7, February 15, 1900, and similar articles at this time.
[295] *Ibid.*, Nos. 6 and 13, March 22 and 29, 1899.

The government favored the demand of industry for the extension of transportation facilities, especially waterways. Although agriculture at first refused the canals' project, the Conservatives in 1904 accepted a part of it. Industry achieved similar success in the matter of rebates on railroad rates to the shipping centers, ship subsidies and the opening of new markets in Asia. The government furthered these demands in the hope of keeping industry prosperous and of gradually diminishing its opposition.[296]

Before closing this brief survey of the Central Union, one should again mention the fact that the Union avoided propaganda. Nonetheless, it concluded as had other propagandistic organizations that Germany had become a world Power. The maintenance of this position, to the realist business man as to the professional politician and agitator, became the political necessity of the age and the hoped-for solution of all ills. No doubt the business man took some of his thoughts from the propagandist and in turn furnished the latter with substance for his agitation. The fact that its enemies referred to the Union as a super-government, the politician *par excellence* of special interests, the arch-enemy of the working-man, and the associate of the bread-usurer shows that they considered the Union to interpret "national interest" as synonymous with its own special interests. "National work," "prestige," imperialism, however, in the 'nineties were common coin everywhere, the only common coin among many conflicting baser interest-coins, which endangered the domestic peace of Germany.

Consideration of the foregoing organizations indicates the battle of interests in the 'nineties and the timely aid which these interests received from the new national imperialism of the period. The fact that in all cases except that of the Central Union of German Industrialists the period of the greatest membership for these organizations coincided with the decade 1892 to 1902 testifies further to the seriousness of the problems facing the country and the government and to the great propaganda activity of the time. As in the

---

[296] Where imperialism is concerned, however, the government was the real initiator. It is almost impossible to tell where industry instinctively felt its interests at stake and where it was convinced by governmental propaganda that they were.

case of the parliamentary groups, these propaganda organizations directed their energies to the tariff question, to the question of agriculture *versus* industry, and that of the expansion of German interests abroad. The objectives of the Agrarian League and the Central Union reveal themselves as closely allied with those of similar interests groups in the Reichstag and Landtag, while the aims and propaganda of the Colonial Society and the Pan-German League show the source from which the nationalists drew their arguments. The Navy League, of whose inner working little is known, presents an interesting example of business interests working behind nationalistic journalism, endeavouring to win governmental and popular support.

The analyses of membership in the propaganda organizations manifest the interlocking directorship of much of the work. Apart from the multiple memberships of many ex-army and ex-navy men, of journalists and of those who may be regarded as professional " joiners," the dual and triple memberships of persons like Prince von Arenberg, Arnim-Muskau, Heydt, Hahn, Hammacher, Krupp, Oechelhäuser, and Kardorff, most of whom held at the same time Reichstag and Landtag seats, indicate the coöperation of parliamentary and extra-parliamentary groups. Undoubtedly, further details about personnel would confirm rather than belie the impression given by the information collected in this chapter. Further knowledge of the sources of the funds used in propaganda would also be enlightening and would almost certainly show greater support from important men than is revealed by the presence merely of their names. Krupp's influence in the Navy League would be typical.

Although one cannot estimate the influence of these organizations in the country at large, the relatively small membership of the societies does not tell the entire story. The propaganda reached and affected wider circles. The organizations accomplished more by stirring up general discussion in the newspapers and by publishing materials in their journals. Furthermore, the greater activity of the organizations at this time shows that the country was more alive than before to the problems discussed. Although the propaganda did not impress the trade unions, its effect must have gone beyond the upper and middle-classes to Centrist workers and to many workers not in the Social Democratic party. Even Social Democrats were not immune to the magic of the word imperialism, as Weber was not to that of Power.

In conclusion it should be emphasized that the propaganda groups found the greatest common denominator in nationalism and imperialism. Whatever the reasons for inscribing these terms on their banners the effect was impressive. The emphasis upon things German increased antagonism toward things alien and when England threatened to infringe upon real or supposed German rights and ambitions anti-English feeling grew.

PART II

ANGLOPHOBIA, 1895-1902

CHAPTER IV

THE KRÜGER TELEGRAM AND ANTI-ENGLISH OPINION, 1895-96

Like an octopus Britain greedily stretches out her navy arms and seeks to embrace the kingdom of the free Amphitrite as if it were her own house.

Schiller

I.

Internal affairs occupied Germany rather exclusively during the first years after Bismarck's retirement. Disturbances in European affairs did not directly concern her. The Sino-Japanese War did not break out until the middle of the decade. American tariffs, reduced by the Wilson Law of 1892, troubled her less than subsequently. Anglo-German relations rested fairly satisfactorily on the Helgoland treaty of 1890. This comparatively peaceful international life endured but briefly; it came to an abrupt end with the crisis in Transvaal affairs, when Germany chose to involve herself in English colonial problems. The foregoing chapters of the present study have sought to explain this new phase of Anglo-German relations from the point of view of German domestic conditions.

When the Emperor William II delighted his countrymen by the Krüger Telegram, Germany was well on the way to an economic renascence. Although the Agrarians grumbled restlessly, commerce and industry were feeling the favorable effects of the Caprivi treaties. In the year of the Telegram the Chamber of Commerce of Crefeld determined to send a commission to explore the East Asiatic market.[1] Even earlier, in 1894, the Chamber of Commerce of Hamburg had spoken with satisfaction of the developing German interests in South Africa, especially in the Transvaal, and had expressed the hope that German industry and commerce would presently reap more of the benefits to be enjoyed there.[2] Herff, the

---

[1] *Jahresbericht der Handelskammer zu Crefeld*, 1896, pp. 1 f.

[2] *Jahresbericht der Handelskammer zu Hamburg*, 1894, p. 4.

German Consul in Pretoria, enthusiastically described German opportunities and in his report for 1894 indicated that German participation in the exploitation of the gold mines of the Witwatersrand had increased.[3] In 1895 the *Dresdener Bank* opened a branch in Pretoria, while export firms annually increased their trade with the Transvaal. Hence it is not surprising that the tense political situation in the Boer Republics upset commerce, banking, and industry in general, and certain enterprises in particular.

Improvement in economic conditions and the growth of German interests in the Transvaal do not alone account for the enthusiasm with which the German public received the Telegram. In the preceding months the official attitude toward German colonial expansion had changed. This transformation, one of the most important post-Caprivi developments, came out clearly in December 1894, during the Reichstag debates on the budget. At that time Chancellor Hohenlohe advocated a colonial policy in the following words:

> The colonial movement is also a national movement. It has grown out of the strengthened national feeling, which after the founding of the Empire sought a field of endeavour for the expansion of national activity; it is a valuable prop for the feeling of unity and no government will be able or will wish to do without this new and strong bond which unites the individual branches of the nation and the various classes of the population. German colonial policy has also an ideal and a religious foundation. It would lessen the German name in the world if the German people could not take part in the mission of

---

[3] On Herff, an imperialist " in the grand manner," see Wolfgang Hallgarten, " L'essor et l'échec de la politique boer de l'Allemagne," *Revue historique* (1936), an article of much interest. It is based on documents in the Foreign Office not printed in *Die grosse Politik der europäischen Kabinette*. The material is in part extracted from the author's book, *Vorkriegsimperialismus*, which for political reasons could not be printed in Germany and came out in abridged form in Paris in 1935.

German investment in the gold fields, it would seem, was both direct and by way of the London Stock Exchange. Herff doubtless referred here to direct participation, which increased German influence in the Transvaal, as he wished to do. There were German banking interests, for example, in Johannesburg helping to finance the opening of new mines. On the other hand, a good deal of German money was invested speculatively in gold mine stocks on the London Exchange. The political effect of the latter circumstance would differ from that of the former, as will be seen.

culture which is to abolish the last evils of slavery and bring the light of Christianity into the dark corners of the earth. To hold our colonial possessions is a demand of our national honor and a sign of our national prestige. We shall know how to defend them.[4]

When Bismarck supported the colonial movement, he did not do so from the considerations or under the conditions given by Hohenlohe as motives for his policy.[5] The movement began as a private undertaking in overseas territories for economic purposes, just as Richter in the same debate in 1894 said. As he also rightly indicated, colonies under these conditions had not proved profitable and the Reichstag itself had refused in 1880 to support the Samoa plantations ventures of the Hamburg firm Godeffroy.[6] In these early days the Reich even relied at times on English aid to restore quiet in a colony. Gradually Bismarck realized that it was not possible to depend upon colonialism to solve his domestic problems. When the original purpose of the colonies, to improve and strengthen German economic conditions and to furnish a "lightning-rod" for the Social Democratic danger, was likewise not fulfilled, Bismarck would willingly have withdrawn from the least desirable of the settlements. In other words, colonial activity was not primarily undertaken for the sake of prestige politics.

Experience with colonies from 1880 to 1890 showed that economic questions and general policy could not be separated and the New

[4] *Sten. Ber. d. Reich.*, IX Leg. Per., III Sess., I, 21. The displeasure of the nationalists toward Caprivi's lack of colonial interest has been touched upon. Hohenlohe was not a colonial enthusiast by conviction, however (Hohenlohe, *op. cit.*, p. 325). In 1900 he knew absolutely nothing of the moves taken in China (*ibid.*, p. 582).

[5] Rudolf Ibbeken, *op. cit.*, pp. 5 f.; 73-89. See also Hellwig, *op. cit.*, pp. 336 ff. and *supra*, pp. 177 f. Bismarck's motives were not so different, for example, a desire to unite the country, especially the bourgeoisie behind him; but Bismarck did not express his real motives openly. The connection between Bismarck's colonial policy and his domestic problems has not been satisfactorily elucidated, in spite of much recent research on the origins of German colonialism.

[6] *Sten. Ber. d. Reich.*, April 22, 1880, IV Leg. Per., III Sess., II, 859 ff. Hohenlohe used the same arguments in this debate over colonies in 1880 as in 1894, but without effect. *Cf.* also *Die Discontogesellschaft 1851-1901* Berlin, 1901).

Course sought to act accordingly.[7]   Caprivi renounced colonial expansion and tried to tighten the Triple Alliance by closer economic relations with Austria and Italy, while his successors, unable to resist colonial ventures, incorporated *Kolonialpolitik* into general policy.   The old Liberals like Richter never acquiesced in the latter move; they protested to the end that the colonies entailed an enormous and unnecessary expense.   But except for the sake of argument the economic value alone of colonies did not concern the new leaders.   By 1895 interest in colonies as such, as a part of a greater Germany, as a sign of her equality with all great nations was gaining ground in the Reichstag.   In 1890 at the time of the Helgoland-Zanzibar treaty only the nationalist press disclosed this attitude;[8] but by 1895 the country as a whole had become more alive to colonial issues.

A third important factor favoring the acceptance of imperialism emerged just before the Jameson Raid.   Already by the autumn of 1895 demands for a larger navy were brought forward.[9]   On November 28, 1895, the Naval Command (*Oberkommando*) asked the Emperor for an increase and induced His Majesty to order the immediate preparation of a bill to this end.[10]   Although the completed plans did not reach the Emperor until Tirpitz presented his memorandum of January 3, the agitation for naval expansion opened on December 14, 1895, with an article in the *National-liberale Korrespondenz* by Count Dürckheim of the Colonial Society.   As soon as news of the Jameson expedition arrived and the Emperor learned that only one cruiser could be despatched to

[7] Ibbeken, *op. cit.*, pp. 80 f.; Lenz, *Macht und Wirtschaft, passim.*

[8] Maximilien von Hagen, *Geschichte und Bedeutung des Helgolandvertrags* (Munich, 1916) ; Manfred Sell, *Das deutsch-englische Abkommen von 1890 im Lichte der deutschen Börse* (Berlin, 1926).

[9] Kehr, *op. cit.*, pp. 51 f.   Thimme notwithstanding.   Also Hallmann, *op. cit.*, pp. 158 ff.

[10] The memorandum of November 28, 1895, outlined the situation as follows: "For a long time now, but especially since the beginning of the 'nineties, not only our probable enemies, France and Russia, but all states which have recognized the importance of the navy for their *Weltmachtstellung* and for the economic interests of the nation have been making great efforts to increase their navies, especially their battle-fleet" (Hallmann, *op. cit.*, 159).

Delagoa Bay, he orally commanded Admiral Hollmann to exploit the latter fact in the press. An article drafted in the Imperial Marine Bureau appeared in *Die Post* and the *Allgemeine Marine- und Handelskorrespondenz,* an organ of the Bureau, and was reprinted in over four hundred newspapers and periodicals. Since the public had already been given some inkling of the new plans and since the Colonial Society and the Pan-German League for several years had preached the need for naval expansion, it was not difficult to obtain a hearing and to focus arguments for a larger navy upon the necessity of maintaining order in South Africa.[11]

A fourth factor, apparent in the published German documents and in the press of 1894-5, should be mentioned. This was the alarm over the activities of Rhodes in Africa and the situation in the Transvaal. Since Germany now desired colonies for their economic and prestige value, she regarded any menace to them and to their rightful development with resentment and fear. In October and November of 1895, the *Neue Preussische Zeitung* (*Kreuzzeitung*) contained frequent articles on dangerous speculation in mining shares in the Transvaal by all branches of German business. The writers discussed whether the German government should not guard against the disturbance caused to the domestic Exchange by the political crisis in South Africa.[12] Another journal noted that the miners on the Witwatersrand came largely of English stock, that the British owned a majority of the mines, that the financing of the gold mines centered in London, and that trouble would very likely arise in the gold market if the Transvaal situation should grow worse.[13] Since the British had invested in German colonies as well as in the Transvaal, the alarm spread. If Rhodes could obtain control of many Transvaal mines, might he not be able to do the same in the weak and insignificant German colonies? The German papers watched with interest the competition for Transvaal trade between the Delagoa Bay Railroad, in which Ger-

---

[11] *Cf.* the way in which the Krüger Telegram aroused the "Trade Scare of 1896" in England, R. J. S. Hoffman, *Anglo-German Trade Rivalry* (New York, 1934), and Langer, *op. cit.,* pp. 244 f.

[12] *Neue Preussische Ztg.,* October 29, November 3, 12, 17, 1895.

[13] *Kölnische Ztg.,* November 25, 1895.

man capital was invested, and the Cape State Road, which belonged to Rhodes and noted Krüger's concessions to Chamberlain.[14] When the *Standard*, an English journal, seemed to be trying to promote better relations with the German " cousins," the *Kölnische Zeitung* rather coldly wrote, " We are of course related to the English through Hengist and Horsa or their forefathers; but beyond that we are Prussians and members of the German Empire and have little in common with them. Prussia is a monarchy and through it has become great, while England is great by means of her parliamentary system." [15] The *Vossische Zeitung* already spoke of Krüger's reliance on German aid as a fact and pointed out how much Germany had at stake in the coming struggle between the Transvaal and England; [16] it hoped that the visit of Dr. Leyds, Transvaal Secretary of State, in Berlin would not be in vain.[17]

During 1895, in spite of some restricted agitation, the press had on the whole been fairly objective in its record of South African conditions and fairly modest in its political claims. The editorials which ushered in the year 1896, however, as well as the article given by the Imperial Marine Bureau on January 3 to *Die Post* announced Germany's entrance into *Weltpolitik*. The latter was the decisive pronouncement to which events had been leading.

> The German people [said *Die Post*] must understand clearly that with every refusal to mingle in world politics the Empire is brought lower from its hard-earned position until finally it will be brought to the point at which the Holy Roman Empire of the German nation ended.[18]

Even without the Jameson Raid or the Krüger Telegram this announcement would have appeared, but these gave it timeliness and force. The fall of Caprivi, the official adoption of a colonial

[14] *Ibid.*, October 15, November 25, 1895.

[15] *Ibid.*, December 13, 1895.   [16] *Vossische Ztg.*, December 28, 1895.

[17] *Ibid.*, December 30, 1895; January 1, 1896. Also an article on Chamberlain, December 1, 1895: "In the near future he will be the most national of all Britons and it will not be surprising if in later history this will be known as the Chamberlain rather than the Salisbury government." See also Hallgarten, *op. cit.*, whose article is especially useful for showing the activities of Herff and of German interests against Rhodes.

[18] *Die Post*, January 3, 1896.

policy of expansion, the determination of the Emperor to build a navy, the rapid development of German interests in South Africa as well as elsewhere, together with the agitation of the nationalists for imperialism, indicated that forces were impelling Germany toward *Weltpolitik*. The Jameson Raid occurred at an opportune moment for Germany's entrance into world affairs.

It is not necessary to rehearse the details of the Jameson Raid and the Krüger Telegram.[19] It is, however, desirable to inquire into the motives behind the German action in order to connect the internal German situation with governmental policy during these events. The Emperor and Marschall von Bieberstein played the principal rôles, although neither drafted the telegram to Krüger. This work was apparently done by Kayser, Secretary for Colonies, who amended the Emperor's own draft of a message. Afterward Marschall, Secretary for Foreign Affairs, took credit for the idea. In addition recent investigation shows that Herff, German Consul at Pretoria, for some years aggres ely encouraged closer German relations with the Transvaal.[20]

The *Vossische Zeitung* for January 1 condemned the Jameson Raid as a breach of the peace. The article concluded that luckily Dr. Leyds was in Berlin to receive the assurance which the German government must give of the maintenance of Transvaal independence. Other journals also requested the government to protect the rights of Germans in the Republic and denounced Rhodes and the Chartered Company.[21] "If the Transvaal government turns to Berlin for protection," they said, "it has a right to do so. In the South African affair German *Macht* stands unquestionably on the side of the Boers. We hope that it will not be necessary to prove this in other ways than by diplomacy."[22] The newspapers watched every visible move of the Foreign Office with passionate

[19] For general discussion see Langer, *op. cit.*, pp. 213 ff.; Reginald Lovell, *The Struggle for South Africa, 1875-1899* (New York, 1934); Raymond Bixler, *Anglo-German Imperialism in South Africa, 1880-1900* (Columbus, 1932); J. L. Garvin, *Life of Chamberlain* (London, 1933), III.

[20] Hallgarten, *op. cit.*, pp. 505 ff.

[21] *Neue Preussische Ztg.*, January 1, 1896; *Berliner Neueste Nachrichten*, January 1, 1896.

[22] *Vossische Zeitung*, January 2, 1896.

17

interest. They interpreted the interviews of Marschall and of Kayser on December 31 with the Emperor at Potsdam as manifesting desired activity and regarded the arrival in Berlin of von Blokland, the Transvaal representative at the Hague, as rightly concentrating in Germany all opposition to England.[23] Everything depended, they thought, on England's realizing the seriousness of the situation and condemning the action of the Company. The press referred to the large German interests in the Transvaal, but it felt so strongly over the independence of the Boers that it relegated financial considerations to a secondary rôle. As the *Kölnische Zeitung* said, the English aimed at ultimate control of the colony and this would lead to similar attempts against German possessions in Africa, especially if Rhodes were allowed to proceed. Every reader, whether interested or not in the Transvaal mines and railroads, understood this menace and regarded with fear and envy the intricate financial control which the press pictured Rhodes as exercising throughout South Africa.

While the public was reading the morning editions of January 3, the Emperor was considering the next move with the Chancellor and several naval officers.[24] His advisers had to dissuade the excited Emperor from one or several ill-considered moves, the nature of which to this day is not clear.[25] In all probability

[23] *Kölnische Zeitung*, January 2, 1896. The *K. Z.* was partly official at the time and Marschall said that he gave Fischer, the representative in Berlin, material on January 4. Holstein also was in almost daily contact with Fischer.

[24] Thimme's effort to get the true story of the sending of the Telegram was the classic work on the subject. Friedrich Thimme, "Die Krüger Depesche," *Europäische Gespräche* (June, 1924). The work has now been added to or amended in details but is still the point of departure for research since it contains hitherto unpublished material and personal reminiscences of those involved. For more recent treatments see H. Hallmann, *Krügerdepesche und Flottenfrage* (Stuttgart, 1927) and *Der Weg zum deutschen Schlachtflottenbau* (Stuttgart, 1933); Konrad Lehmann, "Zur Kaiser Wilhelms II. England Politik," *Historische Zeitschrift*, CXLVII (1932-3), pp. 553 ff.; *Idem, Politik und Geschichte*, V (1925), pp. 159 ff.; Hohenlohe, *op. cit.*; and Langer, *op. cit.*, pp. 213 ff., where is to be found the most recent digest account.

[25] The most recent view is that the Emperor proposed a protectorate over the Transvaal, mobilization of the marine infantry, possibly other

William II wished to support the Boers further than he could be allowed to do. The Telegram of mere congratulation, apparently drawn up by Kayser, was mild compared with the draft which the Emperor himself had formulated and which may even have proclaimed a protectorate over the Transvaal. If the participants in the conference were pleased that they had devised and sent the Telegram as a compromise, they must have been doubly so by its hearty reception in the country and even in France and Russia. In the pages of Marschall's diary for January 3 occur these words: " Our press is excellent (*vorzüglich*). All parties are one; even *Tante Voss* (*Vossische Zeitung*) wants to fight."

It is of course not possible to tell how much the general public opinion of January 1 and 2 influenced the government officials to express sympathy with Krüger. Writers who represent the Telegram as a move to prevent something worse on the Emperor's part do not touch on this question. The Emperor may well have contemplated some bold action, for he appears to have been particularly wrought up by the Raid and was often hasty. But Marschall, who later assumed credit for the Telegram, should have acted deliberately. Did he decide that the Telegram would win acclaim in the country? He and possibly others may have hoped to popularize the navy and imperialism by a move which the Emperor could make with less danger than the Foreign Office. This interpretation does not imply that Marschall wished to go to the extremes proposed by *Tante Voss* or contemplated by the Emperor. It merely suggests that he thought some action indicating sympathy with the Boers would arouse nationalistic public opinion at a time when the government welcomed support for a new and far-flung world policy. Marschall was likewise greatly interested in the plan of uniting Europe against England. He suggested to Lascelles, the English Ambassador, in an interview

moves from which he had to be dissuaded; that he had some form of telegram drawn up, embodying perhaps one, perhaps all of these ideas. The true nature of the " supposed " or reconstructed telegram is not quite certain (Langer, *op. cit.*, pp. 234 f.). The idea of a protectorate having been proposed by the Emperor comes from Konrad Lehmann, *op. cit.*, and is repeated by Langer, who believes it possible that such was the Emperor's intention.

on December 31 over the Transvaal that this might occur,[26] and on the following day definitely posed the question to himself.[27] Under these circumstances it would be of value to him to have public opinion behind him. He watched carefully the reaction of the German, French and English newspapers to the Telegram and " directed " Fischer somewhat.[28] This directing of Fischer resulted in an article in the *Kölnische Zeitung* which bears out the point. In this article the unanimity of the German press was especially commended.

> Only one who knows of our torn internal condition [wrote the journal] can understand the importance of the fact that all parties from the *Kreuzzeitung* to *Vorwärts* are without exception united in their opinion, that even Richter approves governmental policy. . . . But the German government can see that only energetic action, and such was the quick opposition to England, can move the populace to unanimity.[29]

In view of this evidence, the domestic situation undoubtedly influenced Marschall's attitude in January, 1896, toward the Transvaal and especially toward the Krüger Telegram.

Most of the press from the *Deutsche Allgemeine Zeitung* (Conservative and semi-official) to *Vorwärts* supported the government for taking immediate action in respect to the Transvaal. *Vorwärts* wrote: " That a free-booting English adventurer must not endanger the existence of an independent Republic does not concern England alone. All civilized people have an interest in suppressing this robbers' expedition." [30] The articles written about the Telegram did not raise the question as to whether Germany should have interfered. On the contrary, those who feared governmental

[26] Thimme, *op. cit.*, p. 210.

[27] *Ibid.* This is one of Thimme's main theses; but there is the possibility that it was a threat similar to those used by Bülow against England. Marschall wanted to force England into the Triple Alliance.

[28] Thimme, *op. cit.*, p. 213.

[29] *Kölnische Zeitung*, January 4, 1896. This is perhaps misleading in that not all approved of the Telegram; but all did condemn the Raid itself. Naturally, Richter and the Social Democrats did not approve the irresponsible action of the Emperor.

[30] *Vorwärts*, January 3, 1896. *Cf.* also *Deutsche Allg. Ztg.*, January 3; *Neue Preussische Ztg.*, January 2.

apathy were pleased that a definite step had been taken and hoped it would encourage the French government to coöperate with Germany for maintaining the *status quo* in South Africa.[31]   The *Kölnische Zeitung* thought Germany could endure the rage of the English press in the conviction that the government had done rightly; let England show, it said, whether she possessed the sense of fair play so often ascribed to her.[32]   But the industrialist and Pan-German *Rheinisch-Westfälische Zeitung* said proudly:

> It is finally time that another European Power should put in its word in South African affairs against the attitude of the Cape government and especially against the plans of the uncrowned king of South Africa, Cecil Rhodes, and stop England's proceedings. The speedy dispatch of German warships to Delagoa Bay is imperative since no other European is called as Germany is called to act decisively in South Africa. The opportune moment has come to uphold the German name in Africa in honor and pride and to protect from English attacks the independence of the Boer state in the Transvaal, a people related to us.[33]

This attitude coincided with the desire for a navy and imperialism. The local organizations of the Pan-German League in the Rhineland repeated on January 5 the same view in a telegram of thanks to the Emperor. The Colonial Society meeting in Hanover likewise unanimously resolved that the protection of Germany's position in Africa required the action which the government had taken.[34]   In its article of congratulation on the Telegram the *Berliner Neueste Nachrichten* demanded an increase in the navy and added, " If the nation and the Reichstag do not see this need, Germany may as well forsake her position as a world Power."[35]   The Emperor felt that the Jameson affair could well aid German naval propaganda and on January 3 ordered that the press drive home the lesson.

Under the feeling of enthusiasm produced generally in Germany by the Emperor's act even the democratic *Vossische Zeitung* met the counter-attacks of the English press with the Bismarckian

[31] *Vossische Ztg.*, January 4, 1896.   [32] *Kölnische Ztg.*, January 4.

[33] *Rheinisch-Westfälische Ztg.*, January 4.

[34] Cited *in extenso* by the *Neue Preuss. Ztg.*, January 7.

[35] *Berliner N. N.*, January 4.

words, "We Germans fear God and nothing else in the world," [36] and the *Frankfurter Zeitung* remarked, "If the English press is so excited over the Emperor's Telegram, it identifies itself thereby with the disturbers of the peace [that is, Jameson's men]." [37] The *Freisinnige Zeitung* criticized this chauvinism and condemned the activities of Karl Peters and the Colonial Society, who had telegraphed Krüger independently, and the meetings held to collect money for the wounded Boers. [38] It pointed out that Jameson and many of his men were in custody, that England had disavowed the Raid, and that efforts were being made in London to bring the culprits to the bar. Somewhat to justify its position the colonial and Pan-German press now referred to the Zanzibar-Helgoland treaty of 1890 as the original cause of anti-English feeling, a treaty, it said, "much more like that after Jena than after Sedan." [39] In point of fact Germany had not been in the least duped by the treaty; but these remarks show the attitude now taken by the nationalists toward all English moves involving colonies. The Social Democratic press also regretted the Telegram because of the bad blood which it had aroused in England. At the same time *Vorwärts* thought the English public purposely overlooked the fact that the Raid had occurred as a private act. By so doing, it said, England was turning against Germany some of the popular citicism at home of negligence on the part of the British government. [40] This last observation weakened the criticism by *Vorwärts* of the German nationalistic press. Enthusiasm for the Telegram on the part of most of the German journals continued almost unchallenged into the following days. In the papers of the Right the answer to English complaints and counterattacks soon came to be: if we had an adequate navy, the British press would not dare to write as it does. [41]

[36] *Vossische Ztg.*, January 4.

[37] *Geschichte der Frankfurter Zeitung*, p. 870 (January 6). The *Frankfurter* did not participate in the resulting chauvinism, which came later.

[38] *Freisinnige Ztg.*, January 5, 7.

[39] *Berliner N. N.*, January 5. It will be recalled that the nationalists had never approved this treaty.

[40] *Vorwärts*, January 5, 7.

[41] One should not omit to mention that many papers saw the danger, not from England, but from Rhodes and the Chartered Company. This

On or about January 7 the German press perceived that the French press, which at first had welcomed the Krüger Telegram, was veering away from the consequences of its approval. The monarchist *Soleil,* for example, began to write of Germany's " game " to push France against England and in the event of difficulties between them to play the arbiter. Simon in the *Gaulois* also showed wariness. As evidence of the change increased the German press became more convinced that what the Emperor had done was well done: both France and England should see that Germany could not be trifled with.[42] At the same time the more cautious press supported the proposal of an international conference brought forward in the *Kölnische Zeitung,*[43] since it offered a chance of coöperation. As excitement over the Raid and the Telegram waned, many German journals cited from British papers evidence of the anti-German feeling in England, denied rumors in regard to German soldiers being sent as settlers to the Transvaal, and described the outbreaks at the London docks and in the streets against the German and Dutch sailors.[44] They attributed these latter disturbances to the bad feeling in England over the cheaper labor of Germans. The *Vossische Zeitung* which on January 1 was willing to use " other means [for example, war] than diplomatic," now urged that " we wish no war with England " if she would cease to regard Germany as of little consequence in foreign affairs.[45] In short, the moderates in Germany quieted down and blamed England for further disturbance. The *Vossische* wrote: " The split is not becoming worse and with the cool-headedness which Germany shows will not do so. The question can eventually, we hope, be settled diplomatically, as can also that of sovereignty." [46] The warnings of the British cor-

fact did not lessen the fear, however, for South Africa's future. For example, see *Neue Preussische Zeitung,* January 5, 6. There were many excellent points brought out by the left Liberal press, but this opinion, as has been shown, did not carry far.

[42] *Neue Preuss. Ztg.,* January 7, 8.

[43] *Berl. Neueste Nach.,* No. 12, January 8. This suggestion of the *K. Z.* no doubt came from Marschall. *Cf.* also *Dresdener Nachrichten,* January 8, which was favorable to a Franco-German-Russian rapprochement.

[44] *Ibid.,* January 7; *Vossische Ztg.,* January 8; *Freisinnige Ztg.,* January 8.

[45] *Vossische Ztg.,* January 8.

[46] *Ibid.* In these days there was a great deal about the financial side

respondent of *The Times* to England that her attitude in the matter would decide Germany's feeling toward England for the ensuing years were considered in Germany as correct.[47]

The decision of the British Cabinet on January 8 to form a flying squadron of two first-class warships and two first-class and two second-class cruisers and to send a squadron to Delagoa Bay and a force of one thousand men to the Cape State once more stirred up German opinion.[48] Was England giving in to the " capitalists " after all? Nationally minded Germans condemned the formation of the flying squadron as a move against Germany and public demonstrations by the Colonial Society and the Pan-German League increased in number.[49] At these meetings money was subscribed for naval agitation and the flag of *Machtpolitik* was raised high. On the whole, however, others did not share the eagerness of these societies to agitate further. The Conservative *Kreuzzeitung* said it was neither " deceived " by this threat from the British navy nor unduly disturbed over the incipient British boycott of German goods.[50] It stated that the events of the last fourteen days had taught Germany two lessons: 1) the need for strengthening the navy; 2) the impossibility of allowing England to control the underseas cables.

The German press did not believe that the events of January, 1896, would lead England to join the Dual Alliance. It thought

of the Raid and the use of the English press by the " capitalists." See also Garvin, *op. cit.*, III.

[47] Cited by the *Neue Preuss. Ztg.*, January 10. One has to consider that pressure from above was probably exercised on behalf of moderation, especially after Marschall for his own purposes had allowed a glimpse of more impassioned feeling.

[48] The Emperor had agreed to the German consul's suggestion that marines could be landed from the German warship *Seeadler* in Delagoa Bay. Later Krüger asked that this move be deferred. Instructions were also given for the *Condor* to leave Dar-es-Salaam for Delagoa Bay. Both moves helped greatly to arouse English opinion against Germany (Langer, *op. cit.*, pp. 242 ff.).

[49] One cannot say that these demands were directly due to the English action since naval demands were frequent. But no opportunity so good as that of the creation of the flying squadron could be let pass by the nationalists.

[50] *Neue Preuss. Ztg.*, January 12.

the references to this possibility in the English papers were meant only to mislead the English and German publics and to distract attention from the economic issue in the Transvaal.[51] As the storm died down the sentiment was often expressed: " Let us stick to the Triple Alliance and see what happens to the one outside the Dual Alliance." [52] It is interesting to find both in and outside the official and semi-official press this early reaction to hints of alliance, especially since it is known that Marschall was playing his cards to attract England to the Triple Alliance. *Vorwärts* alone believed that Germany had needlessly antagonized England, her "natural ally." [53]

In the meantime the Emperor had not forgotten his naval plans.[54] On January 18 the Empire celebrated its twenty-fifth birthday. During the course of the festivities the Emperor made his first public pronouncement for imperialism. Coming as the speech did during the excitement over the Telegram, it received tremendous applause. The Pan-German League immediately demanded action [55] and newspapers from Right through Center vied with each other in demanding coaling stations, ships, and money for the navy. The Imperial Marine Bureau, probably influenced by Tirpitz and with Admiral Senden in charge of propaganda, began to agitate on a large scale.[56] The Colonial Society under the direction of Karl

[51] *Vossische Ztg.*, January 13; *Kölnische Ztg.*, January 17.

[52] *K. Z.*, January 20.

[53] *Vorwärts*, January 14, 17. In an article " Viel Lärm um Nichts " an attempt was made to show how pressure on the press and Social Democracy had made Germany more like Russia and so more at odds with England than ever. If we assume that all countries used pressure on the press in matters of foreign policy, the point of greater and greater divergence of German and English practice is important.

[54] The Emperor pointed out to Hohenlohe on January 8, 1896 " that a difference is to be noted between the naval plans as laid down by the *Oberkommando* on December 1 and my intentions as evoked by the Transvaal. Both plans complement one another. While the plans for extension must be worked out with the distinct future in mind in order to serve the general world position of the Empire, those which have grown out of the Transvaal affair are to fill a temporary need " (Hohenlohe, *op. cit.*, p. 153). See also Hallmann, *op. cit.*, pp. 171 f.

[55] *Cf.* Chapter III, " Pan-German League."

[56] Kehr, *op. cit.*, p. 56, note 98 f.

Peters added its weight in favor of a navy [57] and important periodicals, such as the *Preussische Jahrbücher* and *Deutsche Wochenblatt,* marched in the van of the movement.[58] The press war over the Jameson Raid preceded something greater. *Vorwärts,* joined by Richter's and often by the Centrist press, tried to combat the exaggerated claims made for the navy and for the introduction of the Power motif into economic questions; but its voice was drowned in the growing waves of enthusiasm.[59] The Right and the nationalists preferred to listen to an article like that in the *Grenzboten:*

> It is the duty and the responsibility of the German government to carry on an aggressive policy. . . . Such a colonial policy in all oceans is naturally not possible without ships. Whoever wishes to belong in the concert of nations must be able to rattle the sabre. The German flag does not have much meaning flying over the house of the consul unless it can also fly over some cannon in the harbor. And have we ships? [60]

Kardorff in the *Berliner Neueste Nachrichten* expressed similar views. " Germany cannot let England alone rule the globe and suppress a free Commonwealth like the Transvaal," he said.

As the agitation proceeded the Centrists undertook to learn

[57] *Ibid.,* p. 57. Kehr held that the Duke of Mecklenburg was influenced by Senden.

[58] *Preuss. Jahrb.,* LXXXIII (1896), especially February and March issues.

[59] *Freisinnige Ztg.,* January 25, 29, February 4. Also *Vorwärts,* January 26. Also *Germania* and *K. Z.,* and Bismarck in the *Hamburger Nachrichten.* The *Freisinnige Ztg.,* feared that the government might have to capitulate to the demands of the Agrarians in order to get the bill through the Reichstag. The *Frankfurter Zeitung* wrote as follows: " In that moment when the demand for a *Weltpolitik* is earnestly made, that is, when a policy of Power overseas is meant, there comes with it a complete break with the former system and the entire political situation of Germany will be changed. Seldom has agitation been stirred up in so important a question with such superficiality as is now shown by many groups in their effort to arouse a nationalistic chauvinism to inaugurate a policy of world expansion. . . . The demand for such a policy for Germany does not mean a strengthening of Germany; rather it endangers the position of the Empire for peace and creates imponderables in politics " (*Geschichte der Frank. Ztg.,* p. 867).

[60] *Grenzboten,* January 30.

definitely from the government the state of naval plans. On February 7 in the Budget Commission Lieber interpellated Secretary Hollmann on his intentions. Hollmann, who did not sympathize with the *Oberkommando* or with the work of Senden and Tirpitz, declared that he would not introduce a new bill in the current session of the Reichstag; furthermore, that when he reported a bill it would not correspond to the boundless demands of the agitators. During the naval interpellation the Transvaal affair naturally had mention. Apparently the Budget Commission had already submitted to questioning in regard to the connection between the Transvaal affair and the unleashed naval propaganda. On February 12 the government presented to the Reichstag a White Book on the Transvaal disturbance. This new material furnished another occasion for opening the discussion. On February 13 Prince von Arenberg (Center) took the floor.[61] His speech was intended to furnish the Foreign Secretary with the opportunity to explain publicly the government's position in the Transvaal. At the same time he pointed out that even after the declarations of Hollmann and Marschall in the Budget Commission fear of unlimited naval expansion felt by some members of the Commission had not abated. He repeated the remark of one member that the increase of trade, used as an excuse for a larger navy, had been most marked in Russia and North America, places where trade could least be protected by a navy.

The close connection between naval propaganda and the Transvaal disturbance suspected by the Centrist and Left members of the Commission actually existed. As previous discussion has shown the original plans for an increase in the navy preceded the Raid and the Krüger Telegram; both incidents, however, furnished the occasion for new agitation in behalf of it.

After Marschall had answered Arenberg in a conciliatory manner and had avowed good relations between England and Germany,[62] the party speakers commented. Hammacher acknowledged that his party had long questioned whether the navy, especially as regards cruisers, was adequate. But he was happy, he said, that the government did not intend immediately to accept the extravagant plans

[61] *Sten. Ber. d. Reich.*, February 13, 1896, IX Leg. Per., IV Sess., II, 931 f.
[62] *Loc. cit.*

being discussed in the Colonial Society and in the press. As to the Telegram, he said:

> All Germans are proud to recognize in this act of His Majesty the German Emperor an expression of true German pride, together with the expression of the real feeling of the German people. If the English people have let themselves be driven by this into an unfriendly feeling, the English press to the most extreme enmity against the German Emperor and the German people, we deeply regret it and must denounce this movement with justified anger.[63]

Manteuffel (Conservative), although of the opinion that the Reichstag should not debate foreign affairs in plenum, approved of the government's conduct in the Transvaal affair. In addition he expressed the hope that the government would attend to the many internal problems, that is, the Agrarian needs preëminently, before it turned to foreign problems and a navy.[64] Lieber, at this time opposed to the navy, praised the government's handling of the Transvaal crisis and added, "We also wish the maintenance of or, when they are disturbed, the renewal of good relations with England, but never at the cost of the rights and the world-power position of the German Empire." [65]

Richter, who vehemently denounced the naval plans, likewise conceded that the White Book showed the German government to have acted correctly. He acknowledged the Telegram to have been " an expression of sympathy which, in view of the events in the Transvaal, was manifest in great and wide circles of the German population." [66] At the same time Richter criticized the taking by a sovereign of such steps when he was not responsible for them to a representative body. Furthermore, he emphasized the great danger during the Jubilee Year of displaying such chauvinism as that prevalent in the colonial and Pan-German groups and the Free-Conservative and National-Liberal journals. Nothing, he said, compared in importance with the necessity for good relations with England. Bebel joined Richter in this warning. The former, although acknowledging that the *Wilhelmstrasse* had acted legitimately, added to his attack on the prevalent chauvinism one on the Telegram itself. He held, as had *Vorwärts,* that the sending of the

[63] *Ibid.*, p. 929.   [64] *Ibid.*, 933.   [65] *Ibid.*, p. 932.   [66] *Ibid.*, pp. 933 f.

Telegram was likely to be misrepresented by those who did not understand the German form of government. Its despatch to the Transvaal implied that Germany intended to exact something from England. He criticized the change of front which Germany had seemed to make during the Sino-Japanese war in 1895, saying that this change in being anti-Japanese had been anti-English, and warned the government that unless the press kept more within bounds, it would cause further misunderstandings abroad.[67] On behalf of the People's party (a small group on the Left) Haussmann also condemned the Telegram. Liebermann for the Right bitterly attacked Bebel's criticism of the despatch,[68] and the extreme Left remained isolated. The debate outlined the pro-English sympathies of the Left against the background of anti-English tendencies on the part of the Conservatives and National Liberals.

Although the Reichstag supported the Emperor's action, on the whole it showed greater reserve than the press in respect to the Telegram. Each party representative felt satisfied that the government had acted cautiously and each emphasized the interest of his party in good Anglo-German relations; each was, with the exception of Bebel and Haussmann, in accord with the Telegram; each was likewise wary of further naval plans. Even the Free Conservatives and National Liberals, while unwilling to close the door to increases in naval appropriations, wished the matter thoroughly discussed in the Reichstag. They showed reluctance to use recent anti-English feeling and the Transvaal episode as incentives to naval expansion. All the left parties, including the Center, objected to a new imperialism and a policy of Power. Lieber asked, " Must we really accept the fact that our foreign policy demands that we read this meaning [*Machtpolitik*] into the Emperor's speech of January 18, a meaning which would be disastrous to Germany? " Marschall assured the protestants that no change in foreign policy had occurred, that the naval plans were in no way connected with recent events in South Africa. Since the Reichstag received no further information, matters had to rest here.[69]

[67] *Ibid.*, February 14, pp. 952 ff.   [68] *Ibid.*, February 13, pp. 948 f.
[69] Hohenlohe wrote in his journal at the time: " I had the impression that there was no enthusiasm for an increase of the navy at this moment " (Hohenlohe, *op. cit.*, p. 157).

The naval agitation did not diminish; in the Pan-German League and in the provincial National Liberal press it grew steadily.[70] During the discussion of the naval budget at the end of February the Pan-Germans under the direction of Admiral Senden began a widespread campaign, which greatly embarrassed Marschall and Hollmann. In the middle of March, shortly before the second reading of the budget bill in the Reichstag, *Die Post, Kölnische Zeitung,* and *Hannoverscher Courier* announced the building of six new cruisers and the replacement of the three oldest iron-clads.[71] The *Kreuzzeitung* regretted that Marschall was having to defend himself against attacks in the Reichstag, while Balfour in the English Parliament needed merely to show that the English government's demands were sufficient.[72] This agitation did not lean on the Transvaal affair; it was becoming strong enough to proceed in its own right.

II.

The task remains of examining briefly the question whether the press and the propagandists in any way influenced governmental policy in regard to England. It has already been mentioned that before the Jameson Raid the Emperor and Tirpitz had begun to discuss plans for naval expansion. The disturbance in South Africa undoubtedly strengthened the memorandum given to William II on January 3 and furnished an opportunity for immediate action on the Emperor's part. The Emperor had already added in a marginal note to one of the despatches from Hatzfeldt, German Ambassador at the Court of St. James, dealing with a conversation about the Transvaal between Sir Edward Malet, former British Ambassador to Germany, and Marschall: "We must make good capital of this story in the eventual demands for a navy to protect our increasing commercial interests." [73] It has likewise been suggested above that the desire for naval expansion on the part of certain leaders, hope of rallying the country to the government at a time when the internal struggle was growing acute, and the recent

---

[70] *Magdeburger Ztg.*, February 14, 15. *Cf.* Kehr, *op. cit.*, p. 59.
[71] Kehr, *loc. cit.*   [72] *Neue Preuss. Ztg.*, March 11, 1895.
[73] *G. P., Hatzfeldt to the Foreign Office*, October 25, 1895, XI, No. 2580, p. 12.

trend in colonial policy may well have led the conference of January 3 to send the Telegram in order to utilize the violent popular reaction against the Jameson Raid. If so, this decision gave the Telegram a value in domestic affairs no less important than any pressure value it was intended to have in foreign affairs.

German documents show that early in 1895 Marschall perceived the seriousness of the Transvaal situation.[74] He also knew that the Transvaal, at least in the view of the British there, relied increasingly on German protection.[75] All that Germany wished, said Marschall at that time, was the preservation of the *status quo,* and he considered Rhodes to be the real menace. At the same time he recognized that the German attitude toward England had changed, primarily, he thought, because of England's lack of generosity in colonial matters.[76] As the reason for his policy of *status quo* in the Transvaal Marschall from the beginning gave the "material interests, which Germany has created for herself through the building of railroads and the establishment of commercial relations with the Transvaal. These interests demand the maintenance of the Transvaal as an economically independent state and the continuance of the *status quo* in respect to the railroads and Delagoa Bay. This characterizes the end and the beginning of our policy in that area."[77] The Emperor wrote "good" beside these remarks. What were the interests which determined this policy of *status quo?*

In October, 1895 Marschall told Malet just before the latter's retirement that if Germany retreated before English threats the German people would "storm with anger." All Germany, he said, had approved the government's steps for the protection of German interests in the Transvaal.[78] Marschall thought that Salisbury, British Prime Minister, agreed with this policy of *status quo.*[79]

[74] *Ibid.*, February 1, 1895, No. 2577, and *Weissbuch*, No. 1.

[75] *Loc. cit.*

[76] *Ibid.*, *Memorandum of Marschall*, October 15, 1895, No. 2576, p. 7.

[77] *Ibid.*, *Memorandum of Marschall*, February 1, 1895, p. 4; also to Malet, October 15, 1895, p. 6.

[78] *Ibid.*, p. 6.

[79] *Ibid.*, No. 2582, p. 13. Malet, when about to leave Berlin, had had a conversation with Marschall in which he had rather plainly referred to the Transvaal as the "black spot" in Anglo-German relations and accused Germany of encouraging the Boers. This might lead, he said, to serious

As the news from South Africa grew more serious, Marschall repeated in December his stand to Sir Frank Lascelles, the new Ambassador.[80]   After the Raid the German Foreign Office was eager that the British Foreign Office renounce any connection with it, primarily in order to be assured that the British government was not party to the attempted overthrow of the *status quo*. Whereas the German people held Jameson and the British government, at least Chamberlain, alike responsible for the Raid, the German government gave the British government full opportunity to deny any connection with Jameson.

The argument that Germany had commercial interests Halzfeldt also presented to Salisbury, who on one occasion inquired of the former what he estimated their size to be.[81]   Between 1895 and 1896 German investments in the Transvaal apparently amounted to five hundred million marks.[82]   This figure seems a conservative estimate in view of the fact that a memorandum on German capital investments in various parts of the world worked out in 1900 for the Budget Commission of the Reichstag assigned nine hundred million marks at that date to the Transvaal.[83]   Of these nine hundred million marks in 1900, one hundred millions were in commercial and banking undertakings, seven hundred and thirty millions in industry, and the remainder, about one hundred millions, in plantations and other real estate.[84]   Only German investments in North and South America surpassed these sums. More important than the total amount invested was the form of in-

complications (*G. P.*, XI, No. 2578). A disavowal by Salisbury of Malet's so-called " strong words " was accepted in Berlin because it was thought that Salisbury wanted the *status quo*.

[80] *Ibid., Marschall to Hatzfeldt*, pp. 15-16; *Marschall to Herff*, p. 16; *Memorandum of Marschall*, December 31, 1895, pp. 17 ff.

[81] *Ibid., Hatzfeldt to the Foreign Office*, January 4, 1896, p. 33.

[82] This is the estimate of Goerz, owner of the commercial house, A. Goerz, with branches in London and Johannesburg (*G. P.*, XI, p. 33, and note).

[83] Tables cited in *Deutsche Kolonialzeitung*, No. 15, Supplement XII, April 12, 1900, p. 160.

[84] *Ibid.* The Koppel firm manufacturing railroad supplies referred often to the situation in the Transvaal (*Bericht der Handelskammer zu Berlin*, 1896, pp. 176-7).

vestment. The above figures show that industry accounted for the greatest part. An analysis of the industries concerned indicates, so far as one can determine, that these were firms like Krupp, who had a factory there and secured large orders, Siemens and Halske, who also carried on a good business, and firms supplying machinery and electric power. In addition individuals possessed capital in such enterprises. Especially important was the dynamite and munitions trade. German and English coöperation had recently broken the French dynamite monopoly in the Transvaal; German interests now controlled this trade and every effort was being made by the German Consul and German interests to surpass Creusot in supplying the Transvaal with munitions.[85] In Germany proper the South African trade especially benefited the *Köln-Deutzer Waggonfabrik* (rolling stock) and the *Bochumer Verein für Gusstahlfabrikation,* which declared later that these orders had aided it in weathering the economic crisis of the early 'nineties.[86] Figures show that heavy machinery, railroad materials, and armaments formed the bulk of German exports to the Transvaal. This fact is easily explicable in view of the economic and political conditions of the region.

The position of industry with reference to Transvaal trade and investments acquires great significance for two reasons: first, heavy industry had suffered during the recent industrial depression and eagerly sought new markets. These markets would be less sure if the Transvaal or the Portuguese colonies should fall completely into British hands, since English steel, iron goods, and building materials would presumably be preferred. Although Germans were not unaware of the fact that British colonies everywhere afforded markets for German goods, the situation in the Transvaal would be somewhat different because here Rhodes' interests would prevail and industrial development would be largely under his companies, operating, as the German press always assumed, for political purposes as well as for economic.[87] In the second place, the heavy

[85] Hallgarten, *op. cit.,* p. 511, citing from an article in the *K. Z.,* November 12, 1895.

[86] *Loc. cit.*

[87] The struggle of the Germans against Rhodes in the Transvaal from 1891 to 1895 is treated by Hallgarten, *op. cit.,* pp. 509 ff. Herff was con-

industries formed the backbone of the Free-Conservative and National-Liberal parties and largely controlled the Central Union of
German Industrialists. The importance of these groups in the
Empire has already been shown. There is every reason to believe
that in outlining his policy of *status quo* Marschall was aware of
their wishes and had already adopted a policy favorable to them
months before the storm of January, 1896, broke loose in the German press.[88] As a member of the government he now faced the
political side of economic expansion just as Bülow would soon have
to do in the matter of the Bagdad Railroad. If the government
were to support this expansion, it must use diplomacy to protect
industry and investment.

In addition Marschall knew both from the work of the Colonial
Society and the Pan-Germans and from his experience in the
Reichstag about the new attitude toward colonies and popular
sympathy for the Boers. To allow England to change the *status
quo* would expose the German government to criticism from colonialists and other nationalists at a time when the Emperor needed
the support of these elements for the contemplated naval expansion.
The criticism would now exceed that of 1890 (the year of the
Helgoland-Zanzibar treaty) because of the greater strength of the
imperialistic movement.

The open declaration by the Hohenlohe government favoring a
colonial movement has been noted earlier. Although the country
had shown increasing interest in colonial affairs, especially within
the Colonial Society and among its sympathizers, this attitude was

stantly bringing pressure to bear on the Foreign Office to support his
projects. At first the Foreign Office showed caution; but one can see how
it was gradually drawn into more active participation.

[88] It is true that "material interests" often became "commercial interests," a term which one might readily assume to mean interests connected with export and import trade in the Transvaal. The above facts
belie this narrower interpretation. In addition, it is a fact that trade with
all Africa was only about 1% of the entire German import and export
trade, while capital invested in the Transvaal alone made up about 15%
of German overseas investments, excluding German colonies. On the other
hand, Germany certainly desired to increase her trade and thought existing
conditions best for doing so, since the Boers were friendly and the Delagoa
Bay Railroad offered a direct shipping route. Herff made every effort to
increase trade.

more marked by 1895-6 than ever before. During the months of
January and March, 1895, all groups attacked the government for
its lax colonial policy. The Pan-Germans in an interpellation by
Hasse, January 14, 1895, were the first to charge insufficient protection to German settlers abroad. The honor in which this group
held Bismarck, who had never approved of its kind of *Kolonialpolitik,* is well illustrated by the way in which Hasse blamed the
New Course for the lack of respect shown to Germany abroad. His
desire for a new naval law might not be so great Hasse said, " if
only another personality were evident in the background "; throughout the world it looked as if Germany were eager only to be left in
peace. He charged the Caprivi era with this indifference.[89]   The
attack induced Marschall finally to concede that:

> We need an increase in cruisers, not from chauvinism, not
> because we wish to mix further in the affairs of distant lands,
> not because of a love of a policy of adventure; we need the
> increase because it is our duty to show the German flag from
> time to time wherever German labor settles in far-off countries
> as a warning to foreigners and to be a symbol to remind our
> own people of their unity with and loyalty to their former
> country.[90]

Richter and the Social Democrats comprised a second group of
critics, which in its turn blamed the government for transporting
to the colonies the Prussian military spirit and effectively destroying any cultural life there. These critics likewise reminded the
Reichstag of the increasing cost of colonies without compensating
returns from them, and indicated the pitifully small success in
settling white men in those colonial areas which Germany had been
able or would be able to acquire.[91]   Ordinarily the government expected this side of the Reichstag to oppose its policies; but in the
present case Count Arnim-Muskau and Hammacher also supported
the attack by opening the question of British concessions in the
German colonies. These men doubted the wisdom of allowing British capital, settlers, and influence to come into the German colonies,
especially to South West Africa. Arnim-Muskau gave their reasons
as follows:

[89] *Sten. Ber. d. Reich.,* IX Leg. Per., III Sess., I, 320-327.
[90] *Ibid.,* p. 332.   [91] *Ibid.,* II, 1553 f.

When I look at South Africa, I must say that the policy of the British has called forth in many circles a certain disquiet; the Chartered Company of Cecil Rhodes, which does not possess the entire land, shows a decided tendency to extend its sphere of influence. I welcome with great satisfaction the fact that we have decidedly vetoed Rhodes' aspirations and that the Boer Republics situated behind Lorenzo Marques, the Transvaal, and the Orange Free State, have found an unexpected support in the power of Germany, that we have declared that we wish to see the *status quo* upheld and will not suffer an attack on the Boer Republics. . . . Our African policy must, according to my view, consist in guaranteeing to the Germans in South Africa that support which will make it possible for them to hold together and which will allow them to coöperate with the Boers, who are bound to us in close and intimate blood relationship.[92]

In answering the questions Kayser, Secretary for Colonies, could not deny that, when it was difficult to attract any German capital to the colonies, large concessions had formerly been given to British companies. He defended the terms laid down by the government to guarantee German interests against territorial robbery and said that the concessions had not been prejudicial to Germany.[93] He did not calm the colonialists. The *Kolonialzeitung* had already carried articles against the British concessions and Rhodes' companies connected with them and continued to do so.[94] The similarity between these articles and speeches in the Reichstag is striking.

In December, 1895 discussion of the new budget evoked a further attack on the colonial appropriations by the Progressives. The Free Conservatives and National Liberals accompanied the attack by demanding new cruisers. As the cost of the colonies rose and the wrath of the left Liberals and Social Democrats increased over the waste of money and effort, the eagerness of the nationalists for a

[92] *Ibid.*, IX Leg. Per., IV Sess., I, 13 f., 26 f.

[93] *Ibid.*, pp. 1610 f.

[94] *Kolonialzeitung*, No. 10, March 9, 1895; No. 11, March 16, 1895; No. 27, July 6, 1895. Arnim and others were certainly influenced by the Colonial Society to which Arnim belonged. The article of March 16 was cited from the Pan-Germans; hence it is evident that this group was thinking in similar vein. *Cf.* with the Reichstag debates of May 19, 1896, 1895-6, IV, 2354 f. The answer to questions on British concessions was contained in a map, *Kolonialztg.*, No. 1, January 4, 1900, p. 5.

bolder policy waxed. The tightening of the situation in South Africa, especially the challenge actually or supposedly offered by Cecil Rhodes' vast schemes, heightened the colonial ardour of the German nationalists. And this ardour was not confined to " material interests " in the Transvaal; it embraced the entire problem of maintaining the *status quo* in South Africa. These nationalists manifested concern for the preservation of German colonies—they frequently condemned as stupid the giving up of Zanzibar and the surrender of Namaqualand on the eastern boundary of German South West Africa—and asked for an opportunity to exploit them with German capital for German interests. Since German capital was reluctant, they thought the government should as far as possible develop the colonies. A full programme of projects to be demanded of the government was not yet worked out in 1895; but the trend of colonial thought could not have escaped the close attention of Marschall and Kayser.

Marschall must also have known of the speculation on the London Exchange in Transvaal mining shares and of the fact that many Germans, probably including members of the Foreign Office, had participated in this speculation. Prolonged disturbance would cause a heavy decline in quotations. He could not have been ignorant of the steps taken by the Germans at Lisbon in 1894 to prevent Portugal from selling to England railroad or harbor rights in the Portuguese East Africa colony or of the manifestations of German friendship with the Boers at the opening of the Delagoa Bay railroad.[95] These activities could hardly be followed by anything less than insistence on the *status quo*.

[95] Hallgarten, *op. cit.*, pp. 510 ff. Hallgarten says that the Emperor had watched events carefully and declared in 1894 that Germany could not allow England to establish herself in the Portuguese colonies. At the same time the German government negotiated in Berlin with representatives of the Boer government, promising to sustain it in the Portuguese question and eventually to make German finance enter the Portuguese colonies if the Transvaal would assume the necessary guarantees. Hallgarten calls the show of friendship at the time of the opening of the Delagoa Bay railroad as expressed in the Emperor's despatch to Krüger " the first Krüger Telegram." Herff called the exchange of telegrams a " pacific demonstration against England which will enforce our position in South Africa." The text of the Emperor's telegram to Krüger on the above-mentioned occasion is worth citing: " I experience a particular satis-

The policy of the *status quo* in the Transvaal had, therefore, been determined upon long before January, 1896. It was intended not alone to protect existing German "material interests" there. Beyond the maintenance of these lay the need to keep open a future market for German industry and German investment banking in the richest gold mining area of the world. The importance of the munitions industry to the maintenance of the monarchy and the power of big business in the Empire impelled the government to act in their behalf. Although at the time of the Jameson crisis the public press of these interests did not directly move the government to take any steps beyond correct diplomatic protest to England, the *Deutsche Bank,* Krupp, and the interests represented by them influenced its stand.

In addition, Marschall, whom the Agrarian-Conservatives hated for his commercial policy, undoubtedly regarded the Telegram as having some internal political value. He could not submit to the demands of the nationalistic press for war or threats of war on behalf of the Boers. But a generous gesture on the part of the Emperor, committing the government to nothing, could rally enthusiasm for the government at a critical moment. This interpretation helps to explain why the reaction of the press to the Telegram pleased Marschall, while it in no way rules out the fact that he likewise strove to impress England in order to turn her toward the Triple Alliance,[96] and does call attention to domestic conditions. It indicates the way in which the German government was being drawn into external affairs in order to satisfy nationalism at home and even to encourage this nationalism as an aid to carrying out the Emperor's naval programme and *Weltpolitik* plans. It is inter-

faction, Mr. President, in sending you my greetings from on board my ship *Condor* in these days when you are celebrating the establishment of a railroad line between the capital of your country and the sea. I congratulate you and the Free State of South Africa on the happy event and you have my appreciation of the success of the achievement. I hope that the new line, rich in promise, will prove profitable for your country in continuing to develop commerce, and that it will equally serve to cement intimate commercial relations with Germany" (Cited by Hallgarten, *op. cit.,* p. 515, note 3. The Telegram was apparently drawn up by Kiderlen of the Foreign Office on a suggestion from Herff).

[96] Langer, *op. cit.,* p. 238.

esting by way of comparison to note that on January 4 Chamberlain wrote the following words to Salisbury: "It does not matter much which of our numerous foes we defy, but we ought to defy some-one."[97] The defiance which he wished was intended to soothe the nationalists in England, whom Jameson's defeat and the bitter attacks of foreign Powers had ruffled. The feeling of the British nationalists resembled that of the German ones, upset by the delay of their government in entering world politics.

III.

In conclusion a few lines may be given to stating the more lasting effects of the events of January, 1896, on anti-English feeling in Germany. That the enemies of the government on the extreme Left knew of the increased colonial and naval propaganda was evident from the attacks by Richter and the Social Democrats in a four-day debate in March, 1896, on the colonial budget.[98] Even the Center joined the attack on Karl Peters and *Vorwärts* was able to rejoice: Peters has as good as fallen and the colonial propaganda suffers thereby.[99] These outbursts against the growing nationalism only excited further manifestations of it such as criticism of the pro-English policy of the government and bold naval demands. The *Kreuzzeitung* thought it necessary to increase immediately the troops in East and West Africa as a protection against the Matabele and the Herreros: race war in South Africa would be inevitable, it wrote.[100] The nationalist press rejoiced that England seemed about to suffer the effects of the Raid in increased native hostility through-out her South African possessions.[101] It approved Krüger's refusal of the English invitation to confer in London on the Uitlander question [102] and grew irate when the *Morning Post,* after a con-

[97] Garvin, *op. cit.,* III, 95. *Cf.* also Langer, p. 246, where occurs the following sentence: "One reason for the despatch of the Telegram to Krüger was indubitably the hope of making a hit with the German public and restoring the popularity of the Emperor." The author, however, does not enlarge upon this idea.

[98] *Sten. Ber. d. Reich.,* March 13-17, 1896, IX Leg. Per., IV Sess., II, 1419-1525.

[99] *Vorwärts,* March 14, 1896.

[100] *Kreuzztg.,* April 22, 1896.

[101] *Ibid.,* April 8, 15, 21, 1896.   [102] *Ibid.* and *K. Z.,* April 30, 1896.

gratulatory telegram from the Emperor to Max Müller on the occasion of an Oxford rowing victory, said that England would be ready to receive His Majesty at Cowes, but only on consideration that beforehand he make his journey to Canossa.[103]

The nationalist press, furthermore, began seriously to consider England's diplomatic and international position and to express satisfaction that she found herself so generally isolated. Although many papers noticed that France quickly turned from enthusiasm for the Telegram to editorials on the " hole in the Vosges," they thought that Russia's Anglophobia was tending to sharpen the Anglo-French enmity in Egypt. England, wrote the *Kreuzzeitung,* would like to have an alliance with Germany similar to the Franco-Russian alliance; England, of course, would try to play Russia's part of dominating, " but fortunately the alliance is not to be had, and it seems in our interest not to get England out of her present difficulties. That might result in turning France and Russia against us." [104] To help England by pressure on the Transvaal would be to cut off Germany's own nose and endanger her position in her own colonies.[105] Germany did not believe France and Russia capable of uniting with England, the *Kreuzzeitung* wrote, and it was well that the Triple Alliance had preserved freedom of action.[106] The Right press rejected out of hand any alliance with England, such as had been rumored the year before at the time of the English proposal over the Turkish Empire, and felt more than justified in this decision as the cipher telegrams were made known.[107] Albion, more accurately the Chartered Company, seemed more " perfidious " than ever.[108]

In May and June the trial and sentence of Jameson and of the

---

[103] *Ibid.*, April 15 and *K. Z.*, April 14, 1896.

[104] *Ibid.*, April 15, 1896.   [105] *Loc. cit.*   [106] *Ibid.*, April 22.

[107] The cipher telegrams were messages exchanged by the Reform Committee in Johannesburg, the Chartered Company, and Jameson. The cipher was found in Jameson's baggage, and the telegrams were made known at the end of April.

[108] This is clear not only in the attacks on the telegrams but in the suppositions about the Metabele War. The press of the Right ascribed the whole to a ruse of the Chartered Company and thought the Company retreated when England threatened to send regular troops into Rhodesia, a fantastic explanation. *Cf. Kreuzztg.* and *K. Z.* during the early days of May.

leaders of the Chartered Company afforded some satisfaction in Germany, and the approval by the Reichstag of the extraordinary budget for German South West Africa somewhat mollified the propagandists. The English press continued to be very disquieting—even *Vorwärts* was appalled by the Offenbach-opera-like fantasy of Fort's article in the Nineteenth Century [109]—but the *Kölnische Zeitung,* perhaps at a hint from above, began to lay the blame for the anti-German attitude of the English press upon the paid press of the Chartered Company. Many of Rhodes' supporters, however, it suggested, were growing silent and England was seriously taking stock of her position. [110]

In the meantime the propaganda of the Pan-Germans and the Colonial Society did not abate. Several incidents in the Reichstag illustrate how sensitive to England public opinion was becoming. In June Liebermann von Sonnenberg, Dr. Förster (Reform party), and Werner (National Liberal) interpellated the government on the Affair Bashford. Bashford acted as the Berlin correspondent of several British newspapers and, according to Liebermann, as confidential man for the South West Africa Company, on behalf of which he had negotiated with Secretary Kayser. He had attacked an employee of the German telegraph service for counting the words of a telegram—so delaying the despatch of the message—and had afterward made some kind of money settlement for the offense. The interpellators demanded to know the truth of the affair. Hushing it up, said Liebermann, was not his way of doing things. No wonder Germans were looked down on abroad: " We wish no chauvinism; but we believe he said that a strong German national feeling is the surest protection to world peace, is the most secure harbor for our kinsfolk abroad." [111] Secretary Stephan of the Post Office Department was able to clear up the matter satisfactorily; but the Affair Bashford showed how extremely sensitive the nationalists had become to any question regarding England or " national honor " and

[109] Seymour Fort, " The True Motive and Reason of Dr. Jameson's Raid," *Nineteenth Century,* June, 1896, pp. 873-880.

[110] *K. Z.,* June 3, 1896. It was thought that the articles in the *Preussische Jahrbücher,* which were in favor of a rapprochement with Russia and France, had affected England.

[111] *Sten. Ber. d. Reich.,* June 18, 1896, IX Leg. Per., IV Sess., IV, 2692 f.

how readily they made use of every opportunity to bring their cause before the public.

In the same spirit the naval question came to the fore again during the budgetary discussions of December. Comparing the British navy with the German Zimmermann (Reform party) said:

> We believe that a policy of imperialism is justified and necessary. After we have attained to national unity, the German eagle may spread its wings over all Germans in whatever land, in whatever part of the world they dwell. We believe that it is the duty of the navy to work to this end: that German property and German honor in more than a thousand places stand under its protection and that many hearts beat for joy when German ships come into sight.[112]

This statement echoed exactly the cry of the Pan-Germans.

In these same days the National Liberals introduced and defended a bill to subsidize steamships. The North German Lloyd should receive a million and a half more marks in order to double its freight capacity and increase the speed of its vessels. This amount would bring the total to three and one-half million marks, a sum still below the French and British subsidies, argued Boetticher, Reich Secretary of Interior. In his speech Boetticher pointed out that German trade had increased, that England's relative share in direct shipping had fallen, that German ships for German trade now replaced British. Especially the British, he said, looked askance at Germany's success.[113]

> We look with envy upon the development of British shipbuilding, of English industry, and of English trade; but no one can blame us if we wish to achieve, if not equality, at least a further increase for ourselves in this sphere. This achievement must be made useful for our national welfare and our national labor.[114]

In making this statement Boetticher and his supporters were looking beyond the Transvaal and South Africa to markets in China. In accordance with the suggestion of the Chamber of Commerce

---

[112] *Ibid.*, December 2, 1896, V, 3668.

[113] Hoffmann, *op. cit.*, p. 67 should be compared here.

[114] *Sten. Ber. d. Reich.*, December 9, 1896, IX Leg. Per., IV Sess., V, 3770.

of Crefeld, they were soon to encourage trade with China by an expedition to the Far East. Germany was growing increasingly aware of new possibilities in the entire field of trade. As the above citation shows, the awareness did not result from hatred of England, but from consideration of internal German interests and represented a current of nationalistic thought which the events of 1896 had strengthened. Hamburg records showed that in spite of the Jameson Raid trade with South Africa had increased and the Hamburg Chamber of Commerce continued as in 1895-6 to urge that German propaganda against England be curbed so that England would not endeavour to check German trade with South Africa. In its report for 1896 it cautioned against antagonizing England as follows:

> We must vigorously deny the recent exaggerated suggestions in England that Germany is trying to crowd out British trade all over the world. . . . Manchester, Birmingham, Glasgow are still the first industrial centers of Europe and German overseas markets and trade cannot yet do entirely without their products. . . . Therefore, we should guard against a chauvinistic underestimate of our competitors; we should strain every nerve instead to see that German industry in the future makes progress.[115]

One last event of 1896 deserves to be mentioned, the great fury against England occasioned toward the close of the year by the strike of the Hamburg longshoremen. The sittings of the Reichstag on December 2 and 3 and all newspapers occupied themselves with this event. Many Germans felt that England had caused the strike. The *Hamburger Nachrichten* wrote that probably the British government was backing the strike in an attempt to embarrass the German government. All the animus against English Social Democracy, the activities of Tom Mann in English labor, and against the English democratic system of government burst forth anew over the strike. That it was unjustified animus reveals how sensitive Germany had grown and how this anti-English feeling did not rest on commercial and industrial grounds alone but represented an antagonism along many lines, not the least of which was the belief that the British example encouraged Social Democracy, the enemy of German progress. Stumm clung to the point that the strike was

[115] *Bericht der Handelskammer zu Hamburg*, 1896, p. 9.

a *Machtfrage* and not a wage question. Germany's entire success in industrial competition lay, he said, in the fact that Germany had " discipline " in her industrial life. If unions were allowed to form, to become successful in strikes, discipline would vanish and industry would lose time through useless strikes and lockouts, dissatisfactions, and class warfare. This showed, he said, how opposite the British and German systems were; German industrial success rested upon the unquestioned control of his workers by the employer; any weakening of this control would react to Germany's disadvantage and to England's advantage in the world market. Stumm believed that Germany must prevent British Trade Unionism from entering. The position of the German employer became almost automatically anti-English.

The Social Democrats and left Liberals defended the workers and in so doing became champions of England.

> It is high time we stopped this constant animosity against England [said Barth], which has grown in some circles to be almost a kind of sport. We have not so much sympathy in the world to lose that we can look upon friendship with England as a matter of indifference. I believe that rather we have a pressing interest to be on good terms with England. German industry competes with English industry all over the world; it has shown in recent years that it does not need to be timid in this. But we do not need to embroil ourselves politically with England over it.[116]

The debate over the Hamburg strike showed that the distribution of anti-English and pro-English feeling in Germany corresponded roughly to the social and economic divisions within the Empire.

Looked at from the point of view of German domestic affairs, what was the ultimate importance of the Raid and the Telegram in the history of Anglo-German relations? It is clear that these actions provoked an outbreak of anti-English feeling in Germany greater than ever before. In fact the outbreak could scarcely have arisen before: first, because German industry and trade up to

---

[116] *Sten. Ber. d. Reich.*, December 12, 1896, IX Leg. Per., IV Sess., V, 3861. *Cf.* Barth in *Die Nation*, No. 10, December 5, 1896. In the latter place he said that there was no rationalism in the anti-English feeling, that one merely saw in it how animosity toward England came to the fore in moments like the strike.

1895-6 had not reached a point of such high achievement and promise; secondly, because German nationalistic propaganda had not been so well organized. A third point might well be added: the German government had not until about this time taken so active an interest in colonial and world affairs. These changes were rapidly producing in Germany a new attitude among nationalists. They had already become vocal; before the Raid occurred they had changed the tone of debate in the Reichstag, had urged new naval laws and secured new ship subsidies for the increase of German shipping facilities. Hence the Telegram was only an incident in the history of governmental use of and adaption to public opinion. The anti-English feeling of the Agrarians and the nationalists had existed for some time; but this feeling now spread more widely with the expansion of the new nationalism. To attack England verbally furnished emotional outlet for the latter; but envy as well fed the attack. England had the navy, colonial empire, and trade *par excellence,* which Germany must acquire to maintain her rate of growth. Through the Raid and the despatch to Krüger opinion crystallized more quickly and more widely than it otherwise might have done and the anti-English direction grew more marked; but the movement for a greater empire had already begun.

That the events of January, 1896, did not suffice to convince the entire nation of the need for imperialism is seen in the fact that new naval plans were not immediately accepted. In spite of the propaganda of the Pan-Germans and the efforts behind the scenes by Admiral Senden and Tirpitz, Hollmann and Chancellor Hohenlohe succeeded in passing their own budget which, though demanding increases for the navy, aimed expressly at stemming the tide of " boundless plans." The Center and the Agrarians still opposed a Tirpitz navy and the Bismarckian press also condemned it.[117] Only a beginning in the new direction had been made; but the nationalistic press had received an impetus which it faithfully sustained. At the same time the nationalistic propaganda for imperialism had become definitely anti-English and this animus did not abate in the ensuing years.

[117] Thimme, *op. cit.*, pp. 221 and 222, note 1.

[118] For a discussion in short compass of anti-English feeling in Germany after 1892 see *Tilly Memorandum on Anglo-German Relations, 1892-1904, British Documents,* I.

CHAPTER V

THE TERMINATION OF THE ANGLO-GERMAN TRADE TREATY AND PUBLIC OPINION

A. *The Anglo-German Treaty Regarding the Portuguese Colonies*

But when the heart's desire of millions of Germans is fulfilled, when 'forever undivided' is echoed from the North German coast to the Danube and to the beautiful Adriatic, when Germany is great and strong enough to challenge the world, then she will need no central European tariff union, at least, not with Slavs, Magyars, and Roumanians.

Richard Denner, *Bedeutung und Ziele deutscher Weltpolitik*, p. 57.

During the years between the Krüger Telegram and the outbreak of war in South Africa Germany developed her hold in the Far and Near East. The time had ripened for the further quest which she had determined to make for spheres of influence and for prestige. In preparation she placed herself under the guidance of Bülow at the Foreign Office (1897) and passed the first naval bill (1898). At the same time she began to reap the rewards of a continued and unprecedented material prosperity. If in these years German public opinion did not fully appreciate the dangers associated with these changes,[1] its ignorance only increased the enthusiasm with which the German press received each move. Bülow's popularity never again equalled that accorded him at the conclusion of the Samoa treaty. It seemed a truism that in Germany nothing could attain to the popularity of successful imperialism.

Germany's entrance into world affairs coincided with the outbreak of acute colonial conflicts, such as Anglo-French rivalry in Central Africa, the Open Door controversy in China, continued bitterness in the Transvaal area, and the Spanish-American War. Germany met abroad not only English diplomacy and ships, but Russian and then American. Several studies have recently revealed

[1] Karl O. Herkenberg, *The Times und das deutsch-englische Verhältnis im Jahre 1898* (Berlin, 1925), Preface by Martin Spahn, pp. 7 ff.

262

that American-German relations, particularly as reflected in the anti-German press of the United States after 1898, were growing worse.[2] England probably had as many overseas problems just before 1900 as she ever faced at one time. Her accumulation of troubles increased sensitiveness to German development and furnished reasons why she desired coöperation with her potential rival. Similarly, it undoubtedly seemed wise for Germany to improve Anglo-German relations and to coöperate with Britain if possible.

During 1897 feeling between the two countries was strained. Although it improved somewhat in the following months,[3] nothing

[2] Alfred Vagts, *op. cit.*; Herbert Zühlke, *Die Rolle des fernen Ostens in den politischen Beziehungen der Mächte, 1890-1914* (Berlin, 1929); Ilse Kunz-Lack, *Die deutsch-amerikanischen Beziehungen*, 1890-1914 (Stuttgart, 1935). *Cf.* also Walter Millis, *The Road to War* (New York, 1935), and a recent bibliographical article, L. B. Shippee, " German-American Relations, 1890-1914," *Journal of Modern History*, VIII (1936), No. 4.

[3] In January 1898 the *Vossische Zeitung*, while protesting its admiration of England, wrote of its regret that the English press should be so anti-German over Kiau-chow (*Vossische Ztg.*, January 6, 1898). Four days later the journal noted that the tone in England had quieted, perhaps because of the projected Anglo-German loan to China (*ibid.*, January 10). On January 13 the same paper wrote: " A right about face has apparently occurred in English public opinion. Most of the English papers, even those which were lately filled with passionate hatred against Germany, have become friendly. . . . In the recent attacks we have made no secret of the fact that we held a *rapprochement* between both peoples and governments as necessary and desirable. If the Chinese loan were to lead to this goal, we should greet it with enthusiasm " (*ibid.*, January 13). These sentiments were echoed by the *Kölnische Ztg.*. Subsequently the *Vossische Zeitung* thought the anti-Russian feeling in England had grown and was greater than the anti-German, which had almost disappeared. Its warning was: " Germany will not be taken in tow by England or Russia but will go with that Power whose interests serve her own " (*ibid.*, January 19). After this all mention of any alliance with England dropped. On February 3 the journal wrote in mentioning talk of an alliance: " These and similar remarks indicate that in England they find a need to wipe out the memory of that hate against Germany which has continued so long in the British press. But it cannot be denied that in Germany the feeling will often pervail that the English are only concerned over our friendship for the present because they find it necessary. Necessity teaches one to beg and to be polite " (*ibid.*, February 3). In 1898 the German press was very wary of and often downrightly opposed to any coquetting with an English alliance. See, for example, the comments on Bülow's speech of

came of the now famous Chamberlain-Hatzfeldt conversations ex-
rept the unfortunate Portuguese colonies treaty of 1898. It is
necessary to review in some detail the treaty between England and
Germany over these colonies because of its bearing on German relations with the Transvaal. In spite of the Telegram and of the press
of 1896 the treaty effected prior to the outbreak of war in the
Transvaal the virtual surrender of the Boers by the German government. The move which Bülow made in negotiating this treaty
illustrated his greed for colonies, as well as the feebleness of the
government's interest in Boer independence *per se*. Immediately
thereafter England deceived Germany over the treaty. Hence instead
of improving relations between the two countries the Portuguese
colonies treaty greatly impaired them and furnished the nationalists
with additional material for warning against coöperation with
England.

For some years German interests in Delagoa Bay and in the
railroad through Portuguese East Africa to the Transvaal had
bothered England.[4] British opinion accused Germany of supporting
the Transvaal in its efforts to obtain possession of the railroad,
while England contested the right of the Portuguese government to
sell it, at least before the announcement of the Berne Award.[5]
From the first Chamberlain and Rhodes appreciated the importance
of Delagoa Bay as a key to the Transvaal situation and they re-

February 8 in the Reichstag by the *Neue Preussische Zeitung*, February
9. *Cf.* also Langer, *op. cit.*, II, 500, where this is also noted.

[4] *Tilley Memorandum, B. D.*, I, 323, 326. Also Langer, *op. cit.*, I, 243 f.;
Hallgarten, *op. cit.*, 515 f. In January, 1898 the *Vossische Zeitung* noted
British interest in Delagoa Bay in the following words: " Delagoa Bay
would be worth for England the greatest sacrifice since it controls not
only the entrance to Maschonaland and Tatabeleland, but it is the harbor
for the Transvaal. Its political importance is thereby clear. It has become a life and death matter to the South African Republic, since Amatonga-
land has been added to the British colony, Natal, and therewith all hope of
the Transvaal securing a direct outlet to the sea has been taken away. . . .
The British have already again a new plan to plant themselves on the
Portuguese Southwest Africa coast " (*Voss. Ztg.*, January 7, 1898). Interest in the question was frequently in evidence and not with any idea of
Germany's granting England her wish.

[5] *B. D.*, I, 323, and Hallgarten, *op. cit.* The tangled questions regarding
concessions had been given to a court of arbitration for settlement.

sented German activities in that area. In 1896 Chamberlain entered into conversations with the Rothschilds to discover whether they would advance money for leasing the Bay from Portugal.[6] Nothing came of these conversations; but in 1897 new ones opened with the Marquis de Soveral, Portuguese Minister in London, touching financial aid to Portugal. Germany got wind of these conversations and, although they had no definite outcome, she recalled von Derenthall, German Minister in Lisbon, for not upholding sufficiently German interests.[7] The following spring England again put out feelers for some kind of financial plan, through which she could strengthen her position in Portuguese East Africa and perhaps directly in Delagoa Bay.[8] Rumor quickly reached Berlin and on June 18 Bülow wrote to Hatzfeldt, " Our attention at present must be directed especially to the question of the Portuguese colonies." He enclosed a list of concessions which would be acceptable to Germany in case of negotiations between England and Germany in regard to Delagoa Bay.[9] That Germany was primarily interested in colonial expansion and not in German rights in the Portuguese colonies or in the Transvaal is indicated by the Emperor's marginal note, " Compensations to Germany need not necessarily lie in Africa," [10] and by the fact that Bülow's list included possible compensations in Asia, the South Seas, and West Africa, as well as in East Africa. Likewise Bülow conceded at the outset that in case of an Anglo-German treaty England should receive Delagoa Bay as her sphere of interest. Support for the Boers he simply did not consider.[11] Since the move came so soon after Kiau-chow,

[6] Garvin, *op. cit.*, III, 308 ff.   [7] *B. D.*, I, 328 ff.

[8] England was to have the right of pre-emption over the Bay should control ever be contemplated, and Portugal could not alienate to a third Power. This came as a result of the Award of 1875 (Garvin, *op. cit.*, p. 308).

[9] *G. P.*, XIV (1), *Bülow to Hatzfeldt, June 8, 1898*, pp. 259 f. Hatzfeldt had already spoken to Kimberley, Rosebery, and Salisbury to the effect that Portugal must not be allowed to grant away her colonial rights without previous agreement between England and Germany (*ibid.*, p. 260). He had also asked on June 3 for suggestions from Bülow about colonial demands, since Chamberlain seemed somewhat conciliatory touching the neutral zone (West Africa) and Delagoa Bay (*ibid.*, p. 242).

[10] *Loc. cit.*

[11] *Ibid.*, p. 269, June 20, 1898. Presented to Salisbury on June 21. It

19

Chamberlain hardly hesitated long as to what he should do to encourage friendly relations. He must undertake some coöperation with Germany.[12]

After broaching the question in London Bülow on June 18 opened negotiations in Lisbon. He directed Tattenbach, the new German Minister in Lisbon, to remind the Portuguese government of the effect which colonial agreement between Portugual and England would have upon German interests. He was to hint at German coöperation with other Powers against it.[13] On the same day he ordered Münster, German Ambassador in Paris, to confer with Hanotaux, the French Foreign Minister.[14]

Bülow's reliance on *Machtpolitik* and national prestige came out in his reasoning on the subject of his policy toward England. He wrote in June as follows:

> This is a question, as with colonial questions in general for us as well as for England, not of a provable right, but of an interest and of a power [the navy] for making this interest good in case of necessity. England is stronger at sea than we are. The English government in the consciousness of its own naval strength negotiates as if it thought up to now that it need not consider Germany. Also, certainly, it acts as if it believed that Germany would have no support from other sea Powers, since Russia wishes British interests directed to South Africa, while public opinion in France, as shown at the time

---

should be noted that during the crisis over Kiau-chow in the previous year Hatzfeldt was empowered to offer England if necessary a free hand in South Africa and Delagoa Bay (Langer, *op. cit.*, II, 453, and *G. P.*, XIV, Nos. 3698, 3702-4, 3708-10).

[12] That England did realize the German colonial lust is amply illustrated by the Bertie Memorandum, *B. D.*, I, 44 ff., May 1, 1898. This Memorandum also mentioned Portugal's fear of the Germans. The Emperor distrusted an English alliance so much that he remarked at the conclusion of one of the early despatches regarding the colonies: " From this despatch, especially from the final passage, it is clear how false and unreliable Salisbury is. That is no way to attract us to an alliance [*Bündnis*]. *Dieu nous en garde!* " (*G. P.*, XIV, 263). In June the alliance seemed desirable to Chamberlain and Salisbury (*ibid.*, pp. 241 f., *Hatzfeldt to Hohenlohe*, June 3, 1898).

[13] *Ibid.*, *Bülow to Tattenbach*, June 18, 1898, pp. 265-6.

[14] *Ibid.*, *Bülow to Münster*, June 18, 1898, pp. 266 f.

of the Jameson Raid, for well-known reasons would be averse to coöperation with Germany.[15]

England, however, must not be allowed to diminish the prestige of the German government " at home and abroad," especially since Bülow thought a continental alliance much more possible now than it would be in the future. Also the Emperor counselled action and regretted that since Germany had no navy she would have to wound German public opinion by sacrificing the Boers, " for years," he said, " the subject of sentimental sympathy not to be explained on logical grounds." [16] As to the question of Germany's sharing in a loan to Portugal, Bülow said, " The means for this could only be found if the German government guaranteed the capitalists; but I do not doubt that the Reichstag would afterward guarantee this loan out of consideration for important national interests." [17] On the whole Bülow wished an Anglo-German agreement excluding France, and he had approached France only to impress England.

Salisbury attempted to separate the financial from the territorial question. He suggested that England deal with the financial alone and make a treaty with Germany covering the eventuality of a breakup of Portugal's colonial empire.[18] Already he was in lively diplomatic intercourse with Hatzfeldt, although Chamberlain and the Portuguese representative still communicated *à deux*.[19] When Hatzfeldt complained of England's putting obstacles in the way of German colonial expansion, Salisbury repeated that he was ready to come to agreement on the Portuguese question. On July 6 Hatzfeldt thought Salisbury firmly decided to go ahead with Germany. Since the Berlin Foreign Office feared an Anglo-American-Japanese coalition to divide the Spanish and Portuguese empires and a possible English attempt to occupy Lisbon, it must have welcomed this news.[20] A few days later, July 13, Soveral definitely

---

[15] *Ibid., Bülow to Hatzfeldt*, June 22, 1898, pp. 272-3.
[16] *Ibid.*, pp. 273 ff.   [17] *Ibid.*, p. 275.
[18] *B. D.*, I, *Salisbury to Gough*, June 21, 1898, p. 48; *G. P.*, XIV, *Hatzfeldt to the Foreign Office*, June 21, 1898, p. 270. The Bertie Memorandum of June 30 favored a secret agreement with Germany and showed some fear of pressure from the continent.
[19] *G. P.*, XIV, 279.
[20] *Ibid.*, XV, July 6 and 7, No. 4154.

refused in London all proposals for a loan to Portugual.[21] Thereupon the negotiations between England and Germany for territorial
compensation entered on a final phase and the financial question
was left to be decided "whenever either government feels it ex-
pedient to accede to a request for money."

It is not ncessary to follow the Anglo-German negotiations. On
August 30, 1898, Balfour and Hatzfeldt signed two documents,
one general and one secret, providing that, if the occasion should
arise, a joint loan should be made to Portugal and excluding any
third Power from certain sections of Africa and Timor.[22] Although
Germany was promised a share in case of a division of the Portuguese colonies, she did not obtain future right to the Volta Delta
and Walfisch Bay. Chamberlain commented privately, "The only
advantage to us is the assurance of Germany's abstention from
further interference in Delagoa Bay and the Transvaal—in other
words, we pay blackmail to Germany to induce her not to interfere
where she has no right of interference. Well! it is worth while to
pay blackmail sometimes."[23]

The opportunity for Germany and England to carry out the
terms of this treaty never came. It remained a phantom feast for
the German colonialists. But for the sake of potential colonial
gain the Emperor and Bülow had renounced Delagoa Bay and
definitely abandoned the Boers. Bülow boldly said, "I wish now
as before an understanding with England, since this is the only
reasonable basis for colonial acquisitions, and *I am free from all
sentimentality toward the Boers.*"[24] He pointed out to Salisbury
that in order to quiet public opinion adequate compensation must
be given for the renunciation; but Bülow did not dare to put the

---

[21] *B. D.*, I, 57. Hatzfeldt said on July 9 that the negotiations had come
to a stop.

[22] Text in *G. P.*, XIV, No. 3872, 347 f.

[23] *Chamberlain to Balfour*, August 19, cited by Garvin, *op. cit.*, III, 315.

[24] *G. P.*, XIV, *Richthofen to Hatzfeldt*, citing Bülow, July 16, 1898, No.
3834, p. 297. Also No. 3840, pp. 304 f., *Memorandum from Richthofen*, to
whom, Hammann said, Bülow assigned an important part of the negotiations (Hammann, *op. cit.*, p. 72). Holstein shared Bülow's view and said:
"The Transvaal is not at all worth our sacrificing the Bismarckian policy
of 'the two irons in the fire' for its sake." (Italics are those of the
author.)

case directly before the public. The treaty remained secret; but news of it leaked out in September in the British papers and appeared with the Emperor's congratulatory telegram to Kitchener on his victory over the Mahdi.[25] Then the German official organs began to moderate their tone. " In fact," wrote the Berlin correspondent of *The Times,* " certain official organs received an intimation from above to pave the way by means of well-timed hints and suggestions in regard to future policy for the announcement that political Germany has altered her helm by a few points." [26] Neither the Pan-Germans nor the other friends of the Boers liked the pro-English policy. In fact, the *Alldeutsche Blätter,* suspecting that the treaty provided only for an eventuality, from this time on grew more afraid of Britain and more insistent on Germany's being treated as an equal. Uncertainty about the treaty increased distrust in a way that forthright dealing would have obviated. The semi-official *Kölnische Zeitung* strongly denied " that an offensive and defensive alliance has been concluded between Germany and Great Britain. . . . This does not mean that Germany and England may not have agreed on particular questions, for example, on the subject of a mutual loan to Portugal for the purpose of relieving more or less quickly the bad finances of that country." [27] The *Kölnische Zeitung* limited itself to remarking that while Delagoa Bay had figured in the negotiations it did not know in what respect. The papers sought for some days to secure more information. They worried over the effect upon Russo-German relations of an Anglo-German treaty.[28] *The Times,* however, grew more definite. On October 8 it wrote, " This much can be said, namely, that in the event of fresh trouble between England and the Transvaal the Emperor William could certainly not despatch a second Telegram to President Krüger, who in his differences with England has little or no sympathy in that quarter." [29] Thus some weeks after the treaty

[25] Hammann, *Vorgeschichte des Weltkrieges* (Berlin, 1919), p. 72.

[26] *The Times'* Berlin correspondent in *The Times,* September 7, 1898, cited by Herkenberg, *op. cit.,* p. 87, p. 134.

[27] Circular note from the Belgian Foreign Office, September 17, 1898, cited by Herkenberg, *op. cit.,* pp. 134-5.

[28] Hammann, *op. cit.,* and Herkenberg, pp. 87-89.

[29] Herkenberg, p. 136.

it was clear that the German government had both repudiated the country's "sentimental" interest in the Boers and abandoned Marschall's "material interests" of 1895-6.[30]

Some light has recently been thrown on the reasons why the German Foreign Office reversed its position in regard to the Boers. As has been indicated in the preceding chapter, banking and heavy industry had done much to determine Marschall to defend the *status quo* and to regard the Telegram with satisfaction. It is reasonable to suppose that if conditions had not changed Bülow could not have ignored these interests in 1898. Herff, German consul in Pretoria, promoted German industry no less energetically than before and the German armament industry continued to hold a market there. Although the French armament firm of Creusot had succeeded in making contracts with Krüger, the majority of the armament business still went to German firms. In 1896-7 Krupp secured contracts to the value of £400,000, the Löwe firm, financed by the *Discontogesellschaft,* £159,000, while £250,000 were placed at the disposal of a German firm for fortifications in the Transvaal. Creusot received orders to the extent of only £105,-000. Herff reported that up to May 3, 1897, Germany had sent to the Transvaal war material worth £550,000 and France £78,750.[31] These figures exclude other business done with the Transvaal.

Lack of interest in the Transvaal, therefore, was not due to loss of the munitions market. It came from another source. In 1897 the gold mining boom suffered a partial collapse and the Transvaal government set up a commission of inquiry into the condition of the mines. Though Herff held firmly to the dynamite trust and the position which he had won for German influence in the Boer Republic, the principal German banks interested in the area became anti-Boer. Görtz, representative for the *Deutsche Bank,* led the forces which now began to criticize instead of supporting Herff. Those industries the Transvaal market of which depended on min-

[30] Germany was eager to keep the treaty a secret from France and Russia, at least until a treaty with Portugal was completed. *Cf. G. P.,* XIV, Nos. 3874 ff.

[31] Hallgarten, *op. cit.*, p. 518, citing from Herff's reports to the Foreign Office, March 28 and May 3, 1897. The figures refer to the period after the Telegram of January, 1896.

ing now became anxious and aligned themselves with the *Deutsche Bank,* especially after the latter and other banks began to refuse funds to the Boers. Toward the end of 1897 the *Kölnische Zeitung* and the *Norddeutsche Allgemeine Zeitung,* as if inspired from above, began to turn against the Boers. Herff, exasperated by this show of official disfavor, said that he was having to defend his post against Görtz and Rhodes at the same time.[32] Since the Portuguese government had rejected Krüger's offers of financial aid, Herff feared that it would seek assistance from Rhodes and the British and lose its colonies.

In this situation financial circles seem to have pressed Bülow for a settlement of the Portuguese problem. Bülow himself wrote in his memoirs, " The opportunity was favorable. Portugal, the bad debtor, found herself in financial straits in which her creditors, both Germany and England, suffered for years because they no longer got any interest payments." [33] Hence financial considerations may have actuated Bülow's move.[34] Germany made every effort to share in a loan to Portugal, even though the Reich might have to guarantee the capital invested,[35] but from the outset she assumed the Delagoa Bay must be given up. The *Darmstädter Bank,* in which, incidentally, the Emperor was personally interested, appeared to be particularly eager for stabilization of Portuguese finances. This fact again lends credence to the proposition that Bülow acted, at least, in part, for finance. As if to confirm the wisdom of the move, after the conclusion of the Anglo-German treaty mining stocks rose greatly on the Exchange.

If this explanation is plausible—and it fits in remarkably both with more recent understanding of modern imperialism and with German *Interessenpolitik*—it indicates that Bülow at times deserved the reputation for cleverness which he enjoyed with the

---

[32] *Ibid.,* pp. 519 ff., citing the papers referred to and Herff to the Foreign Office, November 29, 1897.

[33] *Denkwürdigkeiten,* I, 274.

[34] Hallgarten, *op. cit.,* p. 525, note 4. Hallgarten also points out that Salisbury thought Hatzfeldt wanted a German loan to Portugal and that Hatzfeldt's desire must have rested on some concrete bases, though all this is omitted from *G. P.*

[35] *Cf. supra,* p. 267.

Emperor. He broke a lance for better Anglo-German relations without committing himself to an alliance, secured compensations in return for giving up a long-disputed area to which the British had better claim, and satisfied the German banks. On the other hand, as so often happens in the case of a compromise of interests, the results did not equal expectation, except possibly for the bankers. England eventually nullified the agreement with Germany by the "Windsor Treaty" of 1899 with Portugal, while the nationalists in Germany were not sufficiently satisfied with the "compensations" to overlook the Anglophil tendencies of the government and to forgive Bülow his treachery to the Boers. The affair helped to build up support for them among the Pan-Germans, the South German Liberals and the anti-Semites; it increased the distrust of England, of the German government and of Jewish international finance.[36]

B. *The Anglo-German Most-favored-nation Treaty*

Termination by England in 1897 of her most favored-nation treaty with Germany occupied the press greatly in the months before the Boer War.[37] Germany worried particularly lest England turn to a tariff policy of protection. Russian protectionism and the increases made under the Dingley Tariff of 1897 in the United

[36] Hallgarten works this out in more detail. He concludes that the Pan-Germans became more anti-Jewish at this time because finance was in Jewish hands. This may be an exaggeration; Class, for example, was already thoroughly anti-Jewish. He assumes, however, that the press understood the part of finance in the deal. There is some doubt about this, although a lack of understanding would not nullify the influence of the press on the growth of pro-Boer, anti-English sentiment.

[37] In 1897 the Board of Trade published in London a report on *Trade of the British Empire and Foreign Competition* and in 1898 the British government put out a Blue Book entitled *Foreign Trade Competition*. Both were symptomatic of increased interest on the part of England in German competition. For general discussion of the question see Ross J. S. Hoffman, *op. cit.*; Cornelius Penner, *Anglo-German Trade Rivalry in South Africa* (Unpublished dissertation in the University of Chicago Libraries, 1935); Karl Rathgen, *Die englische Handelspolitik am Ende des 19. Jahrhunderts, Verein für Sozialpolitik*, XCI (1901), pp. 123-171; *Preussische Jahrbücher*, LXXXVI, 481-523.

States already disturbed German industry;[38] it would be further deleterious to German trade if England should adopt the plans proposed to the chamber of commerce by Chamberlain in 1896 to create an imperial tariff union for the British Empire. The new threat that she might do so was doubly alarming, for commercial restrictions actually had checked or seemed likely to check German ambition abroad.

Ironically enough Germany was alarmed by the same movement abroad which she sponsored at home. The departure of Marschall and Boetticher at the end of June, 1897, meant that Germany herself released the last of the Caprivi personnel and would succumb to the demands of the *Sammlung* for higher grain and industrial tariffs. Marschall had already been attacked by the Agrarians and industrialists, who in April, 1897, had interpellated the government on the impending American tariff and seemed ready to undertake a German-American tariff war.[39] In the debate Kanitz, the Pan-Germans, and other groups also urged revival of the plan for a Pan-European tariff union. After the British action all of these readily endorsed the plan as a possible defense. In April Marschall had made every effort to counteract the evil effect in America of the debate and a few months later neither Bülow nor Posadowsky dared to risk a tariff war against America or England. Their reasoning remained the same as Marschall's: Germany would be harmed more than she could possibly benefit. She would lose necessary imports and would force either or both of these countries, as the case might be, into new markets. Germany would then be

---

[38] *Schmollers Jahrbuch*, 1896, pp. 1380 ff. Here von Halle, economist for the Imperial Marine Bureau, asked in the autumn of 1896 for a European union against the probability of a new McKinley tariff. See also Rathgen, *ibid.*, 1897, pp. 1369 f., where the point was made that the British move was rather unexpected inasmuch as the British Cabinet had formerly always refused to denounce the treaty. *Cf.* also F. Moos, " Der kanadische Zolltarif," *Hilderbrands Jahrbuch*, LXIX (1897), 424 f.; Paul Voigt, "Deutschland und der Weltmarkt," *Preussische Jahrbücher*, XCI (1898), 240 f.

[39] Kanitz and Heyl zu Herrnsheim: *Sten. Ber. d. Reich.*, 1897, VIII, 5701-28. *Cf.* also Vagts, *op. cit.* From hitherto unknown material the latter has shown the concern of the Hansa towns over the probable change in policy of the German government (Chap. III, 121 ff.).

excluded from the latter or would have to compete for them, while losing her own export markets in America and England.[40] Unfortunately, such facts did not impress a nationalistic public.

Public opinion, however, did not want a tariff war in 1897. Its thinking was confined to speculation about the future dangers inherent in closer British imperial unity, to desire for the protection of national labor by means of an autonomous tariff with higher rates for imports, and for a navy. Coupled with these desires ran a feeling of uncertainty, which business deplored and which disturbed Anglo-German relations.[41]

The German chambers of commerce united in recognizing the need for friendly Anglo-German relations. At the same time they eagerly asked from the government aids to industry without, apparently, realizing that these aids because of their nature would antagonize England. In the east the termination of the most-favored-nation treaty confronted the Chamber of Commerce of Breslau, the center of the region which before 1897 considered England largely as a sugar market and which ascribed the unsuccessful competition of Silesian coal with English coal in eastern Germany to poor means of transportation, with an event before which, as its report said, " all other developments of foreign policy retreat into the background." [42] The Chamber spoke with regret of the insecurity to business created by the termination of the Anglo-German commercial treaty and by the unfriendly atmosphere resulting to " the relations between two Empires economically so dependent on each other." [43] It urged German newspapers, in spite of England's jealousy of Germany, to avoid arousing unneces-

[40] Vagts, Chaps. II and III. As for the tariff union, it was not as yet regarded by all as impossible, but soon became so. In many circles by 1900 it was a dead issue, while official circles had given it up by 1895 (Francke, *op. cit.*, in *Schriften des Vereins für Sozialpolitik*, XC (1900) 189 f.).

[41] The uncertainty is described by Hoffman, *op. cit.*, pp. 284 ff., but it must not be over-emphasized, since the effect of the termination of the treaty was to emphasize the probability of future difficulties from other commercial policies as well as England's, especially from those of America and the British colonies.

[42] *Bericht der Handelskammer zu Breslau*, 1899, p. 21.

[43] *Ibid.*, 1897, p. 4.

sary bad feeling between the two countries. Although Breslau did not share the fear that in time England would go over to protection, the Chamber took a new interest in general politics after 1897 and for the first time regarded England and Germany as each other's chief competitor.[44] But it emphasized the need for good relations between rivals. The Chamber's report of 1898 said that German export trade gained in importance in the world market through competition with England. Hand in hand with the increase of overseas trade must go, it asserted, the increase of the German merchant marine and the upswing " in our ship-building industry which will use an ever-increasing amount of our own domestic material." The Chamber wished Germany to be everywhere prepared to meet English competition.

Berlin, the center of numerous finishing industries, was always dependent on England to a certain extent, especially on the price of English coal and coke and on the English iron market. In 1897 the Berlin coal market showed for the first time since 1890 a decline in the importation of English coal and a noticeable increase in the use of Upper Silesian coal. The Berlin Chamber, although accustomed to Anglo-German competition, was nonetheless disturbed by the termination of the commercial treaty. In a memorandum presented to the Chancellor and to the Prussian Ministry of Commerce the Chamber expressed the fear that the Canadian tariff of 1897 had begun a movement which would close the British Empire to foreign trade.[46] The Chamber did not believe, however, that Imperial Federation would immediately follow and by 1900 the Chamber reported that the movement showed no signs of progress.[47] Fear of British imperial unity lessened, so far as one can judge from the Berlin reports, and gave place to demands for the erection of chambers of commerce abroad, to discussion of the harm suffered by industry from the rise in prices due to the Boer War—coal, freight, raw materials—, to the downswing of the

---

[44] *Ibid.*, 1899, p. 1. [45] *Ibid.*, 1898, p. 4.

[46] *Bericht der Ältesten der Kaufmannschaft zu Berlin*, 1897, pp. 14 f.

[47] On the contrary, only Barbados had already allowed English and American goods to come in under a preferential tariff, and the Empire Conference in London had shown more enthusiasm for the system in the colonies than in England.

business curve in 1900 and to the demands for a navy.[48] The
Chamber did not regard the navy as a *Macht* factor and wrote:
" The acceptance of the naval law would be of decisive importance
to the domestic market and might make possible a more brilliant
continuation of the prosperity phase of the business cycle than had
ever been expected." [49] In spite of the English export tax levied in
1901 of one shilling a ton on coal and the tax of four pence a hundredweight on sugar imports, both war measures, the Berlin Chamber no longer contemplated the probability of a British tariff union
or of a British protectionist policy. When it saw that an Agrarian
majority in the Reichstag limited the emergency duration of the
most-favored-nation treaty with England to one year, it objected.[50]
Because of this situation the report of 1902 did not criticize England for terminating the commercial treaty in 1897; rather it
took the German government to task for the insecurity of the
commercial-political future and for the lack of good laws regarding
the Exchange. It attributed these deficiencies to " the over-power-
ing influence of Agrarian tendencies on the law and administration
of Germany." [51] This analysis was a telling one and shows conclusively that some business opinion in Germany did not blame
England for every ill.

The city of Hamburg had long been wedded to free-trade
theory.[52] It had complained since 1890 that the German government was more and more restraining in Germany the freedom of

[48] *Bericht der Ältesten der Kaufmannschaft zu Berlin,* 1899 and 1900,
and special reports, Nos. 49-50, 151.

[49] Special report No. 48, 1899, p. 100. Also *Bericht,* 1900, p. 1. Imports
of English coal were increasing in spite of the war because German coal
could not supply the demand. This fact was clearly realized by the
Chamber, just as the government saw the need for American imports.

[50] *Ibid.,* 1901, pp. 1 f. The Bundesrat was empowered to extend the
treaty with England until a more lasting arrangement could be made;
but such an extension was made every year from 1898 to 1901, then from
1901-1903, instead of lessening the uncertainty, as desired by business, by
extending the treaty for the entire time needed. The cause for this arrangement is given below.

[51] *Ibid.,* 1902, p. 3.

[52] Erwin Wiskemann, *Hamburg und die Welthandelspolitik* (Hamburg,
1929), p. 308.

trade to which England owed her superiority.[53] The termination of the commercial treaty created no alarm in the Hamburg Chamber of Commerce, which looked upon protectionist moves abroad as partly caused by protection in Germany.[54] At the same time Hamburg also showed an increasing national consciousness in desiring to invest German capital at home, to ship in German bottoms, to free Germany from British commercial tradition, and to develop German colonies.[55] In the report of 1897 the Chamber stated, " In view of these efforts [those of other countries to increase their trade] it is doubly desirable that the development of the German navy should neither lag behind that of the merchant marine and the overseas interests of Germany nor that of foreign navies." [56] The Chamber did not connect this reaction with anti-English pronouncements. It fully realized the value to Germany of English trade and industry. It even urged that certain prohibitive proposals of German finishing industries against importation of British competitive wares be rejected as impracticable. It recognized that " a seeming protection of home industry may in fact work destruction to it." [57] Moreover, Hamburg regretted the effects of the Boer War on English industry, and for the sake of German trade rejoiced that England had survived as well as she had. English peace and prosperity were pronounced desirable to Germany and to the world.

Essen in the center of the iron and steel producing area faced squarely the possibility of preferential tariffs within the British

[53] *Bericht der Handelskammer zu Hamburg,* 1893, p. 4.

[54] Ernst Baasch, *Die Handelskammer zu Hamburg* (Hamburg, 1915), II, Pt. 2, 862 f. This was the view of the *Frankfurter Zeitung.* In February, 1897 a proposal was made in the Reichstag to have an investigation of the results of the Caprivi treaties. The Agrarians opposed the study, as the *Frankfurter Ztg.* thought, because they wished to avoid official confirmation of the favorable effects of the treaties. When Canada and England took the steps which they did in the summer of 1897, the *Frankfurter Ztg.* maintained that the attitude of the Agrarians in demanding protection encouraged protectionism abroad. It undertook an investigation on its own initiative of the effects of the treaties and published the results, which were favorable. Subsequently, it opposed the new tariff law and the Agrarian League (*Geschichte der Frankfurter Zeitung,* pp. 785 ff.).

[55] *Bericht der Handelskammer zu Hamburg, passim* before 1898.

[56] *Ibid.,* 1899, p. 8.   [57] *Ibid.,* pp. 18-19.

Empire and protection in England; but it did not think Germany in a disadvantageous position to negotiate a new treaty. The Essen Chamber recommended continuation until 1903 of the previous most-favored-nation rights to England and suggested that every effort be made " to maintain the ground gained [in world trade] and to pursue energetically world competition. The strengthening of sea-power is inevitable; a purposeful colonial policy is demanded for securing new markets; and we must have a larger canal network as well as a reduction in railroad rates." [58] The Düsseldorf Chamber shared the opinion that Germany occupied a favorable position for negotiating a treaty with England, and proposed a change in general tariff—the immediate hope of the heavy industrialists for 1903—which would be high enough to force any country into a most-favored-nation treaty with Germany. Düsseldorf, with Crefeld and other manufacturing cities, signed a petition to the Chancellor requesting him to preserve full most-favored-nation treatment with England until 1903 and desired earnestly to avoid a tariff war. [59] Heavy industry was more interested in receiving various governmental aids than in the danger of English competition. The Düsseldorf Chamber of Commerce reported as follows:

> Our commercial policy must have a definitely national character. It must protect home industry in every way as over against foreign industry and especially it must help to overcome the difficulties of agriculture by moderately raising the tariff on agricultural products. It must at the same time not lose sight of the fact that Germany has an increase in population of 800,000 a year for whom work and bread are needed and that a large part of our products are dependent on foreign markets. [60]

It is true that the spinning interests headed by Augsburg and with the *Verein deutscher Baumwoll-Industrieller* and the *Verein rheinisch-westfälischer Baumwollspinner* sought to use the opportunity afforded by the termination of the commercial treaty with

[58] *Bericht der Handelskammer zu Essen*, Appendix, " Bericht der Börse zu Essen," 1897, Pt. I, 41.
[59] *Bericht der Handelskammer zu Düsseldorf*, 1988-1899, pp. 46-7.
[60] *Ibid.*, 1901, pp. 7-8.

England to petition the Chancellor for exclusion of English thread from most-favored-nation treatment.[61] But the weaving industries in Crefeld, Bonn, Bielefeld and other cities opposed this step energetically, since it was a fact, they said, " that the weavers and finishers of the German textile industry cannot get on without English yarns whether cotton, wool, or linen." [62]

Although the chambers of commerce in Germany clearly recognized the dangers inherent in the Canadian tariff and the subsequent action by England, it is evident that they did not use the occasion to denounce England. As in the case of America they did not want a tariff war or any reprisals which would disturb trade. But they did want as protection against development of English imperialism an immediate furtherance of German imperialism. They disregarded the probable increase in Anglo-German competition which would result therefrom in the hope that German business would be assured a successful and lasting future. Most of the chambers objected to limiting the continuation of the old treaty with England to one year, for they wished to avoid insecure or unpleasant relations with Germany's best customer. Every business was alive to the opportunity offered to state again its most pressing demands, a navy, new markets, and Agrarian-industrial tariffs with higher schedules, steamship subvention, and their like.

On June 16, 1899, a long debate occurred in the Reichstag over the renewal of the temporary commercial Anglo-German treaty.[63] Kanitz led the discussion by pointing out that the colonies were becoming more independent of England and that as a result England would all the more try to bind the Empire more closely together. Since a development of this kind would affect Germany gravely, she must recognize that she would not be able to make

[61] The memorandum to the government contained intimate details of English competition in this industry. The writer has not been able, however, to find the memorandum in the archives of the Chamber. *Die Nation* gave the Crefeld opposition to the spinners' position (*Die Nation*, Nos. 34, 35, 36, May 21, 28, June 4, 1897).

[62] *Bericht der Handelskammer zu Crefeld*, 1897-1898, p. 36.

[63] *Sten. Ber. d. Reich.*, June 16, 1899, X Leg. Per., I Sess., III, 2576-8. *Cf.* with the debate over the proposed Dingley Tariff in 1897, *ibid.*, May 3, 1897, IX Leg. Per., IV Sess., VIII, 5701-28. Kanitz interpellated at this time also.

another treaty with England which would include the English colonies. It is regrettable, Kanitz emphasized, that Germany depends upon treaties and does not have an adequate autonomous tariff which can be used in a case like this. He wished, " a tariff with such high schedules that we are in a position to meet the tariffs of other countries, that in this way we may be able to move other countries to concessions." [64] The Agrarians proposed to grant the Bundesrat power to renew the treaty for one year only; for they sought to keep alive the issue. On the second day of the discussion Hahn, Director of the Agrarian League, again expatiated on the tariff question as follows:

> The more friendly we are, the more understanding we have for the rights of others as opposed to our own rights, so much the more do we suffer in prestige in the eyes of the British. . . . How have we during the centuries won the recognition and respect of England? Through our national, ruthless action as a German nation and a German Empire.[65]

Or as Roesicke said:

> England has acted in the belief that Germany no longer has her full strength, that weakness has taken hold here. I believe, of course, differently. You will agree that we have our former force and strength. But we shall not manifest these to the world by continuing to retreat, but only by showing that the old spirit which ruled in Bismarck's time is still here. If we do this, we shall also make better commercial treaties than before.[66]

---

[64] *Ibid.*, p. 2578.   [65] *Ibid.*, p. 2603.

[66] *Ibid.*, p. 2583. The Bismarck paper, *Hamburger Nachrichten*, urged that advantage be taken of the situation to force England to give compensation for " the most-favored-nation treatment which she cannot do without." Many newspapers held the view that now was the time to " show " England and to dictate terms to her. The extreme Agrarians added to the proposed law a resolution to allow the Bundesrat to act only in case German products received no harm in the British Empire or in parts of it through changes in the most-favored-nation treatment or from being treated by the colonies more unfavorably than the products of England (*ibid.*, Amendment No. 389, Appendix III). The amendment was not adopted; the Center considered it too anti-English to be taken seriously and it was withdrawn. Hahn and Roesicke contrasted unfavorably with the quieter Kanitz and Kardorff; they veered from fact to nationalistic

Paasche speaking for the National Liberals also urged an autonomous tariff, not only against England and her colonies, but against the United States. He advocated as well a law to require evidence of the origin of goods, the sugar premium, and an *ad valorem* tariff, so that as many means as possible might be given the government for combatting the protectionist dangers everywhere. But in his discussion Paasche cautioned his audience, including the Agrarians, that these tariffs and special taxes were not levied against Germany alone, even where she might suffer more than others. He was not more anti-English than anti-American or anti-Indian. Nonetheless, he saw the remedy for everything in a strict protectionist commercial policy. The Center, too, warned the Agrarians that Germany must not harm the English market.[67] Lieber said:

> We wish the present discussion to show not only to the British Empire, but to all with whom we have tariff relations that we are resolved to protect German production and commercial interests with all our powers. On the other hand, we are of the opinion that it may be harmful to our purpose to adopt at the moment too sharp a tone.[68]

At the time of this debate preparations were going forward for the new tariff law. It was not necessary to win Posadowsky over to an autonomous tariff scheme, but only to emphasize the value of speed and to obtain a law of sufficient stringency to calm the feelings of the Agrarians. Posadowsky reminded the Reichstag of the work already under way and suggested that before the new tariff law was completed nothing be said to disturb relations with any country. He pointed out the importance of Anglo-German trade to Germany and said that a tariff war, while aiding some interests, would seriously harm others and could hardly be justified to the German people for the sake of the one hundred and seventeen millions of export trade with Canada.[69]

propaganda and would have entered upon a tariff war with pleasure, or so it seemed.

[67] Speck: *Ibid.*, p. 2607. The Center was, however, for the Agrarians' law, but opposed the amendments attached.

[68] Lieber: *Ibid.*, June 17, p. 2600.

[69] *Ibid.*, p. 2584, and May 26, 1900, p. 5793. At this later time the matter came up again briefly on the occasion of renewing the treaty for another year.

20

On the whole the Reichstag debates over the renewal of the
Anglo-German commercial treaty kept relatively free from anti-
English feeling except on the part of the representatives of the
Agrarian League. Even the Agrarians acknowledged the value of
Anglo-German trade. Many recognized that the treaty difficulties
arose out of a world-wide protectionist movement, that it was impossible to separate the discussion of the English treaty from that
of the Dingley Tariff and *ad valorem* duties. Both of the latter
aroused quite as much demand for nationalistic retaliation as did
the English action. The United States and England followed a
like tendency, said Hahn, and England had to draw close to the
colonies because her exports to the continent had fallen off and she
could not recover them. The representatives realized that Germany
should not enter into a tariff war. Hence it was unfortunate that
the otherwise quiet tenor of the debate should have been interrupted
by bursts of nationalism and ideas of *Machtpolitik* from Agrarian
elements. The economist Lotz in writing of the situation said truly:

> It is not the symptoms of the present economic depression
> occasioned by what we hope will be a temporary crisis that fills
> one with care and sadness over Germany's development at the
> beginning of the twentieth century, but the symptoms of a
> spirit of faint-heartedness, expressions of a belief in the power
> of state intervention as the only means of holding off competi-
> tion. And at the same time we think we march in the van of
> social policy and imperialism.[70]

The Agrarians led in the attempt to force the state to assist special
interests. For all groups, however, each new crisis which aroused
fear in Germany led for one reason or another to an increased
demand for ships, state subsidies, and new tariffs to promote the
German cause in the markets of the world.

At the time of the debate in 1899 the Reichstag did not regard
the plan for a Pan-European tariff union against the United States
and England as a serious possibility. The plan had been continually
put forward since 1890 and had been warmly supported on various
occasions by the *Kreuzzeitung,* Posadowsky, the Pan-Germans,

---

[70] Walter Lotz, "Wirkungen der gegenwärtigen und Ziele der zukünftigen
Handelspolitik," in *Schriften des Vereins für Sozialpolitik*, XCVIII (1902),
149. Also Vagts, *op. cit.,* I. Chap. III.

Kanitz, Hammacher, and others; but Kanitz now said it was hopeless.[71] In the press, however, the ideal still lived. One finds it cropping up in the *Preussische Jahrbücher* and among the Pan-Germans, who considered it the logical way for Germany to establish a counterpart to the world empires of England and Russia.[72] Even among enthusiasts the plan did not carry great weight. In the final reckoning reliance was placed on the improved *Machtstellung* of Germany as the surest means of maintaining the economic position. All groups from the Emperor and the government down to the free-trade economists and Hanseatic cities agreed that the termination of the Anglo-German commercial treaty by England demonstrated the need for a German navy.[73] Some observers, even men outside the Social Democratic party, understood the commercial policy involved and counselled a sane and careful line of action.[74] The Emperor himself felt certain that England would not go over to protection even if her colonies did so.[75] Economists pointed out that the colonies would maintain and in all probability increase their tariff independence of England if it were to their interest to do so. Hence, they said, wherever her trade competed successfully Germany need not fear discrimination against her. The dependence of Germany upon English and American trade received emphasis again and again. On the whole, therefore, it

[71] Francke, *op. cit.* Details of the movement are given here.

[72] See articles by Paul Voigt, *Preuss. Jahrb.*, 1898, and following issues.

[73] *G. P.*, XIII, 34-35. Marginal note of the Emperor to the effect: " After the realization of the superiority of German industry England will soon set about its destruction and will undoubtedly succeed if we do not energetically and quickly fend off the danger by a stronger navy." *Cf.* with Rathgen, " Die Kündigung des englischen Handelsvertrags und ihre Gefahr für Deutschlands Zukunft," *Schmollers Jahrbuch*, XXI (1897), 1398: " Is Germany to go ahead or only let others take the first place? If we do go on, we must be clear that only a navy will enable us to succeed."

[74] Paul Arndt, *Mitteilungen des Vereins zur Förderung der Handelsfreiheit* (Berlin, 1900), No. 1; *Idem, Volkswirtschaftliche Zeitfragen* (Berlin, 1899), Nos. 167-168. These gave sane counsel.

[75] *G. P.*, XIII, 34, Marginal note. See also an argument to the same effect by *Die Nation*, No. 45, August 7, 1897, and a contemporary book by W. H. Breymann, *Deutschlands Wachsende Bedeutung als Industriestaat* (Hamburg, 1897), which treats the question as a practical business man would.

seems doubtful whether an Empire tariff union and British protectionism so freightened the German public as has been represented.[76]   Certainly it was no more freightened than by protectionism in the United States.

It cannot be said that the termination of the Anglo-German
commercial treaty brought about the new tariff of 1902; but the
problems raised by the tariff policy of the United States and Canada
helped to effect the ministerial changes of 1897, which in turn
removed the last vestiges of sympathy with the Caprivi system and
paved the way for the power of the Agrarians. It is also impossible
to say where fear of England ended and where desire to advance
special interests began. The action of England in the summer of
1897 added to concern about the future of foreign trade and offered
in 1897 and in ensuing years an excellent opportunity to drive home
the need for the new tariff. Opinion among the nationalists
crystallized against the English competitors, a possible British
tariff union and the United States. At the same time opinion
among all increased in favor of *Machtpolitik* and especially in
favor of the navy as the best means of repelling these dangers.

[76] Hoffman, *op. cit.*, pp. 284 f.

CHAPTER VI

PUBLIC OPINION DURING THE BOER WAR,
1899-1902

But the Boer asked indifferently, "Man, is it really true that the German Emperor has so many soldiers? When will the German Emperor send his soldiers to take back the land, which belongs to us, from the English red-coats, so that we can have room enough again to live as we should?" And he added quickly, whispering, "Man, are you perhaps yourself one of these German soldiers?" Cornelius Friebott answered, "No, I'm no soldier," and asked, "Who's been putting fleas like that in your ear?"

Hans Grimm, *Volk ohne Raum,* I, 394.

A. *Opinion Before and After the Outbreak of War to December, 1899.*

In a long speech in the Reichstag on December 12, 1899, against the new naval bill Bebel spoke scornfully of the change in the official attitude toward England since the Krüger Despatch. "At that time," he said, "they [the members of the government] were enthusiastic over the Boers; today, I won't say that they are enthusiastic over their opponents, but to all appearances very well satisfied that it has come out as it has." [1] Surprising as it may seem, this observation applies to a large extent to German public opinion up to the end of 1899. If one follows through the files of the *Vossische Zeitung,* of which Marschall wrote in January, 1896, "Even *Tante Voss* is ready for war," one is struck by the mildness of its tone in 1899. The tone is particularly noticeable because the French and Russian papers showed less moderation. [2] It is true

[1] *Sten. Ber. d. Reich.,* December 12, 1899, X Leg. Per., I Sess., IV, 3322. In the annual meeting of the Pan-German League in Munich, August, 1898, the League took the government to task for its changing attitude toward the Boers. This came just at the time of the Anglo-German treaty over the Portuguese colonies.

[2] *G. P.,* XV, 395, 413-20, with editor's notes; *B. D.,* I, 302.

that the moderation did not extend to the colonial and Pan-German press, nor to the Agrarian papers and some of the industrialist journals. In the case of the two latter, however, internal circumstances rather than the Transvaal affair shaped their attitudes.[3]

The German press in 1899 followed carefully the negotiations between England and the Transvaal and reported the moves in Krüger's diplomatic game, but with quiet comment and with little assertion of " the German interests " involved.[4] When the *Berliner Neueste Nachrichten* (Krupp and Free-Conservative) published in January a leading article on the migration of English capital into Germany territory in Africa, the *Norddeutsche Allgemeine Zeitung* (Conservative and semi-official) answered by welcoming the influx of British capital as an indication of an improved economic condition in the German colonies. It wrote:

> It cannot be denied that a new day is dawning for our colonies. Life and work, trade and commerce are springing up where formerly economic lethargy obtained. And for the opponents of our colonial policy [Richter *et al.*] it will be a good lesson to see that the value of our colonies is recognized abroad. The Stock Exchange is always regarded as a barometer. If now German, as well as foreign financial circles, compete for participation in German colonial undertakings, then these colonies will become more than the ' sand wastes ' they are so often called. We believe we should rejoice in a new epoch in the development of our colonies.[5]

In the same conciliatory spirit this paper seemed gratified that the government did not intend to present a new naval plan [6] and in March it noted without comment an increase of about three million marks in the British naval budget.[7]

As the year advanced the calmness of the *Norddeutsche Allgemeine Zeitung* did not everywhere exist. In March a serious debate took place in the Reichstag over the purchase or support by the German government of a railroad which the East African Company had begun to build and which it threatened to abandon as too expensive.

---

[3] *Cf. Alld. Bl.* for January and February, 1899, where the possibility of a French alliance was discussed *pro* and *con* and where it was a foregone conclusion that England was the chief enemy of Germany.

[4] See *Norddeutsche Allg. Ztg.*, January 1, 6, 22, 1899.

[5] January 24, 1899.

[6] *Ibid.*, January 12, 1899.   [7] *Ibid.*, March 10, 1899.

The debate exposed new fear of British competition. England, it was pointed out, was endeavouring to complete a road from Mombassa to Uganda, which the German colonialists feared would attract all the trade from the interior of the German colony. Arenberg (Center) and Stolberg (Conservative) supported a proposal to grant one million, seven hundred and fifty thousand marks for the construction of the German railroad. Stolberg said:

> According to my opinion this question is of national import-ance and extends far beyond the immediate economic value of the object under discussion. It is a question of the first rail-road built with German money in a German colony at a time when the world, especially mighty England, is reaching out its hands toward Africa. If the undertaking is liquidated, I believe the outside world will laugh at us.[8]

Richter accused the nationalists and their sympathizers of hiding behind the "national banner" exciting jealousy of England to cover the extravagance of the project. His truths had no more effect than usual upon those eager for colonial enterprise.

On the second day of the debate, March 11, Cecil Rhodes came to Berlin and interviewed the Emperor. The Conservatives, National Liberals, the Center, and even Hasse all approved in the Reichstag of Rhodes' visit and were willing that a Cape-to-Cairo telegraph line and railroad should go through German East Africa.[9] Count Stolberg, who on the day before had raised the English bug-bear, now asserted that foreign capital was welcome in German colonies "on condition that the companies are German and that railroads especially are administered by German officials and are under the supervision and control of the German Empire."[10] Here was proof that fear of England furnished a convenient argument for moving the German government to action in a case where German investments needed to be rescued; but fear did not neces-sarily extend to barring England when hope existed of improving these same investments through financial coöperation with her.[11]

[8] *Sten. Ber. d. Reich.*, March 10, 1899, X Leg. Per., I Sess., II, 1443.

[9] *Ibid.*, March 11, 1899, II, 1488-9; also Hasse in *Alld. Bl.*, No. 14, April 2, 1899.

[10] *Ibid.*, p. 1488.

[11] The writer has not been able to discover whether Stolberg had invest-ments in East Africa. Arenberg probably did, and members of the

Rhodes' visit aroused much discussion in the German press. In his memoirs Bülow characterized the press speculation about Rhodes as petty and *spiessbürgerlich;* [12] but Richter thought the discussion, especially that in the British press, dangerous to Anglo-German relations.[13] Actually, *The Times* in London and most of the German press hoped that the visit would improve relations between England and Germany. The attacks against Rhodes were to be expected; he acted as a " red rag," said Bülow, just as Chamberlain did; but these did not develop into attacks against England as they would have in 1896.[14] The country seems to have been quieted by the assurances of the government that in any agreement German interests would be fully protected.

Colonial Society, which stood back of the proposal above, certainly did. Such investments reached no large proportions, however, and need not be taken as accounting entirely for the anxiety.

[12] Bülow, *Denkwürdigkeiten*, I, 290.

[13] *Sten. Ber. d. Reich.*, March 21, 1899, X Leg. Per., I Sess., II, 1644 ff.

[14] *Norddeutsche Allg. Ztg.*, March 12, 1899. The Hamburg representative Klügmann wrote home at the time: " Cecil Rhodes, or rather his visit instituted by the Foreign Office, aroused much attention at the party at Posadowsky's last evening. He is to be received by His Majesty on March 11. It will depend on the personal impression he makes and on his offers how far we shall be willing to coöperate with him in his plans for carrying his transportation facilities through our East African colony. In any case it is a cause of rejoicing that the ground will be cut from under the agitation of our newspapers against England. Many were of the view that this surprise should not be given directly to public opinion (*Cf. G. P.*, XIV, 617). Baron Richthofen told me he intended to publish the news immediately. After a few days everyone would have quieted down " (*Hamburger Staatsarchiv, Klügmann to Versmann*, March 10, 1899, No. 62. From notes of Dr. Vagts).

[15] Buchka: *Sten. Ber. d. Reich.*, March 10, 1899, *passim*; Bülow; *ibid.*, March 21, p. 1645. Klügmann wrote on March 11: " Rhodes made a not unfavorable impression here. In the morning he appeared as a very much tanned colonial farmer and in the evening as an English gentleman. The prolongation of Rhodes' project through the East Africa colony with German capital under German control and with the addition of a railroad to the coast is being considered here. Already a financial group for it is in the process of being organized on the basis of a yearly guarantee from the Reich of three millions. After the turn which ideas recently underwent in regard to the productive value of our colonies and in view of the debates over this year's colonial budget the success of such a proposal

Unfortunately for the cause of continued calm the Samoan question grew more acute in March and April and nationalism flared up during this crisis. Naval propaganda spread and the German interest in Samoa strained Anglo-German relations. The Pan-Germans had always watched Samoa. Now they moved quickly. Dr. Lehr interpellated the government, local groups sent sixty-one resolutions and petitions to the government expressing dissatisfaction with existing conditions, especially after the shooting at Apia, and in June the executive committee of the League asked for a more speedy execution of the First Naval Law in order to hasten Germany's defenses.[16] An article indicative of the growing distrust of England appeared in *Die Nation* and expressed fear that England in Samoa and elsewhere was drawing nearer to the United States and arousing the latter against Germany.[17] In his interpellation of the government over Samoa Lehr deplored the fact that because the Germans owned no cables news from Samoa had to come over British and American ones. Furthermore, he endeavoured to launch a campaign for a new naval law to create a navy, which should, he said, prevent any recurrence of the humiliation that Germany had just suffered in Samoa. The parties of the Left and even those of the Center and beyond condemned this uncalled for chauvinism; but emphasis upon naval expansion continued in the Pan-German papers and elsewhere in the press. The *Preussische Jahrbücher,* which in general favored better relations with France, regarded the Samoan affair as Germany's Fashoda and urged *rapprochement* with France. But these matters, continued

for guarantees in the Reichstag and Bundesrat is counted on. The strong rise of the market for South West Africa shares is attributed to the fact that a financial consortium with a capital of forty millions has been organized to exploit the copper mines in South West Africa " (*Hamburger Staatsarchiv*, March 11, 1899, No. 67).

[16] *Alld. Bl.*, April 23, 1899, No. 17. Later the *Alld. Bl.*, admitted that Samoa was not very important commercially (*ibid.*, No. 40, October 1, 1899) and, when an exchange of Samoa for something else was mentioned, seemed willing enough for this. So long as Germany had her due the League felt satisfaction. England did not receive forgiveness from the League, however, for causing Germany humiliation.

[17] *Die Nation*, No. 26, April 8, 1899. *Die Nation* wished good relations with England but saw no way to secure them.

the article, were not easily arranged; in the meantime, Germany should not allow herself to be unavoidably estranged from England and the government should negotiate with the Center so that the navy could be enlarged.[18] *Die Post, Berliner Neueste Nachrichten, Berliner Tageblatt,* and other papers, largely those of industry and capital, took up the cry for a new naval bill. Although they were not all equally bitter over the Samoan question or even anti-British, their agitation for ships excited public opinion unnecessarily in the direction of chauvinism.[19] Each time that the navy was brought forward in a crisis, the facts of the situation were slighted in favor of *Machtpolitik.*

The change of popular interest from Samoa to a naval bill offered one advantage: the Agrarian-Conservative press, which either directly or indirectly opposed more ships, immediately drew rein and by June the entire agitation, except in Pan-German and colonial circles, had died down. Every nationalistic outburst, however, helped to keep the country sensitive to English relations. The dangerous effects of arousing hatred of England seem either not to have been weighed, except by the Social Democrats and the Progressives, or else to have been thought unimportant, although industrial and commercial circles recognized Germany's economic need of England. In the midst of the Samoan agitation, for example, the Reichstag considered a petition from the Saxon industrialists, especially textile manufacturers, and from those of Silesia asking for better railroad connections to the coast as an aid to trade with England. The petition stated that England, one of the best customers of the industry, was accustomed more and more to buy on short notice. Since this change in practice made competition with French and Belgian textiles very acute, German manufacturers must have more facilities for filling orders as quickly as pos-

---

[18] *Preussische Jahrbücher,* XCVI (May, 1899), 382-3.

[19] For interpretation of the motives actually behind this new naval enthusiasm *cf.* Kehr, *op. cit.,* p. 175. These motives are not so important here as the fact that the Samoan question was used to stir up a renewed anti-English feeling of which the naval agitation was always able to take advantage. The nationalists quickly attributed to England any embarrassment abroad for Germany and demanded naval expansion. The naval propagandists easily linked the two further.

sible.[20] Unfortunately, neither the textile manufacturers nor the chambers of commerce protested at all against the anti-English agitation of the nationalists. The chambers of commerce were indifferent to it, doubtless because it promoted naval construction and other of their own demands upon the government.

In June the German press began to carry more news of the Transvaal. On the ninth Chamberlain declared that negotiations between Krüger and Lord Milner had broken off. Already in May Bülow had ordered the German Ambassador in London and the representatives in Pretoria and Capetown to telegraph the details of the Transvaal's position. On the basis of their answers he had laid down German official policy.[21] This policy, one of strict neutrality, he now announced and he maintained it consistently throughout the crisis and the war.[22] His spokesman, the *Norddeutsche Allgemeine Zeitung,* for example, reported the rupture of negotiations of June ninth (confirmed June eleventh) without comment.[23] The *Preussische Jahrbücher,* however, could not forbear to point out that England had freed herself for action in the Transvaal and was preparing to raise the number of troops in South Africa. It will now be full steam ahead against the Boers, it wrote, but England will have a hard time, since the Boers are equal to any army England can send to the Transvaal on short notice.[24] Quite frequently in 1899 and 1900 the German press regarded England as a weak military power, whom the war would greatly harm. Only a few persons like Bebel realized that England would revise her military system and emerge strengthened in national feeling and prowess.[25] The idea of a " decadent England " pre-

[20] Fischbeck: *Sten. Ber. d. Reich.,* April 11, 1899, X Leg. Per., I Sess., II, 1692-4.

[21] *G. P.,* XV, 367. The details sent by the representatives are contained in a memorandum, *Bülow to the Emperor,* May 10, 1899. The consul in Pretoria wrote secretly that there were negotiations between Krüger and Milner. The negotiations were concluded and an agreement reached at the end of May; but this agreement was subsequently abrogated (see editor's note).

[22] *Ibid.,* pp. 372, 382, *Memorandum to Holstein,* June 8, 1899; *Bülow to the Foreign Office,* August 12, 1899.

[23] June 10, 11, 1899.   [24] XCVI (June, 1899).

[25] The Pan-Germans wrote in 1900 that England would have to introduce

vailed at the close of the century in various circles of German opinion, but in the idea there was an element of reassurance. It seems to have taken the place of the eagerness with which the press of 1896 had demanded the protection of German rights. In June, however, the German government and press were not yet convinced that war would occur.

By July the Pan-German League spoke of war as unavoidable and referred bitterly to the Anglo-German treaty, which condemned Germany to neutrality.[26] On July 28 sharp debates took place in Parliament which in turn excited Germany. In the House of Commons Chamberlain declared bluntly that the condition for England's non-interference was that the Transvaal take decisive steps for the political equality of the Boers and the Uitlanders. Salisbury in the House of Lords added a new note when he said that, while England did not intend to destroy conventions like the London Convention of 1884 so long as they had an honorable purpose, few Englishmen would wish this convention to stand in its original form.[27] The Emperor expressed horror at what he called Salisbury's "convention theory" and, although Hatzfeldt and Lascelles tried to reassure the German government, he no longer believed that war would or could be averted. From the end of July Germany was wary of the future and regarded Chamberlain as an agent whose duty would be to arouse public opinion to support a war. No one doubted that England would be united in a matter touching her colonial interests; but Bülow felt that England wished friendly relations with Germany and would act with circumspection.[28] Whether the Chancellor communicated his optimism to the country or whether, after the failure of naval agitation, German interests in the Transvaal were no longer urging the press forward, is difficult

military service and this innovation would take many young men out of business so that competition with England would be easier for Germany! (*Alld. Bl.*, No. 6, February 4, 1900).

   [26] *Ibid.*, No. 28, July 9, 1899.

   [27] *G. P.*, XV, 378, *Hatzfeldt to the Foreign Office*, and editor's note.

   [28] *Ibid.*, p. 382, *Bülow to the Foreign Office*, August 12, 1899. To this report the Emperor added: "The Prime Minister forgets India and Persia. The Russians in case of war in the Transvaal will still be sensible. And then the price of our friendship will rise in the market, especially in London."

to say. Only extreme nationalists like the Pan-Germans remained active for official sympathy with the fated Boers.[29]

At the end of the summer, as the negotiations between the Transvaal and England shifted from the question of concessions to the Uitlanders to that of sovereignty, the situation changed for the worse. The German press clearly recognized that the problem of sovereignty was the real point at issue and noted, " There is no doubt that a war party is winning the upper hand in the Transvaal." [30] Instead of demanding that the German government interfere, the *Nationalzeitung,* for one, in contrast to the *Alldeutsche Blätter,* excused England by pointing out that the majority of the British people wished no war; [31] " that England should help to create an independent state in the middle of South Africa," it continued, " is unthinkable and nobody else would act differently in her place." [32] The journal even blamed Krüger for his uncompromising attitude and certainly did not grow unduly heated against England. When a correct account of the English note to the Transvaal was received, many papers printed the full text with favorable comment.[33] " The proposals of the British government, if one does not intentionally interpret them wrongly, are thoroughly moderate and acceptable for the Transvaal," wrote the *Nationalzeitung.*[34] The German government hastened to make clear in Pretoria that Germany would not participate in any plan for the coöperation of France, Germany, and Russia in behalf of the Boers lest this plan arouse public sympathy and encourage the Boers to war.[35] That the press was not belligerent is seen in the fact that on September 14 Chamberlain thanked Eckardstein for its moderate tone and found it not unfavorable. Bülow himself, with the Portuguese treaty and its implications in regard to the

[29] *Kolonialzeitung,* No. 18, May 4, 1899, p. 151.

[30] *Nationalzeitung,* September 8, 1899.

[31] September 10, 1899.　　　　[32] September 11.

[33] *Frankfurter Ztg.,* September 14; *Nationalztg.,* September 14; etc.

[34] *Nationalztg.,* September 14, 21, 29, 1899, had a very generous press toward England.

[35] The writer is not certain as to the origin of the suggestion of coöperation here referred to. It began apparently in the Transvaal, and Berlin was to be sounded by the Goerz House which had connections in the Transvaal.

Boers well in mind, advised the German press to use " quiet, cool and precise language," and he reiterated this advice as the crisis came to a head.[36]

With the approach of the war the German press played up the anti-English interests of France and Russia rather than those of Germany. France, said some of the German papers, would not allow England quietly to secure the whole of East Africa because of the menace to Madagascar. The *Nationalzeitung* wrote that perhaps France, protected by Russia, would attack in favor of the Boers and that Russia would be freer to act in the East.[37] It was realized that England's position as a world Power hung in the balance and that Germany might find allies against England. This attitude echoed the idea of the " continental alliance " in 1896 and preceded that of the *Kontinentigallia* of 1900.[38]

By October war became a certainty and the German press grew a little more openly friendly to the Boers. Pan-German groups

[36] *G. P.*, XV, 395, 413-20, with editor's notes. The Times considered the unity of the continental press, which supported or was said to support the Boers, as dangerous because it made settlement harder for England. It suggested that this harmony in the press could be traced to a secret influencing of the press from the Transvaal. This point raises the question posed to the writer by Friedrich Thimme as to what was the influence from Holland of Leyds, the Transvaal representative there. Unfortunately, the writer has not so far found any definite evidence of whether Leyds constituted an important factor in stirring up the anti-English press in Germany. Apparently, he did have connections with the Pan-Germans. For the suggestion of *The Times* reference may be made to an article in the *Nationalzeitung* from the London correspondent, who thought that this kind of blame was simply an attempt to gloss over England's own responsibility (*Nationalztg.*, September 30, 1899). As is indicated above, the German press was not yet active for the Boers, and the government certainly was not. The Pan-Germans alone seemed belligerent and demanded to know what Germany expected to gain from neutrality (*Alld. Bl.*, September, 1899, *passim*).

[37] October 1, 1899; also *Vossische Ztg.*, No. 462, October 1.

[38] There were rumors, which came especially from the *Neue Freie Presse* in Vienna, that France and Russia had offered intervention. Though this offer was doubted, the *Vossische* thought the fact that England had always refused to submit the question to arbitration showed that she knew she was in the wrong and would not wish to risk arbitration (*Vossische Ztg.*, October 3, 1899).

sent their own " Krüger Telegrams " to the Transvaal or passed resolutions to the effect that recent events in South Africa indicated the importance to Germany of a navy.[39] A more moderate journal wrote: " They [the Boers] are engaged in an honorable war; they were ready for everything but the sacrifice of their independence." [40] But the press, in contrast to that of the Pan-Germans, realized that this sympathy must be shown tactfully in order to maintain the friendship of England. The last efforts for peace on the part of England, including the Duke of Devonshire's speech on October 1, were, it is true, judged to be hypocritically designed to give England respite for preparation; but at the same time the press usually distinguished between the Jingoes in England, especially Chamberlain, and the rest of the country, which it thought sincerely peace-loving. The *Vossische Zeitung* regarded the war as in accordance with the *Zeitgeist,* calling attention in an editorial to the fact that within the last three years Greece, the United States, and now Britain had undertaken imperialistic wars. The editorial regretted that in spite of the International Conference of the Hague public opinion and moral protest had no weight against the lust for gain. Groups of speculators, said the article, including many outside England, had money in South Africa; a defeat of the Boers would send up their stocks because of possibilities for increased business.[41] Another liberal journal, *Die Nation,* although announcing firmly that England must bear responsibility for the war, went on to say:

> The enthusiasm for the Boers as it existed at the time of the famous Telegram to President Krüger grew out of confused political sentimentality and from a picture of the Boers which was about as justified as Cooper's characterization of the noble Indians. We have never shared this sentimental con-

---

[39] *Alld. Bl.,* No. 40, October 1, 1899; No. 42, October 15; No. 45, November 5. The resolution of the Plauen group, for example, read: " The public assembly of the Plauen division of the Pan-German League expresses . . . its deepest abhorrence of the brutal, Turkish attempt by an avaricious England to subdue the Boers who are essentially of German blood (*kern-deutsch*). The Assembly orders all Germans to support these brethren in their struggle for freedom. To prevent harm in the future to German interests, such as in Delagoa Bay and Samoa, we need first of all the increase of the German navy." (No. 40, October 1, 1899).

[40] *Vossische Ztg.,* October 4.   [41] *Ibid.,* October 8.

fusion. The Boers, the form of their state, their lack of ability to adjust to the needs of a free culture make it hard for us even today to sympathize with them.[42]

It was generally argued that Germany must remain strictly neutral in the war. When news of the outbreak came on October 11, the press accepted it calmly, although with the feeling that the Boers should have the protection of a just Heaven. The Berlin Stock Exchange even grew temporarily steadier because the uncertainty was at last relieved. A few papers let off steam by quoting the Russian press, which was more anti-English than the German, and by hoping that Russia would be able to make England's position more difficult. The opposition papers mildly attacked the government for allowing the English to exercise harbor vigilance at Lorenzo Marques.[43] A certain "I-told-you-so" tone in reporting in the German press the early British reverses was not surprising nor especially disconcerting to England, so long as this tone remained within the bounds of moderation. The German press apparently did not grossly misrepresent the facts to England's disadvantage, although in case of two reports of the same military encounter it suspected the more unfavorable of being nearer the truth.[44] Liberals in Germany regretted the increased reliance on *Macht* throughout the world as a result of England's method of handling the Boers.

In November the Emperor planned to visit England. News of his trip appeared in October and neither Right nor Left received it well. On October 18 in Hamburg William II again raised the cry for more ships, and this demand found a lively echo in the industrial press, especially *Die Post* and the *Berliner Neueste Nachrichten*. The Agrarians, who had only recently (August) defeated another of the Emperor's favorite measures, the plan for the extension of

[42] *Die Nation*, No. 1, October 7, 1899, p. 3. At the same time *Die Nation* considered that England's moral reputation had sunk low. "To say this," it wrote, "is especially difficult for us who have always had the greatest sympathy for England. But one cannot close his eyes to the facts" (*ibid.*, No. 2, October 14, 1899, p. 15).

[43] *Cf. Vossische Ztg.*, October 19, 1899, which does not share actively this criticism.

[44] *Cf. Nationalzeitung*, October 21, 1899, *in re* Glencoe.

the canal system, were uncertain as to how they should react to the new proposals, which they felt would be as beneficial to industry as the last.[45] The democratic press was shocked that the government should try to break its promise not to demand a new bill until the end of the Sextennate.[46] For some weeks the country remained upset over the whole question and it was inevitable that England and South Africa should be brought into the discussion. Even though no journal, except the industrial and Pan-German ones, desired the naval increases and most papers decidedly combatted them, the country became more nervous. Many persons did not know whether or not the Emperor had spoken on the spur of the moment; if he had, they feared what he might say or do in England; if he had not, they were afraid of what was being prepared behind the scenes. The heated discussion aroused further internal controversies. The *Berliner Neueste Nachrichten* charged the Pan-Germans with petitioning the Emperor to postpone the visit to Engalnd and wrote of the League:

> Perhaps the Pan-German League is ready to send from its ranks a statesman who will be responsible for taking over and leading a world policy in opposition to England. . . . Perhaps the wisdom of the League is great enough to decide whether Germany can be of more use to the Boers by arousing England against Germany.[47]

Vorwärts asserted the purpose of the naval expansion to be the increase of *Weltpolitik* and the enchaining of the masses.[48]

The sum of these comments made a bad press in Germany for the Emperor's trip to England. It was not a question of such hatred of England that no one wished to have the Emperor visit his relatives, but one of fear of the results, for which the Emperor might be as responsible as the English. If England tried to profit politically from the visit and regarded it as sanctioning the war,

[45] *Cf. Kreuzzeitung*, October 27, 1899; *Deutsche Tageszeitung*, November 2, 1899; Kehr, *op. cit.*, pp. 178 f.

[46] *Vossische Ztg.*, October 24, 19; *Frankfurter Ztg.*, October 19.

[47] *Berliner N. N.*, No. 503, October 26, 1899. The Pan-Germans denied the charge, but it was generally believed and the *B. N. N.* article cited everywhere.

[48] *Vorwärts*, October 20.

21

Germany would feel disgraced before the Boers and the world. Germany must try, reiterated the papers, to keep her neutral position throughout and the German press must see to it that the Emperor went to England only out of politeness and in no official capacity.[49]   No one trusted England or the German government or the Emperor.[50]   The *Vossische Zeitung* grew angry at the Pan-Germans and went so far as to say, " What is the Transvaal to us; what is it to us who rules in Pretoria or Johannesburg? The policy of the Reich is determined not by feeling but by interests." *Tante Voss* even thought that Bismarck would probably have done what England was now doing.[51]   When *The Times* seized upon the antagonism of the Pan-Germans to England and cited it as typical of anti-English feeling in Germany, the moderate press was annoyed by this unjust display of animosity. It tended to censure Britain more than before, a result of the fact that the Pan-Germans had again effected evil by their vehemence.[52]   Even *Die Nation,* though reluctantly, deserted its time-honored tradition of English friendship to quote from Kant, " The English people as a people is the most estimable of mankind, but the English as a nation is the most destructive, forceful, lustful, and warlike of all." The press decided that since the visit was planned, it must take place; but it was not favorably regarded and there was much resentment against the Pan-Germans, who had sharpened the issue.[53]

The moderates welcomed the conclusion of the treaty with Samoa as an aid to better feeling toward England. All factions were pleased. Bülow received great praise and a measure of faith in his government was restored.[54]   Even in the midst of the general

[49] *Vossische Zeitung,* October 21.

[50] According to Bülow's memoirs, even the Empress was filled with apprehension of the trip.

[51] *Vossische Ztg.,* October 25.

[52] *Nationalztg.,* October 28, 1899, in an article which attacked the idea of an English alliance as no longer compatible with German interests.

[53] See *Hamburgischer Korrespondent* for a severe article to this effect. The article is also cited in *Vossische Ztg.,* November 2.

[54] The comment of *Die Post* may be given as typical: " Samoa German! This cry will everywhere find echo in German hearts, and all the more because in recent months the fear found expression that the Empire would probably give up its claims to Samoa for a compensation. For a while it

approval, however, the press warned, " We have always emphasized the necessity of close coöperation in affairs outside Europe, but England, of course, follows her own interests, which are not Germany's; therefore, she ought not to be supported by Germany." [55] This warning against the discussion of a general alliance with England during the coming visit could be found in papers from Left to Right. The same journal wished for good relations with Russia—the Czar and Czarina were in Potsdam on November 8— and with England; but German interests were to be pursued at all cost and these dictated neutrality in the Transvaal, friendship with all nations, and no further alliances. Bülow's decision to accompany the Emperor revived agitation on the part of the Pan-Germans and the Agrarian press; but the rest of the parties, from the National Liberals to the Social Democrats, let the matter drop.[56]

By December the German attitude toward England changed. Before entering into this phase it is convenient to consider some of the reasons why German public opinion up to this time had been reasonably moderate and why it had supported the government policy of neutrality. Since 1896 conditions and simultaneously the attitude toward England had modified.

appeared also as if we should have to strike our flag before the two sea-Powers, England and the United States. That now, in spite of our weak position in the South Sea, Samoa has been given us will be greeted with the greatest satisfaction in wide circles of the German people " (No. 309, November 9, 1899).

[55] *Vossische Ztg.*, November 10, December 1.

[56] See attack on the press of the Right in *Vossische Ztg.*, November 15. Here it is asserted that Agrarian opposition was due to discontent with the government, especially with Bülow, and to impatience over German policy. " According to these critics," said *Tante Voss*, " the leaders of the Reich must rattle the sabre and threaten war or tariff war. If they do not, they are no statesmen." *Cf.* Bülow's statement to Lascelles, *B. D.* I, 302, in which he likewise blamed the Agrarians and laid their antagonism to internal causes. Why the Pan-Germans showed impatience is clear. The Agrarians had no intention of letting the government and the industrialists secure a navy without granting concessions to their interests in the matter of tariffs. For anti-alliance propaganda see *Bitter Not tut uns eine starke deutsche Flotte* (Berlin, 1899: Pan-German Publication). The fact that the division of the Portuguese spoils did not materialize had much to do with increasing the feeling that Germany had been betrayed by England (*Alld. Bl.*, No. 16, April 15, 1900).

Mention has already been made in preceding chapters of the fact that the forces for nationalism increased between 1896 and 1899. If the earlier nationalism of 1894 and 1895 partly occasioned the violent outburst of the German press in 1896, it would be logical to expect an even more intense anti-English feeling in 1899. But Germany was no longer so naïve as to hope to secure her ends by a vehement press campaign. The Pan-Germans, as has been indicated, persisted in anti-English attacks; the Agrarians sympathized completely with the Boers, whom they regarded as a kindred agricultural folk unjustly driven to resistance by a large industrial nation. This feeling, added to their resentment against the government over the long fight for the canals' project and against the recurrent naval propaganda, increased their opposition to England and to the government's policy of neutrality. But England did wrong to regard these two groups as representative of all German feeling. The German press, because of German interests in South Africa, did not share the view of the nationalists and the Agrarians. Mention has been made of the decrease of the interest of bankers in the Transvaal. Export of materials of certain kinds also decreased. In 1896, for example, Germany delivered 9,528 tons of railroad supplies; but by 1898 this amount, due to a decrease in need, had fallen to 825 tons. Purchases of rolling stock had also declined at this time, as had that of munitions, while shipments of glycerine, cyancalcium and chemicals increased.[57] Thus, though business declined, it still continued. The truth seems to be that the uncertainty in the Transvaal, involving the Orange Free State and even the Cape Colony trade, put a strain upon commerce. Stability would be increased if the political status of the Transvaal were settled, and business interests preferred to have it settled in England's favor. Evidence of this is not lacking. A special report to the Berlin Chamber of Commerce, for example, from the firm of Arthur Koppel on the conditions in the narrow gauge railroad industry in 1899 asserted that even before the war the Transvaal had held orders back. Although the war had brought business to a complete standstill, it said, surely afterward there would be increased activity. The report remarked significantly that the anti-English feeling in certain of the newspapers might

[57] *Die Post*, No. 291, October 22, 1899.

harm German trade with South Africa and with all the British colonies.[58] The *Vossische Zeitung* wrote that speculators wished the war to end in favor of England, because of the renewed business activity which British success would bring.[59] Long before the war quotations on the German Stock Exchange had fluctuated and, the movement away from gold-mine stocks (in 1897 and thereafter) depressed other stocks. Germany had, according to the press, at least eighty million marks in gold mine shares with which speculators were playing havoc by driving down the price in order later to pocket the gains. If war were to continue, there would also be a real scarcity of gold in the world market. Furthermore, pursued the *Vossische Zeitung* the Boers, who were planning to take over the mines, might find it necessary in a moment of crisis to confiscate for immediate use their entire proceeds.[60] In case of war, England's eventual success could not be seriously questioned. To arouse England as in 1896 would, therefore, be completely mistaken; to coöperate with her would be impossible because of Russia. Hence only a policy of neutrality would safeguard Germany's position in Transvaal enterprises and help to encourage post-war trade there. Such were the views of business circles. Since the alternative to British rule was chaos, it was not surprising that their tone toward England should be milder than in 1896, when the alternative was less clear.

This change of view on the part of business paralleled the abandonment of the Boers by the German government through the Anglo-German treaty over the Portuguese colonies. A policy of neutrality was considered true *Realpolitik,* which in turn was thought of, in the sense of the "misunderstood Bismarck," as clever pursuit of German advantage. The pleasure derived from the settlement of the Samoan question in Germany's favor during the time of England's need is worthy of note. The press often discussed the possibility of interference in South Africa by the Dual Alliance as if to suggest that Germany was not alone in her hostility to British schemes. In short, Germany found friendship with Eng-

[58] *Jahresbericht der Ältesten der Kaufmannschaft zu Berlin,* 1899, No. 51, p. 111.

[59] October 8, 1899.

[60] *Vossische Ztg.,* No. 461, October 1, 1899.

land, or a semblance of it, a better bet for her. If she were to approximate England's greatness, she would do best to keep on good terms with England in order to get what she could from her.

> We have so far developed into *Realpolitiker* [wrote one journal] that we are ruled not by sentiment but by our interests; but it is too much to ask that our feelings should never be expressed. The English press shows often enough how hard that is. Perhaps *The Times* may use the sojourn of the Emperor to make clear to iself how it happens that the German people, who for many years in the past gazed admiringly at Britain, now has not preserved its earlier attitude of England.[61]

The feeling toward England had not changed fundamentally since 1896, but German understanding of what Germany wanted and of how to get it had developed.

What goals were to be achieved in coöperation with England or through a policy of neutrality such as the press supported during most of 1899? The most important, *Weltpolitik,* has been suggested.[62] Even the Pan-Germans hoped to attract British capital into German colonial enterprise so that these colonies might develop more rapidly and become worthy of their name. English investment in German colonies encouraged German investment, and private investment made more possible the winning of governmental aid for the colonies. In 1896 the public knew about the British investments; but the movement for governmental assistance was still young and hopeful. By 1899 there was proof that the government could not proceed rapidly, that German laws excluded the issuing of small shares of stocks—the German minimum share being one thousand marks, the British often as small as £1—and that the colonies must have more money or would become worthless. Coöperation with England in this matter seemed logical since she was an investing country; France had her own colonies and the Russian market; Russia was seeking capital from abroad and had already found that she could not obtain it in Germany.[63]

Another aspect of the investment problems becomes manifest in connection with the navy. To put the wharves, harbors, and shipyards in shape and to build the navy would require capital, which

---

[61] *Vossische Ztg.*, November 14, 1899.

[62] *Vide supra,* p. 311.   [63] *Cf.* Ziekursch and Ibbeken, *op. cit.*

would not be available, therefore, for foreign investment. Due to the Transvaal crisis and the armament needs, recent foreign investments of Germany dropped from seven hundred and ten million marks in 1898 to two hundred and thirty-four million marks in 1899, while domestic investments rose from one thousand six hundred and seventy-five million marks in 1898 to two thousand one hundred and eighty million marks in 1899.[64] These figures suggest the need for assistance from foreign capital in German colonies.

The navy constituted a further point in the programme of imperialism. Germany was aware of her deficiency in this respect and of England's superiority; but in 1899 the majority of the German public did not want further naval expansion. It preferred to coöperate with England and to spend money on the continued development of the overseas market rather than on the navy. The government had given ship-subsidies, secured Kiau-chow, the Caroline, Marianne and Palau Islands and made the treaty with England over the Portuguese colonies without a larger navy and without an English alliance. The upkeep of the navy already imposed a heavy expense; Germany should wait. In the meantime, declared the *Vossische Zeitung*:

> Germany has not the least interest in pursuing a world policy against England, not to mention paying any such price for it [that is, the price which it would cost Germany to ally with the Dual Alliance against England in the Transvaal crisis]. Germany will not choose between England and Russia but will maintain good relations alike with them. . . . Friendship with one Power is not enmity with another; Germany is and remains independent on all sides.[65]

The *Hamburgischer Korrespondent* also stated:

> For us in Germany there is not the least excuse for wishing to push our government into a war with England. Do these

---

[64] Arnold, *Handelsbilanz*, p. 163; Kehr, *op. cit.*, p. 263, note.

[65] *Vossische Ztg.*, November 8. That trade was grateful for the above benefits given it by the government is evident from the *Bericht der Handelskammer zu Essen*, 1899, I, 1; *Handelskammer zu Hamburg*, 1899, p. 2; etc. Practically all the chambers agreed that foreign markets were the crying necessity and wished further aids of the kind mentioned, for example, a colonial bank.

nouveaux [the Pan-Germans] think Paris has forgotten all idea of revenge? And have they no idea of the joy which would reign on the Neva if Germany were so stupid as to pull chestnuts for others out of the English fire? . . . Germany must preserve a policy of independence, keep on friendly terms with all Powers, love none, hate none, always keep to this goal: Germany's honor, well-being and power.[66]

One might equally quote from Stumm's pacific *Post*. A policy of friendship with England was a matter of expediency while Germany mapped out her new road. The public in 1899 supported Bülow's policy of neutrality and obeyed in large part his orders for a "cool" press. It realized that he had abandoned the Boers and, except for the Pan-German, the colonialists and the Agrarians, it approved his actions. These exceptions formed the bulwark of anti-English feeling in Germany.

Last of all, although probably not without some value, was the opinion that German neutrality insured the peace of Europe. Few persons could ignore the fact that armed intervention for the Boers would mean war, not in South Africa, but in Europe, and no one wanted that. It was necessary to admit that England would not be deterred by bluff and to put the best face possible on her decision to go ahead as she pleased.

B. *Second Phase: December 1899 to December 1900*

I.

In November instead of sending a "second telegram," as the Pan-Germans wanted, the Emperor and Bülow went to England.[67] Bülow has always emphasized his desire for good relations with England; but his friendly attitude toward England did not lack *arrières pensées*. After his fall he summarized the German position as follows:

The relations between the Germans and the English had oscillated in the course of the century. By and large, John

---

[66] November 1; also *Grenzboten*, No. 1, January 4, 1900.

[67] *Denkwürdigkeiten*, I, 303 f.; *G. P.*, XV, 413 ff. The subjects of the conversations between Chamberlain, the Emperor, and Bülow, and Balfour, the Emperor and Bülow are summarized in Langer, *op. cit.*, I, 656 ff. Langer recognizes that the Germans were " on their guard ' from the outset.

Bull stood on the ground of wishing to favor and protect his poor German cousins, to use them now and again for dirty work, but not to recognize them as equals. Fundamentally, all the others did not like us. Antipathy against us already existed before the envy of our power and well-being created by Bismarck had increased the distaste for us abroad. Our lesser favor was also to be traced back to the fact that we underestimated the importance of form, of appearance. . . . The serious, thorough German, who always went to the heart of a matter so that the external was indifferent to him, could only with difficulty imagine [the value of these things].[68]

If such reservations actuated Bülow at the time of his English trip, they did not constitute a sound basis for " friendly discussion." That they probably were present is indicated by subsequent developments. On November 29 Chamberlain proposed at Leicester an Anglo-Saxon alliance of England, Germany, and the United States. On December 11 in the Reichstag Bülow did not refer to an alliance, touched lightly on " mutual consideration," and went on with the naval budget. In doing so he acted not only in accord with the immediate reaction of the German press against the Leicester speech, but in response to the deeper public opinion which he had already recognized in 1897.[69] He was committed to a policy of achieving " equality " with England under the guise of good relations; he did not want an alliance.

German opinion certainly did not receive favorably the proposal of an alliance suggested by Chamberlain. The papers had already warned against any political consequences from the Emperor's trip and did not relish the apparent attempt by Chamberlain to exploit it. " What induces him to make such a proposal? The conversations with Bülow and the Emperor? " asked *Tante Voss* on December 1. The press was filled with editorials headed " A New Grouping of the Powers? " most of which rejected out of hand a hard and fast alliance. For purposes of world trade and colonial policy they approved coöperation, they said; but they did not approve an alliance for general policy. The papers called attention to the coolness with which the English public received the speech

---

[68] Bülow, *op. cit.*, I, 27.

[69] If Bülow's account is correct, Chamberlain had no cause to be so encouraged as he was, or appeared to be.

and felt justified in their own rejection of the suggestion made in it. They also thought Chamberlain's speech in the nature of a threat to France, and they refused to be used by England for combatting anti-English opinion in France. The *Vossische,* it is true, thought that England and the United States might enter the Triple Alliance, a step which would certainly give France reason to hold her tongue.[70] But as a general rule the German press repulsed Chamberlain's invitation.[71]

On December 11—Tirpitz had been busy since October 18—Hohenlohe laid before the Reichstag a plan for doubling the number of battleships. The introduction of the bill centered the budget discussions around the navy and at the same time around Anglo-German relations. In his speech supporting the naval bill Bülow said:

> We do not wish to be again, in the words of Friedrich List, the slaves of humanity [*die Knechte der Menschheit*]. We can only maintain ourselves at the top, however, if we realize that we can have no power without a strong army and a strong navy. The means of fighting through the struggle for existence without strong armaments on land and sea for a nation of sixty millions living in the middle of Europe, which at the same time is stretching out its economic antennae in all directions, have not yet been discovered. In the coming century will the German people be the hammer or the anvil? [72]

Such words furthered the passage of the naval bill far more than they encouraged an alliance with England or any nation. They made thoughts of an alliance almost impossible, because Germany would fear to fall back into serfdom if she were bound by treaty to raise a hand for a country greater than she was.

In the end support for a new naval law rallied around Bülow and crystallized in opposition to England. Liebermann von Sonnenberg came forth for a navy as necessary to Germany's imperialistic programme. Germany, he conceded, was no longer an agricultural state; she was partly agricultural and partly industrial and she must not become entirely industrialized. " The present

[70] *Vossische Ztg.,* December 2, 1899.
[71] *Cf. G. P.,* XV, *Hatzfeldt to Hohenlohe,* No. 4401, pp. 422-26, editor's note.
[72] *Denkwürdigkeiten,* I, 356; *Reden,* I, 88.

fate of England, I think," he went on, " speaks warningly enough against this." He meant that he would vote for the navy but in return the government must see that he was protected against the fate of the English landowner. The connection made between the navy and England seemed to imply a choice between the naval law and an English alliance, and from the Agrarian point of view every interest opposed the alliance.[73] Germany sympathized, Liebermann went on, with the Boers because of their bravery, because of kinship with them, and because " there our own problem is being fought out, the question of whether for all time South Africa is to be English or Dutch, that is, German." Limburg-Stirum, an Agrarian, also declared for the navy. He recalled the long antipathy of England to Germany after 1870 and asked Bülow to found his policy on the Triple Alliance and Russia, because English policy would not change toward Germany and Germany must have a navy. Although everyone realized that Germany could not build a navy equal to that of England, his statement implied that Germany needed the navy in order to make her way against England.[74] Since the acceptance of the new naval law depended on the attitude of the Agrarian-Conservatives, Bülow could congratulate himself on having effected a tie-up between their pro-Boer, anti-English sentiments and interests and the proposed naval expansion. Most of the foreign newspapers commenting on Bülow's speech missed this point and ascribed to the Chancellor wider schemes but less important ones, because they were less realistic.

The visit to England failed to improve the feeling of the German public toward England. Criticism of England even increased after it and the chances of the new naval law infinitely improved.

In the meantime British arms in South Africa were faring badly and their difficulties encouraged sympathy for the Boers and made it more incumbent upon the continental Powers to maintain strict neutrality. Various groups in Germany had already collected money for the Boers in open meetings, while German officers and men, after leaving German service, had enrolled in the Transvaal army. On the other hand, Krupp, as was brought out later in the Reichs-

[73] *Sten. Ber. d. Reich.*, December 14, 1899, X Leg. Per., II Sess., IV, 3398-3400.

[74] *Ibid.*, December 12, 1899, p. 3312.

tag, contemplated filling munition orders for England.   Hence, when at the end of December news arrived that England had seized German steamers carrying alleged contraband, the industrialist press protested less noisily than other journals.   The *Berliner Neueste Nachrichten,* Krupp's paper, discussed the international law of the situation without showing any great feeling against England.   During the first days of January this journal did not immediately turn toward a greater navy as did *Die Post,* but it approved of the Emperor's speech on January 1, in which he declared that he must promote the navy as his grandfather had the army.[75]   *Die Post* was not anti-English and like the *Nachrichten* it criticized the Pan-Germans; but both papers at every possible opportunity advanced the cause of the navy and did not neglect to do so on the occasion of the seizures.[76]   The Emperor has told the story that reports of the seizure of a second ship came to him while he was consulting with Bülow and Tirpitz.   After reading the telegram, Bülow observed, "It is an ill wind which blows nobody any good."   Tirpitz ejaculated, "Now we have the wind we need to bring our ships into port; the naval bill will go through.   Your Majesty must really give the English commander an Order in gratitude for making the navy possible."[77]   Whether the story is altogether true or not, it represents the thought of all three: the seizures would furnish the necessary impetus to public opinion to accept the proposed doubling of the navy.

As was to be expected the press reacted instantly to the insult to national feeling given by the seizures.   In a leading article on January 3 the *Kreuzzeitung* bitterly attacked British imperialism. It pointed out that as the three gold fields of the world, the Klondyke, Transvaal, and Australia, were under British control, England could determine the price of gold.   It demanded satisfaction from England for the accusation of carrying contraband and spoke warmly for a navy, although the article recognized that under no circumstances would Germany fight England.[78]   The Colonial Society issued a pamphlet which contained these words:

[75] *B. N. N.,* No. 3, January 3, 1900.

[76] *Post,* 1899, *passim,* especially in October and November; in 1900.

[77] Ziekursch, *op. cit.,* III, 127.

[78] *Neue Preuss. Ztg.,* No. 2, January 3, 1900.

The fact remains that the disregard of Germany because of her deficiency in sea-power has struck such roots in the minds of the British people that the commander of an English ship breaks international law when Germany is involved. Their lack of fear of our flag must be corrected now and fully, since there exists in it a dangerous fire which can lead to more serious developments. Also the most stubborn opponents of the creation of a strong navy must clearly see the danger which exists daily for the German Empire because it is so powerless on the sea.[79]

The Pan-Germans expressed similar feeling.[80] The *Tägliche Rundschau* concluded that England was possibly not so much attacking Germany as trying to win an occasion for pressure against Portugal in order to take Delagoa Bay;[81] but this paper likewise thought the seizure a warning to prepare for a conflict with England. " We hope for the best from the government's dealings with England, but cannot count on too great success, since England knows well enough that in the last analysis nothing can happen because we have no ships." [82] The *Korrespondenz des Bundes der Landwirte* reacted in a characteristic way by blaming the government for the pass to which things had come. The government, it said, served exporters and industrialists and neglected the interests of agriculture, which was going to ruin.[83] Once again the Agrarian-Conservatives wished to make clear that they would support the naval law only if the government helped agriculture. They even implied that the neglect of agriculture emboldened Britain to proceed in this way against a great Power! The *Kölnische Zeitung* suggested that England, knowing that her navy could not be opposed, had decided to substitute might for right and to give vent to some of her pent up feelings over the defeat of her armies. England had taken away what sympathy was left her in the country, wrote the *Kölnische,* and the case of the *Bundesrat* showed clearly that German naval power must correspond to her land power and

[79] Cited by *Tägliche Rundschau,* No. 5, January, 1900.
[80] *Alld. Bl.,* January, 1900, *passim.*
[81] *Tägliche Rundschau,* No. 5, January, 1900.
[82] *Ibid.,* January 7, 1900.
[83] *Korrespondenz,* January, *passim.*

commercial position.[84] At a meeting of the directors of the East
Africa Line to discuss the capital increase for building new ships
for the company, the bankers present declared that before the
question of compensation from England could be settled, no one
would dare to invest a cent of money in the enterprise.[85] It is well
known that Woermann, the nominal head of the line, actively interested himself in naval agitation; he could use this experience
with his bankers to promote the naval cause. Shortly afterward
the harbor cities asked for the new naval bill. This move on their
part was especially important, a true service to Tirpitz, because in
1897 commercial interests had not unanimously approved a larger
navy.

The more liberal papers did not always show themselves so violently pro-navy; but their calm was greatly ruffled. The *Berliner
Tageblatt* showed distress over the fall in the market following
the seizures. Industrial and bank stocks had declined one to two
points and ship stocks had fallen off steadily. This decline led
the *Tageblatt* to criticize the complicated and vague definitions of
"contraband" and to encourage the government to be firm. It
spoke hopefully of rumors of intervention, since business longed
for the end of the war.[86] The *Vossische Zeitung* also urged the
government to stand firmly on its rights, especially since England
would not dare again to defy world opinion by repeating her
action.[87] The *Nationalzeitung* tried desperately to arouse some
opposition to the meetings of the Colonial Society, which carried on
demonstrations beyond all reason and made demands which could
not possibly be backed up without a strong navy. The journal concluded that a navy which would stop these injuries to national
pride and remove the cause for propaganda furnished the only

[84] *Kölnische Ztg.*, January 3, 1900.

[85] Kehr, *op. cit.*, p. 191, citing from the archives of the Hamburg Chamber
of Commerce.

[86] No. 4, January 3; also No. 6, January 4. Cf. also *Neue Preuss. Ztg.*,
No. 6, January 5; No. 12, January 9; No. 26, January 17 for reference to
the business situation. A journal with the anti-capitalistic point of view
and opposed to the *Tageblatt's* attitude toward the situation was the Agrarian *Deutsche Tageszeitung*.

[87] January 4, 1900.

logical means of quieting the disturbance.[88] Also *Die Nation* and
the National Socialist organ, *Die Hilfe*, knew of no remedy but
seapower against England's violation of international law.[89]

The capitalistic and industrialist press believed that the feeling
over the seizures had no practical value and did not share it; but
it used the feeling, as did, for example, *Die Post*, to pursue cleverly
naval propaganda. Bueck perfected the technique, which he employed publicly soon after, of demanding the navy because it
enhanced Germany's political power and position rather than
because economic interests wished it. He supposed this appeal
to nationalism much better calculated to win public support than
reference to heavy industry's profit from further ship orders. He
mentioned orders only when he needed to call attention to the
work which would be created by them for the benefit of " national
labor." [90]

The socialist papers wasted little space on the seizure of the
Bundesrat and other ships, for they needed to strengthen and
energetically pursue the campaign which they had been waging
since early November (after the Emperor's speech of October 18)
against the naval bill. The Social Democrats understood clearly
the change which had taken place in the Agrarian-Conservative
attitude toward the navy; [91] they perceived the tactics of Bueck
and Woermann.[92] *Vorwärts* cited effectively from speeches made
at a meeting of the Agrarian League in Düsseldorf at which Hahn
spoke for naval expansion. During the discussion the Agrarians
had shown their real attitude toward the navy in the words:

> We Agrarians have up to now regarded everything from a
> patriotic standpoint. Shall we continue to do that? I say,
> ' no.' We cannot pursue a national policy if industry follows
> exclusively an economic policy. We cannot agree to a navy

---

[88] *Loc. cit.*

[89] *Die Hilfe*, No. 6, January 14: " For Germany's whole future policy it
can only be of advantage when the anti-English instinct in the nation
grows." The growth of this instinct was considered helpful to naval expansion. Also Lujo Brentano, *Die Nation*, No. 15, January 13, 1900, pp.
205-208; No. 16, January 20, pp. 217-220.

[90] *Industriezeitung*, No. 4, January, 1900, p. 41; No. 7, February 15.

[91] Kehr, *op. cit.*, p. 184.   [92] *Vorwärts*, No. 7, January 10, 1900.

without further ado. We also cannot rely on the promises of the government.

Finally this Agrarian assembly had resolved to support the "national point of view," but had added that the countryside had little confidence in the government and that confidence could only be restored by aid to agriculture.[93] Gravely troubled by the internal struggle and its relation to naval laws, the press of the Left disregarded questions of international law. Not anti-British feeling, but the effects of this feeling in Germany disturbed it now more than even in 1896. As *Vorwärts* said, it is as if England had been asked to seize a few ships in order to give the *Reichsmarineamt* a chance.[94]

Quite apart from the developments in regard to the navy arising out of the situation in January, the German press continued to worry over the outcome of the seizures. "There are in all probability," wrote Eckardstein, "few who realize how serious was the crisis in Anglo-German relations during the three weeks that we carried on negotiations for the release of this steamer. We were all the time within a hair's breadth of a rupture." [95] Some of the press suggested, as Eckardstein did, that the entire affair represented only an effort on England's part to pacify English opinion for not taking Delagoa Bay, but Germans still thought it a strange act for a friend to perform. Was England a friend then? Was she not again "perfidious Albion"? Business continued to be upset because ships feared to sail, especially after an American ship was searched, and it derived small comfort from the fact that other flags showed timidity. The Hamburg Chamber of Commerce acknowledged that, in view of such injuries to its trade, its attitude toward England had changed.[96] The Berlin *Boersen-Courier*

---

[93] *Loc. cit.*   [94] *Ibid.*, No. 4, January 7, 1900.

[95] Eckardstein, *op. cit.*, p. 112. For the negotiation, *G. P.*, XV, CII. It is not necessary to go into these since they can be found in all accounts of the diplomatic relations between England and Germany. Eckardstein probably exaggerated, as was usual with him, in making the statement cited above.

[96] Cited by the *Vossische Ztg.*, January 2. The *Bundesrat* was an East Africa Line steamer and the *Hans Wagner* belonged to another Hamburg firm.

and the *Berliner Tageblatt* took renewed interest in the probable post-war trade between Germany and the Transvaal. They hoped the government would think of this trade in handling the matter of the seizures and provide future safeguards.[97] In order to encourage the government to press for a release of the ships so that the stock market could improve, they frequently mentioned the rise of interest rates due to the scarcity of gold. Many of the papers, including the *Vossische,* the *Kölnische,* as well as the financial sheets, held to the facts and avoided any heated anti-English sentiment, alert though they were to the prevalent bad feeling.[98] When, however, the publication of the *Bundesrat's* papers and the testimony of the Hamburg lines about their ships showed everything to have been legal, feeling against England increased, especially in the nationalistic journals.

In the midst of the growing agitation occurred an event which the *Tageblatt* considered to be a disparagement of the Boer cause as much as the seizures had been of the English. The Transvaal decided to levy a new tax on gold sufficient to replace all other taxes. The tax demanded thirty percent of the profits of all persons, companies, and firms working their own mines and fifty percent of those from mines run by the government. The law was to be applied as from October, 1899. The European Powers friendly to the Boers judged this act severely, because, said the *Tageblatt,* if the Boers should win, millions of marks would be confiscated. It might be that confiscation was intended, added the financiers. If the law stood, the mining interests of all neutrals would raise questions for their governments. The *Tageblatt* itself had immediately approached the consul in Pretoria. Of course, it added, if England should be victorious the law would remain only on paper.[99] For the bankers and investors press fury and anti-English propaganda could not prevail against this point, although a paper like the *Tägliche Rundschau* answered the argument by

[97] *Berliner Tageblatt*, No. 4, January 3, 1900; No. 9, January 6.

[98] *Kölnische Ztg.,* January 5, 1900. Here even the fact that the Boers could prepare beforehand, while England could not because she must give the appearance of desiring peace, was pointed out by way of trying to square England.

[99] No. 8, January 5, 1900; also *Boersen Courier,* No. 11, January 8.

22

denying that a probably greater economic security under England was important; the German people felt aroused, it wrote.[100]

During the first two weeks of January all the German papers, apart from the Agrarian and Social Democratic, expressed confidence in the government. Bülow rewarded their trust by securing the peaceful release of the *Bundesrat* on January 17 before any discussion of the incident had taken place in the Reichstag. He rewarded them likewise by publishing in the semi-official *Norddeutsche Allgemeine Zeitung* that Krupp had been told to make no further sales to England.[101] There was general satisfaction among moderate papers, which had been disturbed over the incompatibility of the energetic naval demands of the *Neueste Nachrichten* and the seeming friendliness of Krupp to England.[102]

On January 19 by way of an interpellation discussion of the government's policy toward the seizures began in the Reichstag. Representatives of all parties except the Social Democratic signed the interpellation, which fulfilled the express desire of some groups, especially the Agrarians, for a public airing of the episode. At first the interpellation, conducted by Moeller-Duisberg (National Liberal), proceeded calmly. Moeller stated the facts of the case, discussed international law and the violence done it by England,

---

[100] *Tägliche Rundschau*, No. 4, January 6. This paper could afford to make such comment because its readers were largely officials with fixed salaries. It was, in any case, a nationalistic organ.

[101] *Berliner Tageblatt*, No. 22, January 13, 1900. The fact that the semi-official *Norddeutsche Allgemeine* was used indicated that Krupp had intended the deliveries and that the government had the facts at its disposal. The notice said that the question of the legitimacy of such sales had been answered in the negative.

[102] It is difficult to know just how much Krupp had undertaken. His intention to supply England was generally believed in and on the theory of no smoke where there is not some fire there is some ground for the belief. Kehr cited orders to the Ehrhardt cannon factory for one hundred and twenty pieces of artillery (Kehr, pp. 190 f., citing from Ehrhardt, *Hammerschläge* [Leipzig, 1922], pp. 70, 81, 82). The first news of Krupp's intended sale appeared apparently in *Der Weckruf*, the Essen Social Democratic organ (*Vossische Ztg.*, January 13, 1900). Krupp's journal, the *B. N. N.*, was less mild than *Die Post* and quite often disdained British methods. It even urged the German government not to feel always that it must in its foreign policy pursue German interests to the exclusion of justified sympathies.

suggested that England had erroneously assumed that Germany was helping to arm the Boers, and declared that England should have examined the facts before she acted. He asked for compensation and guarantees for the future. Bülow answered immediately that he gladly satisfied public opinion openly, that he wished no disturbance of good relations with England, and he explained what he had done. His speech closed the interpellation; [103] but unfortunately the matter did not rest here. Before the sitting adjourned bitter words, such as the *Vossische Zeitung* feared would be the result of a Reichstag discussion of the incident, were exchanged.[104]

For the interpellation itself most of the German press had nothing but praise. The government's handling of the episode satisfied most reasonable people in the country.[105] It was different with the ensuing remarks. After the interpellation the discussion in the Reichstag turned to the budget for the Chancellery. It opened with a speech by Kardorff bristling with the hatred and jealousy felt by agriculture over the government's treatment of domestic affairs. Liebermann continued the onslaught. Not confining himself to Prussian or internal politics, Liebermann attacked the Chancellor for his foreign policy, which, he said, had in no way conformed to the vast antipathy aroused in the country by recent experiences with England. His words were strong:

> It is already buried [that is, Anglo-German friendship], at least for the German people, and in the long run no foreign policy can be carried on against the entire people's feeling,

---

[103] *Sten. Ber. d. Reich.*, January 19, 1900, X Leg. Per., I Sess., IV, 3595 ff.

[104] *Vossische Ztg.*, January 18, 1900. *The Times* objected to Bülow's speech on the ground that it was not fair to use delicate international subjects for promoting internal policy, that is, for the navy. This accusation was, in this instance, unjust; as the German press pointed out, the Reichstag would not have closed the debate if any chance had been given to discuss the navy. The German press praised the speech, with the exception of the Agrarian and Social Democratic papers. The Agrarian League attacked the government as usual; *Vorwärts* called it all a "pointless comedy."

[105] The Exchange improved on the following day, although the *Tageblatt* attributed the improvement only partially to Bülow's speech and gave credit to British military successes and to German naval plans (*Berliner Tageblatt*, No. 36, January 20).

. . . The more clearly and thoroughly we express ourselves here, the better it will be for the whole country and the more convenient for the government in its future encounters with England, encounters which, after what we have gone through with, will not fail to occur. . . . The German people thinks otherwise than the government. It doesn't believe that good relations with England should be preserved, but that it lies in the interest of our country to make as clean a break as possible with England. The inability of the British war leaders in South Africa has been so clearly demonstrated that one hardly needs to wait for further proofs. One is reminded of the words of Napoleon III when he said. . . . 'I can't ally myself with a corpse.' [106]

On the following day Hahn further chastized Bülow for not following public opinion by taking a more emphatic stand than he had on January 19. He criticized the conduct of foreign policy, accused Bülow of failing to separate economic and foreign policy as Bismarck had done, and urged him to proceed energetically against the United States in the interests of German " national labor." [107]

The nature of the criticism is sufficiently illustrated by the examples given. When Bülow told Lascelles that much of the worst anti-English feeling came from the Agrarians and formed part of their anti-government policy, he was correct. Nothing is better proof than the debates of January 19 and 20, 1900. When all parties from National Liberals to Progressives and the press as well supported Bülow in a moderate English policy, the Agrarians pressed their own cause in speeches which attacked in the bitterest fashion the moderation of the government toward England. The Agrarians were accustomed to use every opportunity to press their interests; but a matter of foreign policy did not often adapt itself so well to their needs as the Boer cause. The Social Democrats understood the entire display.[108] They approved of Bülow's moderation in the *Bundesrat's* case. But because the government would not adequately combat the Agrarians, they stood aside or joined

---

[106] Liebermann: *Sten. Ber. d. Reich.*, January 19, 1900, X Leg. Per., I Sess., IV, 3615. It is interesting that he also denied the charges against Krupp, but said the government should prohibit the sale of arms, because large capital made for internationalization, that is, for international goodwill!

[107] *Ibid.*, January 20, pp. 3621 f.   [108] *Vorwärts*, January 21, 1900.

the latter in attacking it. The lack of a clear policy on Bülow's part exposed the Chancellor to constant criticism; and the more he was attacked, the more foreign policy in general and Anglo-German relations in particular suffered.

The *Vossische* and the *Kölnische Zeitung,* which had done their best to preserve calm and moderation during the crisis of January, 1900, and the *Norddeutsche Allgemeine,* which had also been almost free of provocative discussion, sincerely tried to better feeling. Interest shifted to the pending naval debates. The *Vossische* and the *Berliner Tageblatt,* for example, almost ignored discussion of Anglo-German relations and in them, as in other liberal papers, news of the navy and naval bill remained unaccompanied by anti-English propaganda. Their discretion did not characterize the Pan-German press, for which every event was grist to the nationalistic mill. The press was also beginning to watch with concern for plans of the probable reorganization of the English army, which, it thought, would take place after the war on a large scale.[109]

It is generally said that the seizure of the ships had great influence on the passage of the new naval bill. This statement though true must not be over-emphasized. Tirpitz and the Emperor constantly worked at perfecting plans and winning friends for the navy. Events like those of January, 1896, and of January, 1900, assisted them in demonstrating to the public what the navy could mean, that is, what public opinion thought it could mean, in defending Germany from such events. It is easy to understand the connections which were made, but harder to discover logic in the arguments put forth. Most of these arguments implied, when thought through, that, if Germany had had a navy, England would not have dared to act, a conclusion perhaps tenable in the case of the seizures, but not in the case of the Boer War itself; or that there would have been a war with England, which German public opinion, even the Pan-Germans, did not want. It is interesting testimony to the popularity of imperialism that the German press could analyze the way in which British imperialism had drawn England into the

---

[109] *Boersen-Courier,* No. 54, February 2, 1900. The press did not know of the Emperor's now famous " aphorisms " or *Gedankensplitter,* which he sent to his grandmother and uncle. See Lee, *King Edward* VII, I, 745 f.

Boer War and made her commit acts which all German opinion denounced without seeing that German imperialism would involve Germany in similar dangers.[110]

II.

During December, 1899, and January, 1900, the German press occasionally carried rumors of proposals for intervention and mediation. According to the documents now available these rumors were not unfounded: in London, Paris, and St. Petersburg soundings had been taken to this end, at first without successful issue. On January 11 Count Osten-Sacken, Russian Ambassador in Berlin, put out a feeler as to what Bülow would think of common action of the Powers in case England attempted to seize Delagoa Bay. He indicated that Russian opinion eagerly awaited the answer.[111] But nothing came of his attempt and the German press apparently learned little about it. If the nationalistic papers had known, they would have been glad to use Osten-Sacken's view of the seizures, as given to Bülow, to support their own strictures. Instead Eckardstein found *Die Post, Kleines Journal* and *Berliner Neueste Nachrichten,* all journals of heavy industry, particularly friendly to England and making a good impression. Suddenly on February 6 the French *Éclair* published anti-English articles reported to emanate from the Duke of Mecklenburg, President of the Colonial Society.[112] The articles, which were believed in England to be authentic and were thought to support a Franco-German coalition against England, were badly received by the British press, although the *Mecklenburgsche Zeitung* promptly and officially repudiated them. It is quite probable that the Duke may have talked too much, and such garrulity would also have been censured by the moderate press in Germany; but the German press suspected that this publication was a piece of intrigue against Germany.

[110] There is plenty of evidence that the German press appreciated the dilemma of the English Liberals and saw the difference between their attitude toward the war and that of those favoring a Greater Britain. See also G. P., XV, *Münster to Bülow*, December 25, 1899, Appendix to No. 4459.

[111] *Ibid., Memorandum of Bülow*, January 12, 1900, p. 506.

[112] *Ibid., Eckardstein to the Foreign Office*, February 6, 1900, No. 4467, p. 511.

On February 2 the *Vossische Zeitung* had carried a long article repeating the fears of a Berlin writer in the *Pester Lloyd*. According to this article Russian agents were working to sow bad feeling between Germany and Austria and between Germany and England. The agent of the propaganda was said to be the Pan-Slav, Wesselitsky.[113] The *Vossische* could not vouch for the truth of the authorship, but stated that " at present strong forces are active to separate Germany completely from England and to destroy the Triple Alliance." [114] The journal pleaded with the public not to be misled by this propaganda, since it must proceed from influences unfriendly to Germany. The *Nationalzeitung* on February 5 urged that the new burst of anti-English feeling in the Agrarian and Pan-German papers and in the *Hamburger Nachrichten* be quieted, and called upon England to disregard it.[115] The *Kölnische Zeitung* and the *Münchener Allgemeine* shared these warnings, reiterating, " We run after no one, neither England nor Russia." And *Die Post,* always wary of being estranged from Britain, added: " Germany must be forearmed [that is, by a navy] against England, but as soon as she takes any stand against England, France will only draw nearer to her old enemy; as to a continental grouping, in France they want to arouse hostility between Germany and England." [116]

On the day of these warnings, February 5, Radolin wrote to Bülow from St. Petersburg of alleged intrigues to separate Russia and England, communicated to him by the English Ambassador, Sir Charles Scott. He quoted a remark attributed to the Emperor. On the ninth Bülow denied the remark and agreed that slander was a-foot to poison German relations with England. He seemed disturbed.[117] In the following days opinion in the German papers

[113] A follower of Katkov, who was actually anti-German and worked in this direction in London.

[114] February 2, 1900.

[115] This paper did not see so clearly what was taking place, but knew that the coalition gossip held danger.

[116] *Die Post* held repeatedly that in the last analysis France's interests would always draw her toward England; therefore, Germany must keep on good terms with England.

[117] *G. P.,* XV, *Radolin to Bülow,* February 5, 1900, p. 513; *Bülow to Radolin,* February 9, p. 514.

varied from day to day and edition to edition. It became apparent
even to the press that no one knew what was going on or what
should be done. The public feared France, Russia, the Pan-
Germans, and England. On February 8 the naval debates opened in
the Reichstag. The public turned to the navy as a means of
asserting and building up Germany's own position and power and
of restoring her self-confidence. By a stroke of fate on the same
day Theodor Mommsen, a life-long Liberal and contributor to the
liberal *Die Nation,* published his answer to the inquiry of Sidney
Whitman as to what were the fundamentals of anti-English feeling
in Germany. In his letter Mommsen, after reviewing the Anglo-
philism of his younger days, continued:

> Now the whole thing is completely turned about; the il-
> lusions have vanished. The radical mistakes of the British
> system, the trampling upon subject and despised races, the
> supremacy of moneyed interests, the change of national defense
> from land forces to the sea and to sailors—all that becomes
> only too clear. We began to doubt whether Britain and even
> Greater Britain in the long run could keep step with the great
> nations of Europe and America. But not only our judgment
> has changed; the British themselves have contributed greatly
> to change the German attitude.[118]

Taken together with the naval law, this letter seemed to have an
ominous significance for the future. The Germans had followed
England in so many of these changes mentioned that Mommsen,
a Liberal, who opposed his own government and the ruling classes
for what they had brought about in this respect, almost perforce
opposed England, the forerunner of imperialism and industrialism.

At the end of February the Boer General Cronje surrendered.
A rise in the Berlin stock market did not immediately follow,
probably because peace was not yet assured.[119] The German press
had recently been comparatively quiet about England. The Prince
of Wales had just visited Germany and only the nationalists continued to be disturbed by the worse outlook for the Boers. *Die Post*
suggested that the country think for a moment that England's

---

[118] Cited by the *Berliner Tageblatt* (and elsewhere), No. 70, February 8,
1900.

[119] *Boersen-Courier,* No. 97, February 27, 1900.

collapse would mean first of all a strengthening of the Dual Entente. Let it then restrain its press by remembering what Bismarck once said: " For all the foreign windows our press breaks, the Foreign Office has to make redress." [119a] On March 4 the *Nationalzeitung* carried an article entitled " The Beginning of British Rule in South Africa," which calmly accepted English victory in the war. But anew in Russia, in the anti-governmental press in France, and in the ranks of the Pan-Germans the defeat of the Boers and the equanimity with which the government and the moderates received it aroused public opinion. It seems to have been this reaction which led Russia early in March to hint a second time in Berlin at intervention. Holstein and Bülow reacted coolly and when Osten-Sacken suggested that Germany propose mediation to England, Bülow made clear that Russia, who had no interests in the Transvaal, was better able to take the lead.[120] To the Emperor's satisfaction the Prince of Wales had just spoken well of German policy; hence the Emperor agreed with Bülow in opposing the Russian suggestion.[121] The German press quickly noted that France and Russia were calling on Germany to take the first step against England and, in contrast to its eagerness to intervene in 1896, it feared treachery. " Interventions," wrote the *Nationalzeitung,* " belong to the old diplomacy. . . . The British are determined to fight to the end with the Boers, and, though one may condemn the way in which they began the war, the energy with which they have conducted it and the courage with which they have suffered defeat assure them the right of refusing intervention." [122] The press of moderate opinion believed that the demand for intervention came in most of the countries from anti-government groups and was not founded on pure idealism. *Vorwärts* even blamed the *Kölnische* for being as pro-English about intervention as it had been pro-Boer in 1896; [123] in fact, the latter paper made every effort to

[119a] *Die Post,* No. 105, March 3, 1900.

[120] *G. P.,* XV, *Bülow to Radolin,* March 3, 1900, pp. 516 f.; *Bülow to Radolin,* March 7, 1900, p. 520.

[121] *Ibid., Metternich to Hohenlohe,* March 5, 1900, p. 518, and Emperor's note.

[122] *Nationalzeitung,* March 4, 1900.

[123] *Vorwärts,* No. 54, March 6, 1900; cf. *Kölnische,* March 7, which showed distrust of France because of her internal political situation.

soothe the hostile press in England.[124] The *Vossische* even excused England's refusal to allow intervention by the Emperor, when in response to a request from President Krüger he made such an offer.[125] The *Kreuzzeitung* suggested that Nicholas II had perhaps promised England not to use the war for Russia's advantage and now regretted his promise and was tired of the war. If this was so, it said, the moves for intervention took on a meaning which had nothing to do with sympathy for the Boers.

Russia, the United States, and Holland made further attempts at mediation. It is well known that little came of them. Of great interest is the way in which the German press rejected interference. Neither Bülow nor the moderate press saw anything to be gained from it. The latter was able to make a distinction which, judging mainly from British sources, was seldom appreciated, namely, that the sentimental public feeling such as burst out in Dresden in noisy anti-English demonstrations differed greatly from the attitude toward England of the press and opinion supporting the government. The latter included the business and financial interests, the bureaucracy, the liberals, and the moderate Conservatives outside the Agrarian group, although individuals of these circles may often have attended pro-Boer rallies and subscribed to the Pan-German donation funds.[126] The moderates resented mostly the continued anti-German press in England and England's failure to discriminate between the different shades of feeling in the German press.[127] It must, of course, be remembered that in fighting a difficult war British papers were tempted to use material which would arouse support and keep up interest in the fighting. Anti-German sentiment, provoked by constant references to anti-British feeling in Germany, was well suited to do this. Some of the

[124] See also *Vossische Ztg.*, March 14 *et seq.*

[125] *G. P.*, XV, 525 ff.; also *Vossische*, No. 120, March 14.

[126] *Cf.* exchange of letters in *Deutsche Revue*, XXV (April-June, 1900) between Müller on the part of England and Theodor Mommsen. The letters contain many interesting points.

[127] See *Vossische Ztg.*, March 23, and *Nationalztg.*, April 8. For instance, the German press itself denied that the Catholics were ever so anti-English as the Agrarians and anti-Semites. It may be mentioned here that the anti-Semites were Anglophobs because they regarded the war as forced by Jewish speculators and bankers.

German press realized this fact. But German opinion as a whole failed to distinguish between real feeling and propaganda. *Die Nation* urged Germans not to blame the English people for certain phases of government policy and condemned vigorously anti-English propaganda because of its inevitable effect in England.[128]

The attitude of the moderate papers was well illustrated by their discussion in April of the visit of the Boer delegation to Europe. The *Nationalzeitung* wrote that the sympathy in every country for the Boers rested on the conviction of the righteousness of their cause; "but in the present state of the whole South African question a decision over the theoretical rights of the Boers is of no importance. During war laws are silent and the right of the strong decides such matters." [129] It advised the Boers to give up any hope of intervention and treat with England for peace. After the British victories of May the German press regarded the Boer cause as lost and peace as not far distant. Nothing is more noticeable than the calmness with which the moderate press contemplated the conclusion of peace, especially if this attitude is compared with the feeling in 1896. During the summer months only the nationalists, the Agrarians, the *Hamburger Nachrichten,* and the *Rheinisch-Westfälische Zeitung,* which always supported the Pan-Germans, kept up agitation.[130] The action of the Pan-Germans in the autumn of 1900 when Krüger visited Europe to beg for mediation revealed the frame of mind of this group. The Emperor decided

---

[128] *Die Nation*, No. 44, August 4.   [129] *Nationalztg.*, April 20 and 23.

[130] *Cf. Vorwärts*, No. 105, May 8, 1900. *Vorwärts* naturally accused the capitalistic journals of being especially anti-English. It is a mistake to assert this without restriction, because one does not know when these papers are speaking as capitalists, as nationalists, or when they are silently approving the work which nationalists were doing elsewhere. One sees clearly enough from Class's *Wider den Strom* that in the Rhineland there was much sympathy for the Boers. The Dutch had many interests there, and intermarriage had taken place. Hence it would be difficult to say how much the *Rheinisch-Westfälische* adhered to the Boers because of capitalistic interests competing with England or allied with Dutch interests and how much because of sincere nationalism. Certainly, these capitalistic interests wanted naval expansion and anti-English feeling helped this cause. Commercial interests were seeking through their journals to promote steamer subsidies (May-June in the Reichstag), a cause likewise aided by anti-English sentiment.

not to receive him in Berlin and Krüger stopped short at Cologne. "That which now happened," wrote Class, "belongs to the most beautiful and noble manifestations of healthy German feeling." [131] As soon as news of the impending visit of Krüger arrived the Pan-Germans arranged a reception for him which became a wildly enthusiastic public meeting. A delegation of them with Reismann-Grone as spokesman formally greeted him and expressed its sympathy with the Boer cause as well as its anger over the Emperor's failure to receive the President of the Boer Republic. Later a group of Pan-Germans from many parts of Germany went to the Hague to repeat the expressions of feeling so evident in Cologne.[132]

In the Reichstag the debate over the Krüger visit similarly revealed divided sentiments.[133] The National Liberals did not wish the government to do anything which might harm German interests and offend England; they implored Bülow to restrain anti-English outbursts. Bebel also approved the Chancellor's general English policy, but regretted the non-reception of Krüger as diminishing German dignity and independence; it looked, he said, as if the Germans "fear only God and their Grandmother." Liebermann as usual attacked the government vehemently. He charged the press of the Left with working in coöperation with the government and the Jewish papers to create pro-British opinion in Germany and maintained that this coöperation did not represent the German people in its whole-souled cry, "*los von England!*" In his view he was fully supported by Dr. Hasse, who though less violently, regretted the lack of national spirit which had turned back Ohm Paul. Hahn of the Agrarian League again showed the Agrarian view when he challenged the government to prove that

---

[131] Class, *op. cit.*, p. 55. For further discussion see *Alld. Bl.*, Nos. 50, 51, December 9, 16, 1900. The money collected for the Boers by the Pan-Germans totalled by December, 1900, some two hundred and fifty thousand marks.

[132] Compare with this enthusiasm the attitude of *Die Nation*, which also admired Krüger but added: "Politics, especially imperialism, teaches us that a great Power is often painfully bound by circumstances, by consciousness of the fact that its own existence is at stake in every great war and that the emptiest dream of all is the dream of doing away with all injustice" (No. 10, December 8, 1900, article by Mommsen).

[133] *Sten. Ber. d. Reich.*, December 10-13, 1900, X Leg. Per., II Sess., I, 507 ff.

good relations with England would not harm Germany. As it was, he said, Germany had followed England in accepting colonies, the gold standard, trusts, even though the whole structure of German social and economic life differed from the English. Germany could not become an industrial state, he continued, and yet she had lately imitated England in developing her export industry at the cost of her agriculture. From this debate the Chancellor only learned again that he had the agricultural problem with which to deal, that Anglophobia among the Agrarians was not so much a question of sympathy with the Boers as one of life and death to large-scale agriculture.

C. *Third Phase: January 1901 to December 1902*

Historians have said that the German press in the summer of 1900 moderated its anti-English feeling only to reverse its views again at the time of the Krüger visit. In December, 1900, the *Deutsche Tageszeitung* (Agrarian) had written:

> Luckily President Krüger and the entire world have had in these days absolute proof that the German people and the German government go completely different ways in this matter; that, therefore, our present government policy can only be a passing episode. The news of the reception of President Krüger along the whole line from the German boundary to Cologne and especially in that city sounds truly encouraging.[134]

The divergence of paths was to become more marked in the two following years. The reasons for this become a complicated interplay of cause and effect. Bülow held to a course of neutrality, or, as his opponents thought, erred on the side of friendliness to England. In October, 1900 he had made the Yangtze treaty with England; during the first part of 1901 he engaged in secret negotiations with the British government. He had also passed the word to the German press to moderate its tone, and the papers close to the government were much calmer than the Agrarian and Pan-German ones. The hostile English press, however, came to think of Bülow and the government as stirring up German feeling and

[134] *Deutsche Tagesztg.*, December 3.

during agitation for the naval bill the accusation contained some truth. Tirpitz at least knew the value of anti-English feeling for developing naval enthusiasm. After the acceptance of the naval law in June, 1900, the press certainly grew quieter. At the time of the passage the government had promised to provide aid for agriculture.[135] The promise compensated the Agrarians for their support of the navy and should have helped to reduce their opposition to the government. But because the details of the new tariff schedules had still to be worked out, it failed to do so. Consequently, the Second Naval Law brought only temporary respite from attack to the government. Upon new provocation, such as the Emperor's refusal to receive Krüger, the Agrarian press broke out again against the Chancellor, and during 1901 it persisted in a vehement campaign for its tariff demands.

As for industry, it still strove to support the government and to refrain from offending England. Of this effort there can be no doubt. On the other hand, the navy was only one of many aids which industry sought in order to promote imperialism. The China expedition, a greatly increased budget for the protectorates—fifty million more marks than in 1900 with one million more for Kiauchow—, and higher tariffs succeeded the Second Naval Law. Is it not evident that over and above any economic and commercial rivalry with England such a programme contributed, if not toward anti-English feeling, at least toward anti-English policy? It stimulated Germany's self-confidence and made psychologically impossible an alliance in which the new imperialistic nation might play the lesser rôle, as she always feared she would in acting with England?[136]

As for the propaganda groups, their agitation flared up upon any provocation. They desired not so much to make England detested as to arouse in Germany a wish for developing more and more fully German national consciousness, or, if one prefers, chauvinism. To this desire was added some measure of just

[135] Secretary Thielmann: "The Federated Governments have decided upon emphatic protection of the interests of German agriculture relative to the protection of their products in the proposed future tariff law." *Cf.* Kehr, *op. cit.*, p. 202 and note 109.

[136] *Cf.* Ziekursch, *op. cit.*, III, 149-151.

indignation against British tactics in the Boer states and a great deal of resentment against anti-German feeling in England. The German nationalists had done much to produce this feeling in England because they could not restrain their chauvinism. A press war was rapidly coming to a head.

The economic crisis of 1900 and 1902 must not be omitted from the story. In the summer of 1900 a distinct downward swing in the business cycle became evident.[137] For some time it had been thought that the high interest rates were due to the Boer War and to the shortage of gold, but economists now realized that over-speculation had created a demand for money beyond the supply and had produced a difficult world economic condition.[138] It is impossible to decide whether the temporary lull in public anti-English feeling was due in part to this economic setback. The financial journals had been moderate for some months before the downswing set in and they could at most have influenced only a small group. It is just as possible that the temporary feeling of stringency and irritation, as well as the need for more vigorous economic efforts at home and abroad, sharpened the feeling of rivalry and nationalism against England. As yet psychologists do not supply historians with sufficient knowledge of what happens in time of crisis with respect to foreign affairs to say definitely what occurs in a case of this kind. The greatest self-assertion and national assurance appear during the upswing of the business cycle. The naval laws were passed while prosperity prevailed. During a depression it is not uncommon to find carping and backbiting. England, too, was pressed for money—she borrowed in New York—and manifested this feeling from her side both by press attacks and by deeds. The Chamber of Commerce of Leipzig complained in 1899 that higher prices had reduced the sale of German textiles to England and other chambers objected to the English war tax on sugar. The Krupp *Berliner Neueste Nachrichten* was accustomed to reprint

---

[137] *Schriften des Vereins für Sozialpolitik,* 113, *Die Störungen im deutschen Wirtschaftsleben während der Jahre 1900 seq.* The discussion in this volume takes the form of a symposium. It may be noted that in all the debate there is no reference to English trade rivalry as having anything to do with the German crisis.

[138] *Ibid.,* 110, 280-82.

from *The Times* articles which discussed the decay of British industry and urged it to make greater effort against German and American competition. The *Nachrichten* also considered the House of Commons hostile to the German shipbuilding industry.[139]   In these cases German business became more aware of British competition after the beginning of the depression in 1900 than during the early part of the war.   Hence there was a ground bass of dissatisfaction, even though the *leitmotif* in the press sounded less anti-English than before 1900.

The explanation given above for continued anti-English feeling indicates that in the long run the internal situation accounted for this feeling.   German public opinion in diverging from the course of the government did not do so purely out of distaste for its policies, but from more fundamental objections as well.   Other causes of Anglophobia are evident from the discussion of them in the press, and they will appear from time to time in the narrative which follows, where they need no particular comment.

In January, 1901, negotiations for an alliance between the two governments began and the conversations lasted into March and even May.   During their progress the press somewhat quieted down. Eckardstein said to Holstein on April 9 that he had a distinct impression that Salisbury was losing distrust of Germany.[140] Many of the German papers sincerely regretted the death of Queen Victoria (January 22, 1901) and praised the Emperor's generous action in going to her bedside.   Yet so moderate a journal as the *Frankfurter Zeitung,* which in 1897 had wanted some sort of agreement, spoke of alliance as " unthinkable " and considered that the anti-English feeling in the country went very deep.[141]   On April 19 King Edward told Eckardstein that the government and especially Lord Salisbury still distrusted the Emperor and the German Chancellor.   The King mentioned the activity of the Navy League in spreading antagonism to England in Germany.[142]   Eng-

---

[139] *B. N. N.*, No. 27, January 17, 1901.

[140] Eckardstein, *op. cit.*, p. 214.

[141] *Geschichte der Frankfurter Zeitung*, pp. 871-2.

[142] Eckardstein, pp. 216-18.   This was hardly one of the Navy League's greatest periods of activity.   King Edward was either referring more to past months or to the Pan-German League's constant propaganda.

land apparently realized that the favorable change in the German press was not likely to be permanent. In fact *The Times* had greatly antagonized the *Berliner Neueste Nachrichten* by its violent articles against Germany's leadership of the China expedition and the *Nachrichten* in turn warned England that so long as recriminations continued in her press she could expect nothing more than the rebuff of all her offers of friendship.[143] Upon the rumor of a proffered exchange of Cyprus for German East Africa, this journal said bluntly that England must think Germany a fool.[144] So long as no immediate cause for an outbreak existed, it may be that Bülow succeeded in keeping the press in bounds. The *Kölnische Zeitung* seemed to indicate, as in 1900, that every effort was being made to reduce antagonism; but the matter had gone so far that pressure on the semi-official papers did not result in sufficient restraint.[145]

One unpleasant charge appeared early in 1901 and illustrated the increasing recriminatory nature of the press war. The rumor got about, no doubt by way of the opposition journals, that the de Beers Company had bribed the Berlin journals and the *Kölnische Zeitung* to make their columns more favorable to England. On January 5 the *Dresdener Neueste Nachrichten,* the *Kölnische,* and the *Hannoversche Courier* published denials from their London correspondents, who had had interviews in the de Beers offices in London;[146] but some of the papers remained wholly unconvinced that money was not being used in high places in Germany. They alleged that four hundred and ten thousand pounds had been

[143] *B. N. N.*, No. 2, January 2, 1901.

[144] *Ibid.*, January 3, 1901. In fact the *Norddeutsche Allgemeine Zeitung* and *Kölnische* now carried articles on the colonies, manifesting an especially renewed interest in them, possibly due to the depression and the desire for increased markets. The *B. N. N.* wished railroads built by the government in the colonies, thus furnishing a market for iron and steel (No. 5, January 4). The shipbuilding industry also suffered during 1900 to 1901.

[145] See No. 4, January 3, 1901, for an article which tried to show that the Boer cause was not holy and that the Pan-Germans went too far. Also *Nationalzeitung*, No. 6, January 4, which showed the Pan-German reaction to *The Times*. It pointed out the stupidity of the Pan-German premise that " everything the German government does is wrong."

[146] *Volkszeitung*, No. 12, January 8, 1901.

23

spent and, according to *Vorwärts,* Beit and Wernher of the Company had given art treasures to the Berlin museums for similar
reasons. Hasse even carried the charge into the Reichstag that
the columns of the *Kölnische Zeitung* were opened to the influence
of the Company and of other English groups. After a thorough
investigation the *Kölnische* denied all these charges.[147] The story
is very improbable, first, because there is so little evidence in
support of it and, secondly, because the papers accused had from
the beginning of the war been reasonable and greatly opposed to
the exaggerated nationalism of the Pan-Germans and the Agrarians.
At the time of the rumor the *Kölnische* commented unfavorably
on a new Pan-German publication, *" Deutschland bei Beginn des
20. Jahrhunderts,"* which advocated attaching Austria and Switzerland to the Reich and asked if the independence of Switzerland were
worth less than that of the Boers.[148] It is likely that the Pan-
Germans either invented or used the rumor for their own purposes.
Class's own words show what the Pan-Germans were attempting:

> The experience during the Boer War, especially the fact
> that the official policy under Bülow had changed from that
> earlier proposed, the refusal to receive Krüger and the Boer
> generals, the conciliatory attitude toward England—*all these
> things had lightened for us younger men the work of a stronger
> emphasis on a national opposition,* although these years also
> brought about the withdrawal of von Arnim and Count Stol-
> berg and the death of Dr. Lehr, so that I won more and more
> ground with my proposal [that is, for a " stronger emphasis
> on nationalism "].[149]

Shortly after the bribery rumor the Pan-Germans accused the
German consuls of being pro-English and of failing to protect
sufficiently German interests.[150] They also carried this attack to
the Reichstag as a move against governmental laxity and indifference to German interests abroad.

In late January and early February, 1901, the Emperor was in
England for the Queen's funeral and Edward's accession. During

---

[147] No. 26, January 10, 1901.
[148] *Kölnische Ztg.,* No. 23, January 9, 1901.
[149] Class, *op. cit.,* p. 91.
[150] *Kölnische Ztg.,* No. 137, February 19, 1901.

his stay the press of both countries softened its tone even further.[151] It seems, however, to have acted out of politeness and not from conviction. The *Volkszeitung* wrote of Edward VII:

> Even if he intended a change of political direction he would postpone it until after the mourning. Moreover, the fact that Chamberlain enjoys the special favor of the new King is generally admitted and, accordingly, we expect that the true inspirer of imperialistic policy will now formally come to the head of affairs. The effect on South Africa can only be that the irreconcilable opposition between the demands of the Boers for freedom and the speculatory interests of the mine owners will be resolved by a fight to the death.[152]

The same paper accused Edward of being financially interested in the Transvaal, whereas his mother had been a friend of the Boers. The *Berliner Neueste Nachrichten* wrote that the relations between England and Germany would not be affected by the relationships between the courts but " exclusively by interests and needs; but of course royal families will be in a position to moderate differences which come up and to influence decisively differences between the one or the other Power and a third Power." [153] To the warning of the Hamburg papers that England was wooing Germany with no intention of marriage, the *Nachrichten* rejected the fear of betrayal, because, it said, England had begun no such courtship. But if the German papers did not definitely know of negotiations for an alliance, they watched closely Anglo-Russian relations. The *Nachrichten* saw a change in Russian opinion of England, especially in the papers interested in Asiatic policy,[154] and discussed the nature of Anglo-German and Anglo-Russian relations. When the Agrarian League opposed Edward's return visit to Germany, the *Norddeutsche Allgemeine* hastened to announce that the visit had no political implications. Unpleasant rumors of discourtesy toward the Emperor in England also circulated, evidence of more press activity for the sake of keeping alive bad feeling.[155]

Much of the stored up antagonism came out in the Reichstag

---

[151] *Ibid.*, No. 88, February 1.　　[153] *B. N. N.*, No. 55, February 2.
[152] *Volksztg.*, No. 38, January 23, 1901.　[154] *Ibid.*, No. 60, February 5.
[155] *Kölnische Ztg.*, No. 162, February 28; *Norddeutsche Allgemeine Ztg.*, No. 63, March 15.

during a long discussion on March 5 of Anglo-German relations. Oertel summed up the general fear in a way worth reproducing. German opinion felt, he said, that German neutrality had not been very well preserved. Krüger had been refused a reception in Berlin, apparently only out of good feeling toward England in governmental circles. The delivery of munitions also appeared very unfair. The Foreign Office and the departmental offices connected with it were not protecting the interests of Germans abroad. The Transvaal refugees (some of whom had spoken in Germany) were evidence of this neglect. The German government was too intimate with the British Empire. Germany would be only too glad of the intimacy if she did not fear that what she could gain on the one hand would be lost on the other. England had given proof of her unfriendliness in the seizures of the mail steamers, treatment of consuls, and so forth. Oertel concluded his speech of warning by remarking that intimacy with England would harm relations with Russia.[156] The Emperor's visit had given rise to many rumors of mediation and of a formal alliance, and the Reichstag, one member said, had determined to find out what Bülow had to say of them and why the Emperor had dared to confer the Order of the Black Eagle on Lord Roberts " of all people." [157] During the debate the National Liberals as usual spoke mildly. They regretted the popular ill-feeling against England and pointed out that the government could not share it in cases where the political situation demanded otherwise. Bassermann said that he believed the foundation of the fear of England lay in the feeling that in any argument with England Germany usually came out second.[158] He also suggested that the National Liberals would support no agreement which might antagonize Russia. Hasse sounded other notes. What does the average man, he asked, think of the German Crown Prince's receiving the Order of the Garter kneeling before the Prince of Wales? What does he think of the Emperor's being made a Field Marshall in the British army at a time when this army is at war? The bestowal of the Order on Lord Roberts had been very unfavorably received, he went on. Why was

[156] *Sten. Ber. d. Reich.*, March 5, 1901, pp. 1714-5.
[157] Schaedler: *Ibid.*, March 5, pp. 1693-5.
[158] *Ibid.*, pp. 1704 f.

the Pan-German League accused of *Gefühlspolitik* and *Bierbank-politik* for something which five years ago was the official policy of the Empire? Hasse accused Bülow of equivocal language and said that there seemed a kind of " alliance " with England. He declared that public opinion was much more embittered than the newspapers showed, especially in South Germany, where devotion to the Reich and the Emperor was formerly so great. " This has crumbled through the events of the last ten years, and, indeed, in such a way that there is now not much more to destroy. Now is the time to turn about; it is the crucial moment." [159] If any alliance were contemplated, Hasse thought that the reasons for it should be made public. Liebermann touched upon the decay of English power, and even the Social Democrats attacked the government for its pro-British " neutrality." Bülow's answer to the interpellation was designed to allay all fears without disclosing what was going on between the two governments. In his memoirs he criticized the Emperor for giving the Order to Lord Roberts and for suddenly turning pro-British, as he put it; [160] but at the time he continued his conversations with England, undeterred by public opinion.[161]

In July the negotiations were dropped. On August 5 the Empress Frederick died at Cronberg and King Edward came to Germany for his sister's funeral. On the 23rd he visited the Emperor at Wilhelmshöhe. Although the visit was carefully prepared, the Emperor received a bad impression from it. All possibility of the alliance ceased on the part of William II. The final rupture of negotiations diminished the incentive for quieting the German press.[162] English methods of warfare in the Transvaal had already rearoused the press. Letters from concentration camps and occasional refugees made their way into Germany, and during the autumn of 1901 almost all papers condemned the English use of

[159] *Ibid.*, pp. 1711 f.

[160] *Denkwürdigkeiten*, I, 509.

[161] That this public opinion was known and understood was further evidenced by Holstein's despatches (*G. P.*, XVII, No. 4989, February 11, 1901, p. 33).

[162] In February the Emperor had broken up a mass movement initiated by Pastor Bodelschwingh against England and had helped to keep the official papers in line (*G. P.*, XVII, No. 5067, note).

these camps.[163]   On October 22 the Boers appealed to the Hague
Tribunal, which, however, could not act without a request from
both parties.   Hoping for some aid in a joint *démarche* on London,
Russia had tentatively advanced the view in Berlin that the
British methods violated the Hague Convention of 1899.[164]   But
Holstein was wary.   No step had been agreed upon when on October
25 Chamberlain in a speech in Edinburgh turned sharply on the
nations which denounced the war as barbarous and recalled to them
similar action in Poland, the Caucasus, Bosnia, and during the
war of 1870-1.   The nationalistic press in Germany leapt upon
the speech as an affront to German honor and led an attack which
the moderate press was powerless to restrain.   The British public
reacted in the same way to outside criticism of its war methods,
and again great tension developed between the two countries.   Even
the government tended to share the feeling.   From the point of view
of Anglo-German relations it was especially unfortunate that
Chamberlain should have been the one to make this speech, since
in the German press from 1895 to the present the greatest animus
had been directed toward him.   The denial of his connection with
Rhodes and Jameson had never been convincing to the German
press and the fact that he had wished an alliance had always tainted
the proposal in the minds of German nationalists.   Now he seemed
proven guilty.   One pamphlet of the time wrote:

> If isolated German newspapers have sought to place the
> Edinburgh speech in a harmless light, they have only placed
> themsleves in opposition to the public opinion of Germany.
> Public opinion protests against the attack on our national
> honor in a public speech and by a minister.   For once Germans
> are completely united in this.   England has made us more

---

[163] On May 7 there had been an interpellation to find out from the Chancellor what had been done to free German prisoners in English hands and
with what success.   The fact that missionaries had been taken, their goods
plundered, was greatly resented by public opinion, it was said, just as the
concentration camps were.   Hohenberg, the interpellator, said that the
prestige of the German government at home was being harmed by continuing to treat England in so friendly a way.   Hasse came forth also to say
that all the British conduct in the Transvaal was " barbaric " (*Sten. Ber.
d. Reich.*, May 7, 1901, pp. 2603 ff.).

[164] *G. P.*, XVII, Nos. 5069, 5070.

hostile than ever and at a time when she must find her isolated position already very difficult. If Germany were silent, England would only think she acquiesced; it is well that people answered her.[165]

Protest assemblies of soldiers and patriotic organizations were held everywhere. Typical of the general feeling was the remark made in a Christian Socialist meeting, that after the Krüger Telegram it was not logical to have turned a deaf ear to the Boers during five years. The Pan-Germans collected over six hundred thousand marks for those in the concentration camps.[166] In short, not merely anti-English feeling but a storm of outraged nationalism arose all over Germany.

In January, 1902, Bülow poured oil on the fire by a speech which he thought it his duty to give. Metternich, German Ambassador in London after the death of Hatzfeldt, warned Bülow not to do so and the speech was most unfortunate, not so much for what the Chancellor said as because of the violence it evoked in men like Liebermann. The latter declared that Germany had only suffered shame at Britain's hands and that Germany would no longer bear this mistreatment. As for Chamberlain:

> The Colonial Minister Chamberlain as owner of many stocks in dynamite and armaments, as owner of stocks in the gold and diamond mines of the Transvaal, as a friend of Cecil Rhodes and Jameson, can rightly be regarded as the embodiment of the evil instinct which conceived the robber war and

---

[165] Eugen von Enzberg, *Protest gegen Chamberlain* (Berlin, 1901), pp. 12 f. *Cf.* Professor Wagner: " It must be allowed that we express ourselves nationally when we as a nation are hurt." Hatred of Chamberlain was always great. During 1900 rumors were current in the German papers, which copied from the *Independence Belge*, that a brother of Chamberlain was president of a munitions company, that Joseph Chamberlain owned over three thousand shares of the company and members of his family still more, that other relatives owned shares in a company manufacturing small calibre weapons of which another Chamberlain was president, that he also had shares in the Central Bank for South Africa, etc. No doubt some of these charges were true; but the alleged interests did more to arouse anti-Chamberlain feeling in Germany than they did to determine the South African war, in which the shares of many others were equally at stake (*cf. Deutsche Tagesztg.*, January, 1900).

[166] Class, *op. cit.*, p. 65.

gave it the barbarous character which it displays. If I were to express the judgment of the German people on Chamberlain and on the insult to our army, I must do so in these words: Chamberlain is the craziest clown who shames the earth's surface.[167]

The speech by Liebermann indicated the irrational element with which Bülow had to deal and which made his rôle doubly hard. He had to rebuke Liebermann for such violence and by doing so, as Hasse pointed out, weakened the effect of his reprimand to Chamberlain on January 8 and augmented his own reputation for timidity. The debate went far to prove the charge of inconsistency which the Social Democrats made against the German government. In a long attack on the government on January 8 Südekum (Social Democrat) said that the divergency of views of the people and the government in the British question was causing the latter to feel unsure of itself. It was afraid, he said, to maintain strict neutrality by preventing England from buying remounts in Prussia; it also feared to declare what it did want from England. He bitterly denounced the conduct of government by chance.[168] For several days the debate dragged on. The Agrarians used the occasion to stress the importance of Germany remaining strong by preserving its peasantry and army. The Pan-Germans tried to prove that they were at last justified: it was clear, Hasse said, that all Germany felt about England as they did and not as the official press did. The Chancellor had also given a hint of which much was made when in his speech of January 8 he spoke of the value of the Triple Alliance but conceded that it was no longer an " absolute necessity " for Germany.[169] Speakers eagerly asserted that Germany could, indeed, walk alone: " Our position today is so strong," Oertel declared, " that we do not need to run after anyone, so strong that we do not need to fear anyone." [170] Was this not a dangerous sentiment for the future of the Triple Alliance and for any subsequent renewal of Anglo-German negotiations? Yet it logically accompanied Bülow's effort to arouse national feeling in Germany and to acquire equality. Its implications are perhaps more im-

---

[167] *Sten. Ber. d. Reich.*, January 10, 1902, IV, 3278.
[168] *Ibid.*, January 8, p. 3221.
[169] *Ibid.*, p. 3210.   [170] *Ibid.*, January 10, p. 3287.

portant than the whole Chamberlain-Bülow episode. Liebermann expressed these implications in words from Goethe:

> *Doch erquickend sind zu Zeiten*
> *Goldene Rücksichtslosigkeiten.*[171]

Needless to say the British press reached an almost unprecedented degree of fury over Bülow's and Liebermann's speeches. Metternich wrote that the only hopeful aspect of the situation lay in the fact that feeling could hardly be worse.[172] In Germany it also reached a climax; but Bülow persisted in saying to Metternich in March that German opinion was improving and that at least it wished no weakening of England. The Emperor tried to smooth matters over by a cordial invitation to the Prince of Wales to visit Germany, and this visit (January 25-27) did help to restore quiet. Bülow said in his memoirs that he made every effort in Germany to calm the nationalistic organizations;[173] but Lichnowsky, a German diplomat at the time in England, had in February the impression that irreparable damage had been done in London: Lord Rosebery had told him that England must in the future count on the hostility of the German people; Chamberlain's position was stronger than before; pro-Russian feeling in England had increased, he said.[174]

The reaction of the propaganda papers to Rhodes' death illustrated the persistence in Germany of bad feeling. Angry articles appeared against Rhodes' influence and against his legacy of scholarships for Germans to study in England. According to the *Münchener Allgemeine Zeitung,* one of the large South German democratic papers which had maintained a moderate tone throughout the war, these anti-Rhodes articles teemed with untruths and false impressions of England and Oxford.[175] The *Münchener Allgemeine* itself clearly realized Rhodes' deficiencies and knew

---

[171] *Ibid.,* pp. 3278-9. *Vide infra,* Appendix II, p. 368 for Liebermann's answers to the questionnaire of the *German Times* in London. Bülow's statement satisfied the Agrarians and the nationalists and saved his prestige with them.

[172] *G. P.,* XVII, 198 f., note. [173] *Denkwürdigkeiten,* I, 555.

[174] *G. P.,* XVII, February 17, 1902, p. 204.

[175] *Münchener Allgemeine Zeitung,* No. 105, May 7, 1902, Supplement, pp. 249 f.

that the scholarships would help to teach imperialism; but it protested against their being refused by Germany out of false pride and suggested that Germany had relationships worth cultivating other than those with the Boers. It urged the country to let the government set the tone toward the gift, since everyone knew that William II had thought well of Rhodes.[176]

Moderate papers had cause to seize upon any indication of English friendship for Germany, since news began to arrive from Germans in the Transvaal protesting against the anti-British attacks of the German journals. The correspondent in Pretoria of the *Münchener Allgemeine* wrote that these outbursts against British methods in South Africa endangered German residents there. In view of the fact that many overseas Germans depended on England and did not wish to suffer and, secondly, because England was making every effort to use anti-English propaganda to bring about a boycott of German trade in South Africa, meetings were held by Germans in South Africa to devise ways of protecting themselves from this propaganda in Germany.[177] Moderate journals at home, impressed by these points, pleaded the inadequacy of knowledge about British activity in South Africa and appealed to common sense. The attempted boycott of German trade largely failed, proving that common sense did function at times in economic relations if not in the sphere of political relations. On the other hand, after the adoption of an International Sugar Convention in Brussels, the British papers attacked the German delegates to the conference as well as Bülow for not conforming to England's wishes, while the Reichstag attacked the delegates for not sufficiently upholding German interests and honor. The *Münchener Allgemeine* wrote in despair:

> The other side of the Channel seems to think that a German policy which guards German interests, although in all friendliness to England, is nothing but the capitulation of German statesmen before anti-English public opinion.[178]

In the face of English antagonism, if not in a boycott, in *The Times,* the *National Review* and elsewhere, attempts to improve German opinion seemed useless.

[176] *Ibid.,* and articles from No. 90, April 2, 1902, to No. 105, *op. cit.*
[177] *Ibid.,* No. 90, *op. cit.*   [178] *Ibid.,* No. 138, May 21, 1902.

At the end of May, 1902, the peace treaty with the Boers was signed. Anti-British propaganda in France and Russia almost ceased and semi-official and pro-government journals in Germany hoped this would also be the case here.[179] Both the English and the German governments shared the wish. The Pan-Germans, who had founded societies for aid to the Boers and had collected thousands of marks, now encouraged the settlement of Boer refugees in German South West Africa; they wished to further the settlement there of desirable Boer farmers in order to develop the German colonies. Interest shifted in their annual assemblies to *Kolonialpolitik,* the Poles, and Venezuela.[180] The Venezuelan question excited everyone and the tariff began to loom larger on the political horizon. As the struggle in the German press over the tariff law advanced toward its final stages, the controversy between the Agrarians and the government assumed greater proportions. Business conditions improved slightly and projects for increased activity in South Africa appeared in advertisements. In June Metternich told King Edward that in Germany feeling had grown quieter and that he must protest against the virulence of *The Times.*[181] The *Berliner Neueste Nachrichten,* now more anti-English than in 1900, wrote against England, however, and when *The Times* looked about for ammunition, it could not fail to find it in Agrarian and Krupp journals.[182] In August at the King's coronation, Waldersee, under orders from the Emperor, paid a tribute to the English army and even *The Times* calmed down somewhat for a few days. Through the efforts of Fischer of the *Kölnische,* Stein of the *Frankfurter Zeitung,* and Hammann of the governmental Press Bureau the semi-official German press turned more moderate and Bülow endeavoured to maintain it so. Germany realized with concern that England had now assumed a more hostile attitude and found no hope for a fundamental change in Balfour's accession to the Premiership.[183]

---

[179] *Ibid.,* No. 153, June 5, 1902.

[180] *Zwanzig Jahre, op. cit.,* pp. 126-152.

[181] *G. P.,* XVII, No. 5081, p. 208.

[182] It appears from the documents that King Edward tried to influence *The Times* to change its tone, but without success (*G. P.,* XVII, June 3, 209 ff.).

[183] *G. P.,* XVII, *Metternich to Bülow,* July 17, 1902, No. 5089, p. 214. The attitude of the House of Commons was thought unfriendly and Met-

In August the Boer generals, Botha, Dewet, and Delarey, came to Europe on a mission of good will and a search for loans. The German government did not wish to complicate matters by receiving them. Bülow knew from what sources to expect trouble and in a talk with Arnim-Muskau (Member of the Pan-German League and the Colonial Society) tried to make clear his reasons for discouraging the visit of the generals to Berlin. Some papers had already begun to agitate and in case the Boers came to Berlin the government wished to prevent anti-English sentiment from bursting out anew. Arnim told the Chancellor that the government must seek to restrain the Pan-Germans, but added that Stolberg (First Vice-President of the Reichstag and a Pan-German) and Hasse agreed with him about the inadvisibility of the visit.[184] He offered to use his influence in the same direction, especially with the Boer Auxiliary Association (*Burenhilfsbund*), which he thought likely to give even more trouble by demonstrations than the Pan-Germans.[185]

As soon as news of the coming of the generals was confirmed the Pan-Germans invited the Boers to be their guests. Hasse signed the invitations and the committee on preparations had set to work when Class received a telegram from Arnim asking him to prevent the reception. Class immediately surmised that the Chancellor had influenced Arnim and refused to retract the invitation. Following this attempt came further telegrams from Stolberg and from Hasse. To all alike Class refused to give way. At the end of September he called a meeting of the executive committee and by vote won out; the preparations of the Pan-Germans continued, even without Hasse's approval.[186] As was to be expected, the Auxiliary Associa-

ternich felt that Chamberlain would be more important in the new Cabinet. This was likewise the view of the *Münchener Allgemeine*: "If Chamberlain had become the follower of the Cecils, perhaps one could have looked for political surprises; from Balfour they are not to be expected" (No. 191, July 14). Also the following: "One would suppose that after a three-year war of aggressive imperialism, England would have had enough. But the dangers which threatened the Empire are already almost forgotten, the pride of triumph, unjustified as it is, and the feeling of superiority, are all powerful, and the hunger for territorial possessions, for new markets, and for sole control of the world, is as great as before" (No. 194, July 17).

[184] *Ibid.*, September 12, 1902, No. 5090.

[185] *Ibid.*, No. 5091, p. 217.   [186] Class, *op. cit.*, pp. 66-8.

tion participated in the arrangements for the reception. A great assembly was planned for the evening of October 17, when the generals were expected to arrive in Berlin, and the Pan-Germans hoped on the 18th to join in the general festivities.

The British press grew greatly excited at the rumor that the German Emperor would receive the Boer representatives. But the Emperor determined not to give them personal audience. "Under the circumstances," he said, "the audience will not take place since I am the only one through whom our English relations are still maintained and my navy is not ready if these should be prematurely broken. It is much better that the British government denounce it [the reception] and that we adjust ourselves accordingly." [187] William II was apparently allowing himself to be influenced by British public opinion, and, except for the journals close to the government, the German press sharply reproved the Emperor and his Secretaries. To the delight of the triumphant Pan-Germans the public received the Boer generals with unusual cordiality.[188] A moderate journal like the *Münchener Allgemeine Zeitung* resented the violence of the English comments, which made it doubly difficult to maintain an objective attitude in Germany, and praised the relative calm with which the German press met the British attacks.[189] A part of the feeling in Germany was manifestly directed against the Foreign Office for considering Britain's wishes in the matter. The opposition especially raged when news came out that the Emperor would not give audience to the generals. It did not believe the official explanation of October 8 in the *Norddeutsche Allgemeine Zeitung* and thought that Bülow had changed his own and the Emperor's minds on a hint from London. The *Rheinisch-Westfälische Zeitung* attacked the Press Bureau of the

---

[187] *G. P.*, XVII, No. 5101, p. 231, note.

[188] Class, *op. cit.*, p. 71. The question of why the Boers were not received was not a simple one for the press to solve. In the Reichstag as well it was debated as to why the Boers "changed their minds" (the reason given out by the official press as the excuse for their not being received by the Emperor) about the Imperial interview.

[189] *M. A. Z.*, No. 271, October 2, 1902. It is quite probable that Brentano and other university professors, who were Anglophil, influenced this journal.

Foreign Office for its handling of the matter and most of the German press inclined to see some outside influence, probably that of Leyds, at work on the Boers themselves for their quiet acquiescence in the Emperor's decision. The rabid nationalists condemned the stand as unworthy of a strong government. The unpopularity of the Chancellor increased among the extreme Right and extreme Left, who for a variety of domestic reasons already hated or mistrusted him.

In short, the visit of the generals, while passing off well enough and without any unduly anti-English demonstration, re-opened the old wound. In November almost every issue of the *Münchener Allgemeine* carried an article on Anglo-German relations in an effort to promote better feeling between the two countries. It urged that England judge the anti-English papers in Germany for what they were worth, that periodicals such as the *National Review* be more circumspect in the nature of their anti-Germanism.[190] It pleaded for objectivity on the part of both countries, criticized the Pan-Germans and the *Rheinisch-Westfälische*, and emphasized moderation. The journal even feared that unless some change in tone could be effected Britain might be driven into the Franco-Russian alliance. On November 7 the Emperor, who had momentarily revived his pro-English enthusiasm, went to England. But the attitude of the British press did not appreciably improve during his stay.[191] The cause of better relations seemed lost.

Although at the end of November the tone of the two presses grew quieter, the lull preceded a storm over the Venezuelan venture more merciless than ever before. A brief consideration of the reaction of public opinion to the joint undertaking by England and Germany in Venezuela will show in conclusion the impasse which Anglo-German relations had reached. The entire period of coöperation lasted only a few weeks. On December 8, 1902, the British and German representatives left Caracas; on February 14, 1903, the affair came to its end. At first the British press seems to have been the worse offender; Unionists and Liberals unitedly condemned the coöperation with Germany. The German press thought this

<hr>

[190] *Ibid.*, No. 301, November 1, 1902.
[191] *Ibid.*, No. 310, November 10, 1902. November 11.

reaction possibly due to internal difficulties: the unpopular Conservatives might be trying to turn attention from themselves to foreign affairs, while the Liberals might be seizing a good opportunity to attack Lansdowne.[192] Moderates in Germany eagerly sought to keep the nation calm and objective, but they failed. As the British ire mounted and the United States joined with a press attack upon Germany, particularly after the *Panther's* work in the middle of January, 1903, the German press reciprocated in kind.

On January 20 and 22 the German Chancellor faced a double barrage of wrath in the Reichstag from Right and Left. Vollmar, Social Democratic representative, opened on the 20th with an attack on the government's foreign policy, which, he said, completely lacked steady purpose. It had wavered, he continued, during the Boer War and the China Expedition (1900) as it did now in the Venezuelan affair. Germany's present action, he said, only served the interests of the United States at the expense of her own reputation.[193] The speaker and all the Social Democrats, as well as the Agrarian Right thoroughly resented Bülow's opportunism. The Chancellor essayed to appease these feelings by declaring that the two governments had acted in concert and in good faith during the Boer War, as they were now doing. He expressed a hope for the improvement of public opinion in questions like that of Venezuela, where the two countries could act together for the peace of the world.[194] On the following day Liebermann continued the attack. He said that anti-German feeling in England did not date from the South African War, but had appeared at every opportunity since 1870. Bülow, he maintained, continued to pursue a policy contrary to that desired by the German people. His policy passed all understanding; for, if reason was to govern German relations with Britain, some good cause for friendship should be advanced, and, he claimed, none was. England undoubtedly got the better of every

---

[192] *Ibid.*, No. 9, January 9, 1903, Morn. Ed.

[193] *Sten. Ber. d. Reich.*, January 21, 1903, X Leg. Per., II Sess., VIII, 7413 ff. In fact, the Venezuelan expedition, like the treaty of England and Germany over the Portuguese colonies, was in the interests of finance capital, and was, therefore, equally repellent to Left and Right, especially to the Agrarians.

[194] *Ibid.*, pp. 7429 ff.

arrangement with Germany, as the German people knew only too well.[195]   Bebel attacked the Emperor's irresponsibility and added bitter words against the Venezuelan policy of the government.   The expedition, he said, was undertaken at the behest of Krupp and the *Diskontogesellschaft* (which had invested in the guaranteed Venezuela railroad) and was causing bad feeling everywhere against Germany (for example, in the United States).[196]   Hasse, however, who spoke next, did not wish less use of the " mailed fist," as did Bebel, but more of it.

> I should like further to express my regret [he said] over the fact that the time of the South African War was not used by our foreign policy in the interest of our colonial policy.   I ask you in this respect only to compare us with France and Russia. The Russians have used the time well for a mighty advance in Asia and the French no less well for strengthening and improving their already important position on the Mediterranean, in Africa, and in Siam.   Anything comparable it not to be found in our case and I regret that we have only stared across the Channel in these important, decisive years in a kind of stupor similar to the stupor of the French, who have, as we know, stared for decades at the hole in the Vosges to their own disadvantage.[197]

This speech gave the key to the Pan-German opposition to Bülow and to any pro-British policy. Oertel, speaking for the Agrarian League, criticized Bülow, the China Expedition, and the Venezuelan one.   Thus the forces of the opposition all arrayed themselves against the Chancellor.   While undoubtedly the criticism of his policy in the Venezuelan affair grew out of resentment toward and fear of England, it never lacked over-tones of an eager nationalism, an impatience of the slower and more cautious advance of the Foreign Office, and, where the Agrarian League was concerned, self-interest.   Bülow's opponents, in seeking to bring pressure to bear upon him, thrust their frequent attacks into any part of the budget debates, especially those on colonies.   And the pressure was not exerted purely for the sake of being anti-English but in order to force him to be more German and chauvinistic.

[195] *Ibid.*, pp. 7462 f.
[196] *Ibid.*, January 22, 1903, pp. 7467 ff.
[197] *Ibid.*, p. 7494.

The debates of a few days later on the budget for the Chancellery furnished another illustration of the tactics of the opposition. Bülow had just delivered (February 5) a speech before a national meeting of the Agricultural Bureau (*Landwirtschaftsrat*) in which he had gently chastized agriculture for its thankless attitude on the tariff law. On the sixth Roesicke of the League rose in the Reichstag to refute Bülow's charges. He asserted that the Agrarians had faithfully supported all national measures and he implied that in return they were entitled to expect full compensation in the form of legislation ameliorating their situation. In the course of his argument Roesicke said while he was speaking of American grain imports:

> I recognize therein again and again the old weakness, the old conciliatory attitude toward foreign countries. . . . We are friendly and flattering, we give them out of the rich store of our treasure without securing, or, at least, without assuring ourselves of a return. . . . The Americans have every reason to be our friends; we have no occasion to anticipate them. I maintain that in Germany, with the exception of the pure importers and exporters, all classes demand unconditionally that we ask more from the Americans and suffer less from them. The cool restraint of a Bismarck had, according to my notion, better results and brought more respect than the present effervescent activity.[198]

From grain imports the League went on to attack with its usual violence the recent Sugar Convention, whence it was only a step to Anglo-German relations, the Boer generals, and Venezuela.

After the conclusion of the Venezuela affair Hertling and the Center on March 19 brought an interpellation on it into the Reichstag. When Bülow had answered this by giving the facts of the settlement of the Venezuelan matter, Hasse took the floor. He said that he heard with pleasure that England had not left Germany in the lurch, but expressed surprise at the virulence of the press war in England against Germany. He protested against what he called the effort of the Foreign Office and the official press to say that this attitude in England resulted from the German attitude during the Boer War, especially that of the Pan-Germans.

[198] *Ibid.*, February 6, 1903, X Leg. Per., II Sess., IX, 7722.

24

On the contrary, he said, the English hatred went back to 1870, as the British well understood. Jealously of German industry furnished another ground for it. Unable as he was to cry "wolf" now that the Venezuelan episode was successfully past, Hasse regretted the action, because by coöperating with England and Italy without the United States Germany had lost, so he supposed, her influence in South America in favor of the United States.[199] German business might suffer severely from this loss. Oertel on the other hand conceded that the Agrarian League could not regret Germany's coöperation with England because this coöperation made the venture successful and because, after all, Germany had much to learn from her cousin as to how to do these things.

> Only we must draw the conclusion [he added] that others will seek us out if we do not run after them, if we let them come to us, if we wait, if we accustom ourselves to be somewhat more restrained in our search for friends.[200]

Four years had now passed since the Boer War had become a certainty; almost eight since the scare of 1895-6. After having run the gamut of feeling more than once during that time, German public opinion in both press and parliament became quieter than it would have thought honorable in 1896 or in 1900. The change was due in part to the increased and continued press animosity of the English which led Hasse, no less that a liberal and moderate paper like the *Münchener Allgemeine Zeitung,* to plead for a calmer tone in Germany.[201] In fact, the majority of the German press remained noticeably unperturbed by the Venezuelan expedition in coöperation with Britain.[202]

[199] *Ibid.,* March 19, 1903, X Leg. Per., II Sess., X, 8722-4.

[200] *Ibid.*

[201] The writer has not studied English public opinion; but the increase is often referred to and much cited by the London correspondents of the large German papers. In the matter of trade rivalry, Hoffmann, *op. cit.,* may be referred to. He indicates that the war was largely one of the press by pointing out that the trade journals were less anti-German than were the newspapers. The German chambers of commerce, too, did not often indulge in anti-English propaganda.

[202] This view appears in the *M. A. Z.* in an article entitled, "Eine Pflicht gegen uns selbst": "But the inimical voices which were everywhere loud, the complaints, accusations, and threats which were raised against us

Why had German opinion quieted down? That Germany was surprised and disturbed over the hatred of her in England during the coöperative venture in Venezuela offers a partial explanation. So does Bassermann's remark—one which the Emperor and Tirpitz were making behind the scenes—in his speech at the National Liberal party convention in Eisenach in which he said, " We must speak softly to England before we have a navy." The external improvement in attitude toward England represented no fundamental change in the German determination to pursue imperialism. The outlook may have approximated more that sense of " form," the lack of which in the Germans Bülow deprecated and which he may have helped to inculcate through the press loyal to his policy; but even this is doubtful. There existed other reasons.

During the years between 1896 and 1903 Germany had accomplished the most important initial steps in her new world policy. Aroused by the spectacle of English imperialism at work in South Africa, she had passed two naval laws, increased her colonies and naval and coaling stations, passed a new high tariff, and won approval for all these measures from groups previously opposed to them. Since the war was over and its lessons learned and used, the time had come for more calmness, for good relations with all nations and the development and employment of the instruments lately forged. None but a few hot-heads had ever suggested a break with England. The Germans wanted to be equals and they were now on the road to becoming so. The Pan-Germans, colonialists, and the protagonists of the navy had made use of England to begin successfully the work they had in hand; but they could not afford to see Germany pushed to extremities by anti-German feeling in England. So far as English relations were concerned, Hasse's last Venezuela speech in the Reichstag was a rational one, even though it gave no indication of a change of general policy on the part of the Pan-Germans.

should at least caution us; they should give us the comfort that it is hardly so difficult for any other government as for our own to keep to the peaceful road and to further the cause of peace without harming our national honor and national interests. Under such circumstances the representatives of the press should, first of all, avoid that which will raise abroad pointless anger and which can make more difficult the government's own political duties " (No. 211, August 3, 1902).

A large part of the German press had been sentimental about the Boers. With the Boer cause definitely lost, this element grew quiet by force of circumstances. It continued to be interested in the multitude of problems arising out of the reorganization of South Africa and still thought of Chamberlain and his friends as enemies to mankind. Admittedly this group exerted no real influence on the government, but it comprised many who never again felt friendly toward England. It believed with Mommsen and Treitschke that fate had permanently estranged the two nations.[203] To many of these people anti-English feeling meant German patriotism. This represented the extent of their thinking of the subject.[204] The groups which had attacked the German government by waging war against the English policy of 1899 to 1902 did not cease to attack because the war had ended. Their attitude in the case of Venezuela, as well as their position touching the new Tariff Treaties of 1903, showed this to be the case. They used any subject as an occasion for an onslaught on the government. The Agrarians especially made use of these tactics. Violently as they hated England and her industrialized, *laissez-faire*, imperialistic system, they also hated Russian and American competition in grain and meat and were constantly on the alert for opportunities to oppose it and to improve their own precarious existence.[205] The Agrarians would

---

[203] Many historians and other people in conversation today still go back to the Boer War in their remarks about Anglo-German relations.

[204] See *Grenzboten*, No. 7, February 15, 1900, an article by Hans Wagner, "Die deutsche Weltpolitik," or *Deutsche Revue*, XXV (1900), an article by M. von Brandt, "Die deutsche Presse und die auswärtige Politik."

[205] Under the commercial treaty with Russia of 1894 Russia and Austria became competitors in supplying the German market with grain and Russia won out. After 1895 Austria sent almost no wheat to Germany, while in 1898, a year in which even the German harvest was good, Russian exports of wheat to Germany were valued at one hundred and twenty million marks. In all, about forty-five per cent of the entire Russian export or 725 million marks' worth went to Germany by the close of the century, while Russian trade with France and England remained stationary or declined slightly (Francke, *op. cit.*, p. 209). When in 1899 Russian imports declined somewhat, German industry saw this as only temporary (*Die Post*, No. 99, February 28, 1900). The East Prussians felt the competition greatly, because, by a system of railroad tariffs offering cheap through rates to the coast, Russian grain could be shipped to Danzig and Memel and so by sea

have disliked England without any Boer War and the United States without any Spanish-American War; but both wars intensified their fear. Three years more elapsed before Bülow could persuade the Conservatives, with some help from the Agrarian League, to support government policy.

The other great opposition group, the Social Democratic, continued to attack the government after the war. Although the Social Democrats disapproved of the excesses of British imperialism, as they deplored the rise of German *Weltpolitik*, they were anti-Russian rather than anti-English. They did not like the Boer War and many times led the attacks in the Reichstag against the Chancellor almost hand in hand with Hasse and Liebermann;[206] but these were attacks of constitutional principle, emphasizing that the German people and their representatives did not know what was going on, that they were led by an irresponsible government. The Social Democrats had condemned the Krüger Telegram on the same grounds. In fact, their analyses of the situation in Germany, discounting the personal element, did not differ much from the later ones of Bülow.

As for a large block of intelligent opinion, it had ceased since 1900 (after the seizure of the German mail steamers and the passage of the Second Naval Law) to approve an active campaign again England. The National Liberal press, the democratic and

to west Germany more cheaply than Prussian grain could be shipped. When the German government on December 13, 1897, reduced the railroad rates to the coast for Prussian grain, all the grain was drawn toward the coast so that mills in the interior had to shut down. The new Bülow Tariff sought, therefore, to throttle Russian competition as well as American. Russian exports of rye were cut off entirely by the terms of the tariff and after 1905 Russia was forced to export feed rather than breadstuffs (C. Ballod, *Schriften des Vereins für Sozialpolitik*, 90).

[206] For example, Gradnauer made a speech in the Reichstag against the English system of waging war in the Transvaal which led to a general attack on the foreign policy of the government in China and elsewhere (*Sten. Ber. d. Reich.*, March 3, 1902, X Leg. Per., II Sess., V, 4537). As on this occasion, sometimes the attacks of the Social Democrats ultimately led the Right to support the government. Arendt, one of the leaders of the Boer Auxiliary Association, supported Bülow's policy of neutrality, even though the Association had just been refused in England permission to send a sanitary corps to the Transvaal (*ibid.*, March 4, 1902, p. 4562).

financial papers and business journals opposed in varying degrees the violence shown toward England. The *Rheinisch-Westfälische Zeitung* was an exception, but even the Chamber of Commerce of Essen writing to the government at the time put no emphasis on hatred of Britain but pressed for measures to aid industry abroad and at home. The future competition of American iron alarmed it as much as competition with England. *Die Post* and *Berliner Neueste Nachrichten* regarded the enthusiasm for the Boers as a display of sentimentality and preferred to push business by demanding a navy, colonies, and markets under cover of nationalism. Often such efforts were made under cover of anti-English propaganda. Compared with the extreme nationalists the representatives of big business in the Reichstag seemed quiet, although one must not overlook the possibility that the Pan-Germans and colonialists spoke sufficiently for industry. The *Hamburger Nachrichten* was, like the *Rheinisch-Westfälische*, exceptional, but this Bismarckian journal occupied a rather peculiar position in the press world. The *Hamburgischer Correspondent* defended commercial interests more calmly. On the other hand, the moderate papers were all as enthusiastic as the nationalists for colonies and a navy, *Die Post* and the *Nachrichten* dangerously so. Did they ignore the meaning of these demands for the future of Anglo-German relations, or were they temporarily desirous of good relations with England, perhaps only until Germany could force England backward step by step? The two seemingly contradictory attitudes co-existed. The naval question lacked the significance which it later acquired between the two countries and men did not face the ultimate consequences of competing with England in this respect. They had confidence that without a war they could ultimately match England commercially, especially if a German navy stood back of them.

In conclusion one must seek to discover the significance of the Anglo-German disturbance. The period of the Boer War was an extremely emotional, tensely excited one. For an American who has never been bound by a long and close tradition, who has lived in a land of opportunity and quick growth, and to whom practice has been more important than refinement of theory, it ought not to be impossible to comprehend the reckless urge to action and power in the Germany of the eighteen-nineties. " Just at the moment in which we Germans had begun to make history ourselves," wrote the philosopher Windelband, " we wished to ignore history."[207] The psychological background against which anti-English propa- ganda stood forth cannot be too much emphasized. Every sprout of root and stem stirring in Germany since the eighteen-fifties came to flower in the 'nineties, perhaps more vigorously than Bismack had dared hope. The fever of activity created abnormal pressures within the body politic and these had to find outlets; from 1860 to 1870 political longing for national unification had conditioned the nature of these outlets; from 1890 to 1900 national imperialism did so. Added to the emotional state produced under these cir- cumstances was the influence of the press, for which nationalism, imperialism, and righteous indignation always offered fruitful sub- jects for exploitation.[208] Whether or not it was true that Leyds persuaded the German press to favor the Boers, it is easy to see why such an attitude was adopted, just as it is easy to see why the propaganda of the Navy League and the Pan-German League ap- pealed to societies of women and ex-service men. The high ner- vous tension at the turn of the century accounted for much of the pro-Boer, anti-English sentiment. This was not calculating, logi- cal, or often intelligible. Although its ranting might often be a cloak for well-defined interests which feared to come out into the open, it did not rest on any particular interests. What is one to think of a paragraph like the following?

> German world policy must be Protestant; Protestant, that is, freeing and reconciling as corresponds with Christian teaching, not Papist, which means largely enslaving and inciting. And also the external Protestantism of England does not attract the German people, not this pious humanitarianism which seeks to conquer gold and empires; but pure Protestantism. A

---

[207] W. Windelband, *Philosophie im deutschen Geistesleben des XIX Jahrhunderts* (Tübingen, 1909), " Die neuen Wertprobleme und die Rück- kehr zum Idealismus," p. 105.
[208] J. A. Spender, *The Public Life* (New York, 1925), *passim.*

Protestant foundation will protect a justly larger Germany from the hate which is heaped upon pious, self-seeking England.[209]

The thought is so fantastic as to be disregarded until one realizes that journals, sermons, and public speeches abounded in this kind of gibberish, just as they do in present-day Germany. During the Boer War England was the natural enemy of the emotional enthusiast who had no great commercial or political responsibility but felt the urge to make Germany a glorious name in the world. The new navy, the army, the Triple Alliance delighted the enthusiast, while the fact that a Spanish-American and a Boer War brought gains to others as his country stood passively by irritated him. If Germany could have obtained tangible benefits thereby, many of these men and women would have gone with England; many others would have gladly succored the Boers, the consequences notwithstanding. The German government, which had to execute *Weltpolitik*, could not well antagonize England by direct support of the Boers nor could it proceed against the Boers. Hence the pent-up feeling of the nationalists expressed itself in feeling against England: to some she was too great, to others decadent; to all she was treacherous, grasping and not to be outwitted in a bargain; her money market ruled everything in the island and the Empire; her trade methods were unfair; she had no respect for the weak. An endless list of charges against her can be culled from many sources. Why England was a " natural enemy " to these nationalists is fairly clear; she constituted the greatest world Power and already possessed all that Germany wanted to attain; she stood in the way of German advance; she was superior to alliance with a continental Power. The feeling may be summed up in a citation from Friedrich Naumann in his National Socialist journal, *Die Hilfe*:

The Boers defend indeed a piece of Germany's future since they are a thorn in England's flesh. They shoot for us, bleed

---

[209] *Grenzboten*, LIX, No. 7, February 15, 1900, an article entitled, " Die deutsche Weltpolitik," by Hans Wagner. Another article by the same author wrote of the need for furthering *German* education, which, he said, was needed in contrast to the objectionable culture which England had produced under her egoistic system (*ibid.*, No. 3, pp. 429 f.).

for us, for everyone shoots and bleeds for us who fights England. . . . England is the international world Power which threatens all independence, all nationality, a new Rome, who destroys, crushes, strangles national individuality. He who is international may think English; but he who is a nationalist must be anti-English.[210]

Who were the people to whom such propaganda appealed? They seem to have been almost everyone at one time or another and no one constantly. Even the Emperor was now ready to teach England a lesson, now to learn from her. Most consistently they were the lower middle-class, the anti-Semites, officers and ex-service men,[210a] women and hangers-on of the large propaganda societies, probably some journalists who believed what they wrote and some intellectuals who idealized Germany's destiny and thought of England as an obstacle. All parties and economic groups contained many fanatics, who either in accord with their own interests or in opposition to them decried England and loved the Boers. One can have no idea of their real number. The Pan-Germans always said that the number of those outside the League who supported their ideas was larger than anyone thought. It is certain that no two or three thought alike about the problems involved or had any idea of the consequences into which their muddled thinking might lead their country. They got into an exaggerated emotional state which found peculiarly welcome expression during the Boer War period in anti-English, pro-Boer sentiment.

From a study of the press between 1899 to 1903 it is clear that not all Germany indulged in feeling to the extent often indicated by generalized statements in documents and memoirs. It has been shown above that the press in 1896 differed from that of the Boer War. There were intervals such as that in 1900 from January

[210] *Die Hilfe*, No. 10, March 11, 1900. It may be noted that *Die Hilfe* in 1896 was a modest, religious journal. In 1900 it was full of politics, imperialism, and all else which marked the new age. It was pro-navy: " We need the navy to be protected against the attacks of the most powerful naval opponent. That means England " (*ibid.*, No. 5, February 4, 1900).

[210a] For reference to the number of officers in the Colonial Society and Pan-German League see Vagts, *History of Militarism*, p. 418. These officer members, says Vagts, forced " diplomatic language into a sharper key in colonial conflicts."

to March or April, or at the time of the Krüger visit, when the
spirit of 1896 generally prevailed. Even then it was not so belli-
cose or insistent on interference as in the earlier period. Some reasons for this change have been indicated in an earlier part of the
chapter. It has been shown 1) that large sections of German
opinion did not participate very actively in any of the anti-English
propaganda, 2) that in the case of those groups whose members
were pro-Boer and anti-English it was almost impossible to distinguish whether they acted more from motives of genuine hatred
and fear of England or in the hope of advancing their several
causes, 3) that internal problems and objectives and the national
imperialistic movement were so closely bound up with the thinking
of the period that anti-English feeling meant nothing unless
studied in connection with them.

In regard to the first point, the National Liberal party and its
organs, as well as business in the country, did not lead the anti-
English propaganda. It has always been said that English and
German commercial rivalry lay back of the ill feeling between the
two countries, even though exceptions were made of Georg von
Siemens, Carl Fürstenberg, bankers, and of Albert Ballin.[211] If
true one would expect to see this rivalry manifested at every opportunity; but business emphasized more logically the need for
those things which would be useful to it in meeting competition,
such as reduction of railroad freight rates, acquisition of new
markets, construction of railroads in distant prospective markets,
extension of the consular service. In view of what was being asked
from the government in return it is not surprising to find the
National Liberals and Conservatives (the cleft between the Agrarians and straight-line Conservatives increased as the tariff issue
became more bitter) more favorable to the government's policy in
regard to England than the nationalists. The navy particularly
was a gift from the government and the country to big business,
industrial and commerical, and it has been shown that business,
Stumm, Krupp, and Woermann outstandingly, tried hard to obtain

---

[211] It is the opinion of Dr. Vagts that Ballin was rather anti-English at
first; only later did he become friendly to an understanding with England,
when he saw the value of such an understanding to Far Eastern enterprises
of his.

the navy. More fundamental for understanding the industrial, commercial, and financial opinion is not what it said or did not say about Britain, but what it asked for and received while availing itself of anti-English feeling. The latter would determine the future of Anglo-German relations.

It may be said tentatively that financial interests criticized England least. They regarded English imperial rule and English coöperation as desirable for investment and for commercial security. A long editorial in the *Boersen-Courier* during the war, for example, stated that English rule in Egypt had been of great value and importance to Egypt and world trade and concluded:

> If the English should really be pushed out of Egypt [as a result of their situation on the Cape] either the earlier chaos would return or the narrow-minded colonial policy of the French would be introduced there. One would be as bad as the other, and either a serious retrogression for international trade.[212]

Similar evidence has already been given.

Commercial interests did not attack England much more than the financiers did, although they shifted fundamentally in deciding wholeheartedly for the Second Naval Law. By so doing they cut away from their earlier policy, which had always been, especially in the sea-port towns, liberal and sympathetic to England.[213] The change is not hard to explain. A city like Hamburg still kept close relations with England, closer than with any other European country. Yet during the entire 'nineties Hamburg had been freeing its trade from British control. She shipped more of her goods in German owned boats; international agreements, as in the case of the international grain contract of 1903-4, were slowly taking the place of more local arrangements; and Hamburg established a Metal Exchange of her own. The historian of the Hamburg Chamber of Commerce wrote: " It is of special interest that in the efforts for the international grain contract and for the Hamburg Metal Exchange the thought . . . of freedom from the corresponding London market and custom has played a great rôle." [214] Ballin

---

[212] *Berliner Boersen-Courier*, No. 60, February 6, 1900.
[213] *Geschichte der Handelskammer zu Hamburg*, II, 369 ff.
[214] *Ibid.*, II, Pt. I, pp. 64-5; II, 2, pp. 778-800.

was helping to protect his industry from British competition by joining the organization of the Morgan Trust Atlantic Pool; yet he was not anti-English to the extent of supporting propaganda to antagonize her.[215] Stettin, too, had a double English relationship. She competed in shipbuilding and the " Vulcan " wharves located in Stettin eagerly desired German governmental orders in the hope of booming their industry. But Stettin used British coal. In 1900 at the height of the enthusiasm for the Boers the Stettin Chamber of Commerce stated that the city had to import more coal from England and " this shows that Upper Silesian coal no longer gravitates toward Stettin as would be natural, that Stettin can not do without English coal and that measures which have been taken to close the market to English coal are not justifiable." [216] Stettin would not indulge in violent anti-English propaganda under these circumstances and in fact she complained more of competition in shipping and shipbuilding with Hamburg and Lübeck than with England.[217] Naval expansion interested Stettin most, because it would provide her with governmental shipbuilding orders. She rejoiced in the law of 1900, which made possible the continuation of business during the depression of 1900-1902, and in 1902 " Vulcan " paid a dividend of fourteen percent.[218]

Heavy industry showed itself more anti-English than banking and commercial interests, but, as has been suggested, the question of its attitude is complicated by 1) the difficulty of knowing when industry was using anti-English feeling to further other ends such as the navy in 1900, 2) uncertainty as to whether industrial papers expressed the views of journalists and editors who may have been influenced by the Pan-Germans more than by business itself. Industry had to keep the factories going. Competition with England

---

[215] Bernhard Hüldermann, *Albert Ballin* (Berlin, 1922).

[216] *Bericht der Handelskammer zu Stettin*, 1900, p. 44. These measures were those asked for by Silesian mine owners to increase the domestic sale of their product, which was more expensive under existing railroad tariffs for the sea-ports than English coal coming by water. In 1901 Stettin's import of English coal increased still more, even with the export tax of a shilling laid in April for war purposes on English coal.

[217] *Ibid.*, 1901, p. 85.

[218] Report of the Company, cited by *Bericht der Handelskammer zu Stettin*, 1902, p. 26.

was keen; but the potential power of America and Russia threatened to hinder the industrial progress of Germany. The burden of social legislation, the growth of Social Democracy, the support of German agriculture and the problem of the cost of production especially concerned the representatives of heavy industry. Hence, it seems best to give weight not to the immediate attitude toward England, not violent at most, but to the policy of business, which at the worst would ultimately bring the two countries face to face in the outer world. However friendly a feeling for England business men may have harbored—it is probable that the anti-English feeling of business men flourished in after-business hours, heightening their moral indignation but not surviving the night,—their devotion to *Weltpolitik* would have made an alliance difficult to negotiate and impossible to keep.[219]

Finally, it is necessary to repeat that business had its representatives in the Pan-German League, the Colonial Society, the Navy League, where anti-English propaganda abounded. Possibly these organizations did enough toward arousing nationalism and patriotic endeavour to relieve business of the need for doing that work. Clearly, business used any popular argument for its own measures and, when it saw the advantages of propaganda for the furtherance of imperialism, it probably did not protest so much as it might against the anti-English implications of the movement. The truth is difficult to determine; at times business members of

[219] During the 'nineties Germany had surpassed England in the continental markets and she was making strides abroad. Hoffman concludes, writing from British sources, that trade rivalry was the main cause of bad relations. But he also shows that before 1914 greater specialization in goods was working out a balance which eliminated much of the competition between the two countries in specific items of trade. He shows also that trade was less anti-German than the press and that the two greatest periods of tension were 1884-8 and 1894-8, that is, before Germany's new tariff law or naval law. It would seem, therefore, that the political policy and problems arising out of economic competition, not merely competition with Britain, were important in the final reckoning. Further, did popular opinion know much of economic competition? It is doubtful; and the fact that Tirpitz did not rely on it greatly for naval propaganda seems to indicate that he saw the necessity for more popular material. He stressed it for certain groups, but he had many other arguments of a more appealing nature.

the Pan-German League and the Boer Auxiliary Association aided Bülow in defense of moderation; but the *Rheinisch-Westfälische Zeitung* also continued its Anglophobia.[220]

So much has been written above of the motives of the more violently anti-English groups that it is enough to mention the connection between the Agrarians' sympathy for the Boers, their feeling against England and their own dilemma, their opposition to Bülow and their efforts to force aid from him. The method of the Agrarian League, to use any feasible opportunity for wringing from the government further help for the Agrarians, has been described.[221] The Boer cause was peculiarly adapted to this end. The Boers, a simple peasant folk able to hold out for three years against the power of an Empire—a tribute to the moral and physical forces of the man on the land—were being pushed to the wall by industrialists and money-grabbers. England had become thoroughly industrialized so that she had no adequate army to meet the situation, a despicable state of affairs. Germany must not allow her agriculture to fall prey to industrialization or she would find herself exposed to humiliation. Liebermann, the most ardent anti-Semite, put the blame for the entire war on the Jewish money-lenders and speculators. The fact that German financial circles leaned toward England and regarded London as the credit center of the world added fuel to his fire. The Agrarians did not like England; but they opposed her in part as a means of opposing the German Chancellor and of drawing attention to their own needs. The Boer War proved opportune to the struggle for a new Agrarian tariff.

[220] The writer does not possess material for discussing the attitude of light industry except in a general way, namely, from the absence of vehemence in the Chambers of Commerce of Berlin, Leipzig, Frankfurt, etc. These industries should have been friendly to England, since they were exporters and since they were against high tariffs. The *M. A. Z.* was fairly inclined toward England and Munich was the center of the beer industry which exported to England and to her colonies. On the other hand, light industry often followed heavy industry and the Central Union, especially in tariff matters, even against its own interests, so that no general statement can be made without reservations.

[221] The *Deutsche Tageszeitung* carried the Conservative-Agrarian feeling particularly. Its position on most questions followed that of the Agrarian League. *Cf.* No. 59, February 5, 1900, for a good summary.

The opposition of the Pan-Germans and the Social Democrats to the British policy of the government has been fully discussed. If Richter's party has not been mentioned again in this chapter, it is only because he, like the Social Democrats, was anti-Bülow, while friendly enough to England and the Boers. The three groups had in common their distaste for the Chancellor and the political situation in Germany, although they differed fundamentally. At their annual congress at Plauen in September, 1903, the Pan-Germans returned to the same point.[222] All three, however, made good use of the occasion offered them by the Boer War to oppose Bülow. It was somewhat inconsistent of the Pan-Germans to despise England when they beheld her doing what they wished Germany had the courage to do and what they urged should be done with the Hungarian opposition in Austria. The Pan-Germans had more in mind than mere championship of the Boers. They had been gaining confidence and power for a decade to use an occasion like this to rally popular feeling against a weak government and in favor of an energetic national programme. In the years 1899-1902 active propaganda for the navy, colonial development, and the German cause in Austria-Hungary paralleled anti-English propaganda.

The anti-English attitude of the Colonial Society differed somewhat from that of the Pan-Germans. The war created a panic in the *Kolonialzeitung* about the future of the German colonies and German influence in Africa. The colonialists constantly drew up petitions to Bülow and memoranda on the German position. They wrote articles indicating English competition in all parts of Africa and containing pleas for railroads and settlements. They started an editorial campaign for Germans to go to South West Africa in order to forestall a Boer-English majority there. The *Kolonialzeitung* published statistics about railroads and investments and articles on Rhodes and the de Beers Company, the latter often written by highly informed men like Alfred Zimmermann. The material was reproduced in provincial newspapers and many debates on the colonial budgets also used it. In these ways the Colonial Society had as important an influence as did the Pan-German League with its more violent pro-Boer enthusiasm.

[222] *Zwanzig Jahre*, p. 158.

Finally, the experience of the Boer War period greatly increased the nervous tension and the eager nationalism out of which violence grows. Moderate opinion sought to act against powerful forces which at the same time it highly approved. But the War really inaugurated no new policy. It merely sharpened the outlines of some measures and speeded up action on others. It also reduced to rather fixed form the Portrait of an Enemy and this portrait received the name of Englishman, not because all Germans hated Englishmen—an actual majority probably did not—but, on the one hand, because the portrait represented to some Germans what Germany still had to do under her programme of world policy to achieve equality among the nations, on the other, because it represented what others hoped she might avoid. The portrait did not necessarily suggest war with England. Germany knew that she confronted other world empires and industrial organizations as well as those of England. As the *Preussische Jahrbücher* said:

> We wish to become a world Power and pursue colonial policy in grand style. That is certain. There can be no step backward. The whole future of our people among the great Powers depends on it. We can do this with England or against her. With England means peace; against England means war.[223]

The question of whether or not the propaganda campaigns of the Boer War helped to determine the decision in the alliance negotiations of 1901 will be discussed below. It cannot be overlooked that Bülow and the Emperor, although they adhered to a policy of neutrality, gave public opinion cause for unrest and uncertainty. They made visits to England whose purpose was suspect and, in spite of the Krüger Telegram, they introduced a noticeable change in governmental policy toward the Boers. These things forced the Reichstag to interpellate, to discuss foreign policy, and the press to do the same. Along with the frequent attacks on the government came increased criticism, especially of Anglo-German relations, which seemed more disturbed than did those with other countries. Thus Bülow's unsteady policy, not so neutral as he has pictured it, in large degree came to bear responsibility for sharpening the Anglo-German issue.

[223] *P. J.*, XCVIII, November 26, 1899, pp. 588-9. Also Kehr, p. 384, note.

CONCLUSION

It remains to inquire whether or not the anti-English opinion of public and press during the Boer War helped to determine the outcome of negotiations in 1901 for an Anglo-German alliance. Recent research as to the failure of this proposed alliance indicates conclusively, it would seem, that there could have been no alliance for the reason that England made no definite offer of one. The present investigation, devoted to the history of German internal affairs rather than to diplomatic negotiations, shows equally conclusively that the internal German situation rendered a permanent alliance with England improbable. The virulence of anti-English feeling during the Boer War period did not create the improbability, but it did serve to lay bare to all the incompatibility of the two peoples. During the many heated discussions of foreign policy arising out of the problems presented by the War, public opinion within and without the Reichstag rejected the idea of an alliance. Although this public opinion had only rumors and speculation upon which to base its discussion of the intergovernmental conversations on the subject, it made clear to the German government that the latter should preserve a free hand as between England and Russia. Yet Bülow might have disregarded or controlled this attitude had not the fundamental economic and political situation in the country precluded an alliance.

The attitude of the German Agrarians was the greatest obstacle to such a tie. While this group exercised so large a measure of political and social control, a policy so antipathetic to it as alliance with England could not have been undertaken. The Agrarians could not have been reconciled to allying themselves with an industrialized state whose materialistic philosophy they despised. They would not have welcomed closer contact with the liberalism, cosmopolitanism and Trade Unionism characteristic of England. Under an alliance financial relations between the two countries would presumably have become closer. German industry would have expanded, possibly growing impatient of carrying the burden of agricultural relief for the East Provinces. (In these provinces,

25

361

not accidentally, the strongholds of the Agrarians were the regions in which agricultural holdings carried the heaviest mortgages.) Colonial expansion might have been facilitated, thus drawing off capital to other enterprises than the fostering of agriculture at home.[1] Successful development of German colonies might have brought fresh competition with German domestic agriculture. German Agrarians were always careful to legislate that governmentally subsidized ships should not be allowed to carry home food supplies from colonial areas. English capital might even have strengthened Austria-Hungary and have increased agricultural and industrial competition between Germany and her older ally. German labor in all probability would have benefited from and have been encouraged by closer English connections. Such considerations, realized or felt, made the Agrarians and Conservatives oppose England; they suggest strongly that to realize the advantages of an alliance the Foreign Office would have had to choose between England and the Agrarians. In view of the strategic position of the Agrarian-Conservatives no such choice actually lay before it. Public opinion thus coincided with that of a powerful vested interest.

The decadent state of German liberalism and the predominance of the social question in Germany in this period suggest other reasons against a permanent coöperation of England and Germany. The old Liberals to whom English ideals had meant so much now had little influence, while sympathy with and admiration for England on the part of German Social Democracy frightened the ruling classes in Germany away from a democracy in which Trade Unionism was even stronger than at home. The ruling classes in England were thought to have capitulated to bourgeois and proletarian demands in order to reap the benefits of imperialism. Germany was determined not to do this; she did not wish to change the basis of her domestic structure before embarking on imperialism, but rather hoped to preserve it by strengthening the existing state. The condemnation of British imperialism during the Boer War by the old Liberals and Social Democrats did not conceal from the ruling classes the fact that both opposed German imperialism

[1] *Konservatives Handbuch* (Berlin, 1898, 3rd ed.), pp. 84 ff.

even more and sympathized with democracy. A stronger leader than Bülow would have been needed to overcome the fear of democratic infection.

How far economic rivalry operated as an obstacle to the alliance presents a more difficult question. Statements about the anti-English feeling of business men have certainly been exaggerated in the past; it is highly probable that the *fait accompli* of an alliance would have disturbed Krupp, Stumm, Fürstenberg, Rathenau less than historians have imagined. At the same time, the reiteration of the argument " economic competition " by both the English and German press had done much to spread a belief in competition beyond those groups actually suffering from it. Its existence was regarded as axiomatic: Bülow believed in it; historians and economists wrote of it; cautious men founded their support of *Weltpolitik* on the conviction that Germany must expand her markets and hence must come into conflict with England, the greatest possessor of markets. The prevalent fear that something might prevent future economic and commercial development acted as a caveat to any hard and fast contracts. Neither Bülow nor any man in the Empire wished to interrupt the brilliant course which seemed under way for Germany by making an alliance with unpredictable responsibilities implicit in it. In so far as the Foreign Office was sensible of and responsive to such as inhibition, it responded to special interests, but to special interests whose case had been adopted by most of Germany. A similar fear of America obtained wide support among the literate public, and in neither case was there evident so much the working of economic determinism as a mixture of apprehension and exaggerated nationalism. The effect of this latter feeling was, however, much the same as that of economic rivalry. The Foreign Office and press alike avoided forming an attachment for or a contract with the object of national competition and fear.

Important to an understanding of anti-English feeling is the suspicion with which the country regarded William II and his government. The irresponsibility of this ruling group appeared dangerous to an increasing number of Germans genuinely apprehensive of the results of a pro-English policy. They did not trust William II or Bülow to maintain Germany on a par with England;

they feared Germany would easily become a cat's paw and lose the position in Europe which she had achieved. The attacks on the Chancellor during the Boer War showed how little faith existed in his ability to promote unswervingly German development. The new nationalism of the period made public opinion doubly aware of the contrast between Bismarck and his successors and doubly wary of undertaking new responsibilities. Bülow never allayed this fear by a bold stroke; for he could not radically change policy without disturbing entrenched interests. Fearing to do this, his constant compromises only promoted uncertainty about his course.

Finally, the policy of imperialism which crystallized after 1897 nearly if not entirely precluded an alliance. Imperialism brought Germany face to face with all other world empires rather than into close association with one or more of them. Until she had achieved her own "place in the sun" she could not make an alliance which would retard her progress. The growing friction between Germany and the United States over tariff questions provoked public opinion in both countries quite as much as the Boer War provoked that of Germany and England. It is significant also that Germany made no new treaty with Russia, with whom her imperialism brought her into frequent discord, while England in drawing toward the Dual Entente had to settle her outstanding colonial quarrels with France and Russia first. Even then she did so only after achieving a signal victory over France in the Sudan affair and because German imperialism seemed too strong for her to combat alone. That Germany made with England the treaty over the Portuguese colonies, the Yangtze treaty of 1900, and the Bagdad Railway agreement in 1914 does not refute the argument. In each of these cases Germany met a specific situation arising out of her imperialistic policy without any intention or fear or having to assist England in the future. In the case of the first two treaties mentioned, their outcome deepened German distrust of England and hence strengthened German imperialistic endeavor. Moreover, because German imperialism was undertaken in part to escape a thorough-going reform at home, it was in essence and continued to be at variance with British imperialism. The difference between German and British colonial administration and tariff policy illustrates this. Such differences would not have been decisive

however—they were not so in the case of France and England—
if German imperialism had not seemed so determined and formidable, characteristics due to the nature of the interests and forces
behind it.

For these reasons, each arising primarily from internal conditions, Germany could hardly have concluded an Anglo-German
alliance of a permanent nature. The conviction of public opinion
on this point followed national instinct and tradition, although
it cannot be denied that a less chauvinistic and a more realistic
nationalism on the part of the masses might have taken a different
direction and so have determined Britain to make a definite offer
of alliance instead of holding only conversations about one. If this
had been the case, one cannot say what internal changes Bülow
might have been emboldened or forced to make. The innovations
would have had to far-reaching. Thus the formulation of foreign
policy was dependent on domestic conditions.

APPENDICES

I.

The large holdings in the six eastern provinces of Prussia with their owners and the effect upon them of the Bülow tariff of 1902 were as follows:[1]

[1] From Conrad's *Grundriss zum Studium der politischen Oekonomie* (1899), cited by Singer: *Sten. Ber. d. Reich.*, December 11, 1901, X Leg. Per., II Sess., IV, 3127 ff. Conrad undertook the first statistical study of the latifundia. His figures, as indicated above, did not cover the whole of Germany and were not always correct; but some idea may be obtained of the consolidation of holdings and of the probable effect of the new tariff law, at least as estimated by a Social Democrat. *Cf.* the most recent work on the subject, Theodor Häbich, *Deutsche Latefundien* (Königsberg, 1930, 2nd ed.). This study makes no attempt to deal with the effect of the tariff law to the Agrarians.

A. Those who owned 5,000 to 35,000 hectares of land (250 hectares equal 617.5 acres):

> Heinrich IV, Prince of Reuss
> Friedrich Leopold Prince of Prussia
> Ernst Duke of Saxe-Coburg-Gotha
> Ernst Gunther Duke of Schleswig-Holstein
> Wilhelm Duke of Württemberg
> Prince Hohenlohe-Sigmaringen
> Friedrich Leopold Duke of Anhalt-Dessau
> Albrecht King of Saxony
> Sophie Adelheid Henriette Princess of Reuss
> Heinrich XIII, Prince of Reuss
> Ernst Duke of Saxony-Altenburg
> Sophie Grand-Duchess of Saxony-Weimar
> Friedrich Prince of the Netherlands
> Marianne Princess of the Netherlands
> Friedrich III Hohenzollern, now his heirs

The combined extra income of these fifteen persons with two hundred and forty holdings from the three and one-half marks grain tariff was estimated at RM. 2,328,621. It was estimated at RM. 3,492,931 under the higher Bülow tariff "at the cost of the poor."

B. Some of the thirty-eight families who owned rather less than 5,000 hectares.

> Prince Bismarck, now his heirs
> Count Arnim-Boitzenburg

367

Prince Biron of Kurland
Imperial Count Bruel (Brühl?)
Prince Carolath-Beuthen
Prince Hatzfeldt-Trachenburg
Count Henckel-Donnersmarck
Prince Hohenlohe-Ingelfingen
Prince Hohenlohe-Oehringen
Prince Ujest (Silesia)
Prince of Pless
Prince Schönaich-Carolath
Prince Thurn and Taxis
Count Philip of Eulenburg
Von Wladow und Reitzenstein
Herr von Tiele-Winkler
Count Mirbach, etc.

These thirty-eight persons had two hundred and fourteen holdings with 252,153 hectares and an annual income from the tariff of RM. 2,116,888. They would have RM. 3,176,332 under the new law.

C. Ten bourgeois agrarians with seventy-five holdings equalling 82,890 hectares with an income of RM. 695,961. This sum would reach RM. 1,043,441 under the Bülow tariff.

The totals as given by Singer gave 152 owners with 1776 holdings and 1,637,963 hectares. He estimated that they sold their grain under the old tariff at a gain to themselves of 13,754,000 marks; the new tariff would bring them 20,631,150 marks.

II.

At the beginning of 1902 (or the end of 1901) a newspaper was started to assist in reconciling England and Germany. It took the name of *The German Times* and appeared simultaneously in London and Berlin. Bloch, supposedly the editor, sent out a questionnaire to members of the Reichstag (perhaps to others), and this questionnaire was cited by Liebermann von Sonnenberg, Agrarian anti-Semite, in a speech in that body together with the answers which he had made to it. Liebermann did not send in his answers, because he had no sympathy with the enterprise; but they are of considerable interest.[1]

Q. Do you believe that the German Empire would have avoided war with the Boers if it had found itself in the same position as Great Britain?
A. Of course we all believe that. We do not think Germany would ever have committed so shameless a breach of right against a people.

---

[1] *Sten. Ber. d. Reich.*, January 10, 1902, X Leg. Per., I Sess., IV, 3278-9. This represents the opinion of an extreme Anglophob, whose voice was never absent from Reichstag debates on foreign policy.

Q. Do you consider the British nation or individual leaders or the natural development of the history of Great Britain responsible for the war?

A. Both in my opinion: the development of the Empire is responsible, but also the people who are at the present at the head of the nation.

Q. Do you consider a political coöperation of Germany with Great Britain desirable or do you believe or think that the interests of the two countries forbid such a union?

A. As matters now stand, such coöperation (*Zusammengehen*) is no longer possible.

Q. Do you consider a formally agreed upon or silently recognized alliance of the two Empires desirable?

A. I would answer: we would consider this the greatest national misfortune which could happen to us.

Q. Do you think that Germany has only the choice between alliance with Great Britain or Russia?

A. The answer to that was given by the Chancellor on Wednesday. Let Mr. Bloch read it. The German Empire needs alliance neither to the right nor left. It can alone protect its interests against a peaceful world today.

Q. Do you believe that a split between Great Britain and Germany must lead to a weakening of both Powers and as a direct consequence a strengthening of Russia?

A. That is the Jew raging against Russia, which is too anti-Semitic for him.

Q. Do you not believe that a strengthening of Russia would be equal to a strengthening of the absolutistic system in and for itself, that also such a strengthening would be an actual danger for the free institutions of the nations in general?

A. That is a bait at which Mr. Schrader (*Freisinnige*) could perhaps bite.

Q. Do you think that an alliance between Germany and Russia would severely menace the free institutions of Germany, while a union with England would lay the foundation for free development?

A. Nothing is more foolish than this question. One doesn't need to answer it.

Q. How do you explain the widespread outbreak of feeling against England among the German people? Do you consider this feeling artificially aroused and temporary, or in-rooted and lasting?

A. I consider it deep-rooted and lasting because it thoroughly corresponds to historical development.

III.

The following is a letter, published locally at the time of the Boer War but given to the writer by the family of its author, which illustrates well the attitude of the middle-class toward the Boer War and the Bülow government. It speaks for itself.

Berlin (undated)

OFFENER BRIEF AN SEINE EXCELLENZ FREIHERR VON RICHTHOFEN

Herr Staatssekretär:

Die Ausführungen, mit denen Sie die englische Antwort in der Angelegenheit des Burenhülfsbundes begleiten, haben noch keineswegs die Erwiderung gefunden, die ihnen gebührt. Weder im preussischen Landtag noch in der Presse hat man mit genügender Schärfe darauf hingewiesen, dass das Entgegenkommen der Engländer, das Sie mit so heftigen Dankesgefühlen erfüllt, in Wahrheit nichts anderes bildet, als die endliche Erfüllung der dürftigsten Pflichten, die das Völkerrecht einer kriegsführenden Nation vorschreibt.

Es ist schlimm genug und geradezu empörend, dass ganz Europa all den schweren Verletzungen des internationalen Rechts, wie sie von England in diesem traurigen Kriege begangen wurden und wie ich sie als ehemaliger Führer eines Burenkommandos, gleich so vielen andern, mit eigener Kenntnis bezeugen kann, nur mit dem Achselzucken der jämmerlichsten Hülflosigkeit zusieht. Aber noch schlimmer ist es, wenn Sie jetzt, wo die Worte, die vorgestern der Reichskanzler gegen Chamberlain richtete, doch wenigstens den Schimmer einer Hoffnung auf ein besseres Verständnis der leitenden Kreise erstehen liess, dem deutschen Volke, das mit allen seinen Empfindungen auf Seiten der Buren steht, die breite Bettelsuppe der Sentimentalität vorsetzen.

Sie haben in Ihrer Rede die Wendung gebraucht, dass Sie glauben, die Gefühle des deutschen Volkes richtig zu verstehen, wenn Sie annehmen, dass ihm vor allem daran gelegen sei, den Notleidenden in Südafrika nach Kräften zu Hülfe zu kommen, nicht nur den Frauen, Kindern, und Greisen, sondern auch den Verwundeten und Kranken.

Jawohl! aber das Empfinden des deutschen Volkes, Herr Staatssekretär, ist noch ein anderes: Sie scheinen nicht zu verstehen, dass die von Ihnen so oft und pathetisch gepriesene Ehre und Würde der deutschen Nation es in allererster Linie fordern, dass die von uns feierlich mit unserer Unterschrift versehenen Haager Konferenzbeschlüsse voll und ganz befolgt werden, und Sie verstehen es auch nicht, dass die Achtung der Völker vor den Handlungen Ihrer Regierung in jeder Weise herabgemindert wird, wenn man wiederum mit dem Achselzucken der Hülflosigkeit der vollen Missachtung dieser Beschlüsse zusieht. Dankbar zu sein, nur weil England nach langen Jahren wenigstens einem geringfügigen Teil seiner Verpflichtungen nachkommt, das, Herr Staatssekretär, ist nicht deutsche Art.

Sie meinen allerdings, wir sollten in unseren Urteilen und Äusserungen über den Krieg darauf Rücksicht nehmen, dass man sich nicht selbst durch Reizung der englischen Empfindlichkeit Steine in den Weg wirft für die Sicherung der Unterstützung und Hülfe. Nun, es ist weit gekommen, wenn wir das uns aus sittlichen und politischen Gründen verkürzte Recht der Unterstützung und Nächstenliebe durch zaghaftes Verleugen unserer wahren Ansicht erschleichen sollten. Nein, ein anderer und grösserer als Sie hat von dort aus, wo Sie standen, dem deutschen Volke zugerufen, dass ein Appell an die Furcht keinen Raum in deutschen Herzen hat, und wir weigern uns, unser gutes deutsches Wort feige zu verschlucken, um nur ein Recht, das wir fordern können, zu erlangen.

Sie führen den Bericht eines preussischen Generals an, um die, wie Sie behaupten, übertriebenen Auslassungen der Presse über die Gefangennahme zu entkräften. Gestatten Sie mir, hieran zu bemerken, dass das gesamte deutsche Volk, vielleicht mit Ausnahme Ihrer Kreise, sich nicht über die Gefangenenlager, sondern über die jedem Völkerrecht ins Antlitz schlagenden Konzentrationslager und ihren Folgen im Oranje-Freistaat und Transvaal ausgesprochen hat, und sich in dieser Entrüstung, in dieser Empörung einig fühlt mit der ganzen gesitteten Welt, England und Ihre Kreise vielleicht wiederum ausgenommen.

Sie muten uns zu, Herr Staatssekretär, Teilnahme für einen verwundeten englischen General äussern zu sollen unter dem Hinweis, dass dieser Mann als Attaché einst in den ersten Berliner Kreisen verkehrt hat. Na, für einen englischen General, der sich während des ganzen Feldzugs, vom rein militärischen Standpunkte aus betrachtet, als völlig unfähig erwiesen hat, der in bekannter Humanität zur Säuberung des Landes von Frauen und Kindern beitragen hat, der selbst gefangene Buren, die keine andere Schuld trugen, als dass sie für ihr Recht und Vaterland kämpfen, zum Tode verurteilt und dem schmachvollen Tode durch Henkers Hand überantwortet hat, können wir eine grössere Teilnahme nicht heucheln. Nein, so weit ist das deutsche Volk nach Bismarcks Tode noch nicht gesunken, um solche Empfindungen zu teilen und schwachherzig den Mahnungen einer Regierung zu folgen, die alles in der Welt zu fürchten scheint.

Wenn Sie schon glauben, in persönlichen Bemerkungen öffentlich ein Urteil über den Krieg fallen zu sollen, dann hätten Sie es nicht unterlassen dürfen, auch die tiefen Sympathien des Volkes für Delarey, Dewet, und Botha zum Ausdruck zu bringen und denen, die heute noch auf Kommando sind und unter furchtbaren, unerhörten Schwierigkeiten den Kampf für ihre Heimat, ihre Unabhängigkeit gegen einen hundertfach überlegenen Feind kämpfen, Teilnahme, Bewunderung auszusprechen. Wenn Sie wissen wollen, woher es kommt, dass unser ganzes deutsches Volk—arm und reich, hoch und niedrig—sich im Gegensatz fühlt zu Ihnen und Ihren Kreisen, wenn Sie auch jetzt wieder auf eisiges Schweigen und kaum im Lager der Byzanziner auf lauen Beifall stossen, so will ich, ein Sohn deutscher Erde, der für das Burenvolk geblutet hat, der im Ausland wie daheim aufmerksam der Stimme der Völker lauschte, es Ihnen sagen.

Wir vermissen die Stetigkeit, die Gradheit, die Zielsicherheit der Regierung in der inneren, wie vor allem in der äusseren Politik.

Ist auch Bismarck tot, so sollten doch die Männer der gradsinnigen Tatkraft, der klugen Erwägung und dabei doch tapferen Mutes jedermann gegenüber nicht ausgestorben sein; es fehlt uns der Rückgrat, der sich nicht beugt unter jedem Luftzuge von den Höfen her, es fehlt uns jenes Selbstbewusstsein, welches allein eine Nation zur Grösse führt. Ich will Ihnen nur ein paar Dinge ins Gedächtnis rufen, die Ihnen sicherlich nicht entgangen sind. Oder sollte es Ihnen nicht bekannt sein, dass der deutsche Konsul in Bloemfontein Dr. Stollreither, einer der besten Deutschen unserer Beamten im Ausland, als Vertreter Seiner Majestät des Deutschen Kaisers— dieser Titel wird Ihnen imponieren—von der englischen Regierung und ihren militärischen Behörden in Südafrika ganz schmählich behandelt worden ist? Wissen Sie nicht, dass ihm, als er so insultiert worden und sich in voller Dienstuniform zum Gouvernor von Bloemfontein General Prettyman begab, die Antwort zu teil wurde: Ich erkenne überhaupt keinen kaiserlich deutschen Konsul an und habe nichts mit Ihnen zu schaffen? Muss ich Ihnen, Herr Staatssekretär, ein Bild all der Demütigungen zeichnen, mit denen englischen Behörden die Deutschen und unsere Vertreter bedacht haben?

Wie steht es mit der Genugtuung hierfür? Sie werden Antwort schuldig bleiben, weil Englands Empfindlichkeit berührt werden könnte und weil Lord Methuen sein Bein gebrochen hat. Wie steht es mit der Antwort auf die Frage eines Reichstagsabgeordneten über den Neutralitätsbruch, den wir in diesem Kriege noch jetzt begehen, indem wir der Ausfuhr von Kriegsmaterial aller Art von Deutschland nach Südafrika ruhig zusehen? Ich erinnere Sie an den Entrüstungssturm, der 1870-71 durch deutsche Gauen ging, als England um schnöden Gewinnes willen in krämerhafter Weise während des Krieges den Feind unterstützte, und heute müssen wir beschämend gestehen, dass Deutschland auf dasselbe Niveau gesunken ist. Ist Ihnen nicht bekannt, dass wir deutsche Pferde, diese wichtigste Kontrebande in diesem Kriege, an England verkaufen? Nun, das gesamte deutsche Volk steht, Gott sei Dank, auf einem anderen Standpunkt als Sie. Es trauert und wehklagt nicht mit Ihnen um Lord Methuen, den Liebling Londner und Berliner Gesellschaft, sondern es trauert und leidet, es triumphiert und jubelt mit Delarey, Dewet, und Botha.

Ich versage es mir, Ihnen aus dem reichen Schatze meiner persönlichen Erfahrungen in diesem Kriege in englischen Lazaretten, aus denen ich, als zum Krüppel amputierter Kämpfer, zurückgekehrt bin, aus denen ich aber ein deutsches Herz und deutsches Ehrgefühl zurückgebracht habe, eine Auswahl zu geben. Ich füge nur noch eins hinzu: Ich will mit meinen Worten nicht das englische Volk, nicht den tapferen Soldaten und Offizieren zu nahe treten, vor ihnen hatte ich die Hochachtung des ehrlichen Feindes— ich will aber warnen vor jeder Gemeinschaft und selbst vor dem Mitgefühl mit einer rein kapitalistischen von den dürftigsten Geldinteressen beherrschten Regierung.

H. BANKS.
Buchengrund, Schlesien.

INDEX

26